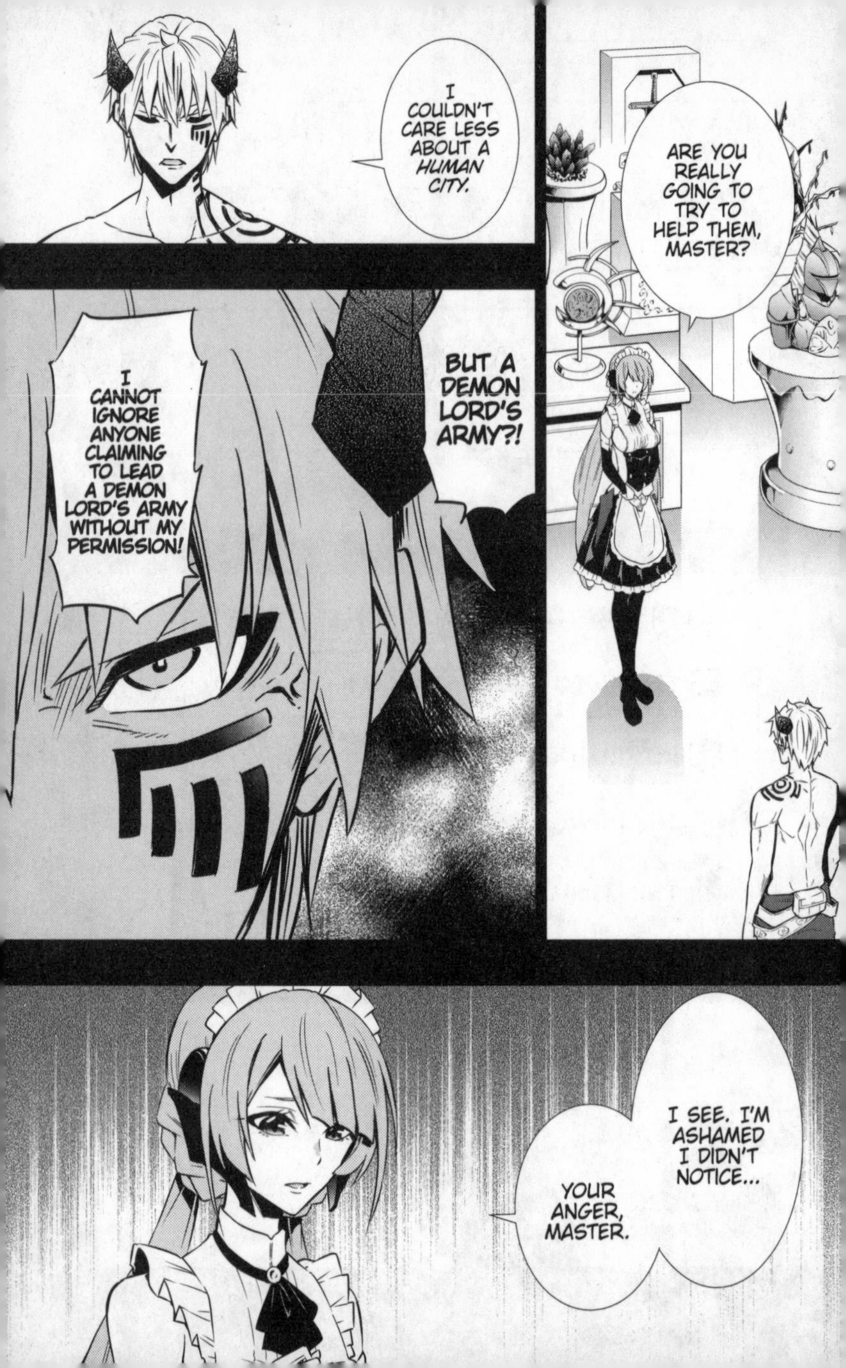
ARE YOU REALLY GOING TO TRY TO HELP THEM, MASTER?
I COULDN'T CARE LESS ABOUT A *HUMAN* CITY.
BUT A DEMON LORD'S ARMY?!
I CANNOT IGNORE ANYONE CLAIMING TO LEAD A DEMON LORD'S ARMY WITHOUT MY PERMISSION!
I SEE. I'M ASHAMED I DIDN'T NOTICE...
YOUR ANGER, MASTER.

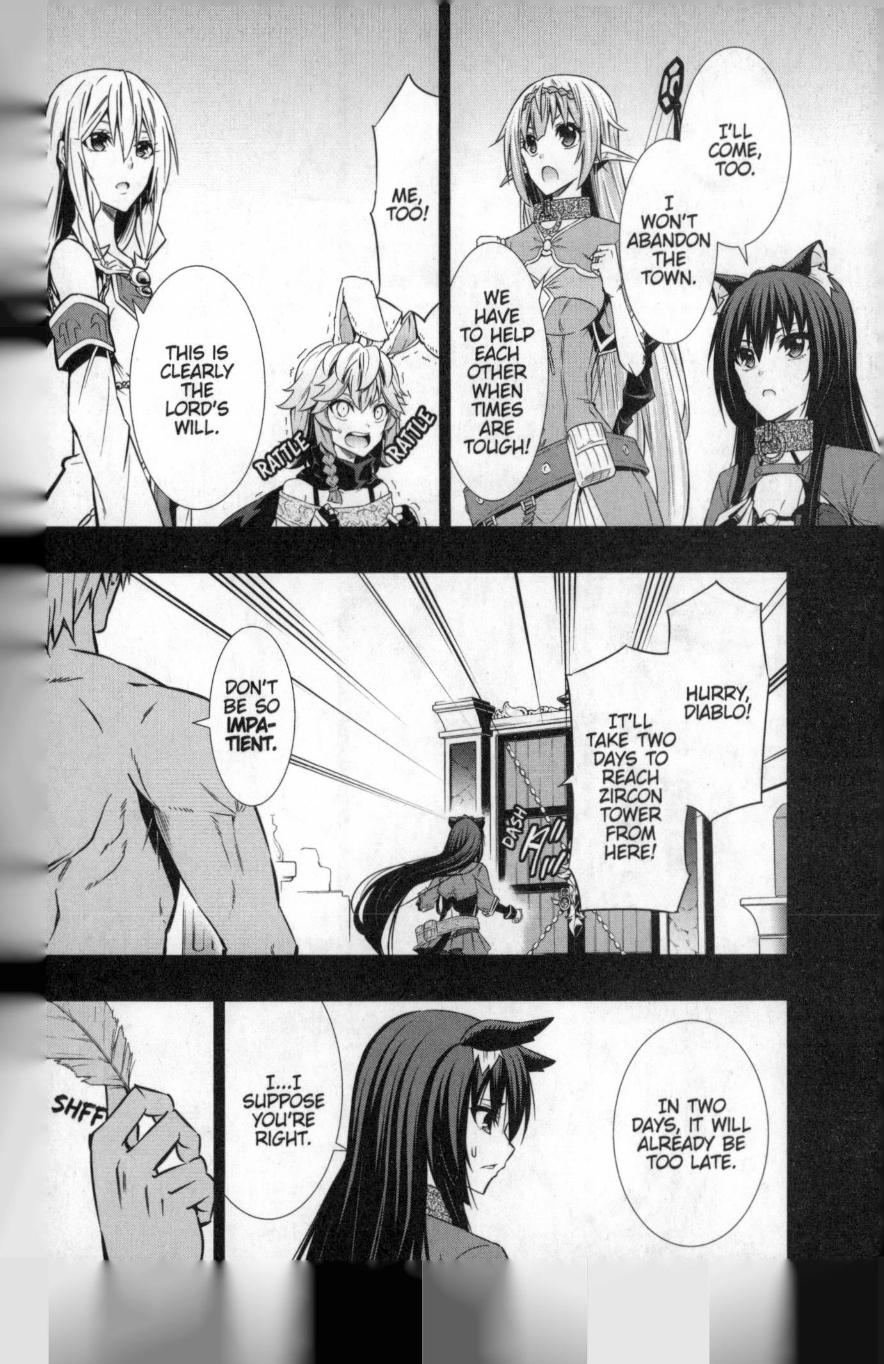
I'LL COME, TOO.
I WON'T ABANDON THE TOWN.
WE HAVE TO HELP EACH OTHER WHEN TIMES ARE TOUGH!
ME, TOO!
RATTLE
RATTLE
THIS IS CLEARLY THE LORD'S WILL.
HURRY, DIABLO!
IT'LL TAKE TWO DAYS TO REACH ZIRCON TOWER FROM HERE!
DASH
DON'T BE SO IMPA-TIENT.
IN TWO DAYS, IT WILL ALREADY BE TOO LATE.
I...I SUPPOSE YOU'RE RIGHT.
SHFF

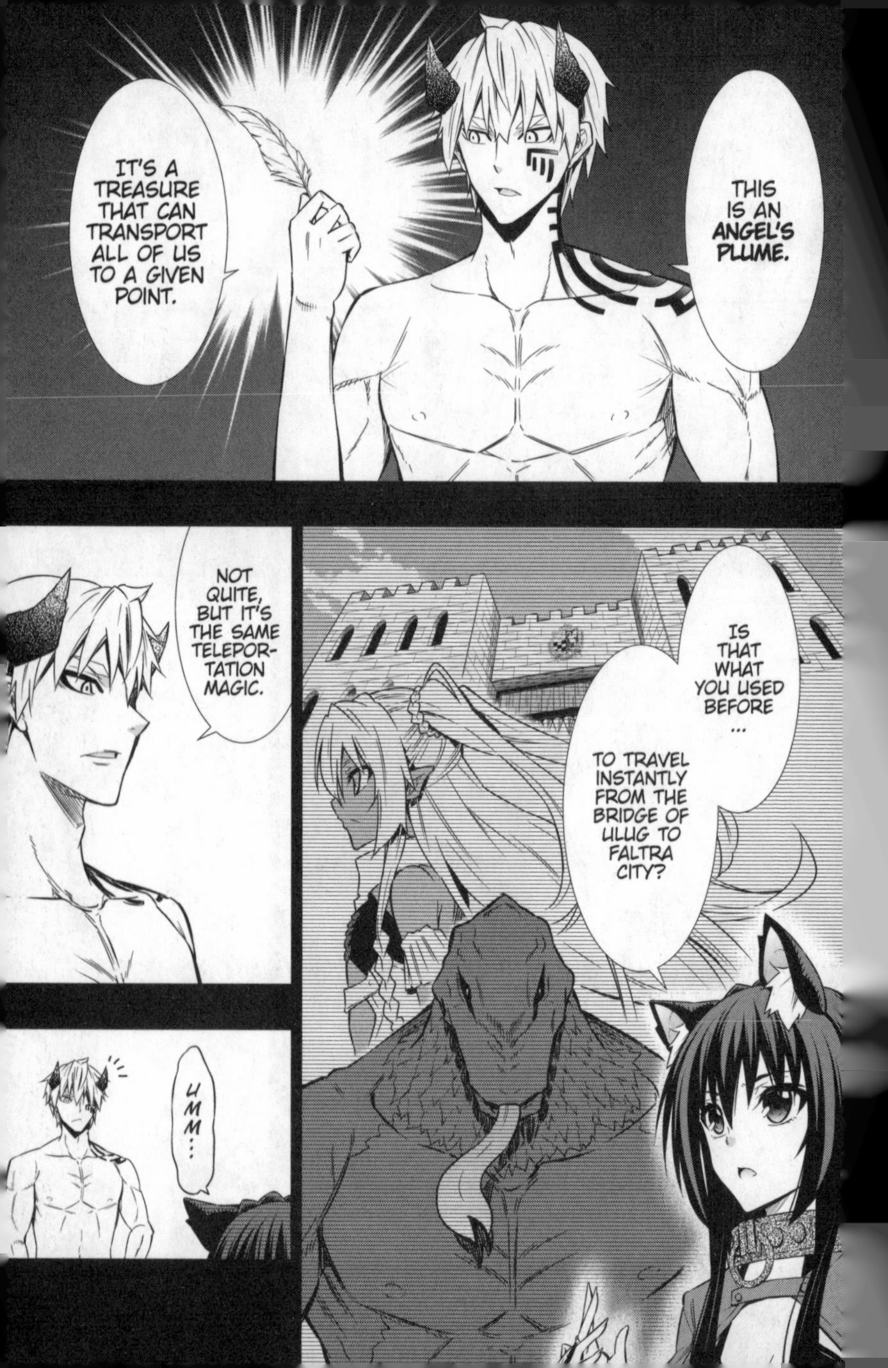
THIS IS AN ANGEL'S PLUME.
IT'S A TREASURE THAT CAN TRANSPORT ALL OF US TO A GIVEN POINT.
IS THAT WHAT YOU USED BEFORE ...
TO TRAVEL INSTANTLY FROM THE BRIDGE OF ULUG TO FALTRA CITY?
NOT QUITE, BUT IT'S THE SAME TELEPORTATION MAGIC.
UMM...

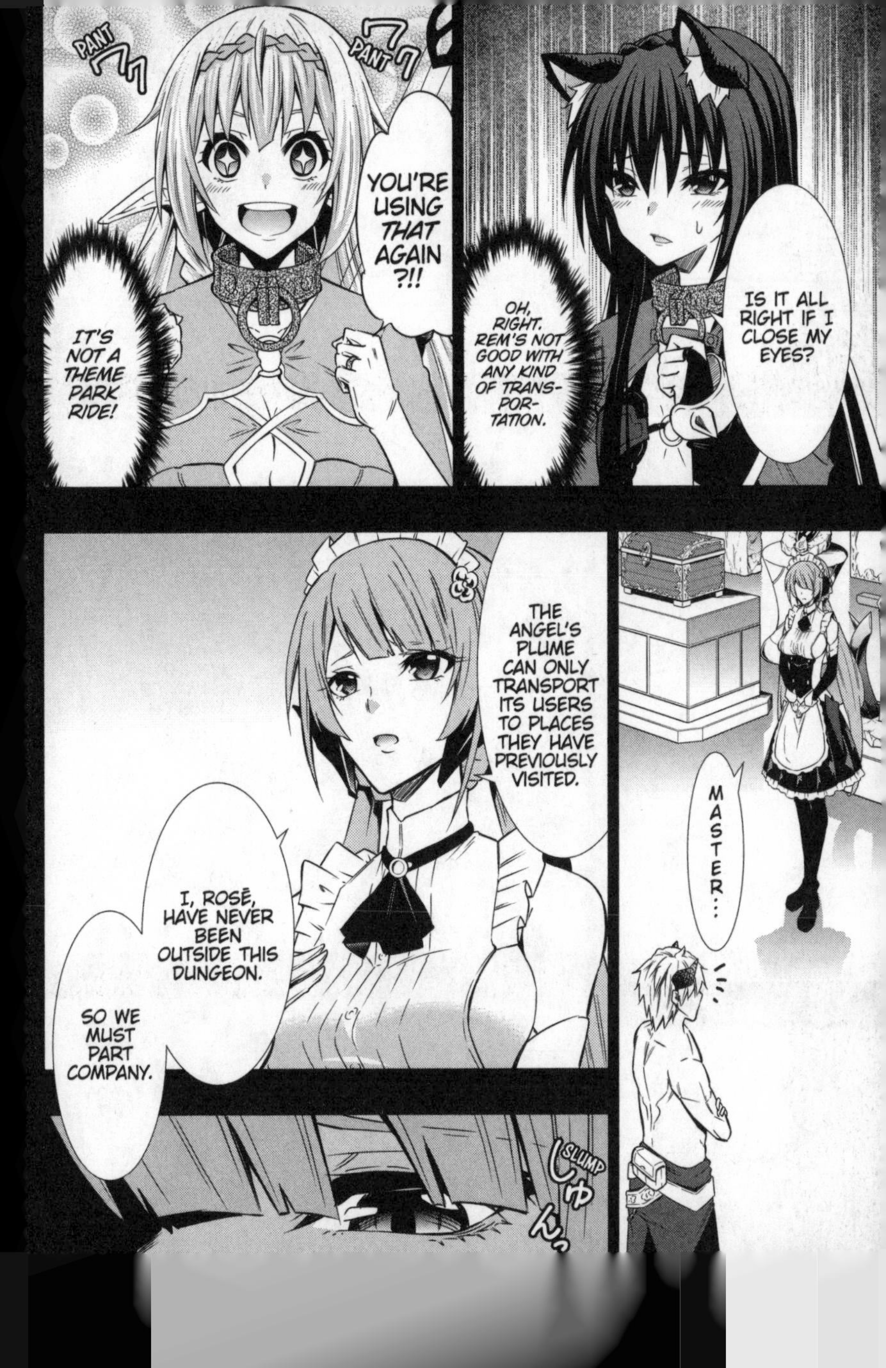
IS IT ALL RIGHT IF I CLOSE MY EYES?
OH, RIGHT. REM'S NOT GOOD WITH ANY KIND OF TRANS-PORTATION.
PANT
PANT
YOU'RE USING THAT AGAIN?!!
IT'S NOT A THEME PARK RIDE!
MASTER...
THE ANGEL'S PLUME CAN ONLY TRANSPORT ITS USERS TO PLACES THEY HAVE PREVIOUSLY VISITED.
I, ROSÉ, HAVE NEVER BEEN OUTSIDE THIS DUNGEON.
SO WE MUST PART COMPANY.
SLUMP

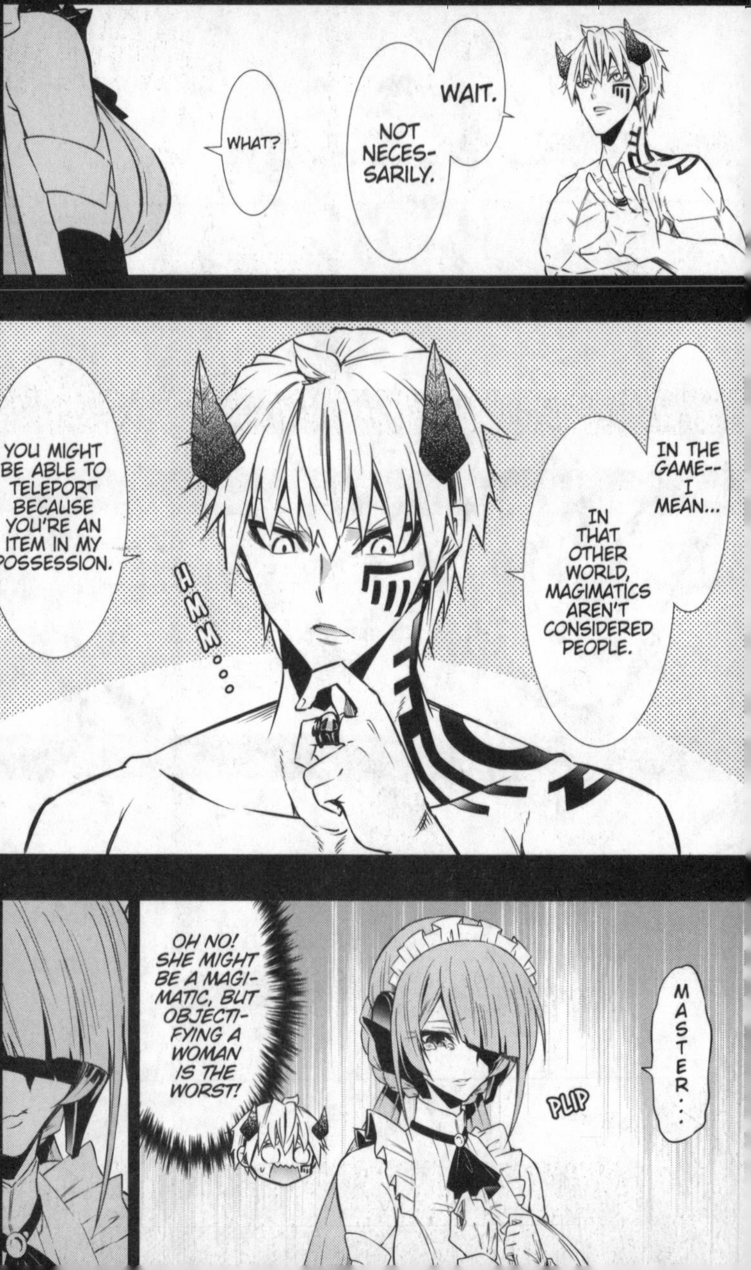
WAIT.
NOT NECES-SARILY.
WHAT?
IN THE GAME-- I MEAN...
IN THAT OTHER WORLD, MAGIMATICS AREN'T CONSIDERED PEOPLE.
HMM...
YOU MIGHT BE ABLE TO TELEPORT BECAUSE YOU'RE AN ITEM IN MY POSSESSION.
MASTER...
PLIP
OH NO! SHE MIGHT BE A MAGI-MATIC, BUT OBJECTI-FYING A WOMAN IS THE WORST!

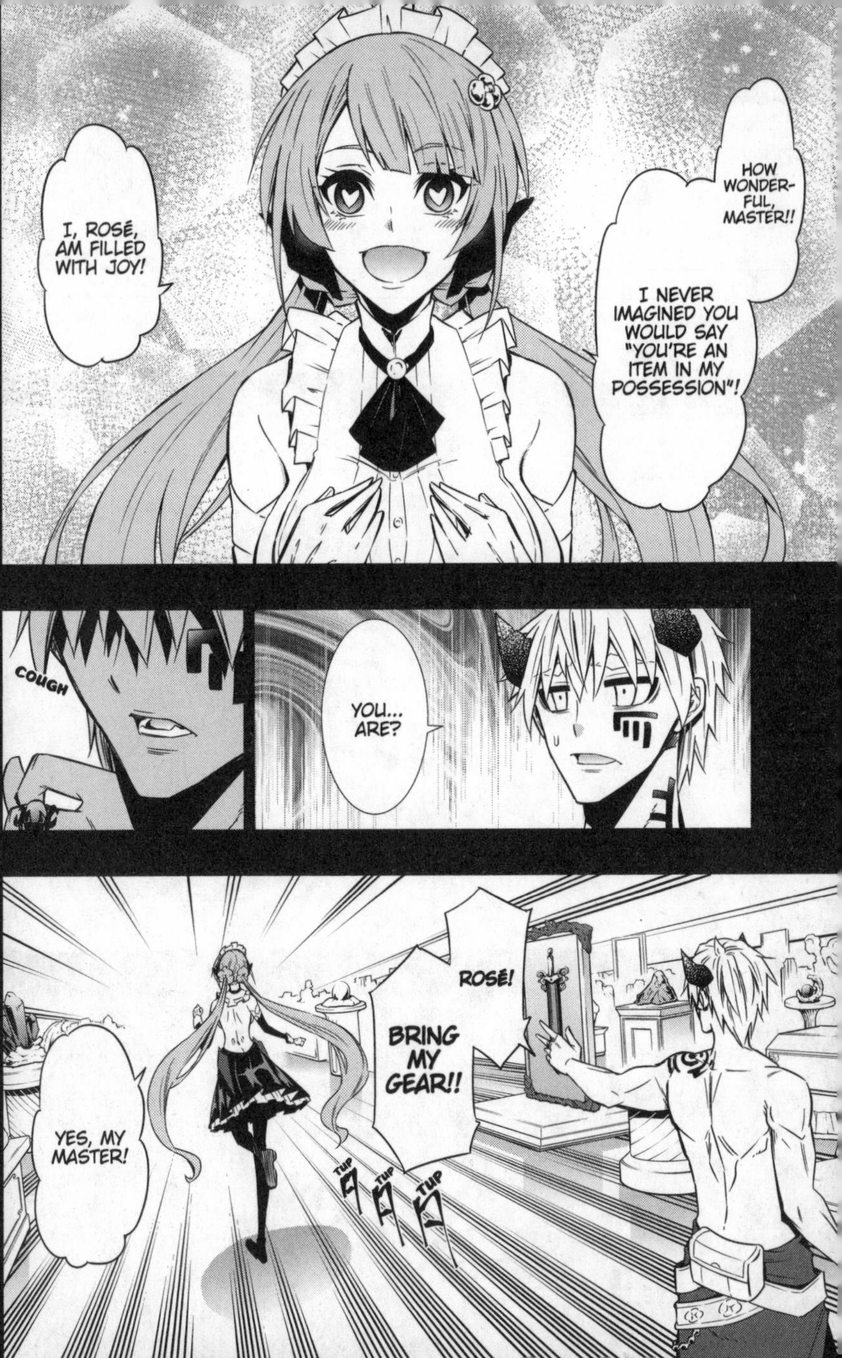
HOW WONDERFUL, MASTER!!
I NEVER IMAGINED YOU WOULD SAY "YOU'RE AN ITEM IN MY POSSESSION"!
I, ROSÉ, AM FILLED WITH JOY!
YOU... ARE?
COUGH
ROSÉ!
BRING MY GEAR!!
TUP TUP TUP
YES, MY MASTER!

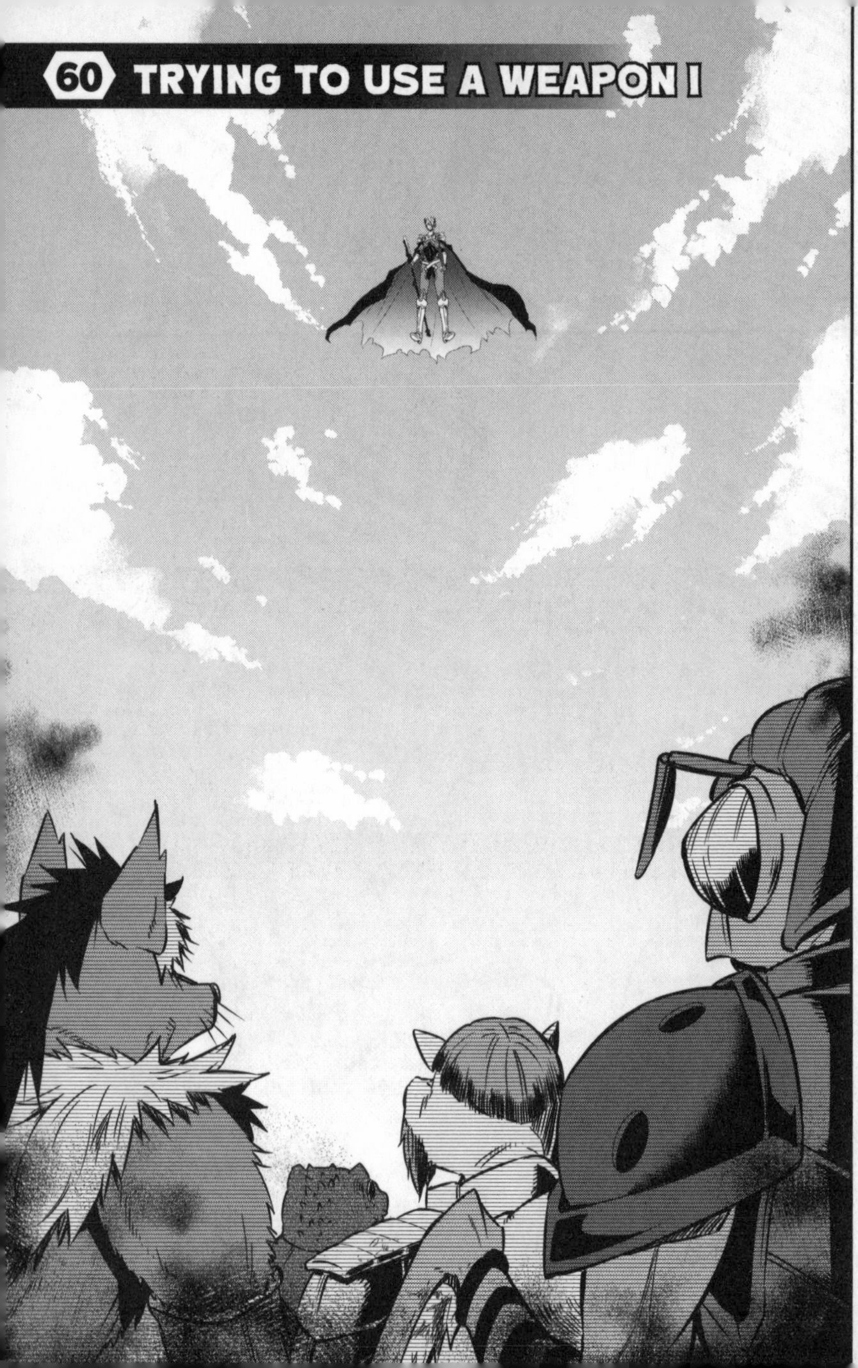
60 TRYING TO USE A WEAPON I

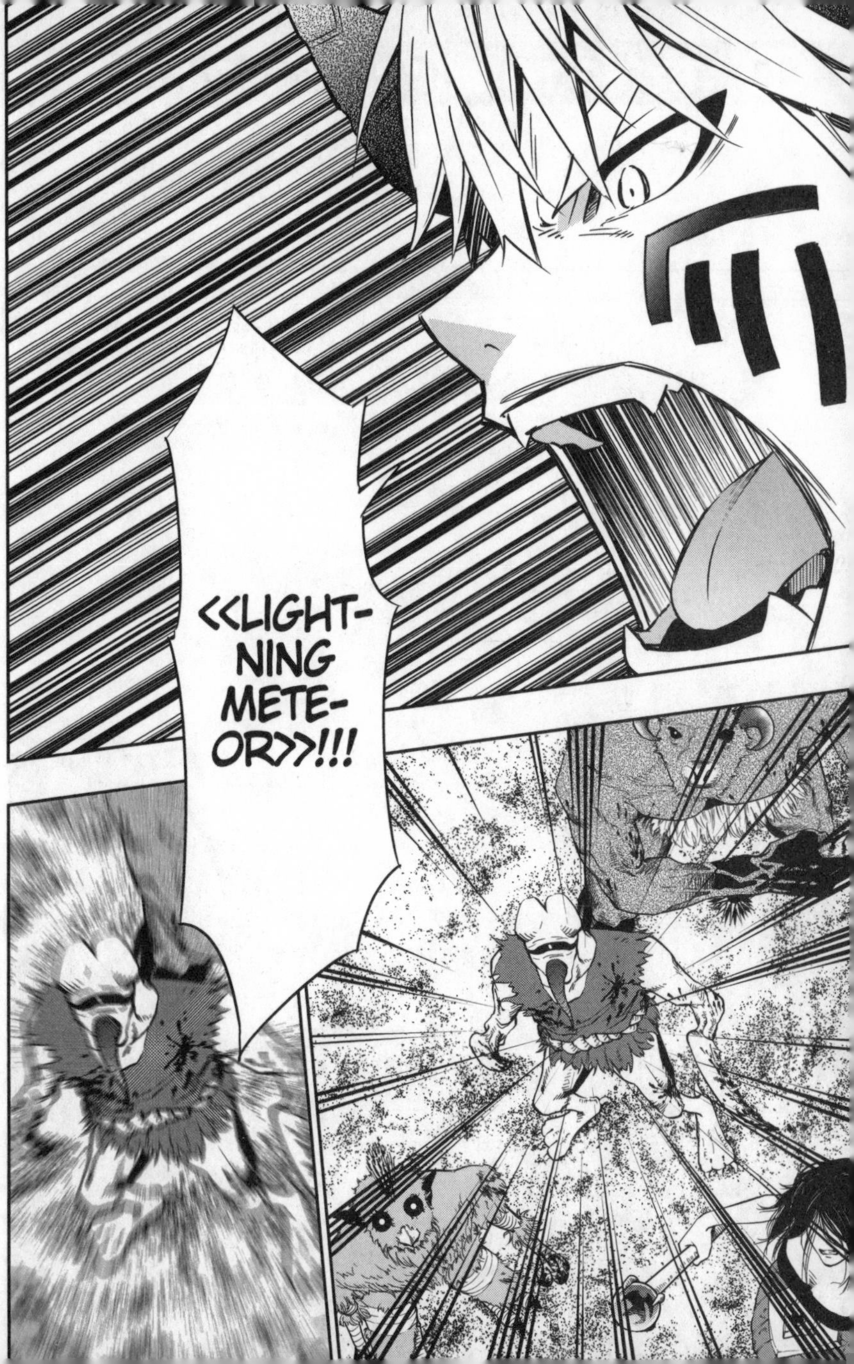

<<LIGHT-NING METE-OR>>!!!

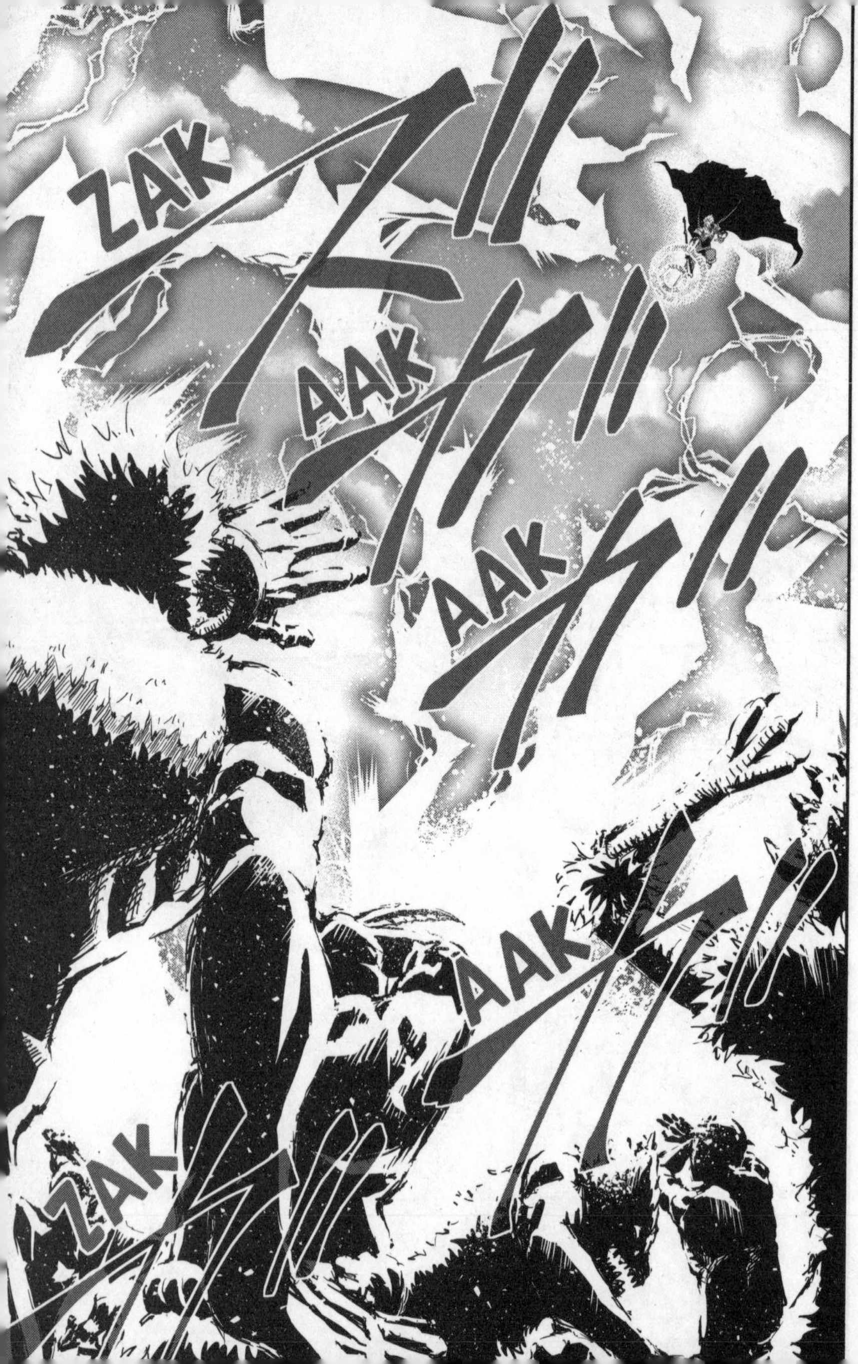
ZAK
AAK
AAK
AAK
ZAK

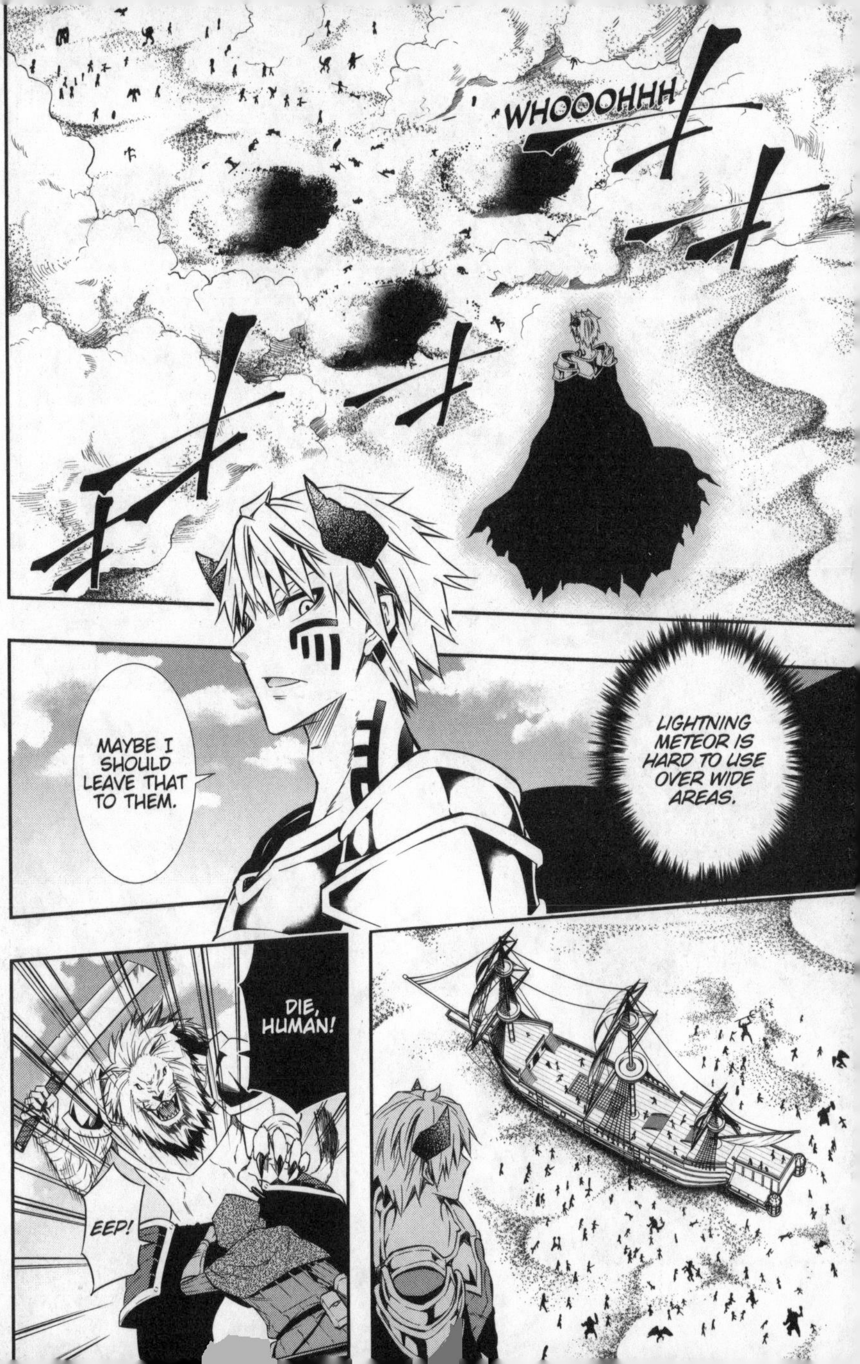
WHOOOHHH
LIGHTNING METEOR IS HARD TO USE OVER WIDE AREAS.
MAYBE I SHOULD LEAVE THAT TO THEM.
DIE, HUMAN!
EEP!

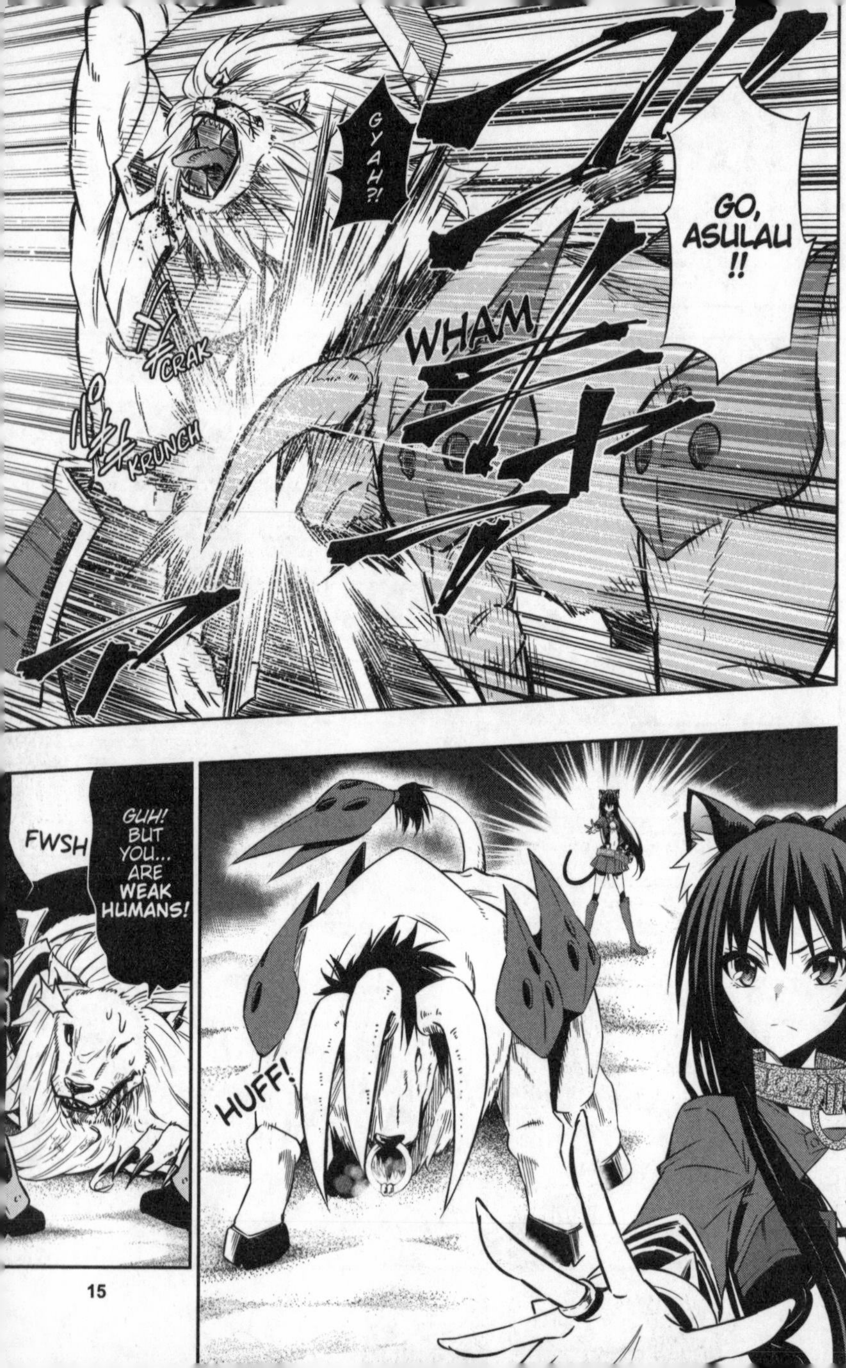
GO, ASULAU!!
WHAM
GYAH?!
CRAK
KRUNCH
HUFF!
GUH! BUT YOU... ARE WEAK HUMANS!
FWSH

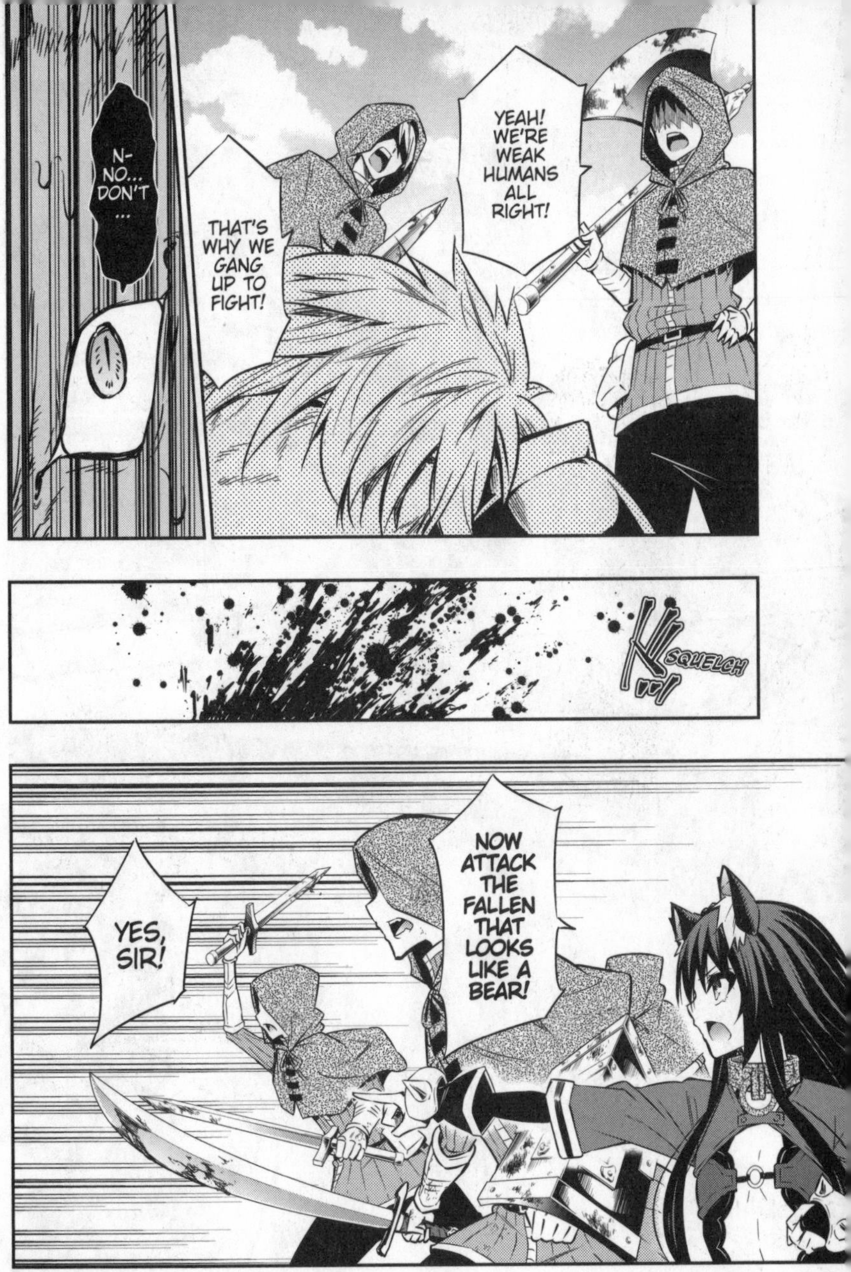
YEAH! WE'RE WEAK HUMANS ALL RIGHT!
THAT'S WHY WE GANG UP TO FIGHT!
N-NO... DON'T ...
SQUELCH
NOW ATTACK THE FALLEN THAT LOOKS LIKE A BEAR!
YES, SIR!

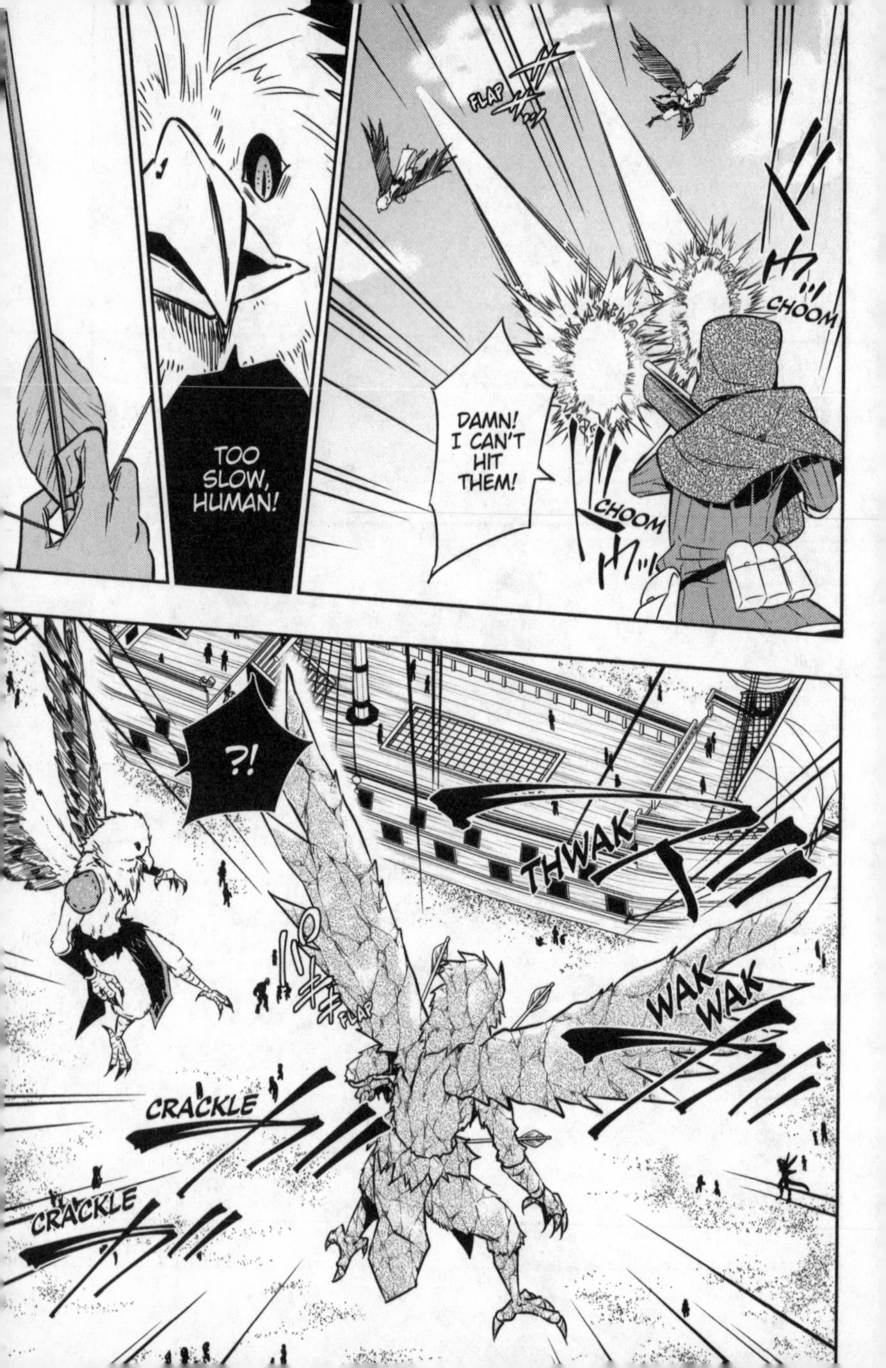
FLAP
CHOOM
DAMN! I CAN'T HIT THEM!
CHOOM
TOO SLOW, HUMAN!
?!
THWAK
WAK WAK
FLAP
CRACKLE
CRACKLE

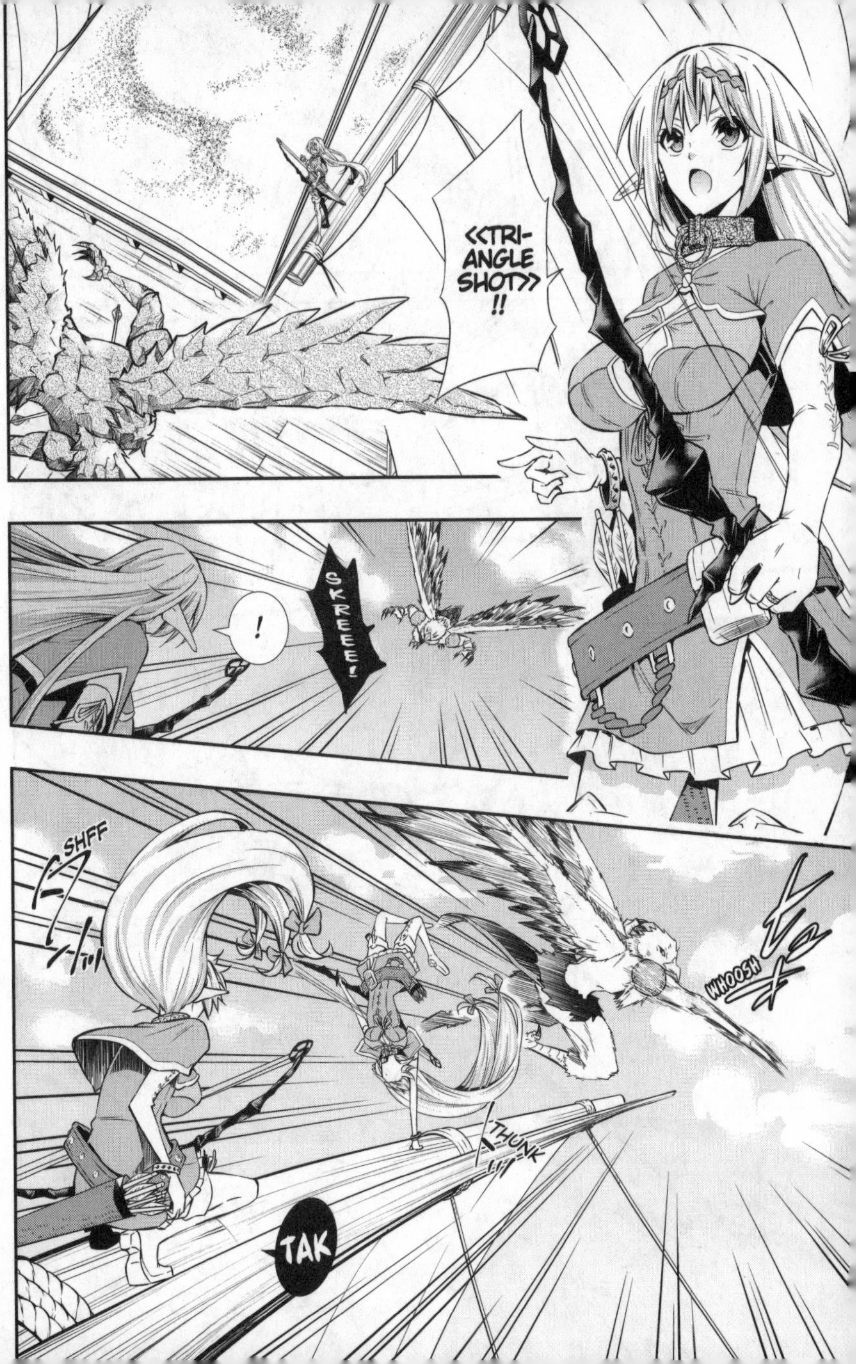
<<TRI-ANGLE SHOT>>!!
SKREEE!
!
WHOOSH
SHFF
THUNK
TAK

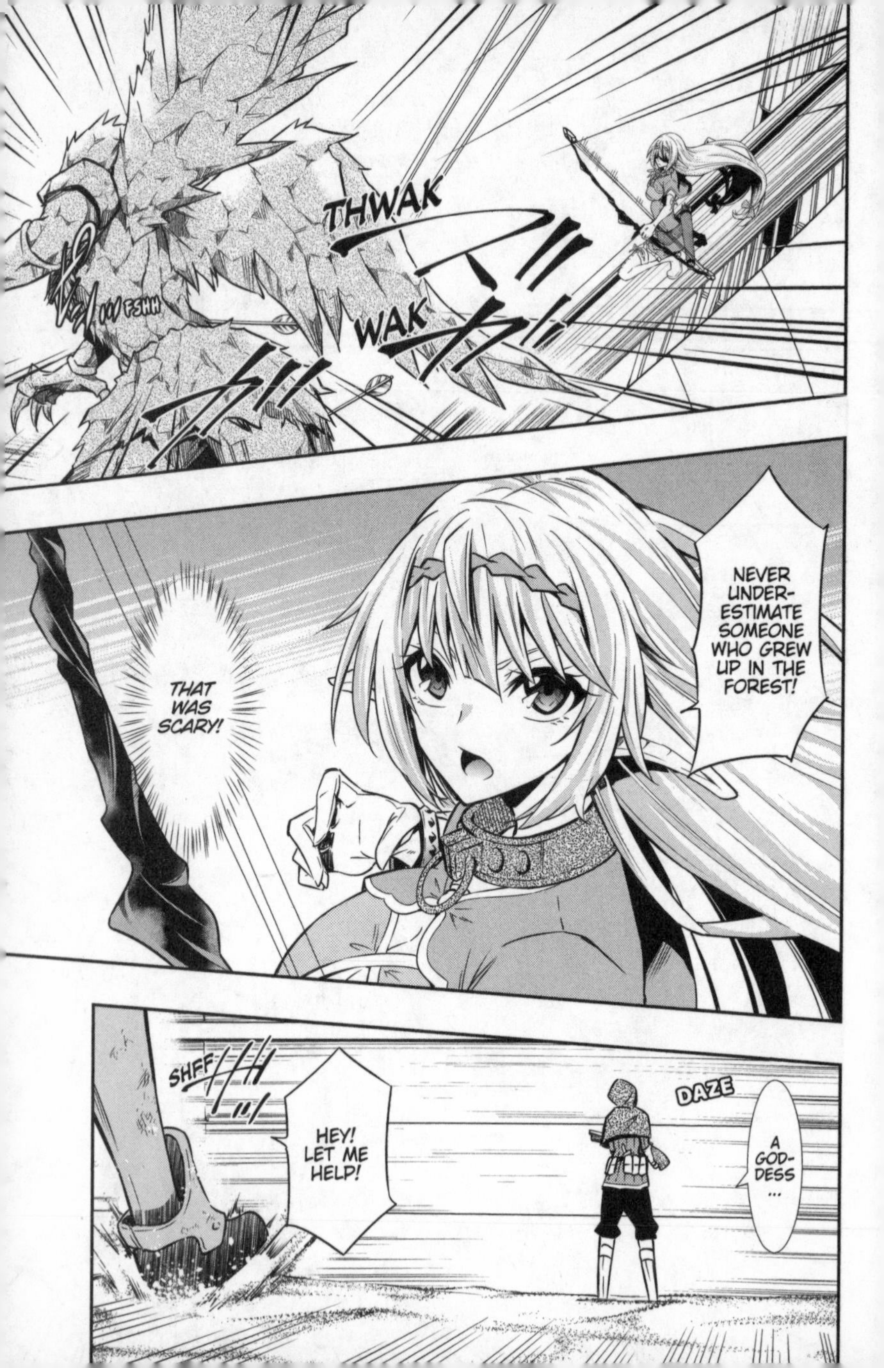
THWAK
WAK
FSHH
NEVER UNDER-ESTIMATE SOMEONE WHO GREW UP IN THE FOREST!
THAT WAS SCARY!
A GOD-DESS ...
DAZE
HEY! LET ME HELP!
SHFF

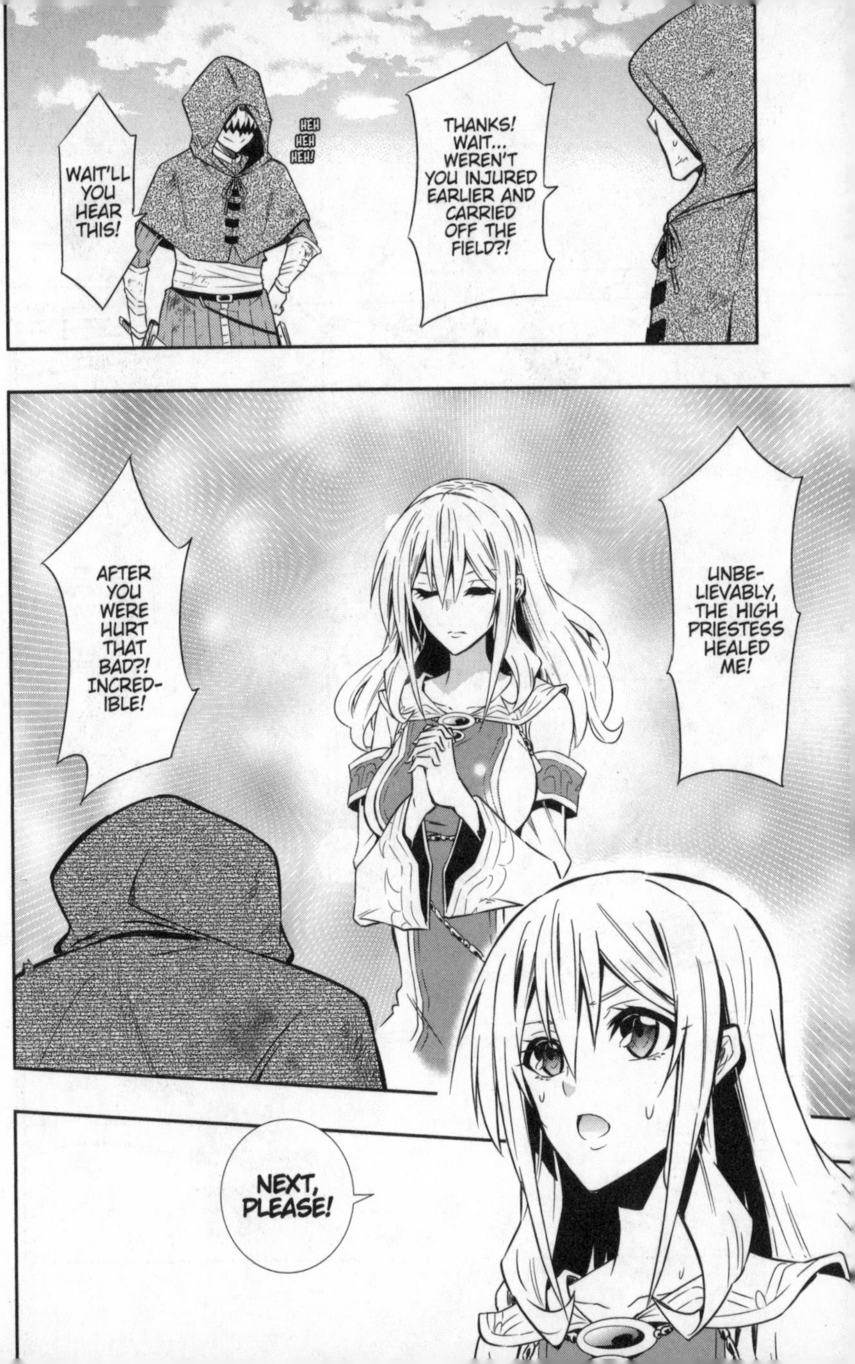
THANKS! WAIT... WEREN'T YOU INJURED EARLIER AND CARRIED OFF THE FIELD?!
HEH HEH HEH!
WAIT'LL YOU HEAR THIS!
UNBE-LIEVABLY, THE HIGH PRIESTESS HEALED ME!
AFTER YOU WERE HURT THAT BAD?! INCRED-IBLE!
NEXT, PLEASE!

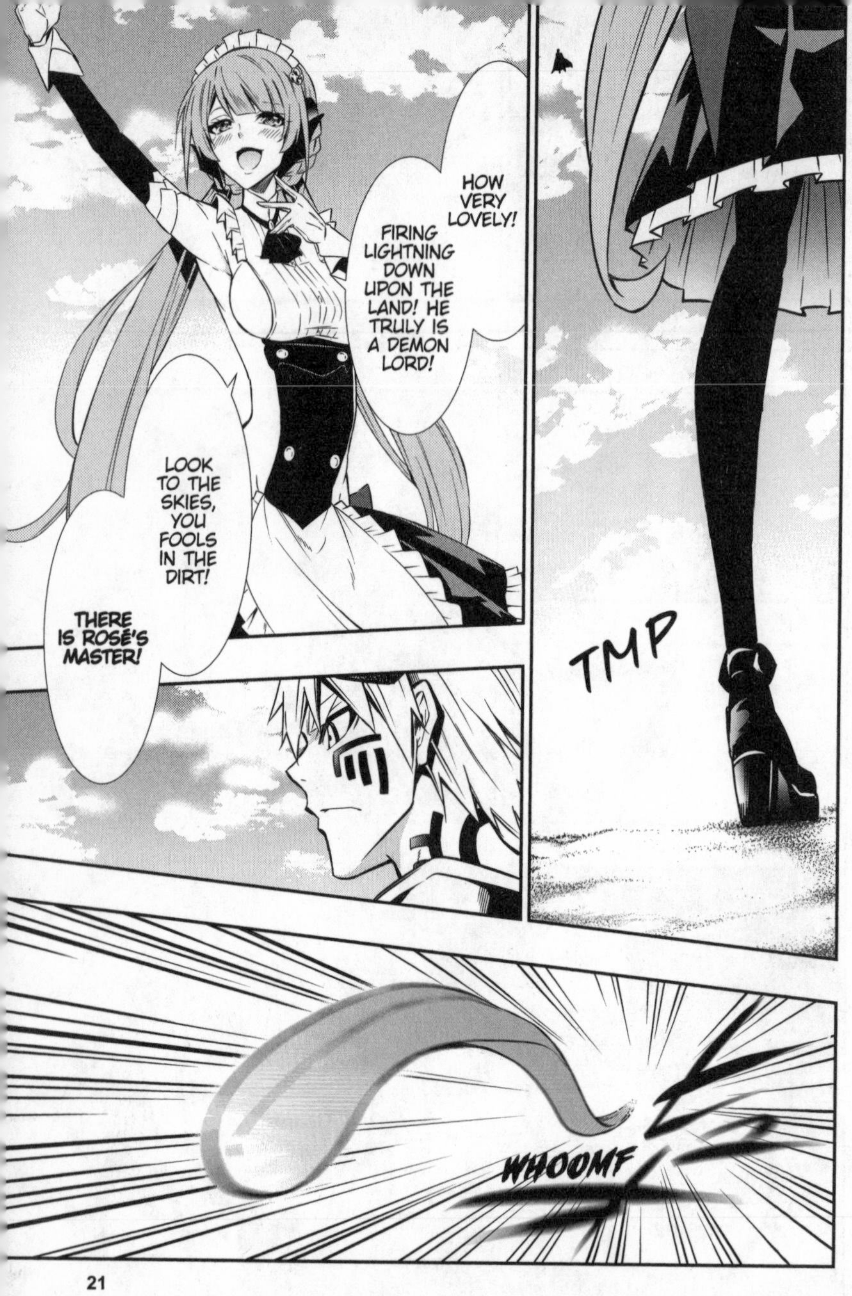
TMP
HOW VERY LOVELY! FIRING LIGHTNING DOWN UPON THE LAND! HE TRULY IS A DEMON LORD!
LOOK TO THE SKIES, YOU FOOLS IN THE DIRT!
THERE IS ROSÉ'S MASTER!
WHOOMF

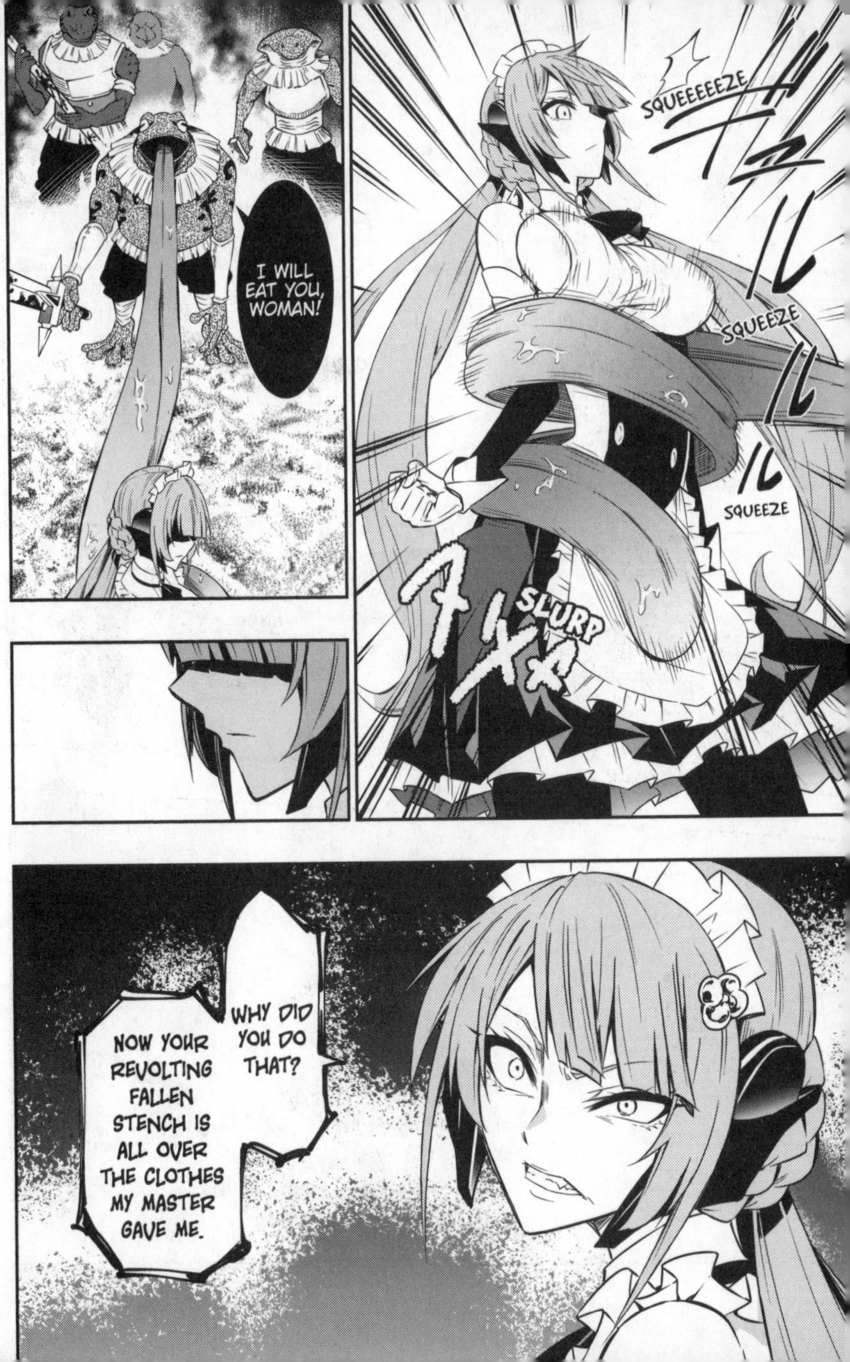
SQUEEEEEZE
SQUEEZE
SQUEEZE
SLURP
I WILL EAT YOU, WOMAN!
WHY DID YOU DO THAT?
NOW YOUR REVOLTING FALLEN STENCH IS ALL OVER THE CLOTHES MY MASTER GAVE ME.

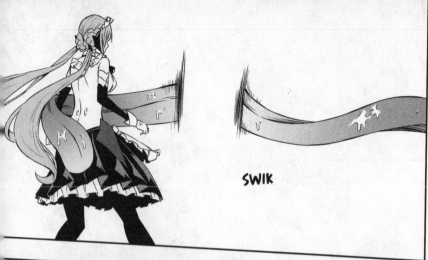

SWIK

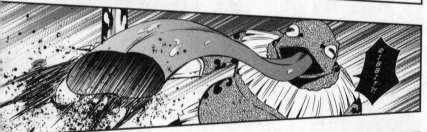

RIBBIT?!

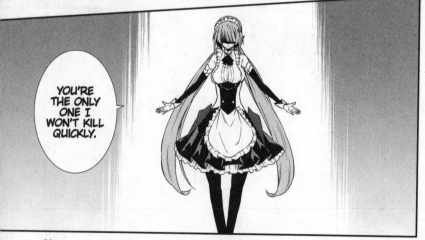

YOU'RE THE ONLY ONE I WON'T KILL QUICKLY.

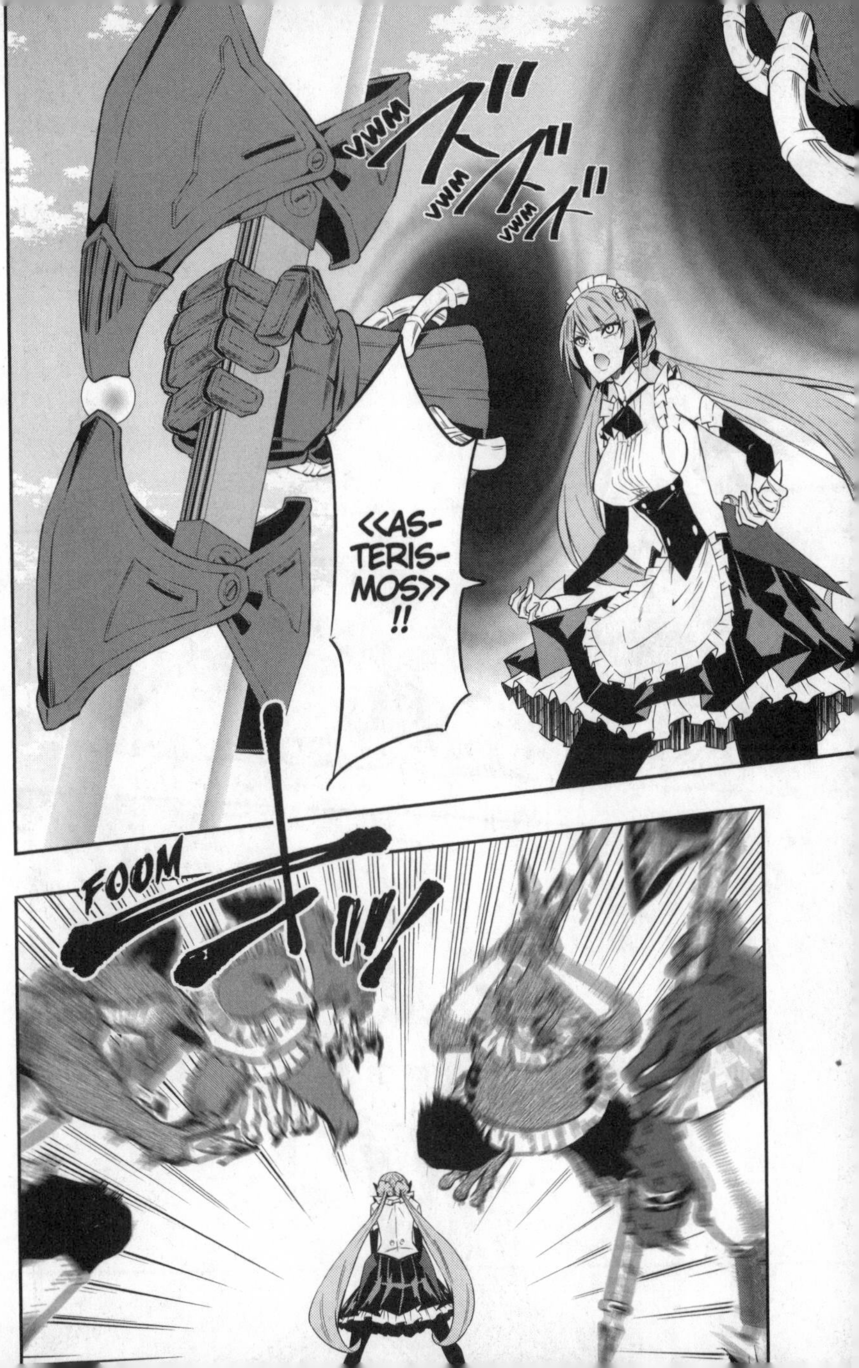
ズ VWM
ズ VWM
ズ VWM
<<AS-
TERIS-
MOS>>
!!
FOOM

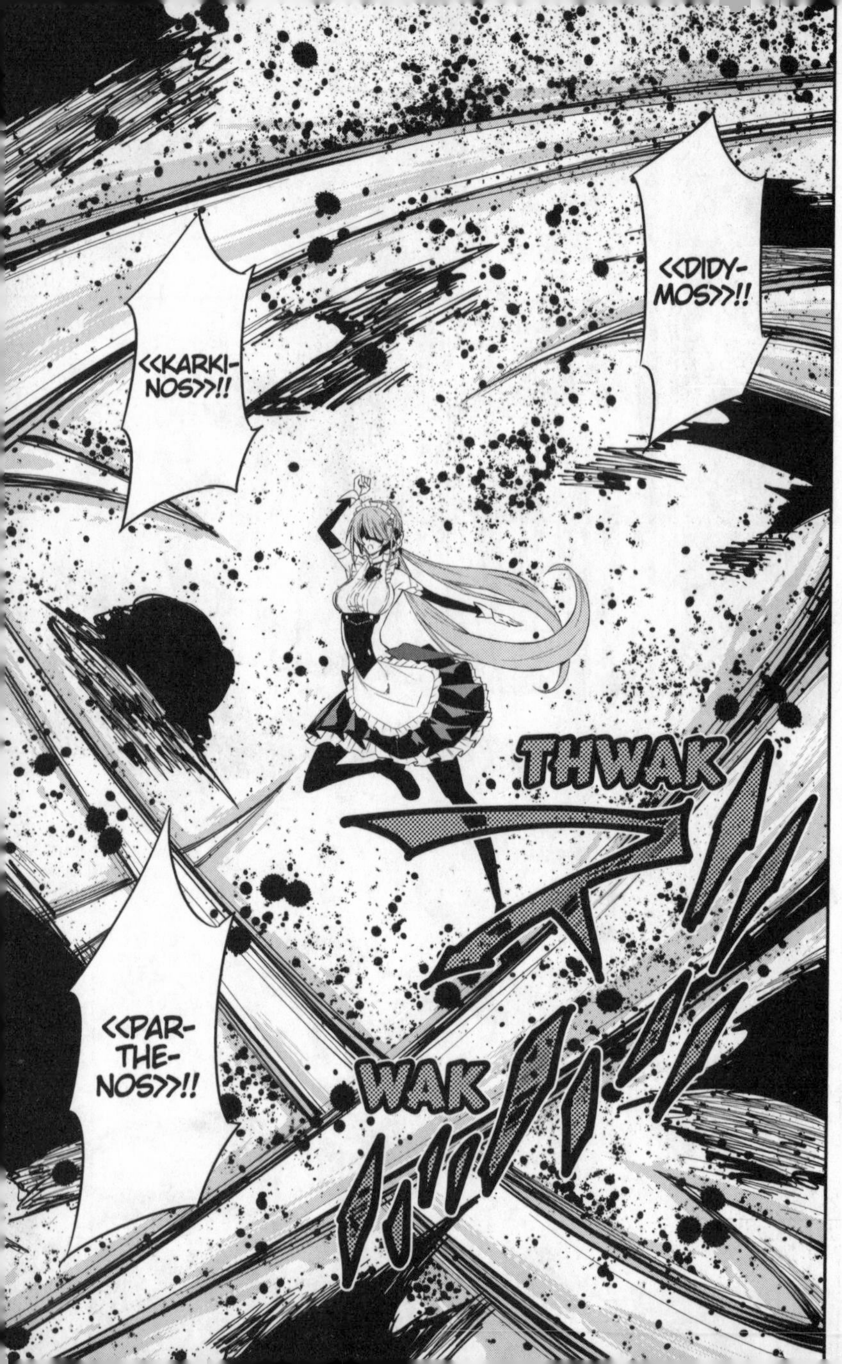
<<DIDY-MOS>>!!
<<KARKI-NOS>>!!
THWAK
<<PAR-THE-NOS>>!!
WAK

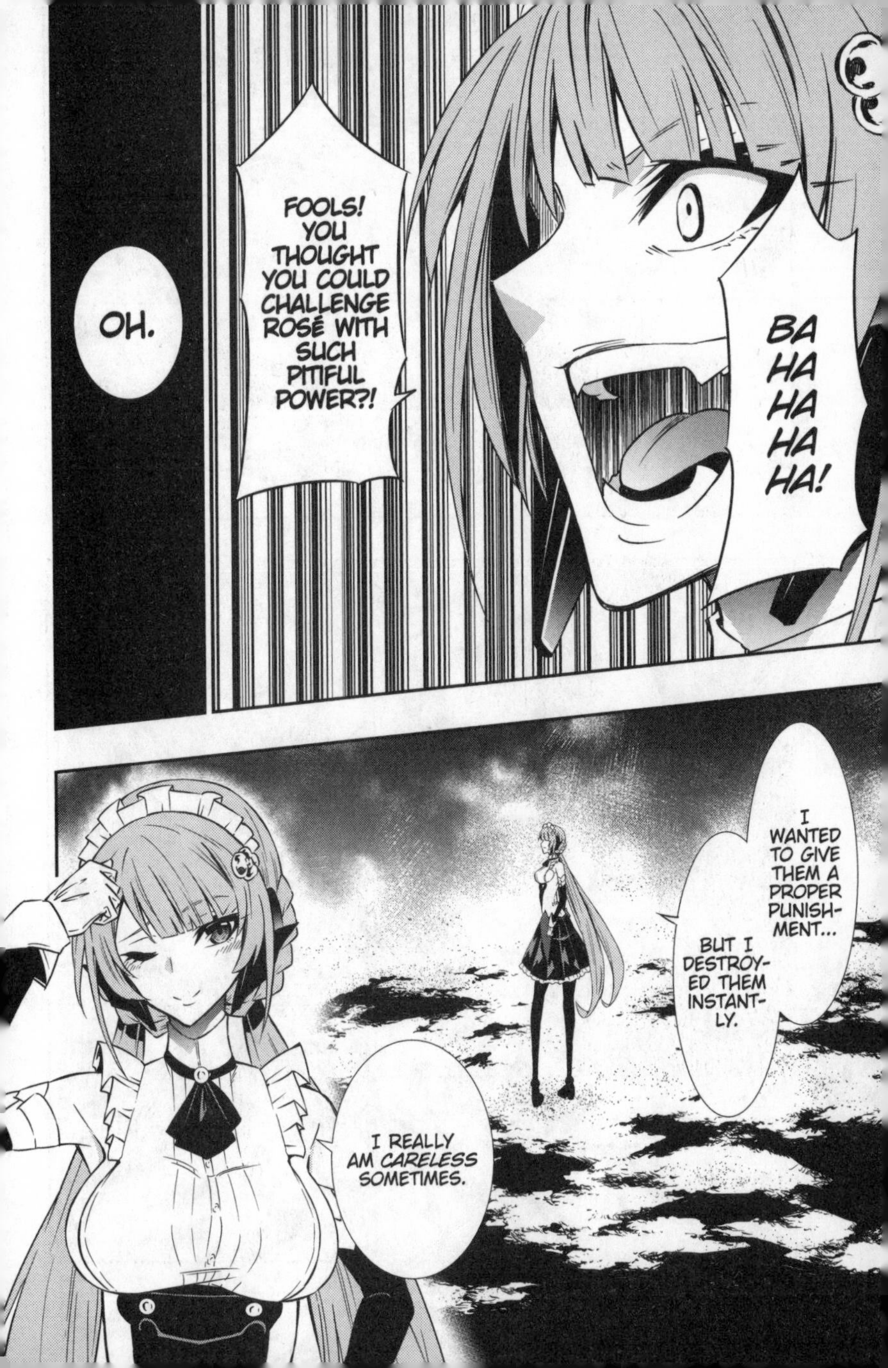
BA HA HA HA HA!
FOOLS! YOU THOUGHT YOU COULD CHALLENGE ROSÉ WITH SUCH PITIFUL POWER?!
OH.
I WANTED TO GIVE THEM A PROPER PUNISH-MENT...
BUT I DESTROY-ED THEM INSTANT-LY.
I REALLY AM *CARELESS* SOMETIMES.

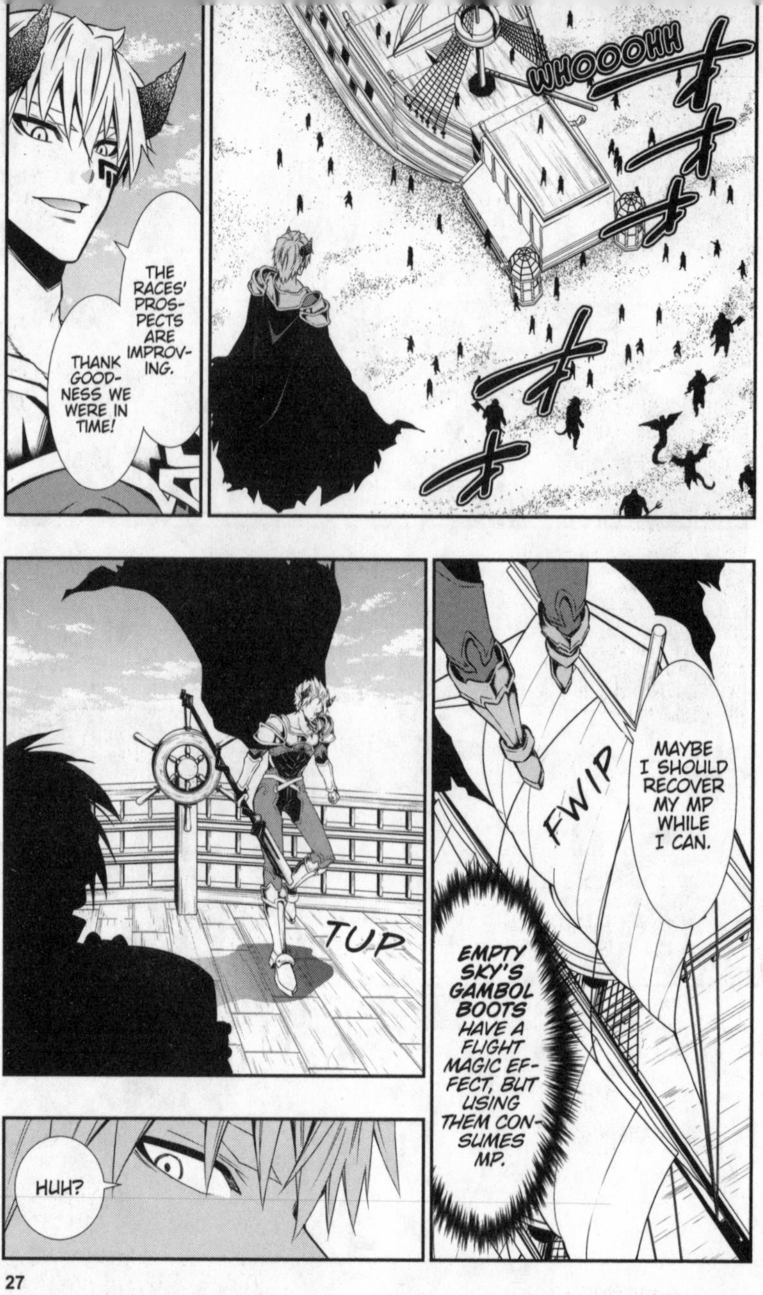
WHOOOOHH
THE RACES' PROSPECTS ARE IMPROVING.
THANK GOODNESS WE WERE IN TIME!
FWIP
MAYBE I SHOULD RECOVER MY MP WHILE I CAN.
EMPTY SKY'S GAMBOL BOOTS HAVE A FLIGHT MAGIC EFFECT, BUT USING THEM CONSUMES MP.
TUP
HUH?

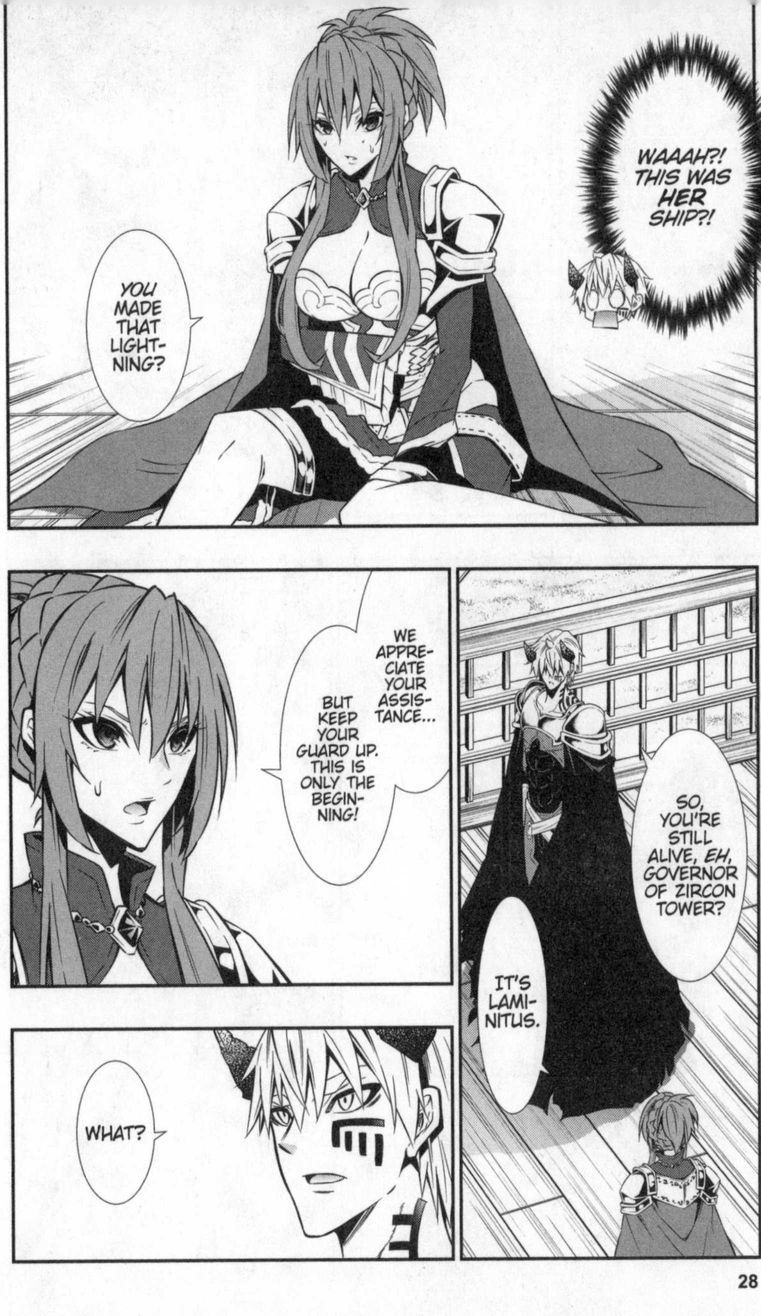
WAAAH?! THIS WAS HER SHIP?!
YOU MADE THAT LIGHT-NING?
SO, YOU'RE STILL ALIVE, EH, GOVERNOR OF ZIRCON TOWER?
IT'S LAMI-NITUS.
WE APPRE-CIATE YOUR ASSIS-TANCE...
BUT KEEP YOUR GUARD UP. THIS IS ONLY THE BEGIN-NING!
WHAT?

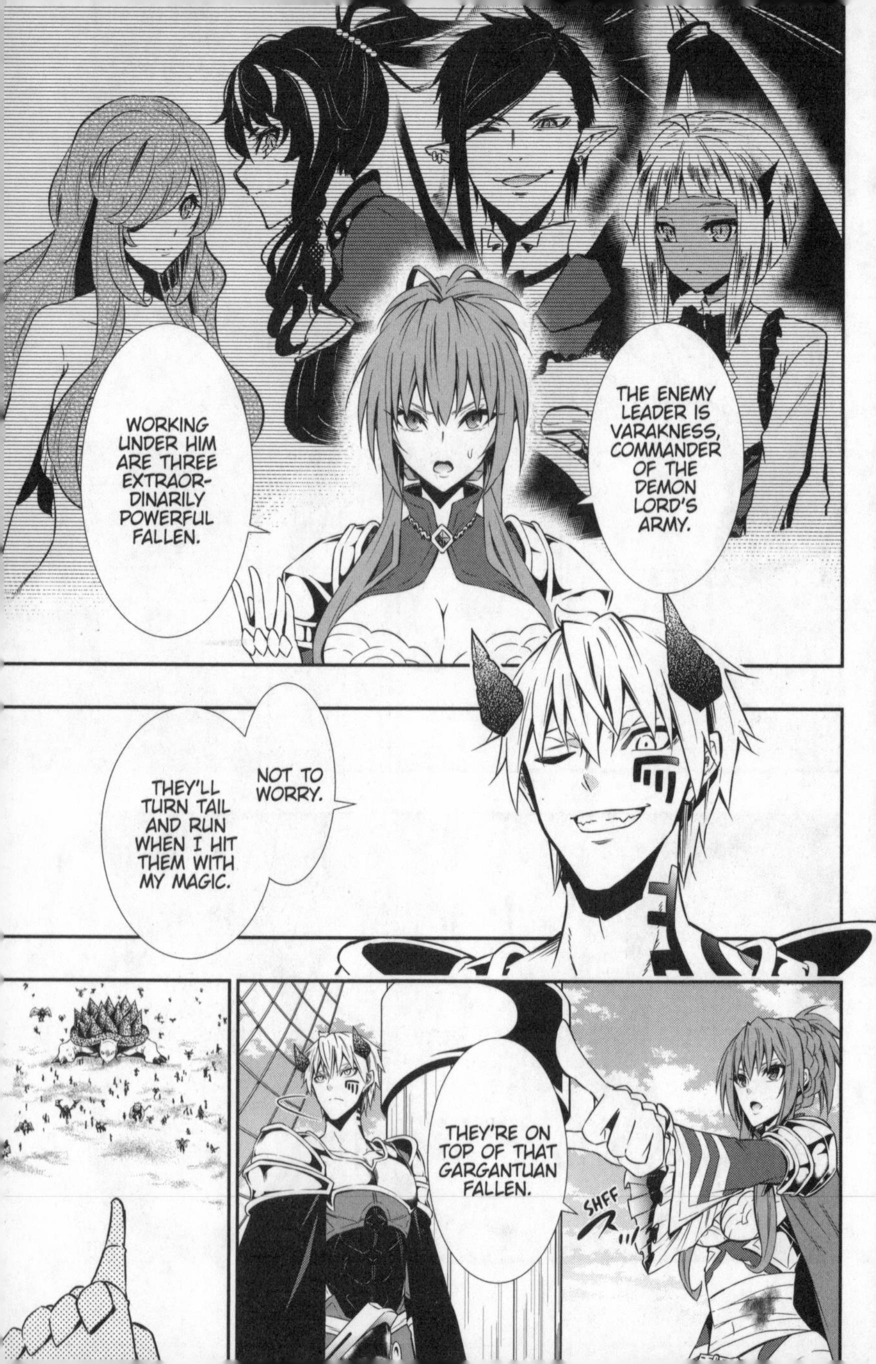
THE ENEMY LEADER IS VARAKNESS, COMMANDER OF THE DEMON LORD'S ARMY.
WORKING UNDER HIM ARE THREE EXTRAOR-DINARILY POWERFUL FALLEN.
NOT TO WORRY.
THEY'LL TURN TAIL AND RUN WHEN I HIT THEM WITH MY MAGIC.
THEY'RE ON TOP OF THAT GARGANTUAN FALLEN.
SHFF

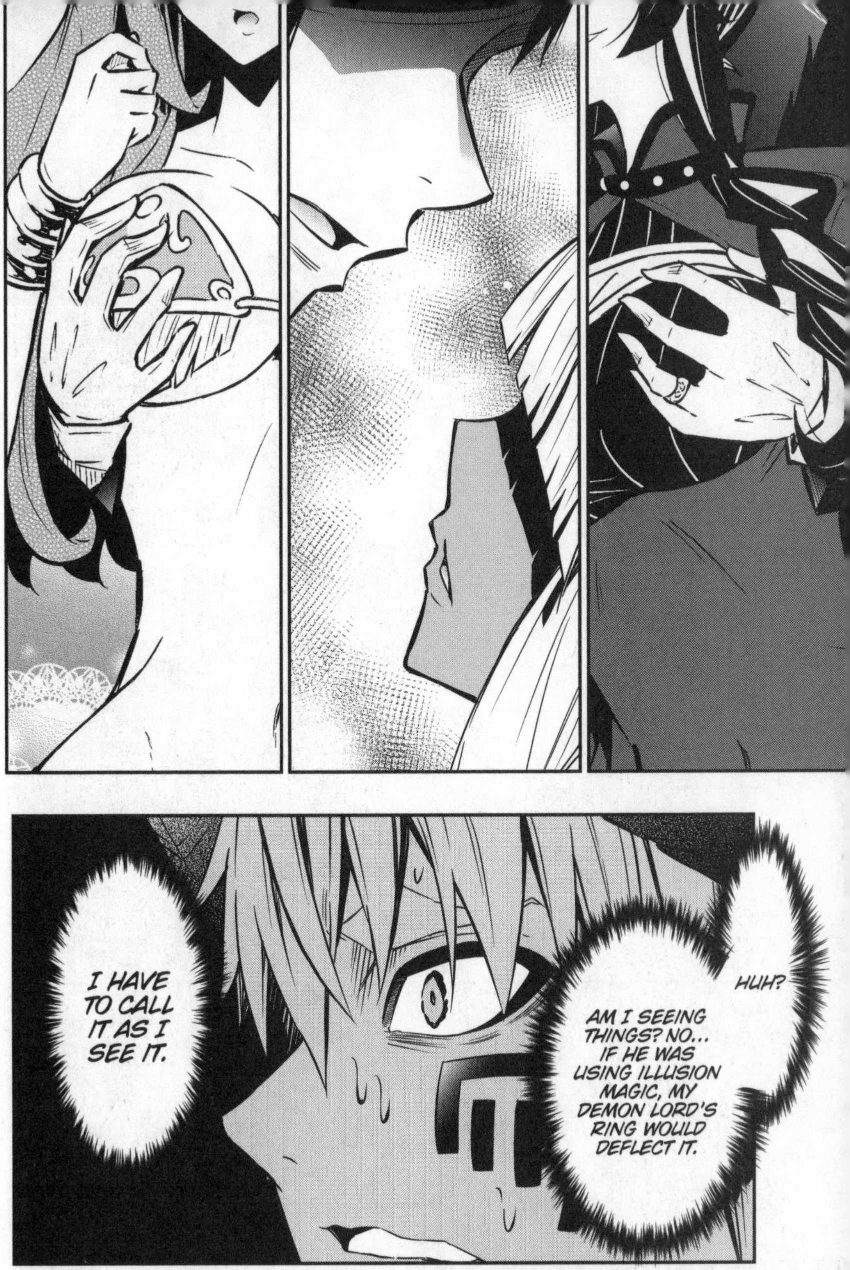
HUH?
AM I SEEING THINGS? NO... IF HE WAS USING ILLUSION MAGIC, MY DEMON LORD'S RING WOULD DEFLECT IT.
I HAVE TO CALL IT AS I SEE IT.

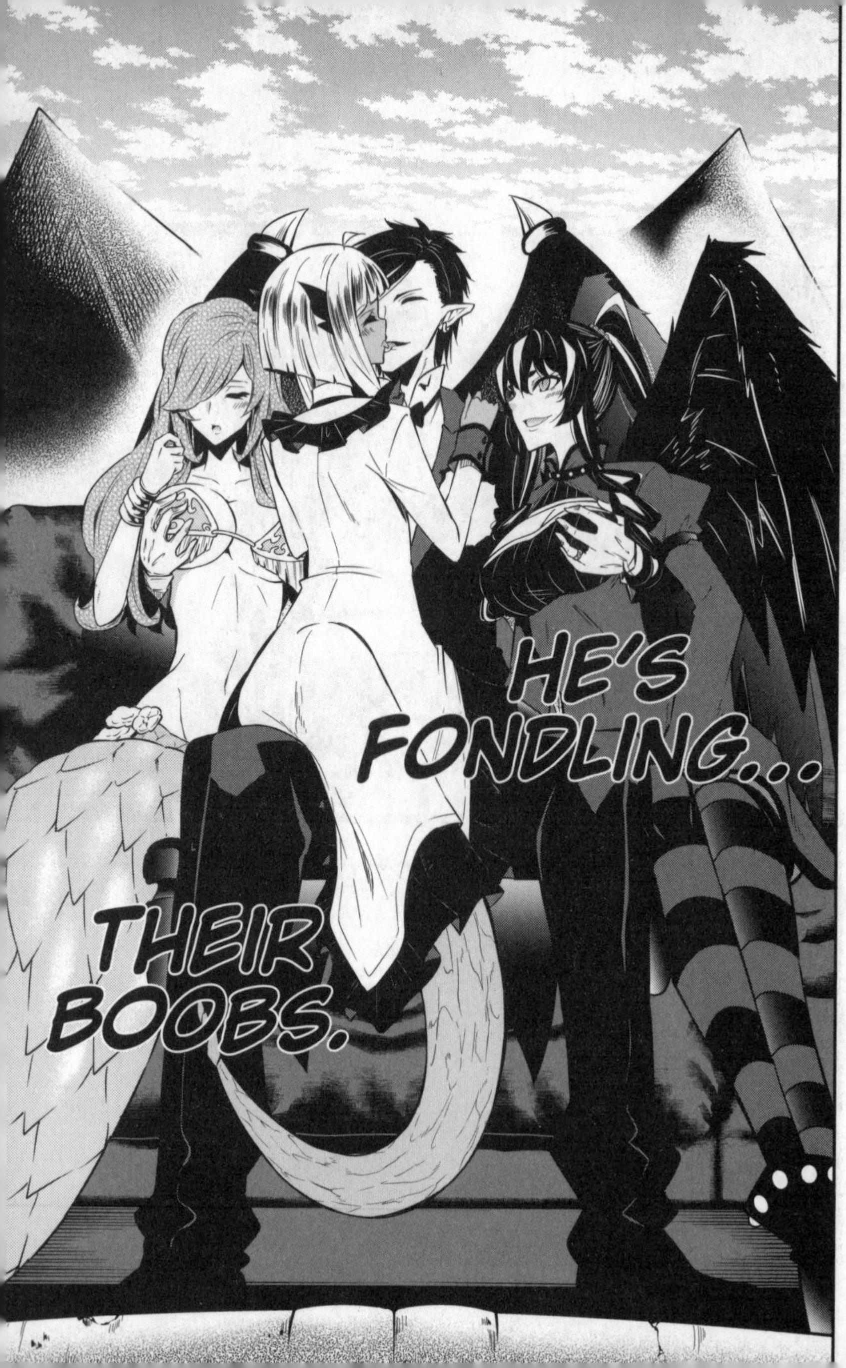
HE'S FONDLING...
THEIR BOOBS.

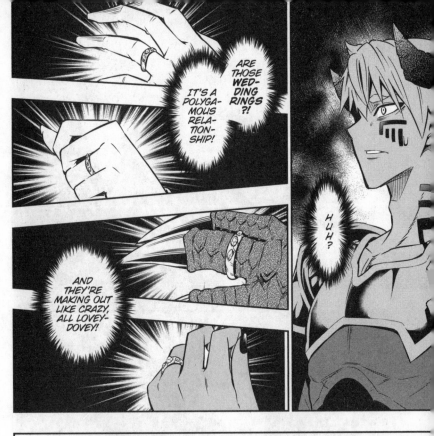

ARE THOSE WEDDING RINGS?!

IT'S A POLYGAMOUS RELATIONSHIP!

AND THEY'RE MAKING OUT LIKE CRAZY, ALL LOVEY-DOVEY!

HUH?

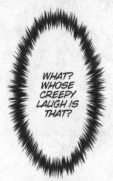

WHAT? WHOSE CREEPY LAUGH IS THAT?

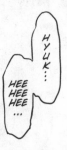

HYUK...

HEE HEE HEE...

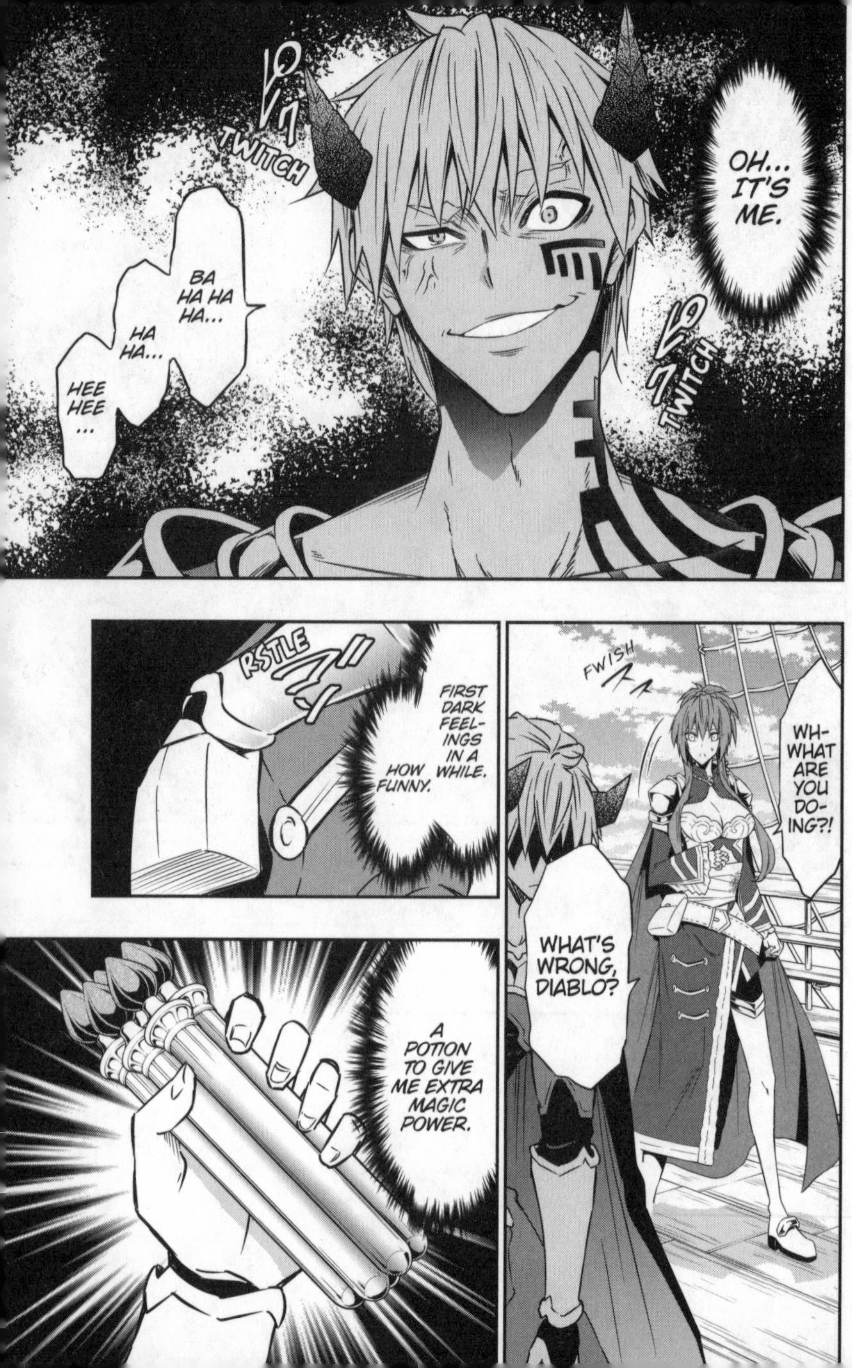
OH... IT'S ME.
TWITCH
BA HA HA HA...
HA HA...
HEE HEE ...
TWITCH
FWISH
WH-WHAT ARE YOU DOING?!
WHAT'S WRONG, DIABLO?
RSTLE
FIRST DARK FEELINGS IN A WHILE.
HOW FUNNY.
A POTION TO GIVE ME EXTRA MAGIC POWER.

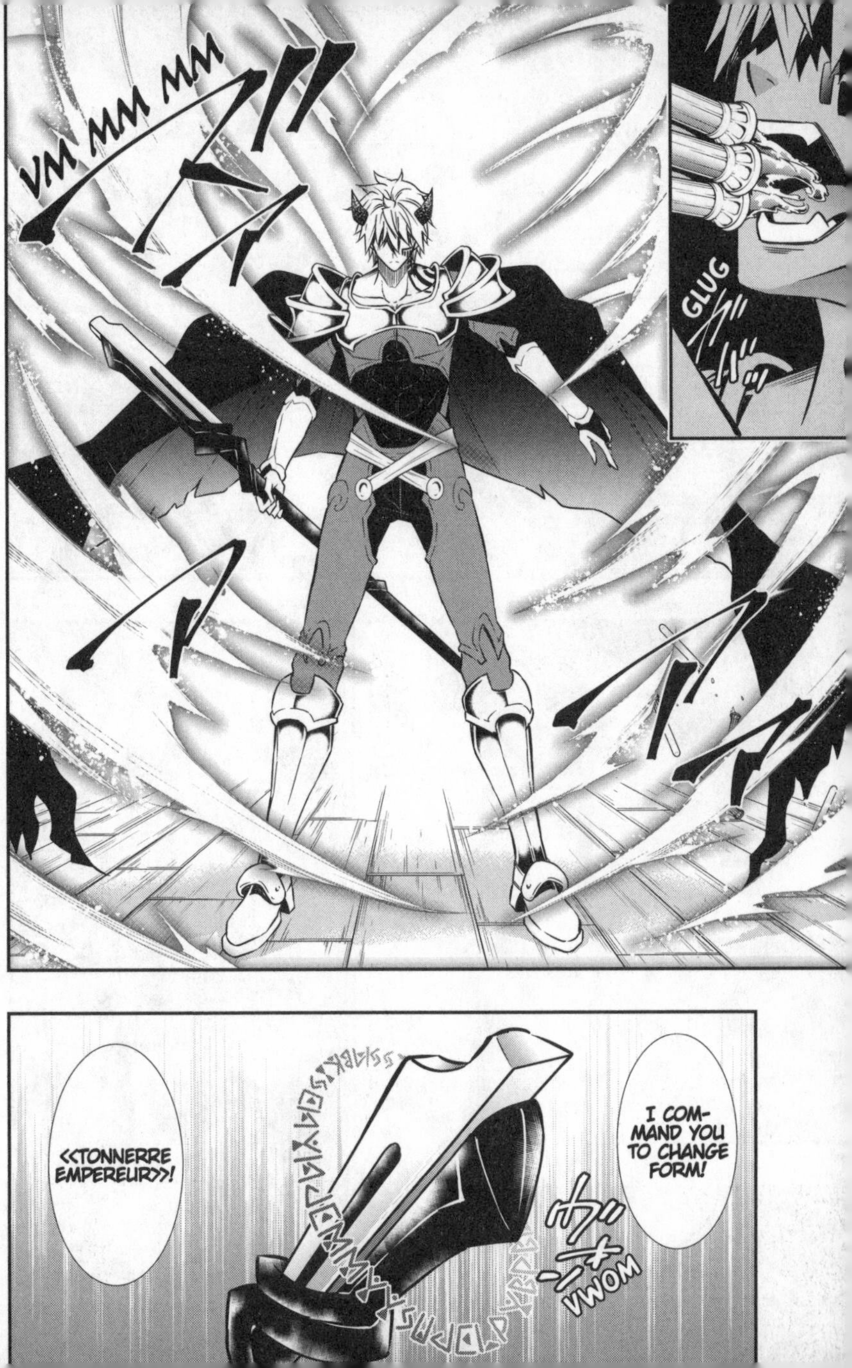
GLUG
VM MM MM
I COM-MAND YOU TO CHANGE FORM!
VWOM
<<TONNERRE EMPEREUR>>!

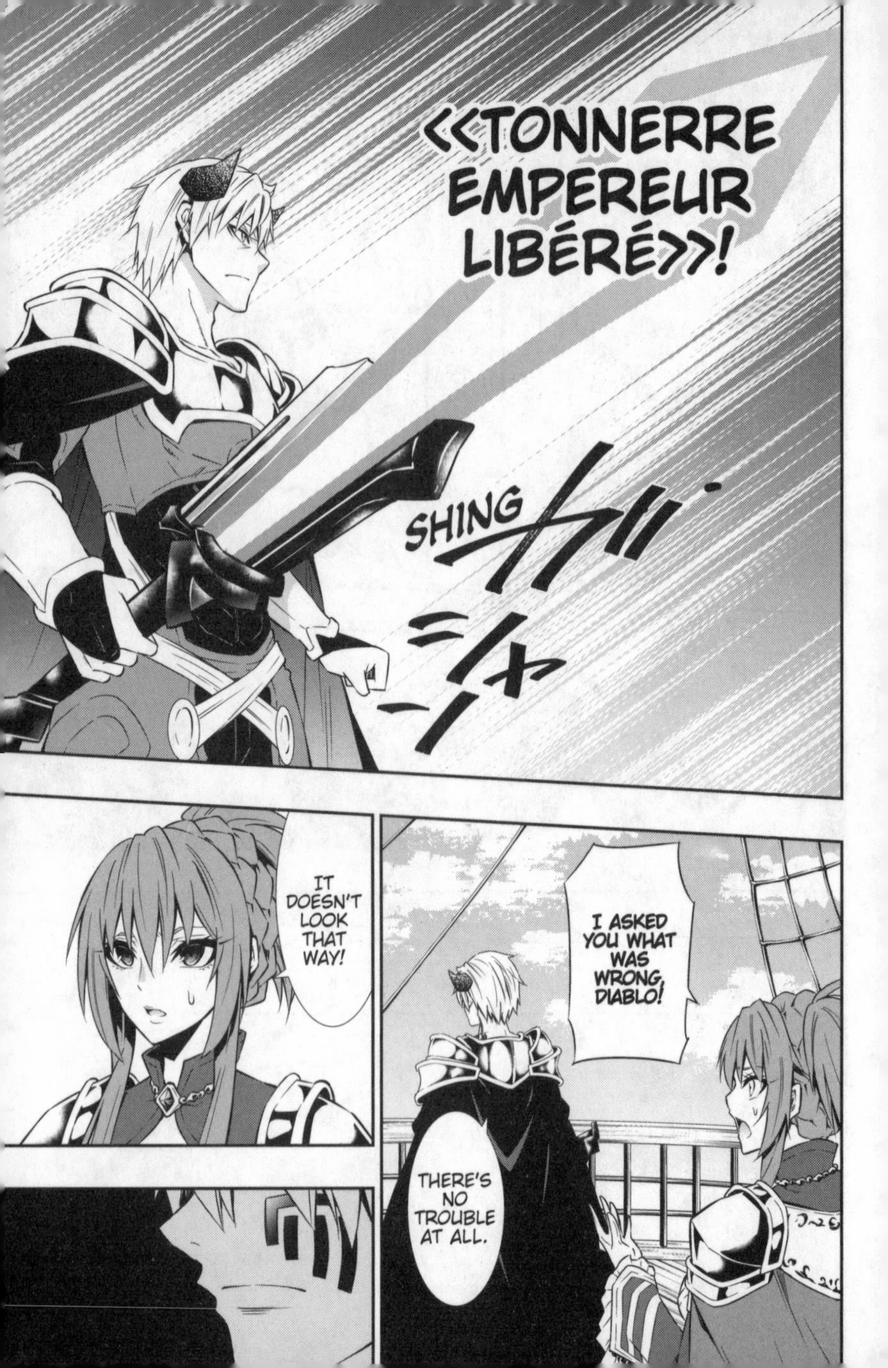
<<TONNERRE EMPEREUR LIBÉRÉ>>!
SHING
I ASKED YOU WHAT WAS WRONG, DIABLO!
THERE'S NO TROUBLE AT ALL.
IT DOESN'T LOOK THAT WAY!

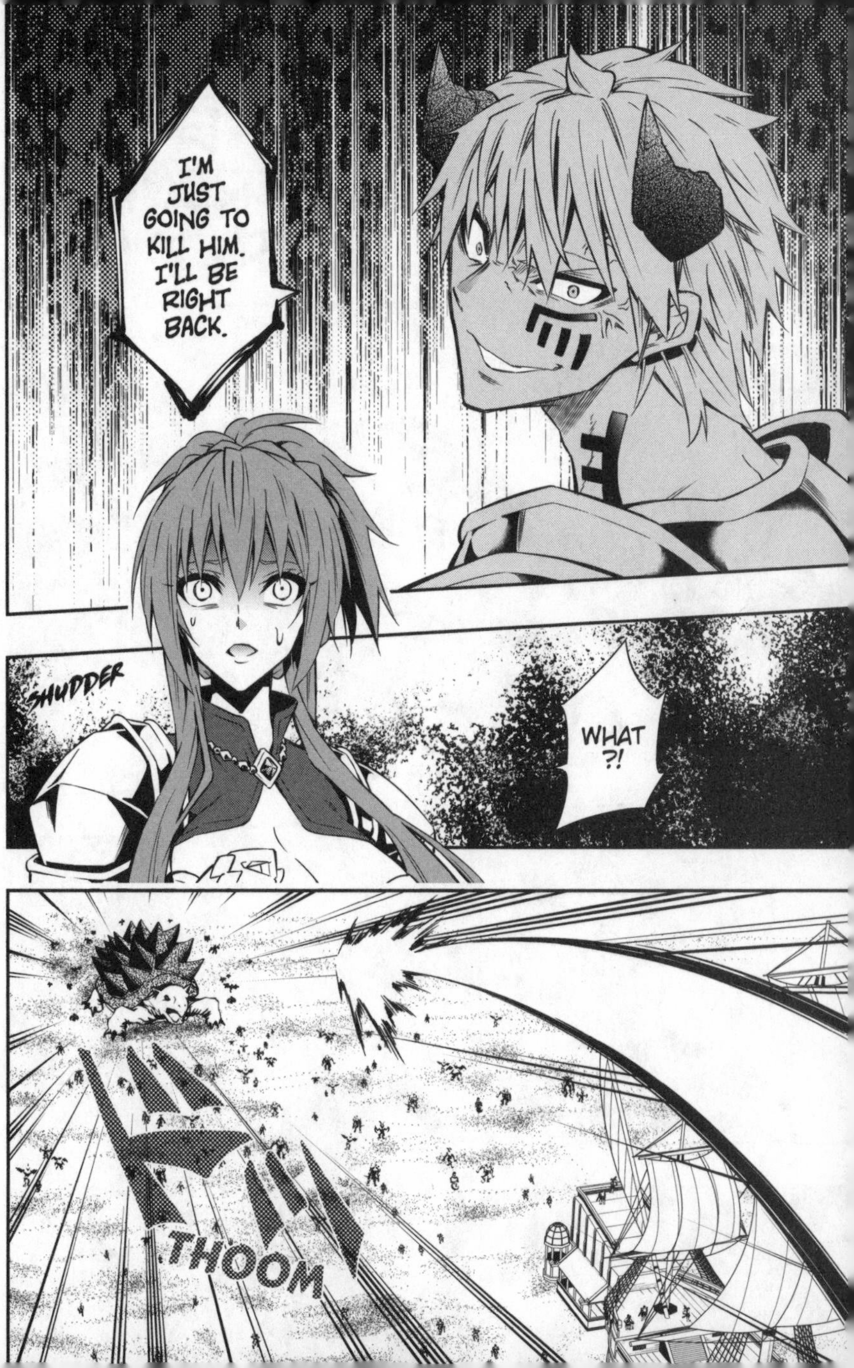
I'M JUST GOING TO KILL HIM. I'LL BE RIGHT BACK.
WHAT ?!
SHUDDER
THOOM

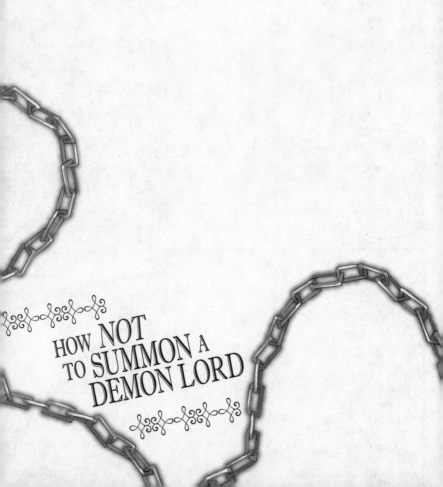

HOW NOT
TO SUMMON A
DEMON LORD

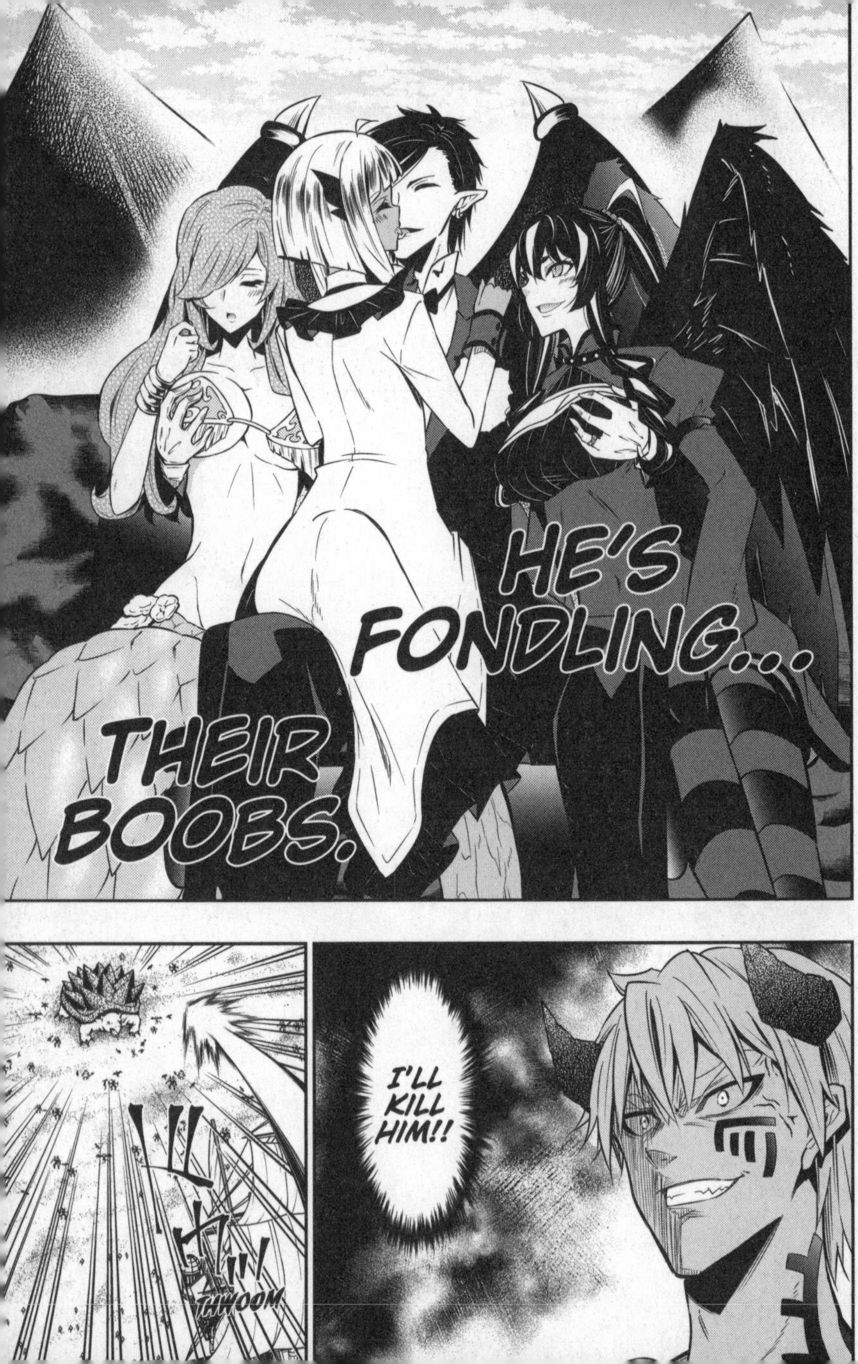
HE'S FONDLING...
THEIR BOOBS.
I'LL KILL HIM!!
THWOOM

61 TRYING TO USE A WEAPON II

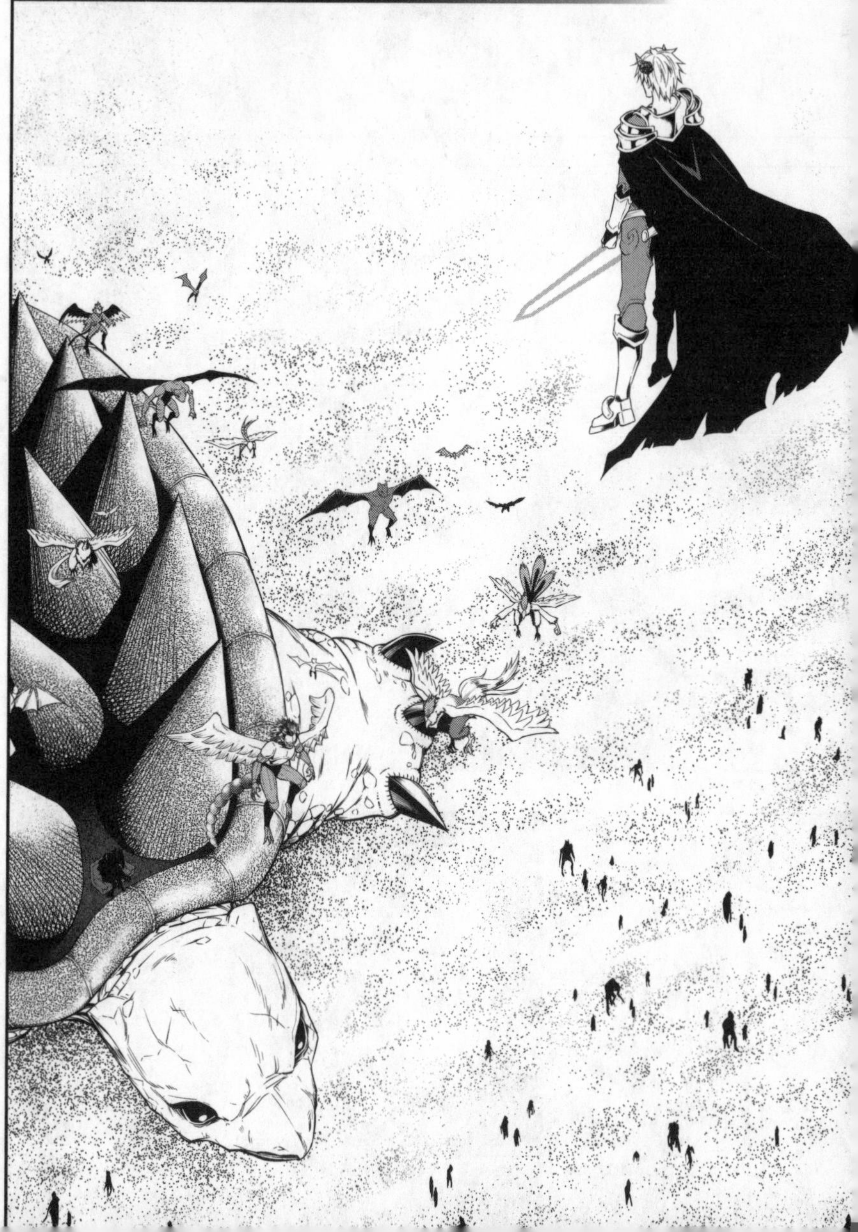

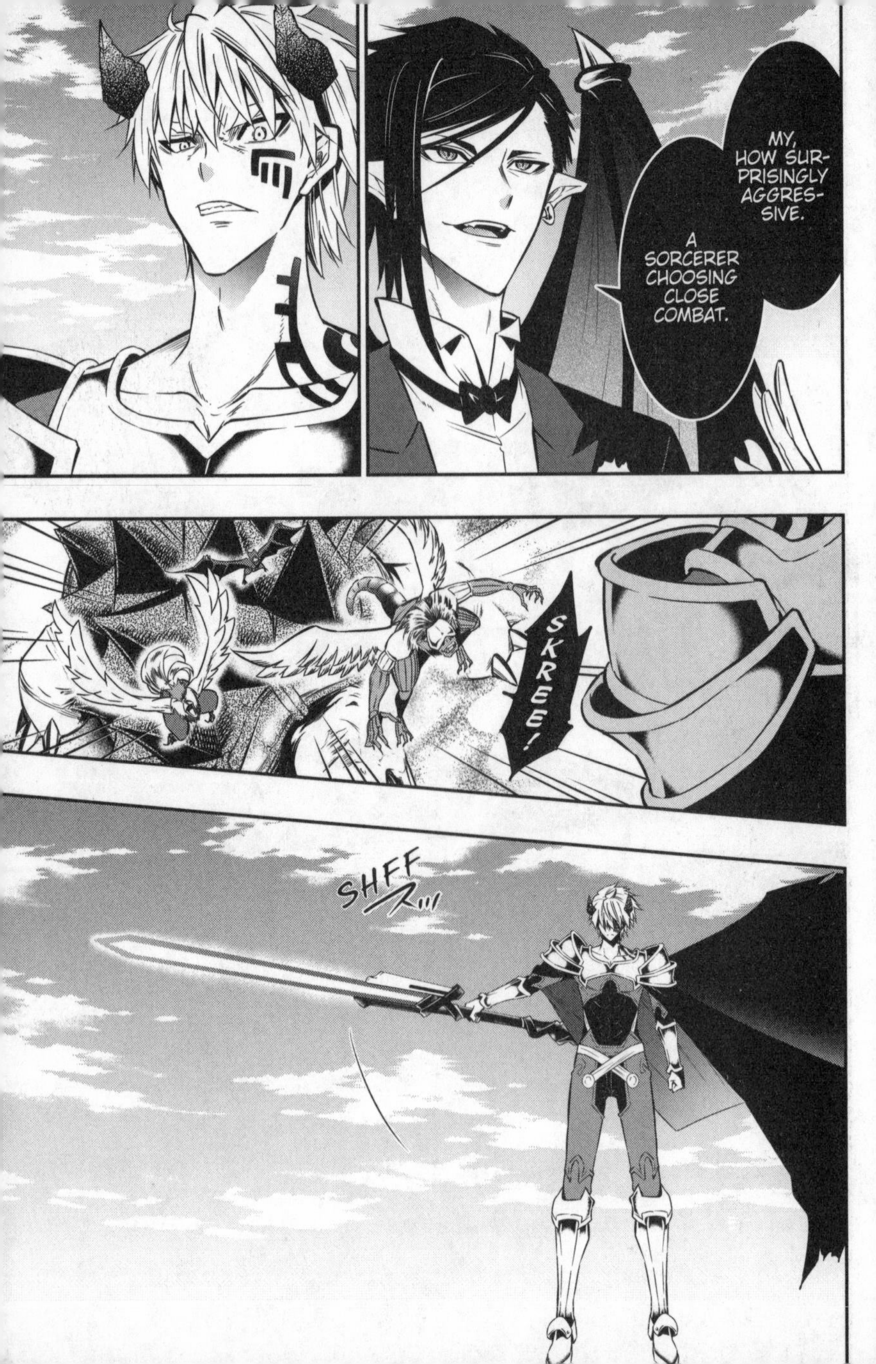
MY, HOW SUR-PRISINGLY AGGRES-SIVE.
A SORCERER CHOOSING CLOSE COMBAT.
SKREE!
SHFF

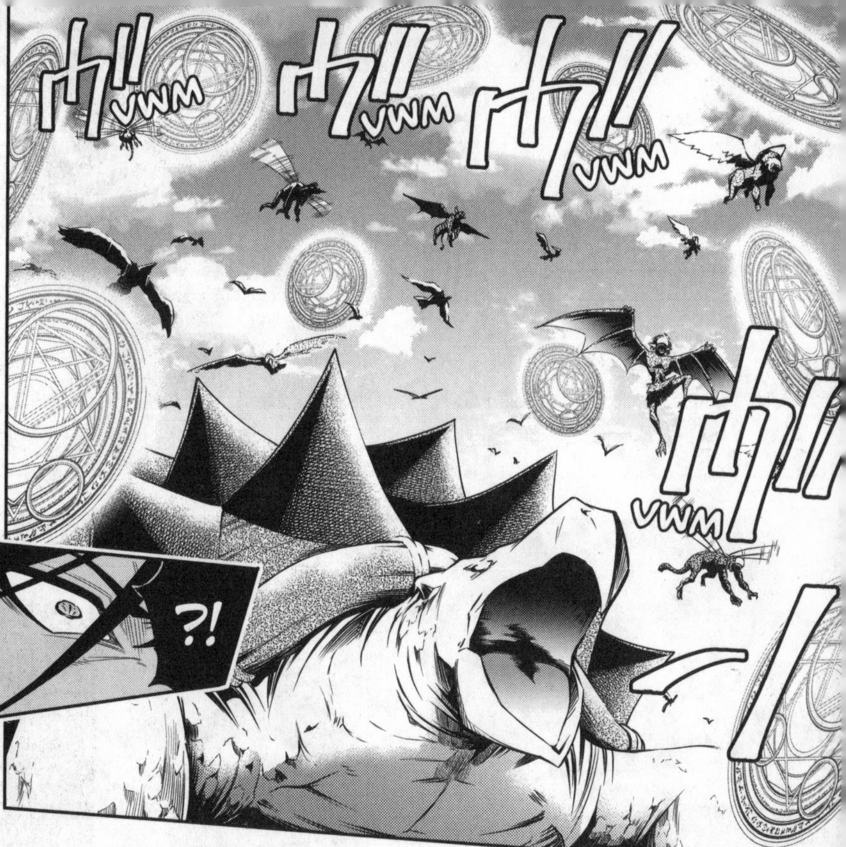
VWM
VWM
VWM
VWM
?!
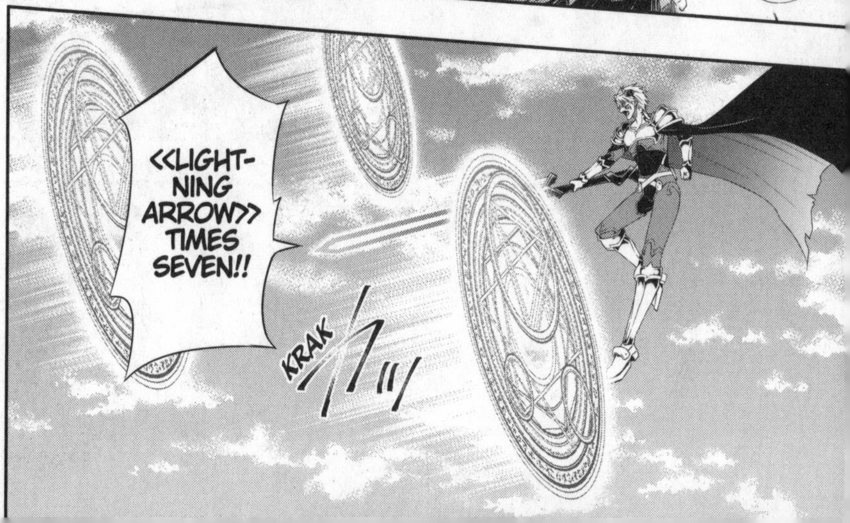
<<LIGHTNING ARROW>> TIMES SEVEN!!
KRAK

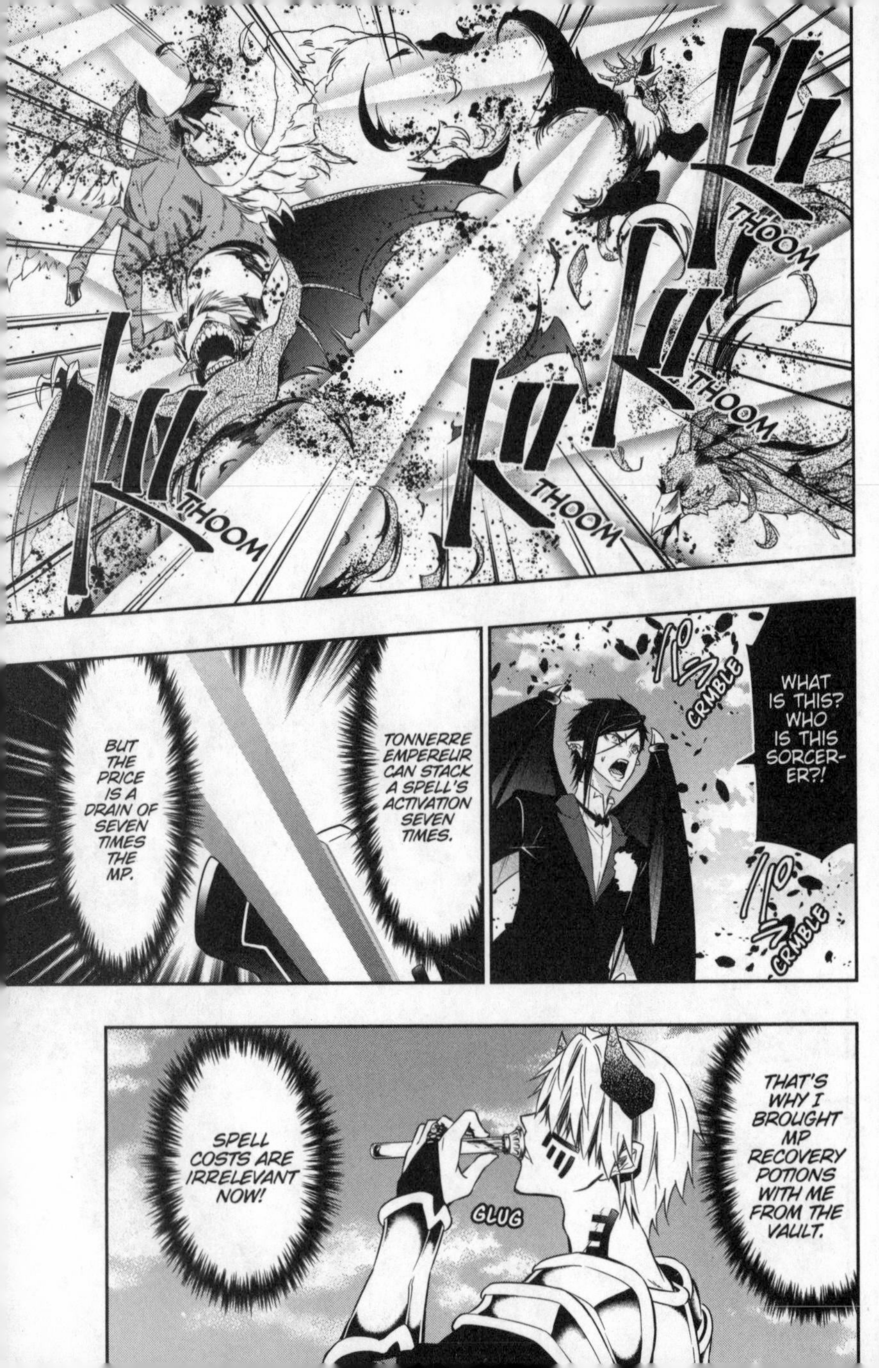
THOOM
THOOM
THOOM
THOOM
CRMBLE
WHAT IS THIS? WHO IS THIS SORCERER?!
CRMBLE
TONNERRE EMPEREUR CAN STACK A SPELL'S ACTIVATION SEVEN TIMES.
BUT THE PRICE IS A DRAIN OF SEVEN TIMES THE MP.
THAT'S WHY I BROUGHT MP RECOVERY POTIONS WITH ME FROM THE VAULT.
GLUG
SPELL COSTS ARE IRRELEVANT NOW!

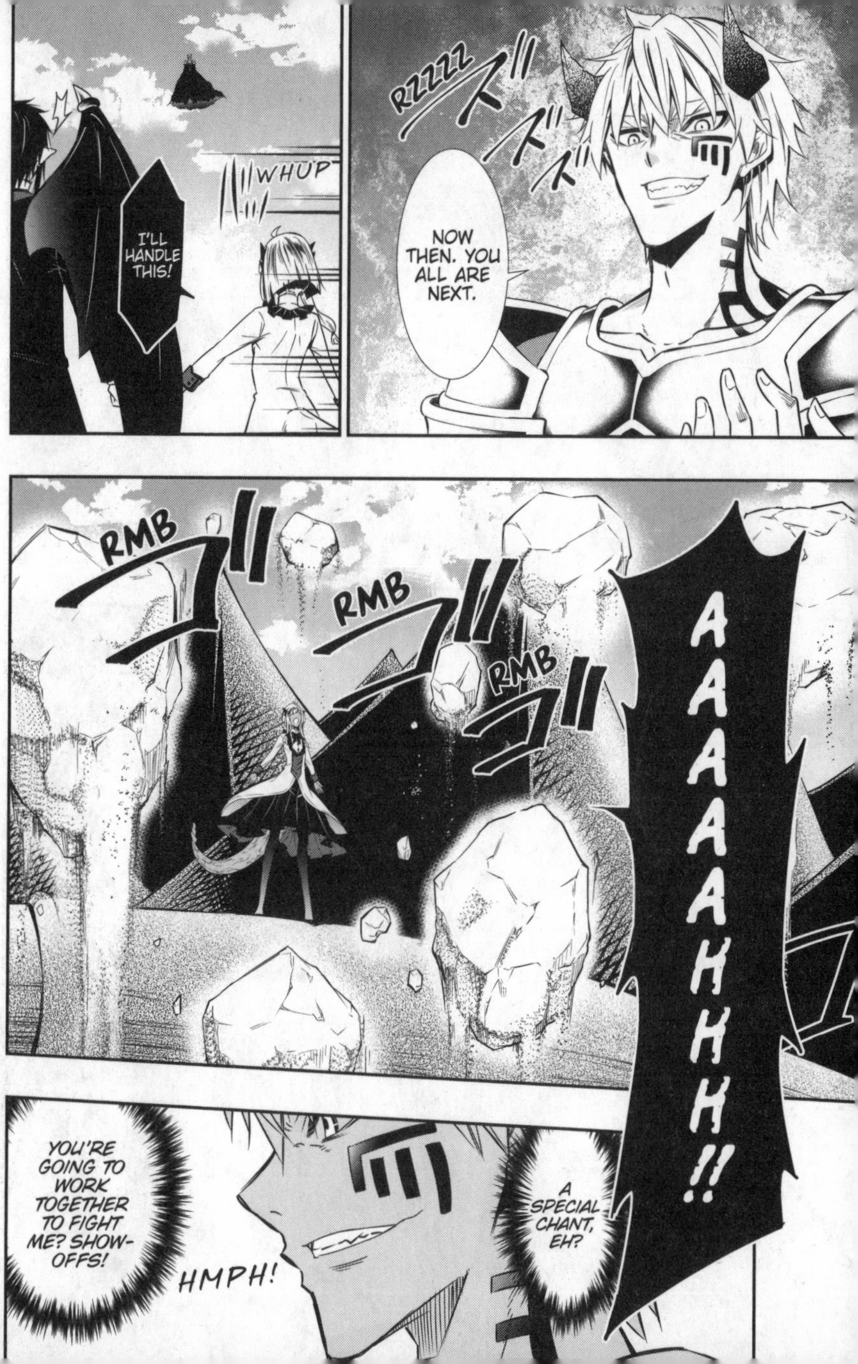
RZZZZ
NOW THEN. YOU ALL ARE NEXT.
WHUP
I'LL HANDLE THIS!
RMB
RMB
RMB
AAAAAHHH!!
A SPECIAL CHANT, EH?
YOU'RE GOING TO WORK TOGETHER TO FIGHT ME? SHOW-OFFS!
HMPH!

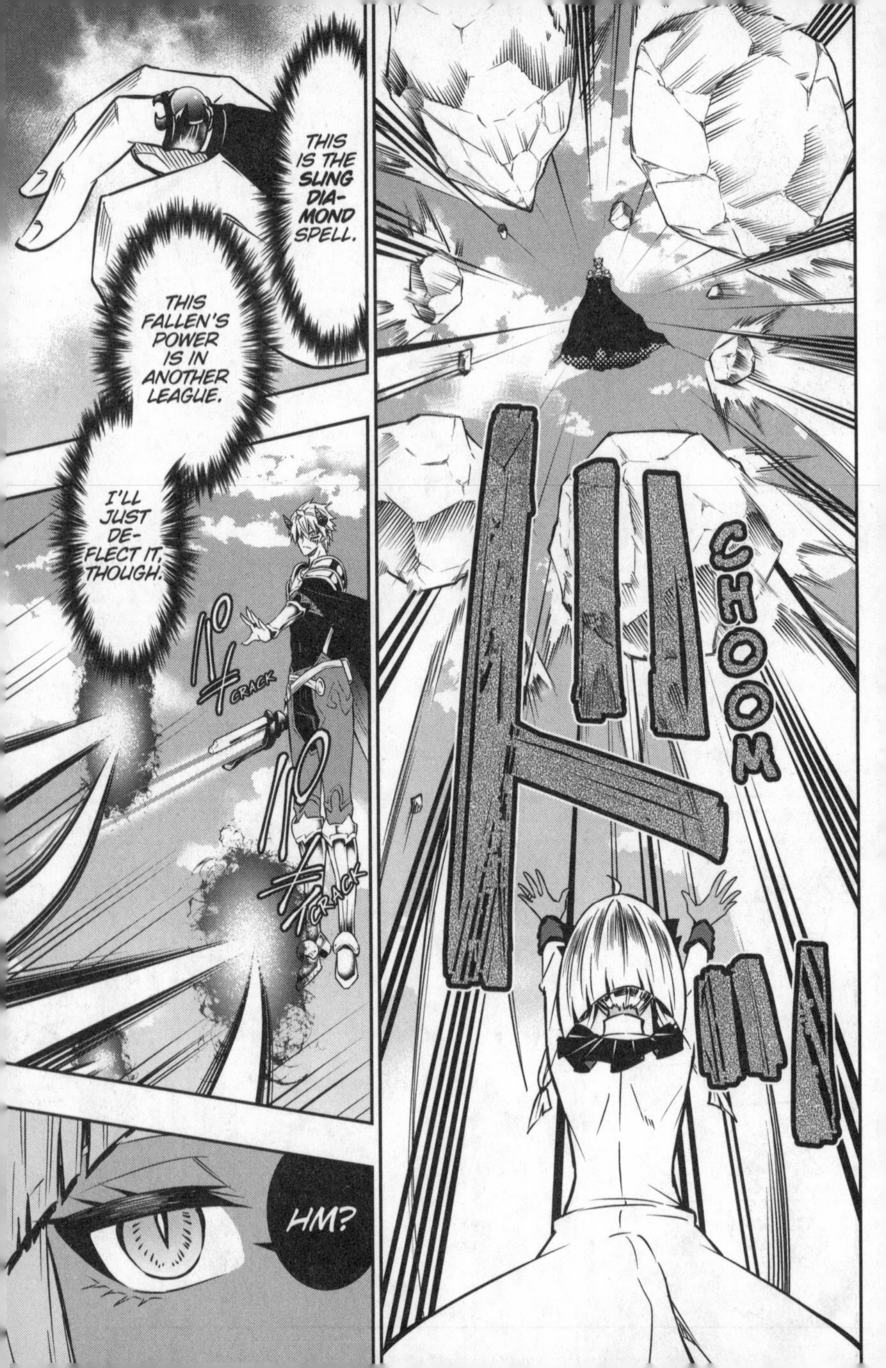
CHOOOM
THIS IS THE SLING DIAMOND SPELL.
THIS FALLEN'S POWER IS IN ANOTHER LEAGUE.
I'LL JUST DEFLECT IT, THOUGH.
CRACK
CRACK
HM?

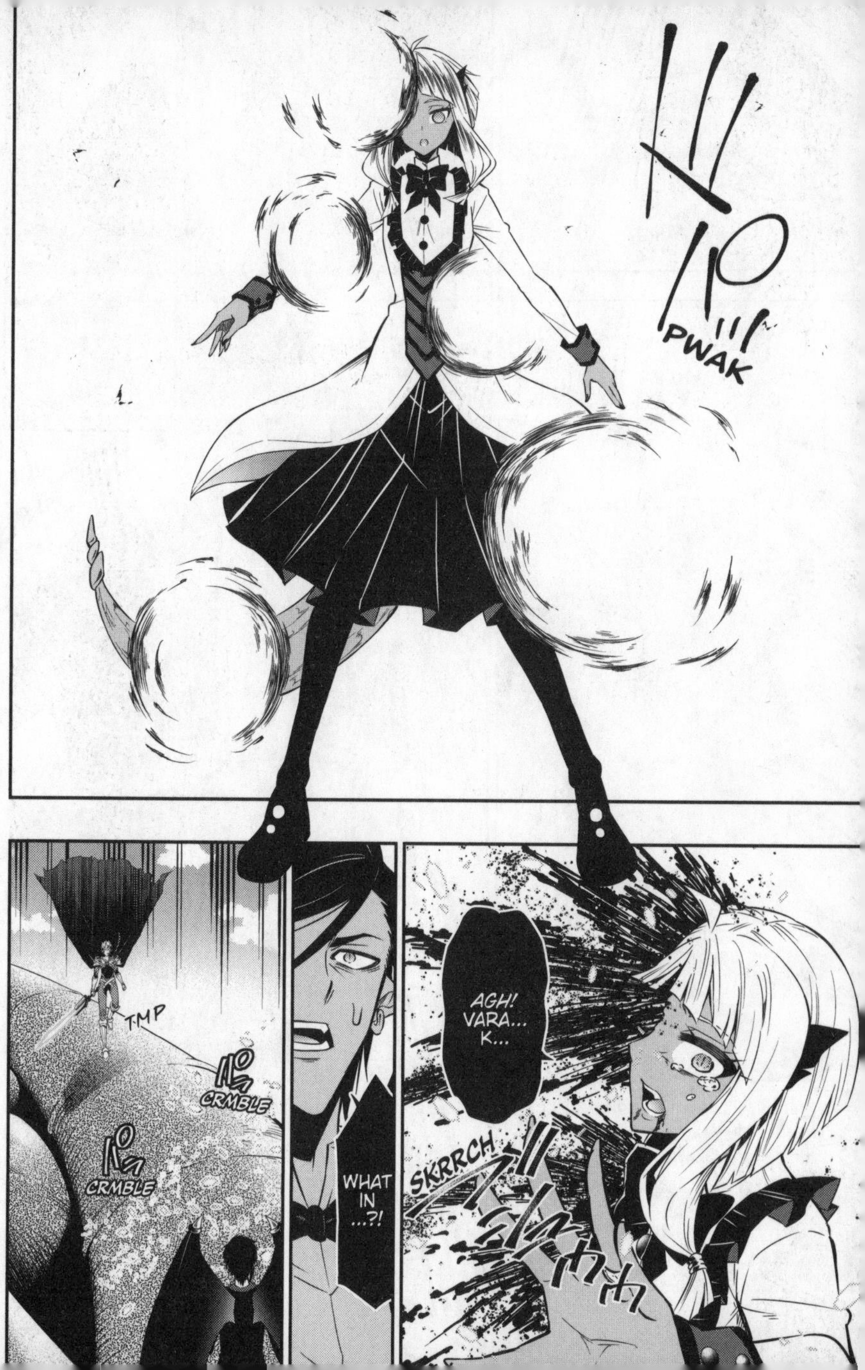
PWAK
AGH! VARA... K...
SKRRCH
WHAT IN ...?!
TMP
CRMBLE
CRMBLE

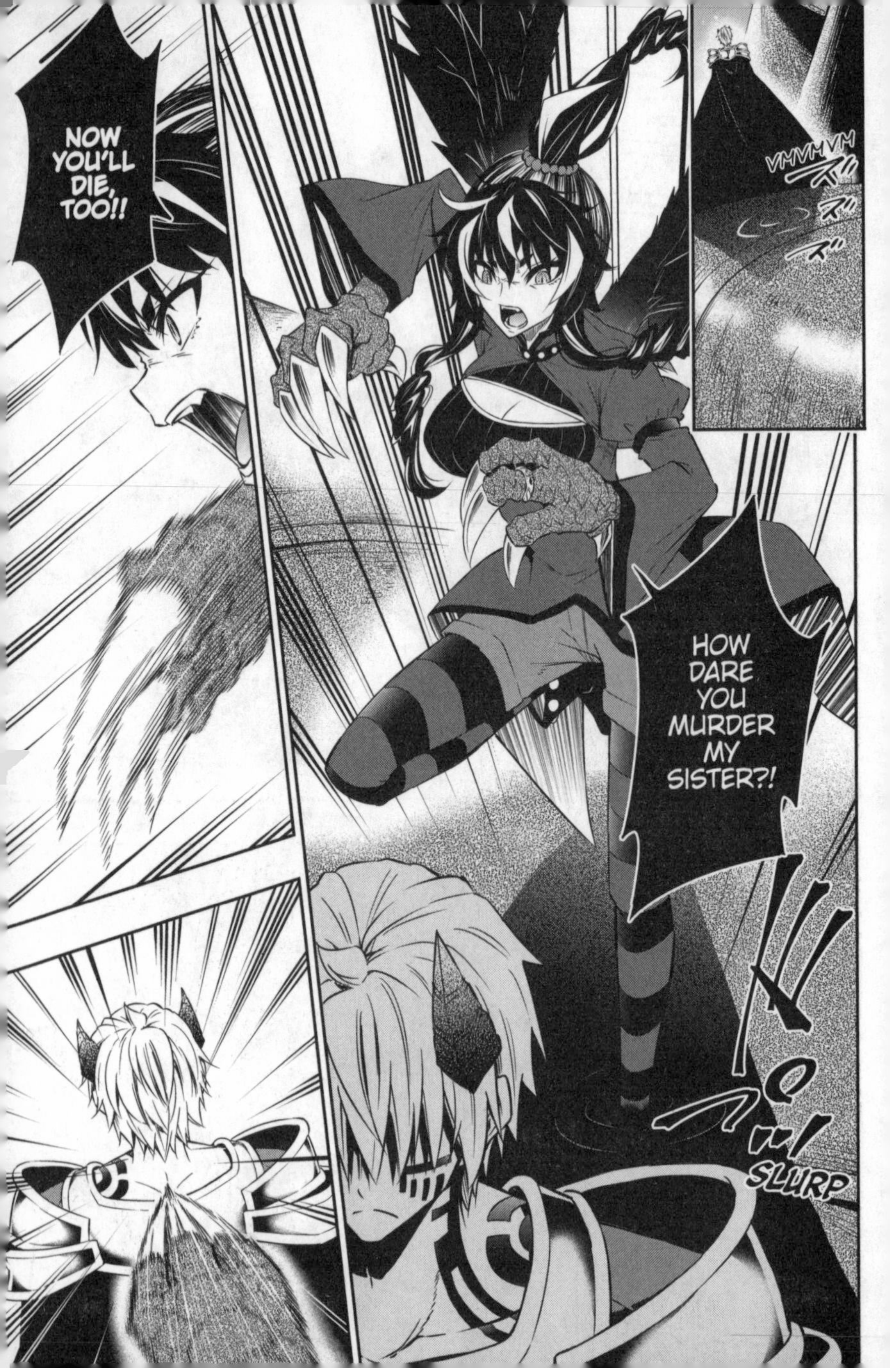
VMVMVM
HOW DARE YOU MURDER MY SISTER?!
NOW YOU'LL DIE, TOO!!
SLURP

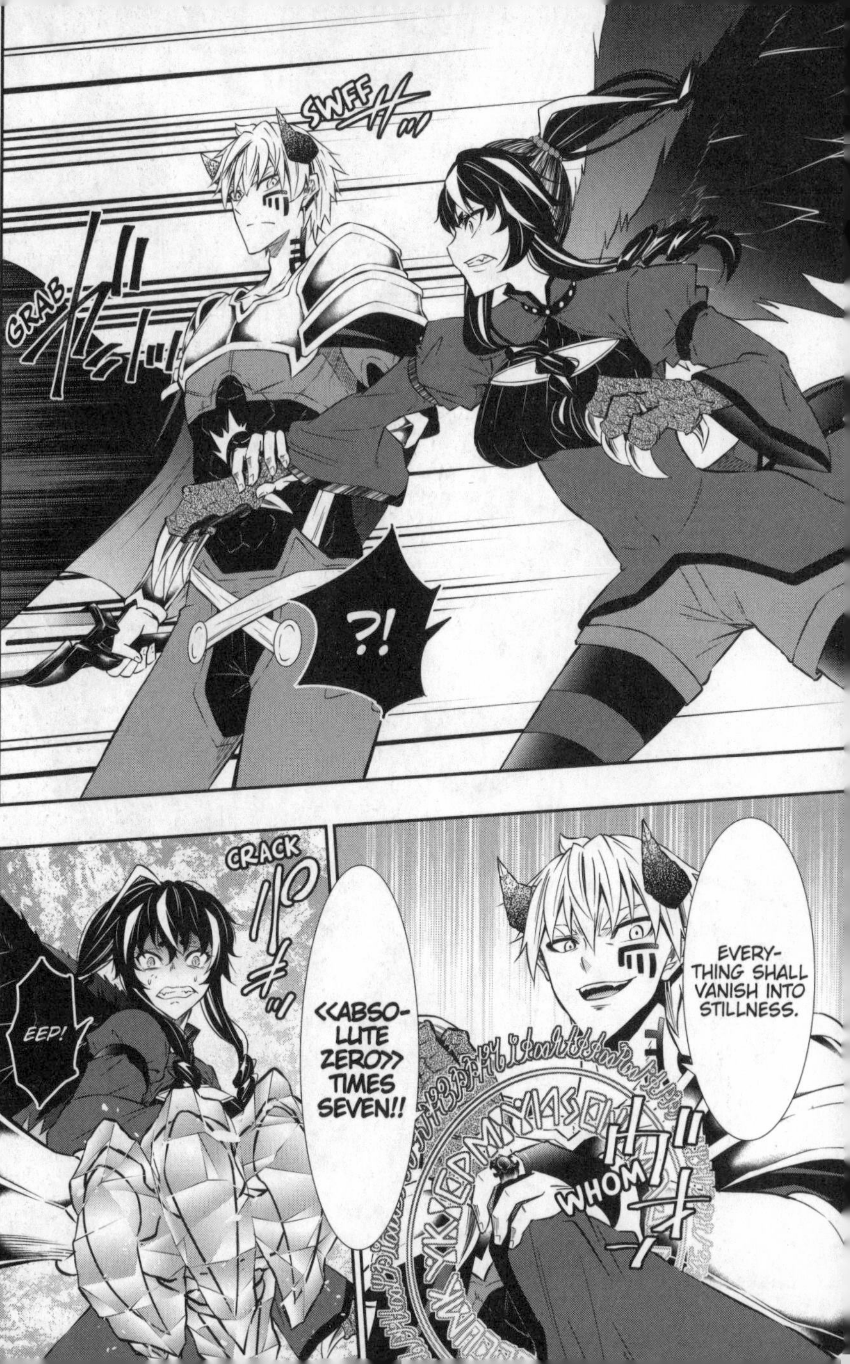
SWFF
GRAB
?!
EVERY-THING SHALL VANISH INTO STILLNESS.
<<ABSO-LUTE ZERO>> TIMES SEVEN!!
WHOM
CRACK
EEP!

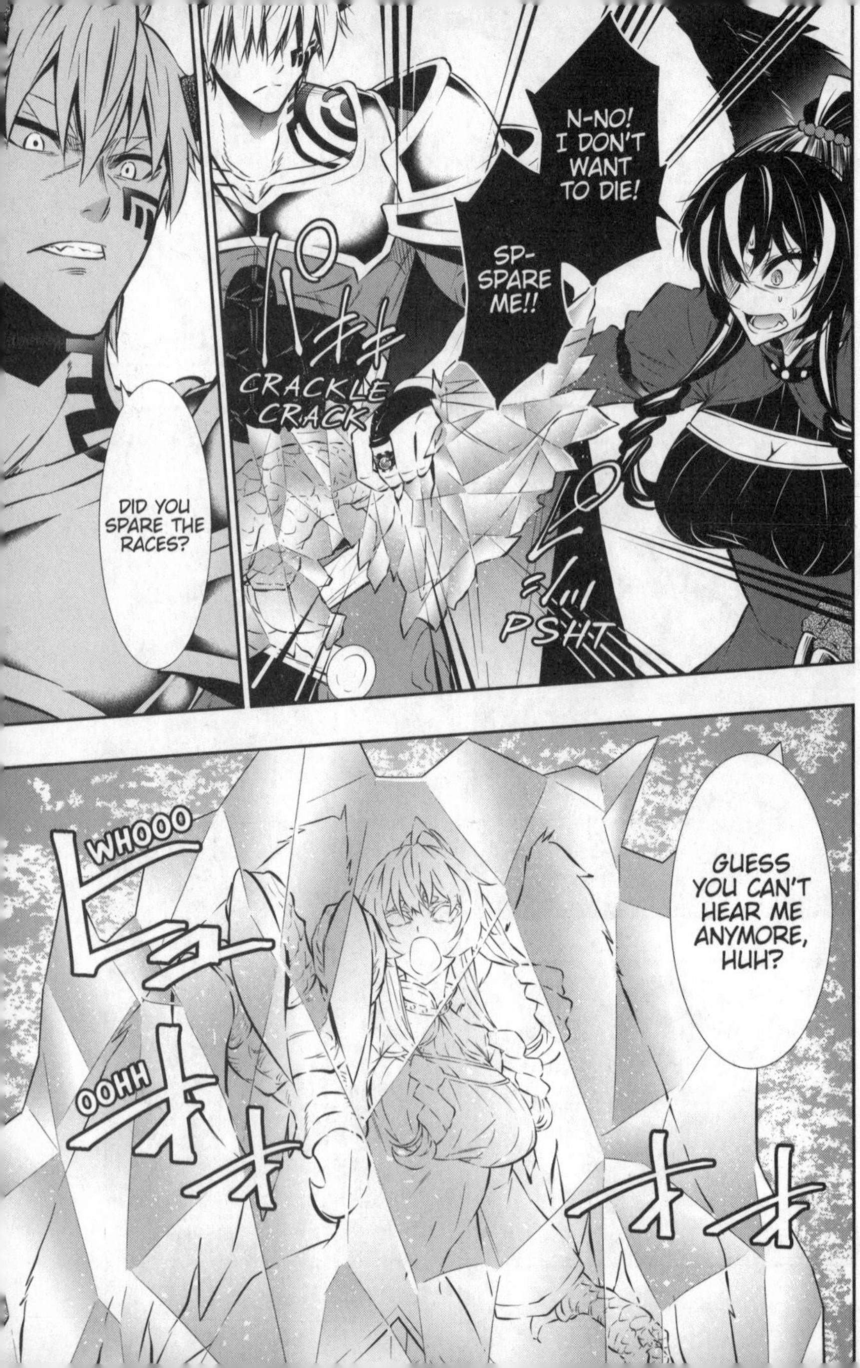
N-NO! I DON'T WANT TO DIE!
SP- SPARE ME!!
CRACKLE CRACK
PSHT
DID YOU SPARE THE RACES?
GUESS YOU CAN'T HEAR ME ANYMORE, HUH?
WHOOO
OOHH

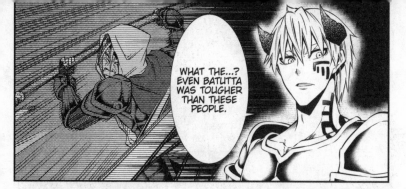

WHAT THE...? EVEN BATUTTA WAS TOUGHER THAN THESE PEOPLE.

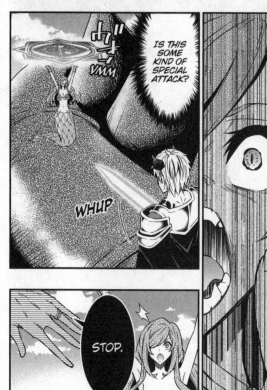

IS THIS SOME KIND OF SPECIAL ATTACK?

VMM

WHUP

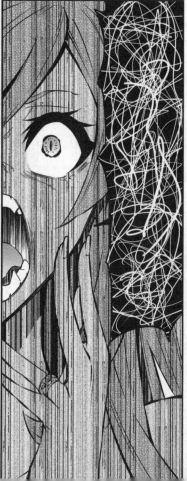

STOP.

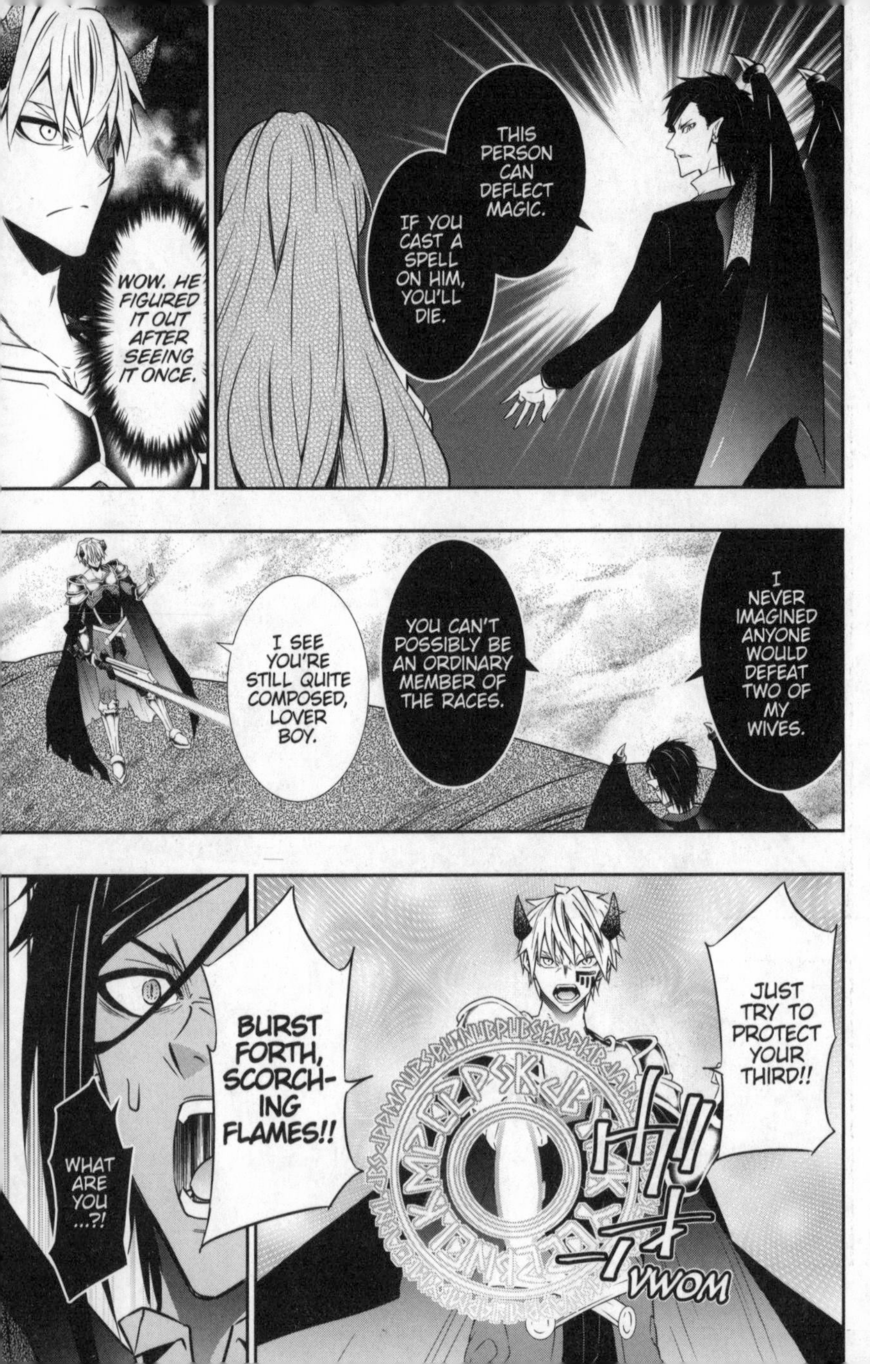
THIS PERSON CAN DEFLECT MAGIC.
IF YOU CAST A SPELL ON HIM, YOU'LL DIE.
WOW. HE FIGURED IT OUT AFTER SEEING IT ONCE.
I NEVER IMAGINED ANYONE WOULD DEFEAT TWO OF MY WIVES.
YOU CAN'T POSSIBLY BE AN ORDINARY MEMBER OF THE RACES.
I SEE YOU'RE STILL QUITE COMPOSED, LOVER BOY.
JUST TRY TO PROTECT YOUR THIRD!!
VWOM
BURST FORTH, SCORCHING FLAMES!!
WHAT ARE YOU ...?!

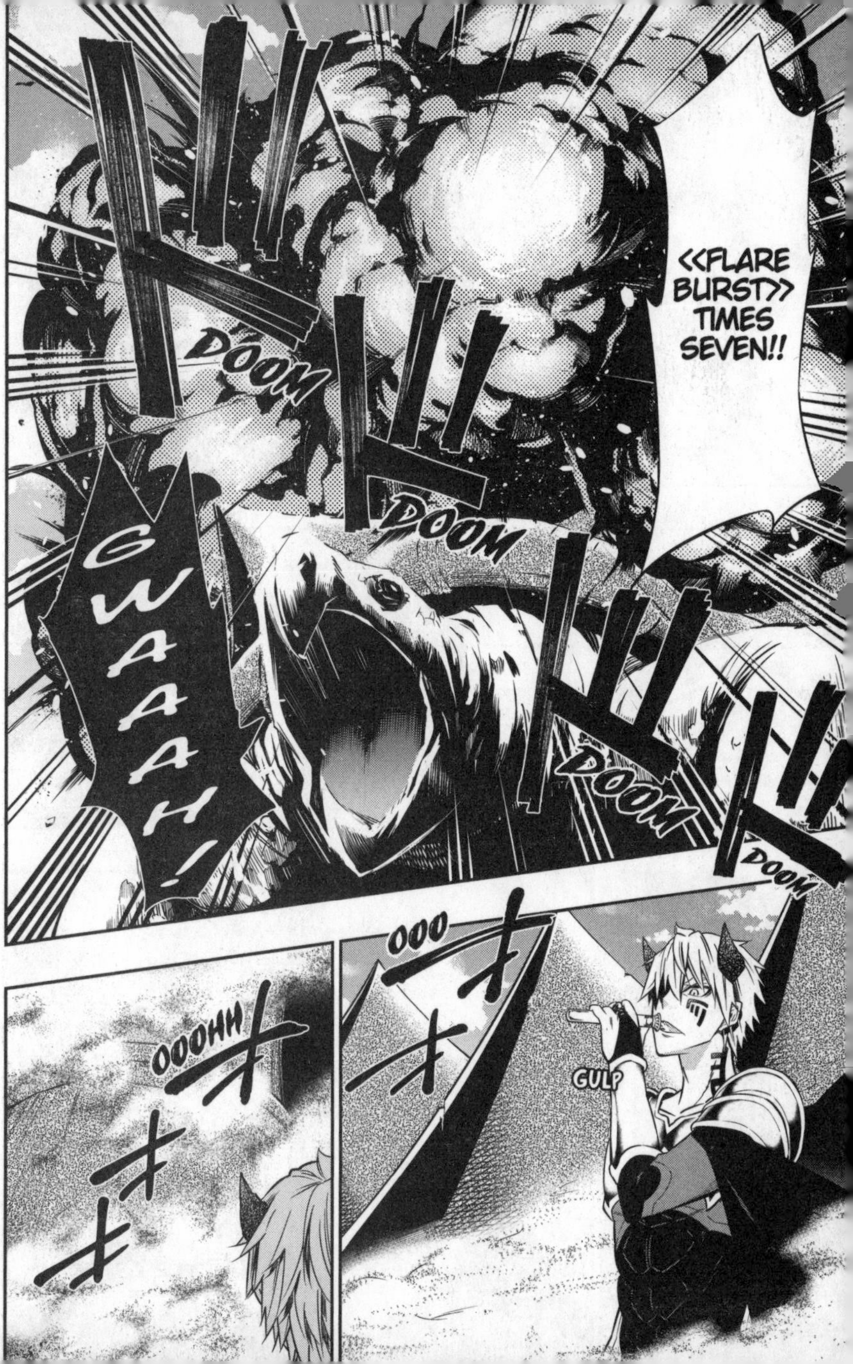
<<FLARE BURST>> TIMES SEVEN!!
DOOM
DOOM
DOOM
DOOM
DOOM
GWAAAH!
OOO
GULP
OOOHH

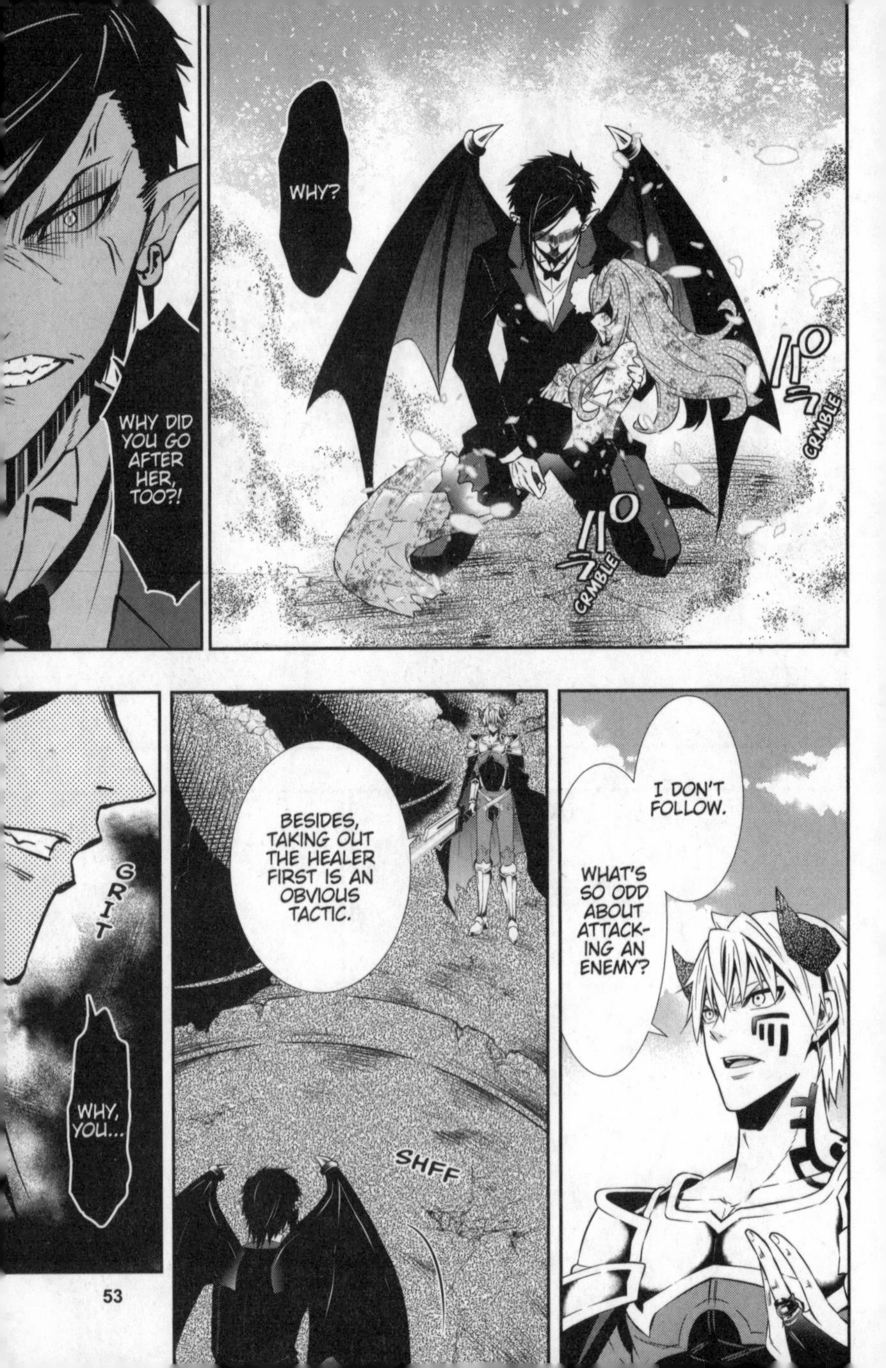

WHY?
CRMBLE
CRMBLE
WHY DID YOU GO AFTER HER, TOO?!
I DON'T FOLLOW.
WHAT'S SO ODD ABOUT ATTACKING AN ENEMY?
BESIDES, TAKING OUT THE HEALER FIRST IS AN OBVIOUS TACTIC.
SHFF
GRIT
WHY, YOU...

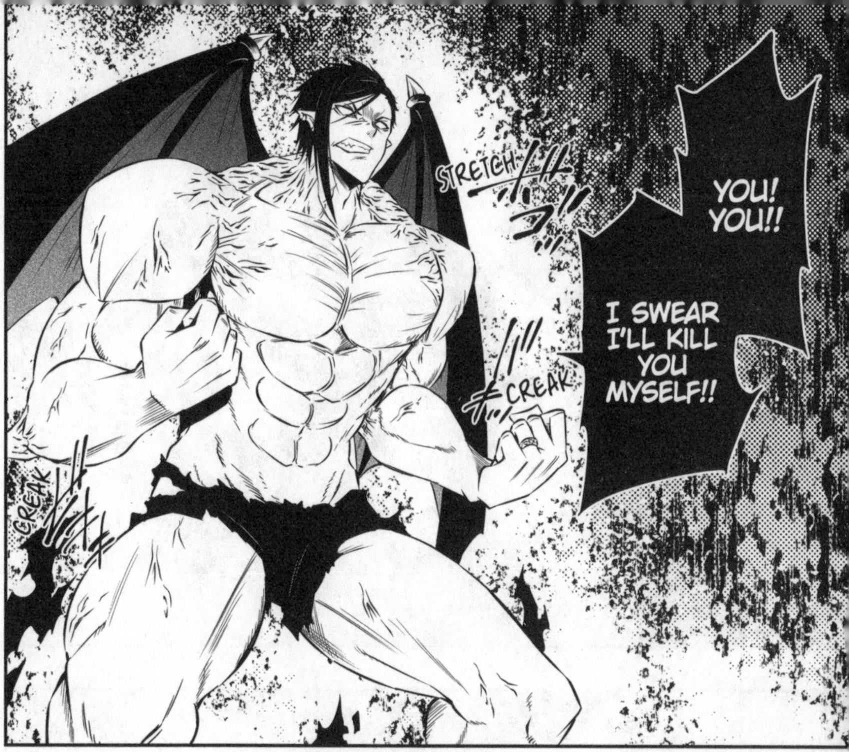
YOU! YOU!!
I SWEAR I'LL KILL YOU MYSELF!!
STRETCH
CREAK
CREAK
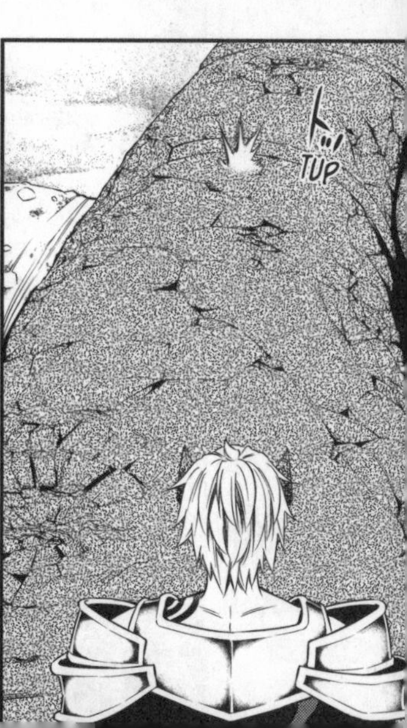
TUP
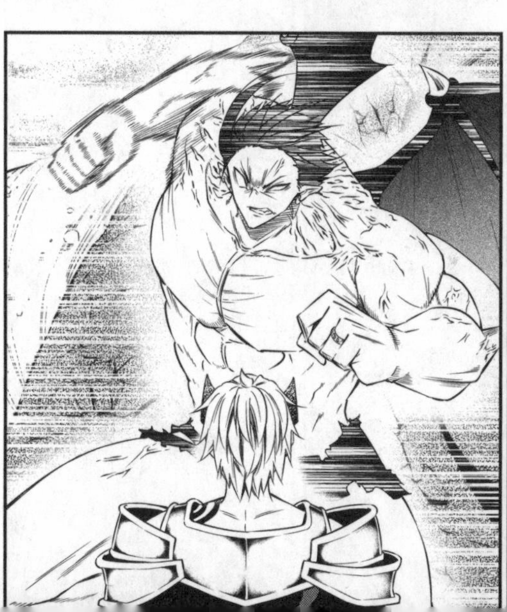

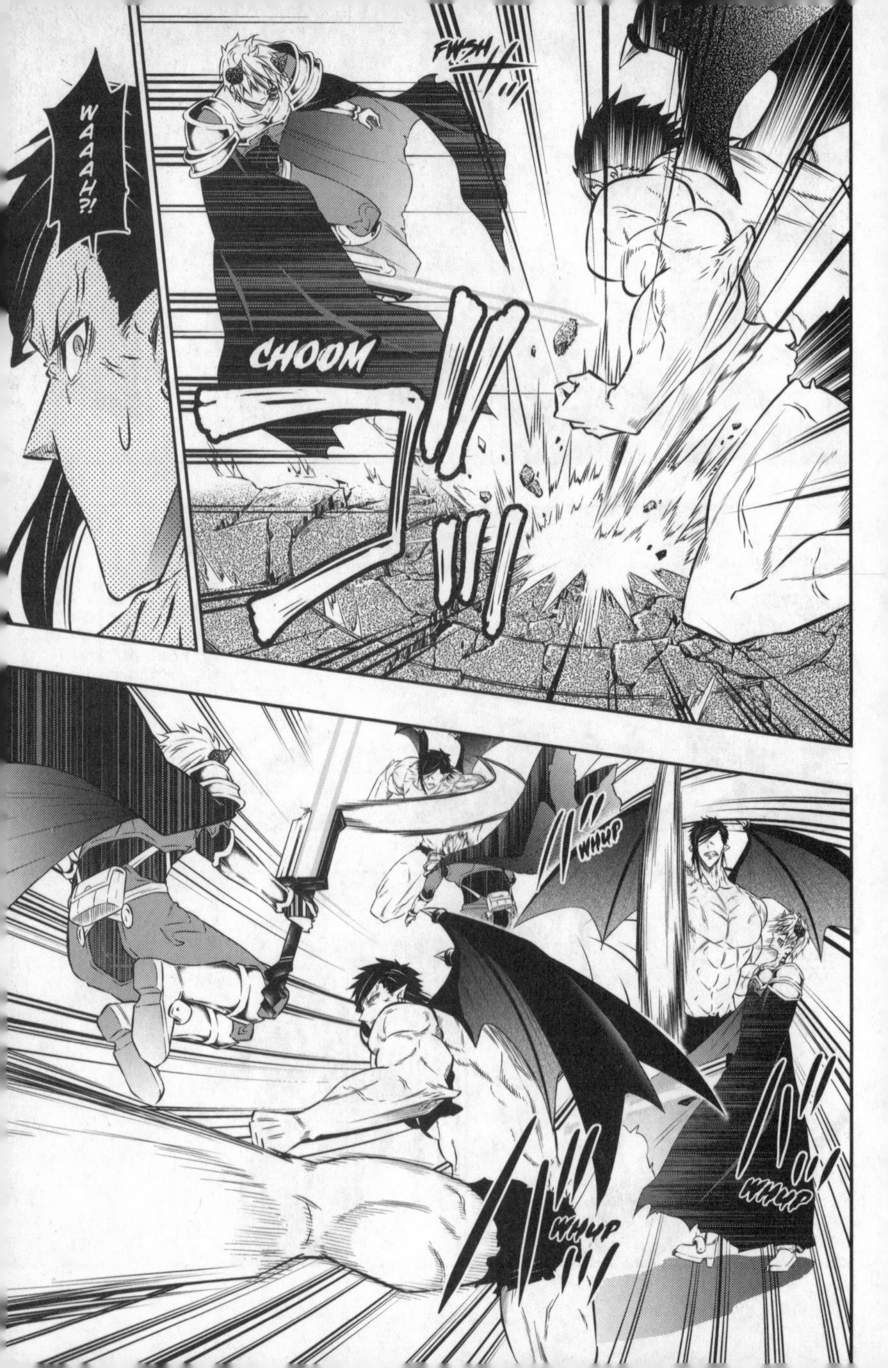
FWSH
WAAAAH?!
CHOOM
WHUP
WHUP
WHUP

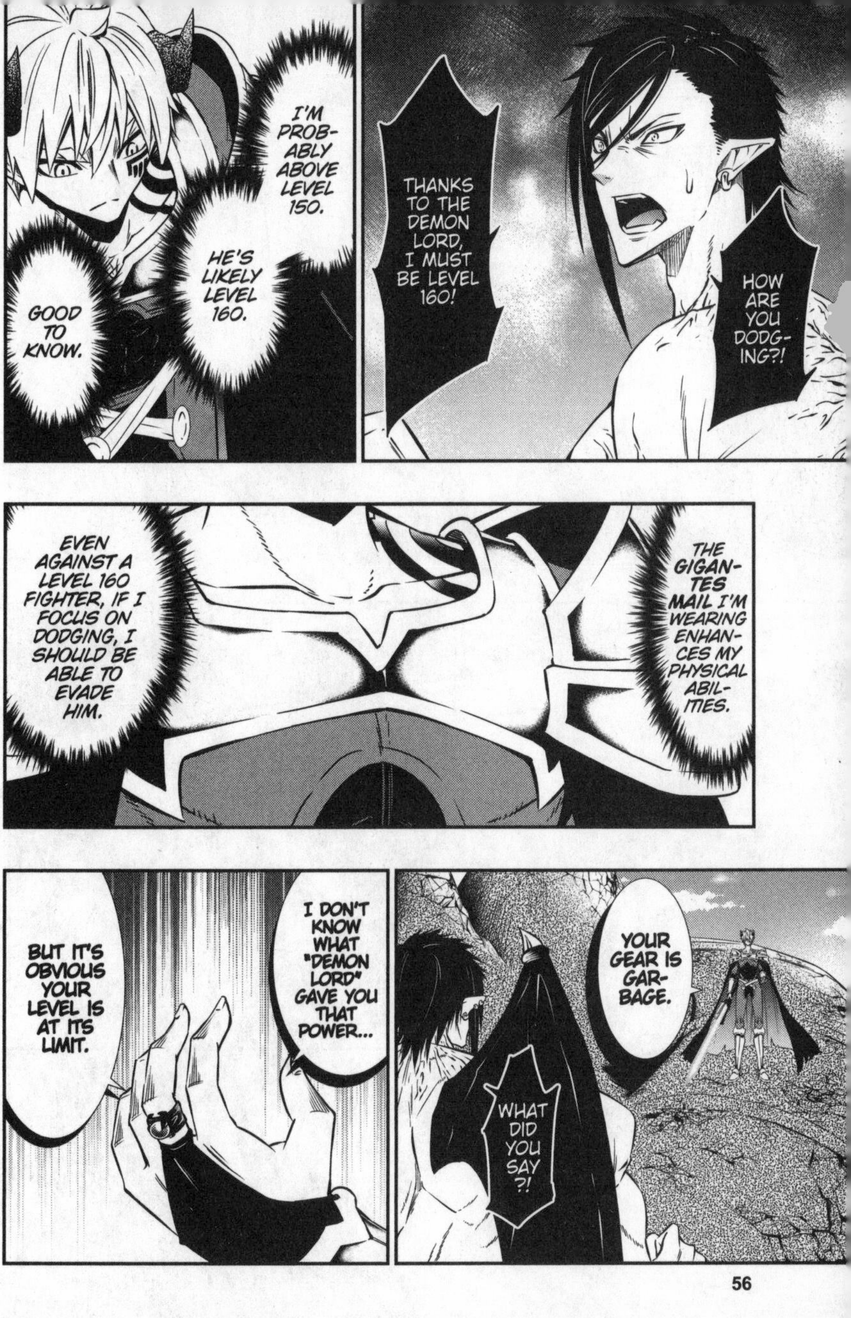
HOW ARE YOU DODGING?!
THANKS TO THE DEMON LORD, I MUST BE LEVEL 160!
I'M PROBABLY ABOVE LEVEL 150.
HE'S LIKELY LEVEL 160.
GOOD TO KNOW.
THE GIGANTES MAIL I'M WEARING ENHANCES MY PHYSICAL ABILITIES.
EVEN AGAINST A LEVEL 160 FIGHTER, IF I FOCUS ON DODGING, I SHOULD BE ABLE TO EVADE HIM.
YOUR GEAR IS GARBAGE.
WHAT DID YOU SAY?!
I DON'T KNOW WHAT "DEMON LORD" GAVE YOU THAT POWER...
BUT IT'S OBVIOUS YOUR LEVEL IS AT ITS LIMIT.

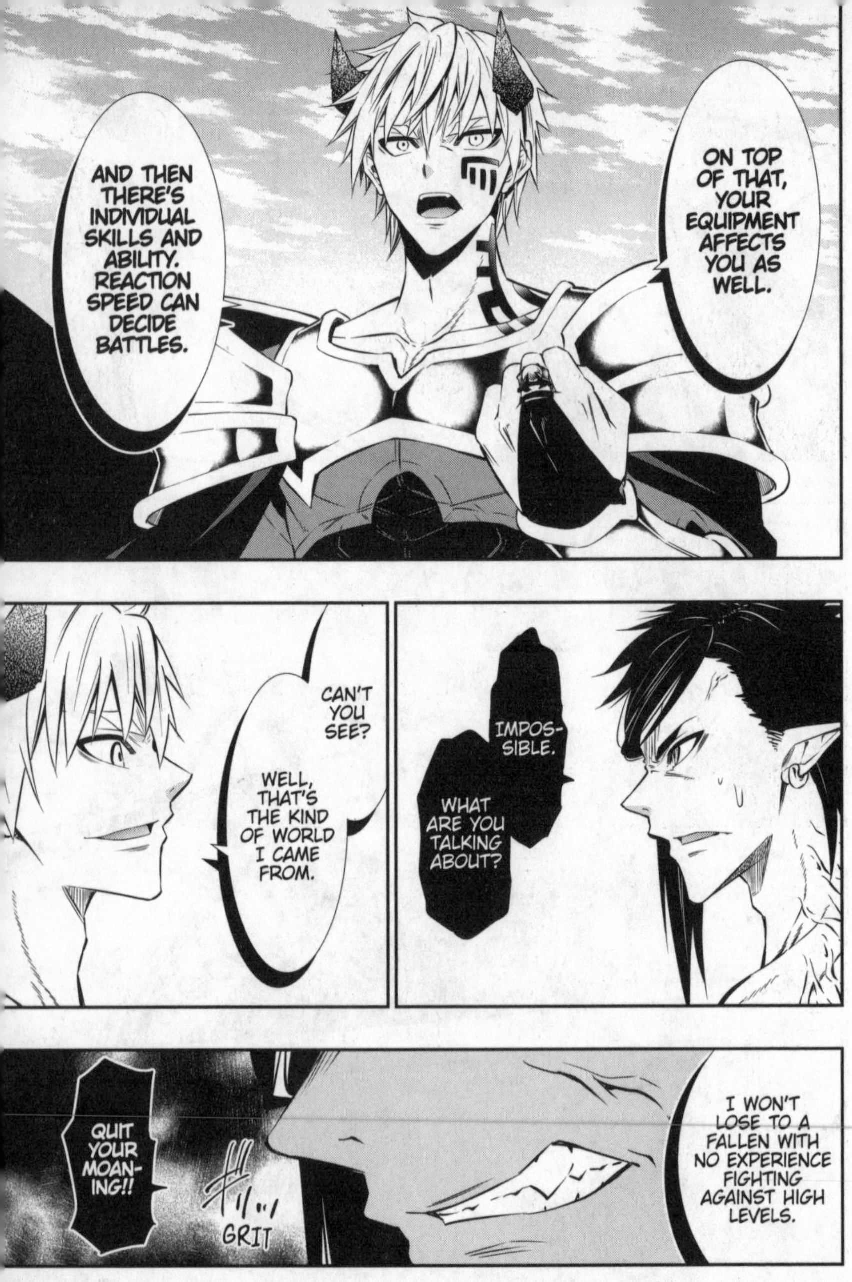
ON TOP OF THAT, YOUR EQUIPMENT AFFECTS YOU AS WELL.
AND THEN THERE'S INDIVIDUAL SKILLS AND ABILITY. REACTION SPEED CAN DECIDE BATTLES.
IMPOS-SIBLE.
WHAT ARE YOU TALKING ABOUT?
CAN'T YOU SEE?
WELL, THAT'S THE KIND OF WORLD I CAME FROM.
I WON'T LOSE TO A FALLEN WITH NO EXPERIENCE FIGHTING AGAINST HIGH LEVELS.
GRIT
QUIT YOUR MOAN-ING!!

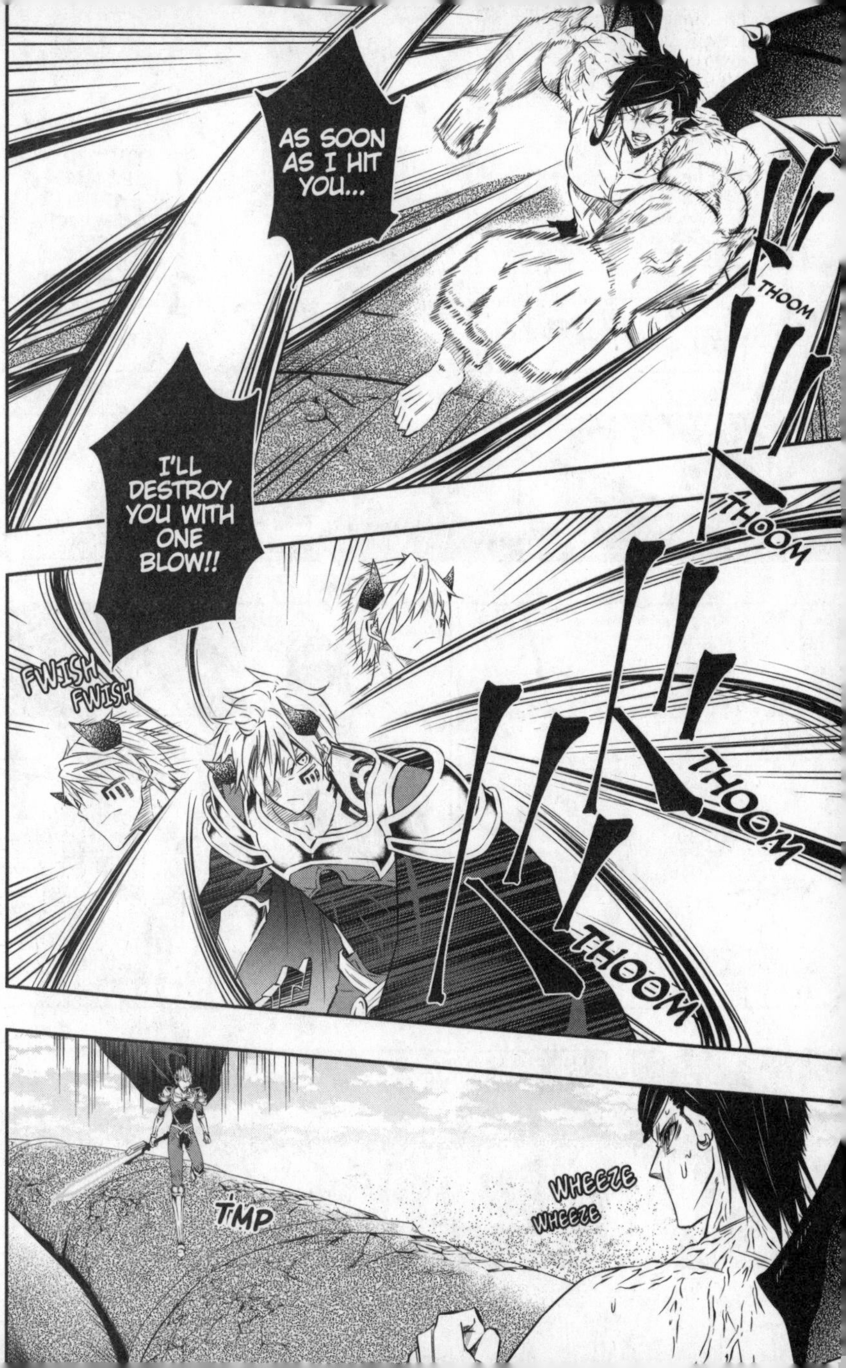
AS SOON AS I HIT YOU...
THOOM
I'LL DESTROY YOU WITH ONE BLOW!!
THOOM
THOOM
THOOM
FWISH FWISH
WHEEZE WHEEZE
TMP

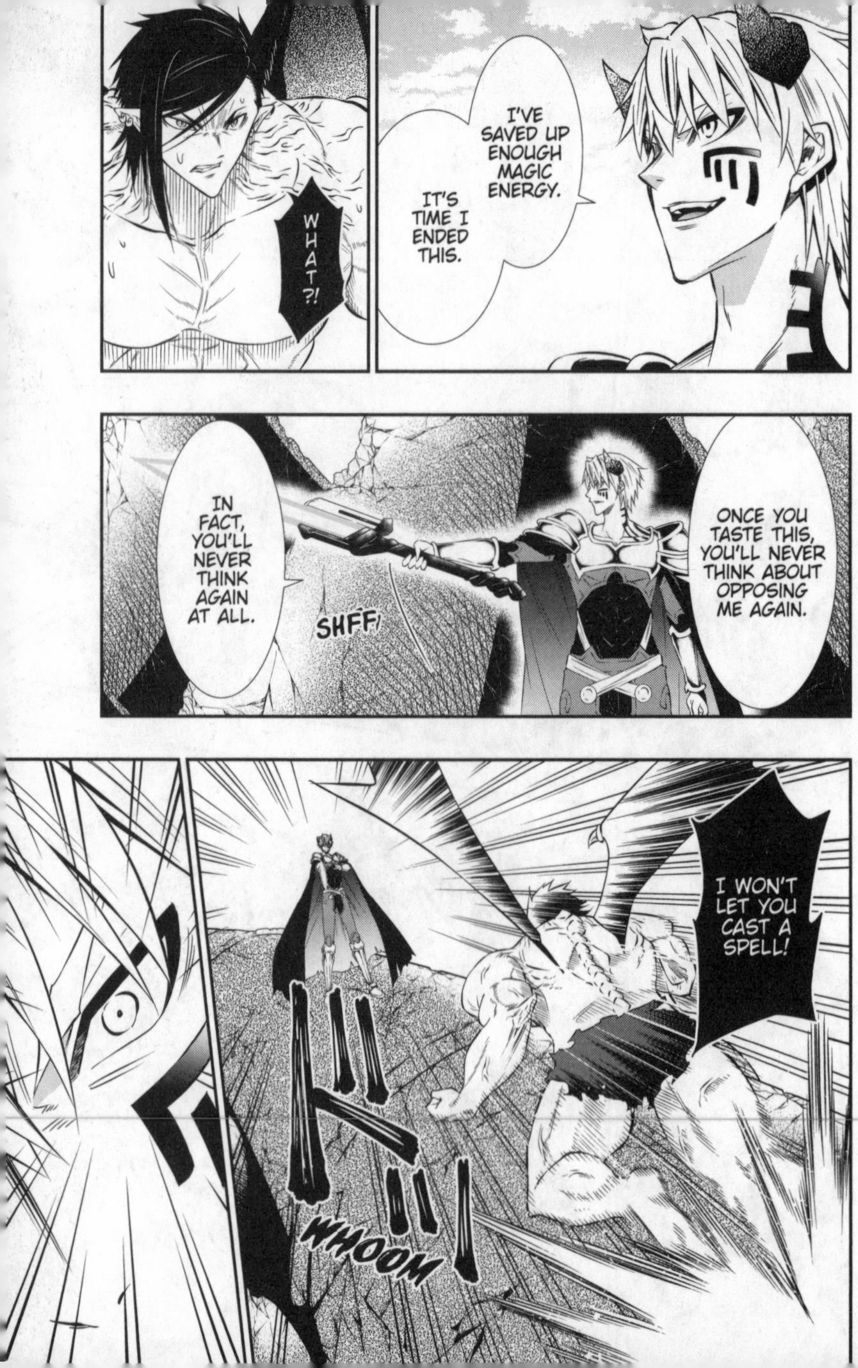
I'VE SAVED UP ENOUGH MAGIC ENERGY.
IT'S TIME I ENDED THIS.
WHAT?!
ONCE YOU TASTE THIS, YOU'LL NEVER THINK ABOUT OPPOSING ME AGAIN.
SHFF
IN FACT, YOU'LL NEVER THINK AGAIN AT ALL.
I WON'T LET YOU CAST A SPELL!
WHOOM

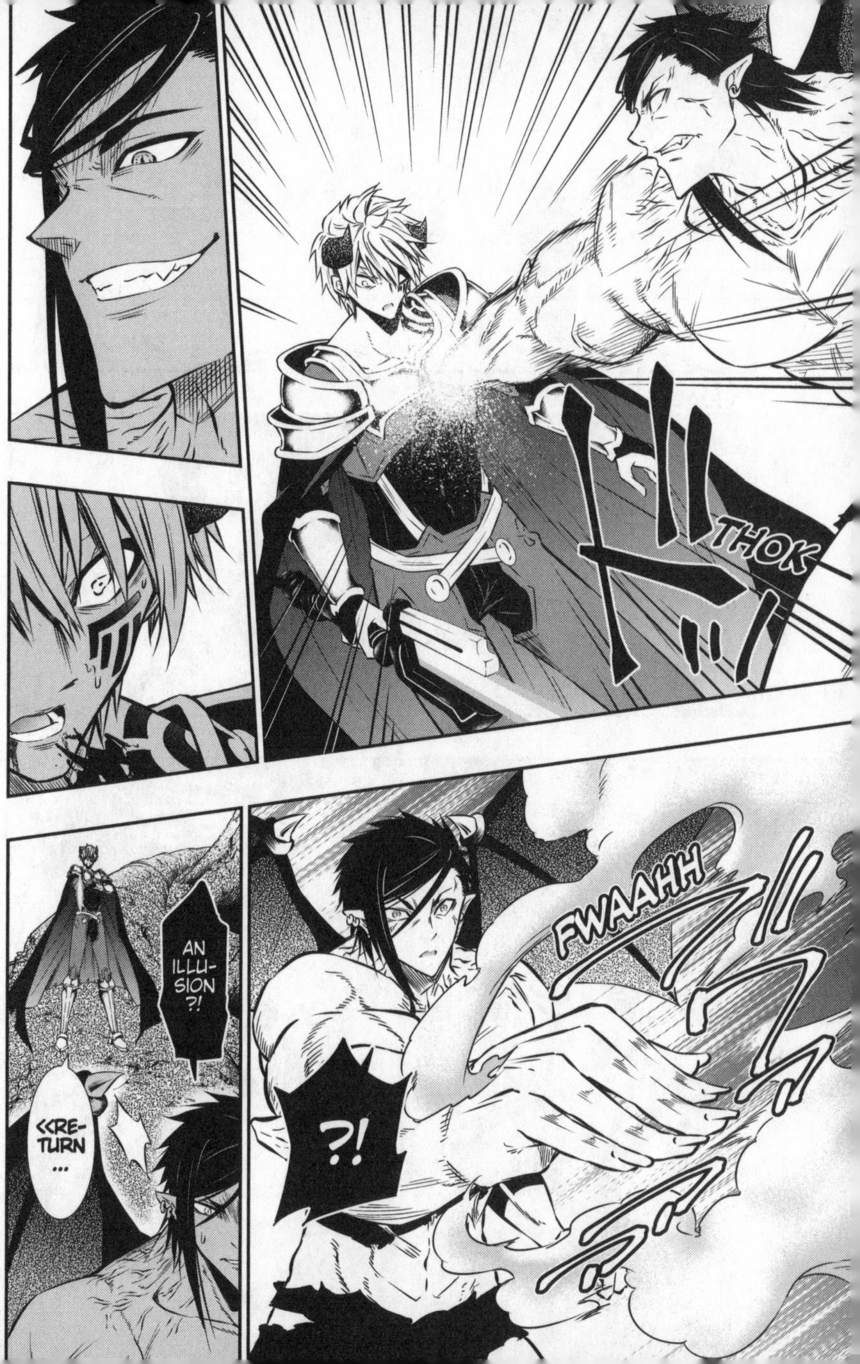
THOK
FWAAHH
?!
AN ILLU-SION ?!
<<RE-TURN ...

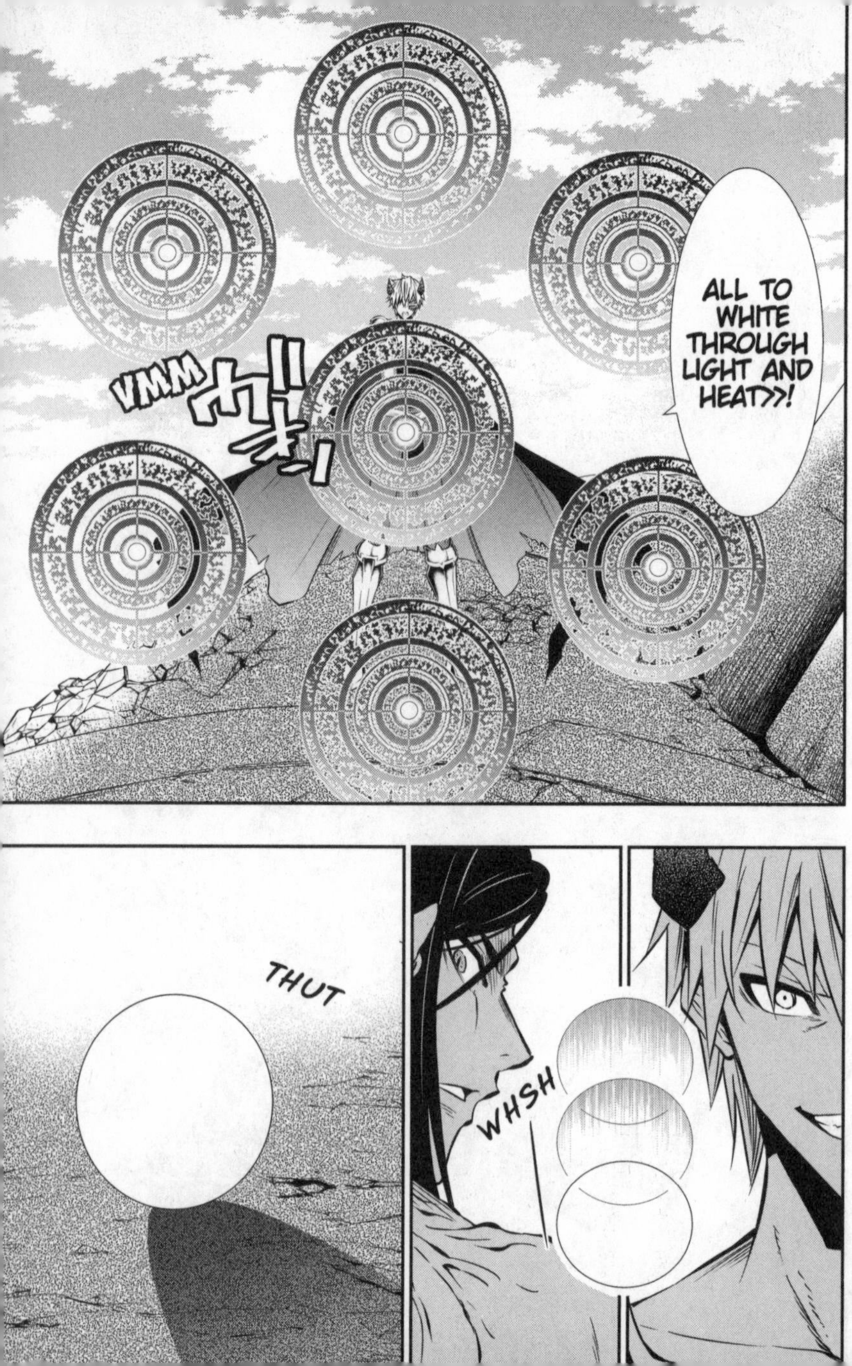
ALL TO WHITE THROUGH LIGHT AND HEAT>>!
VMM
WHSH
THUT

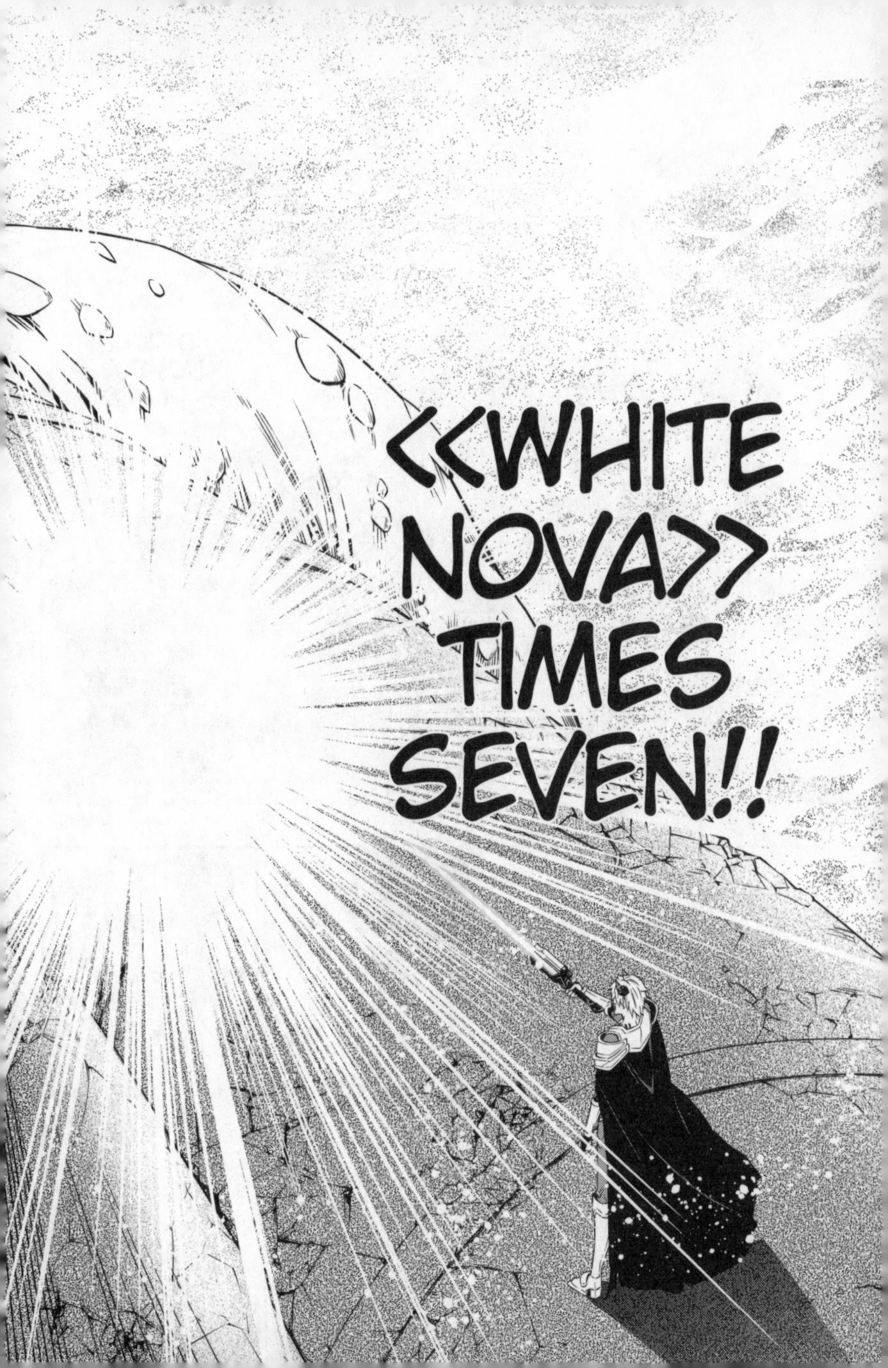
<<WHITE NOVA>> TIMES SEVEN!!

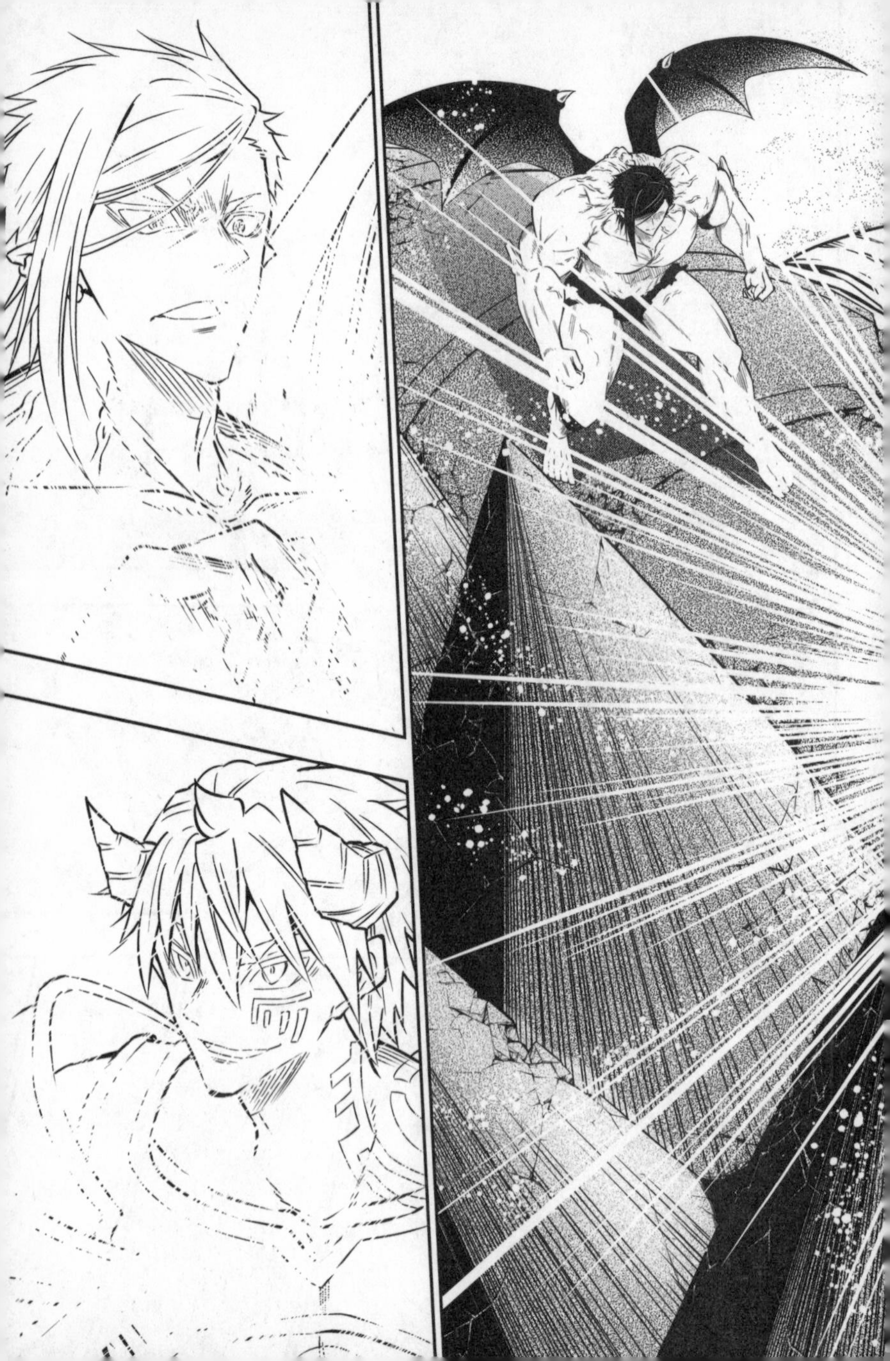

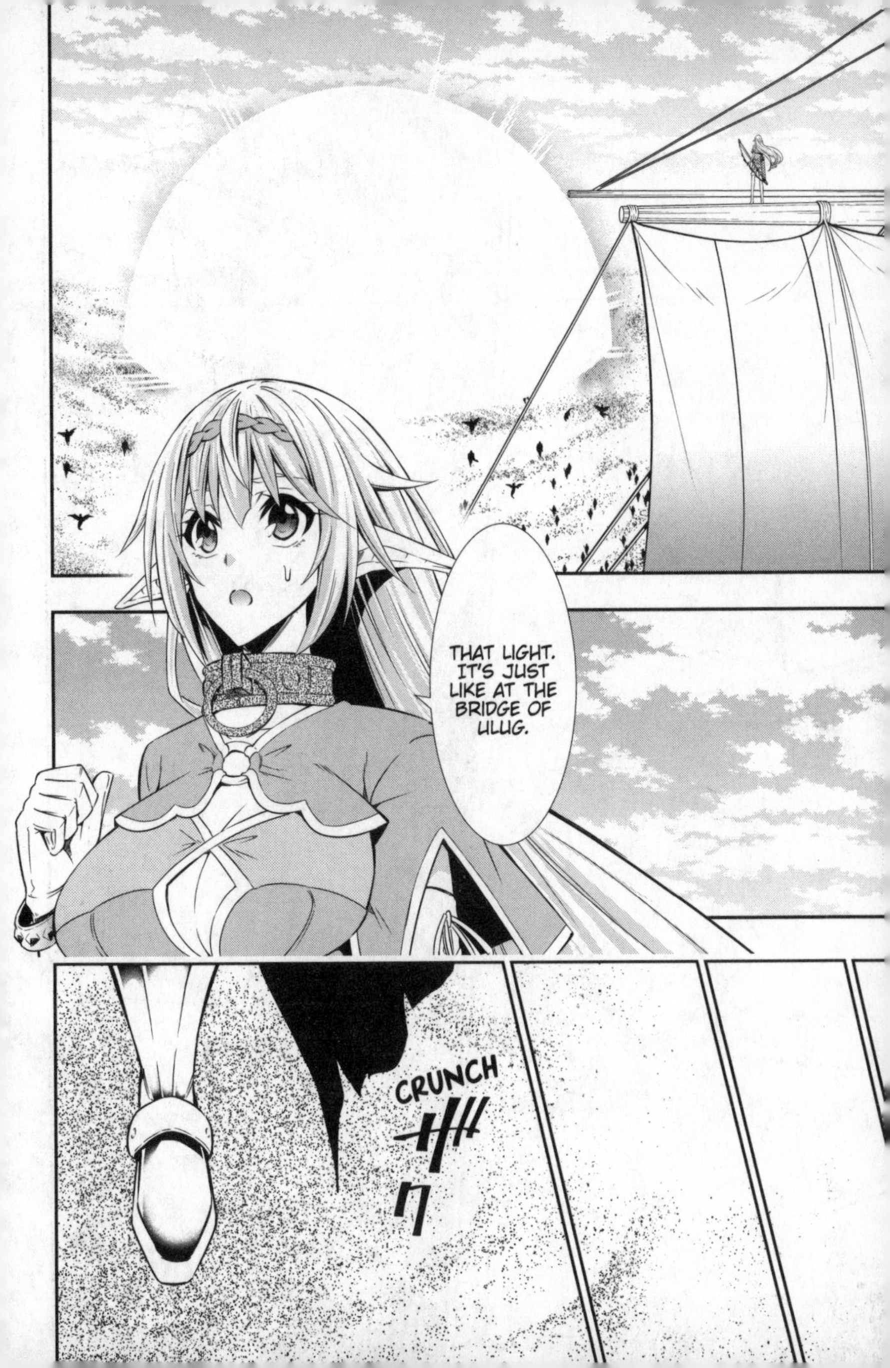
THAT LIGHT. IT'S JUST LIKE AT THE BRIDGE OF ULUG.
CRUNCH

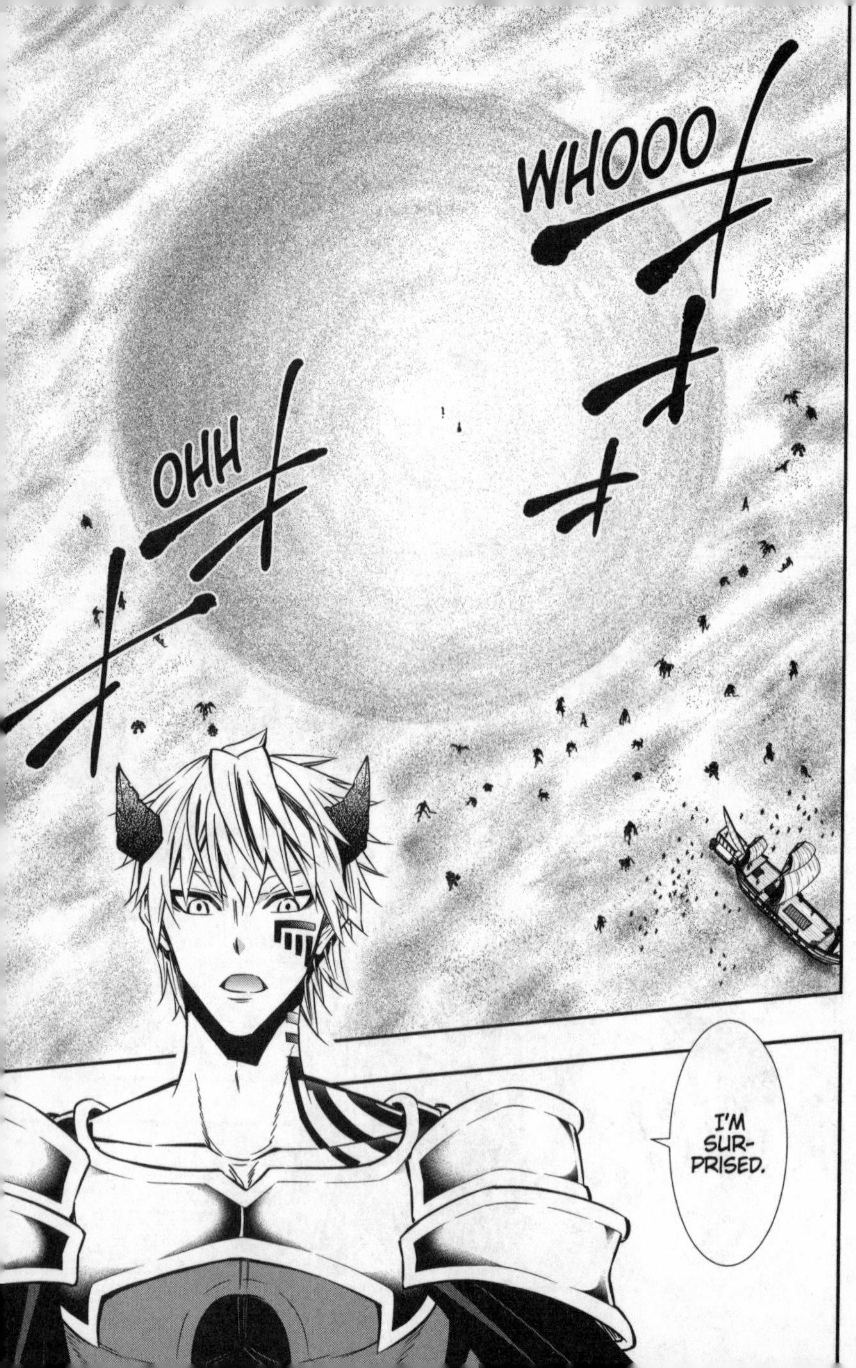
WHOOO
OHH
I'M SUR-PRISED.

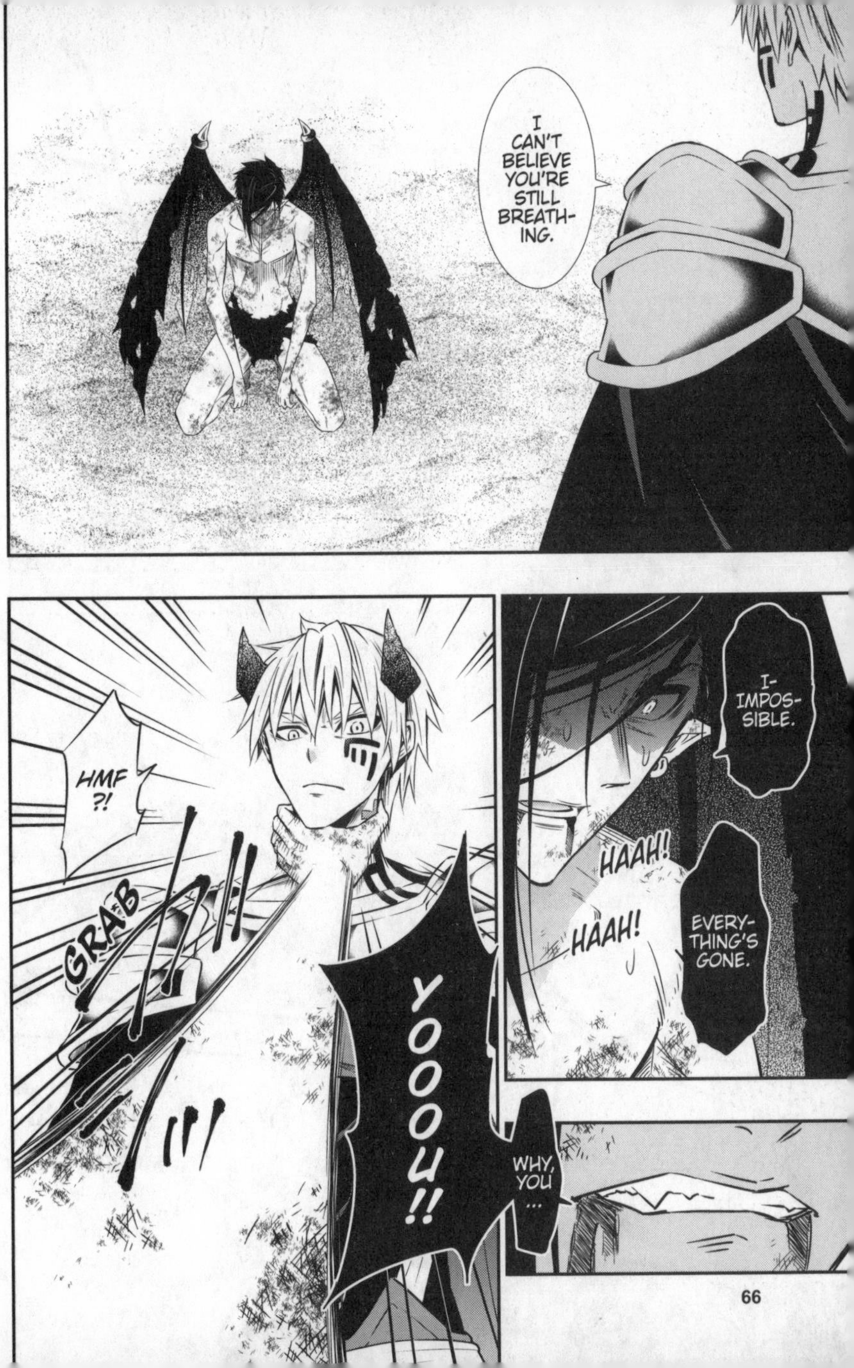
I CAN'T BELIEVE YOU'RE STILL BREATHING.
I- IMPOSSIBLE.
HAAH!
HAAH!
EVERYTHING'S GONE.
WHY, YOU ...
HMF ?!
GRAB
YOOOU!!

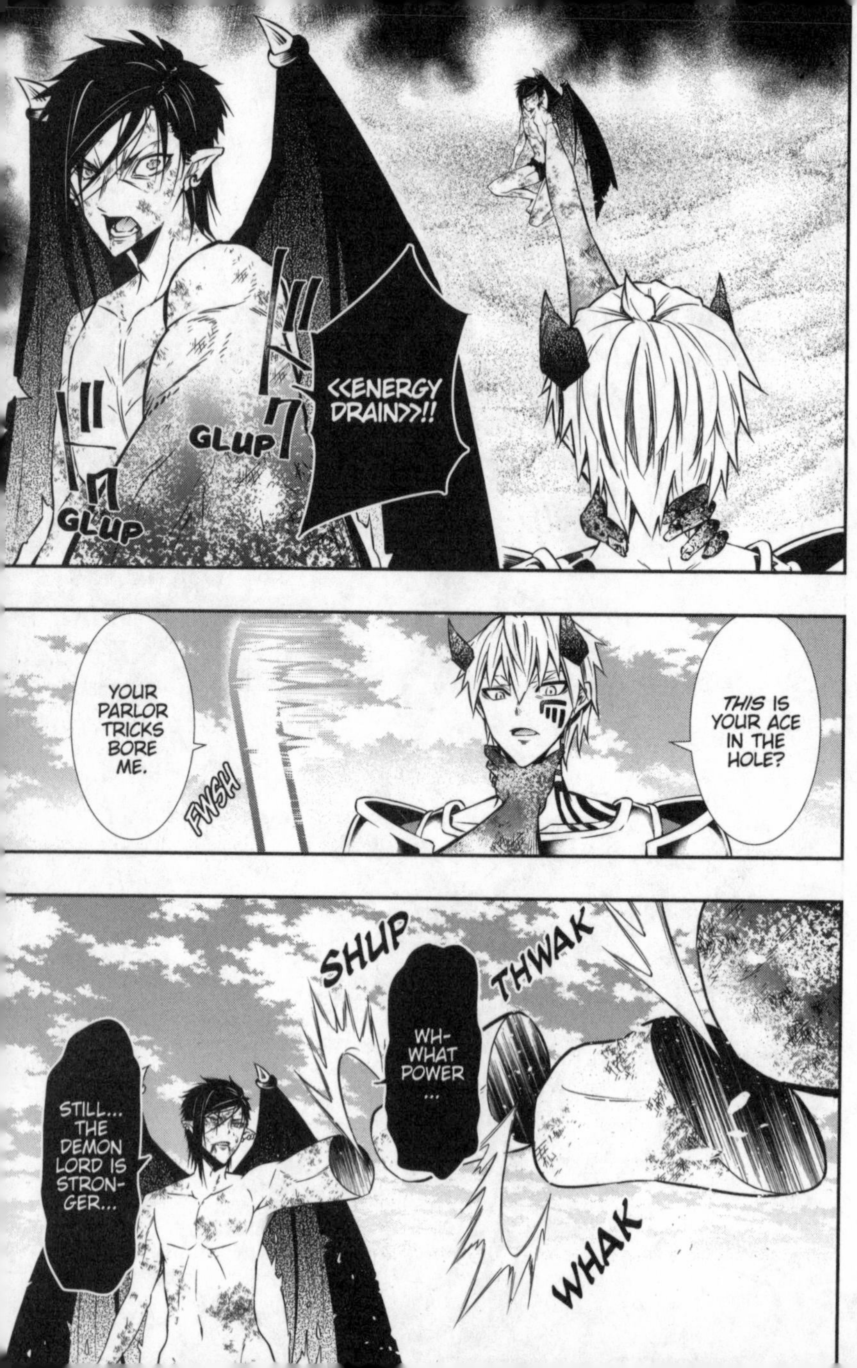

<<ENERGY DRAIN>>!!
GLUP
GLUP
THIS is YOUR ACE IN THE HOLE?
YOUR PARLOR TRICKS BORE ME.
FWSH
THWAK
SHUP
WH-WHAT POWER...
STILL... THE DEMON LORD IS STRONGER...
WHAK

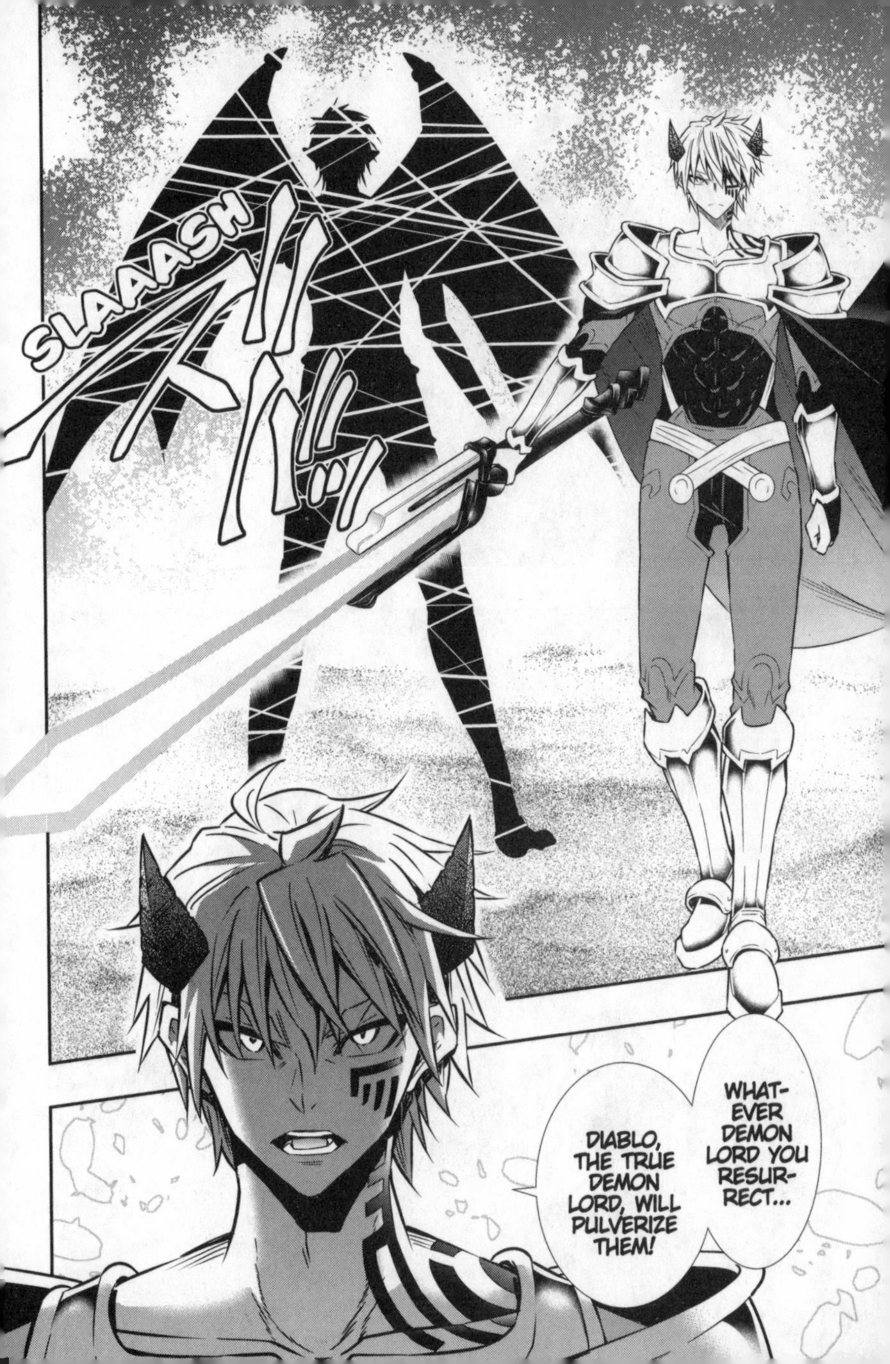
SLAAASH
WHAT-EVER DEMON LORD YOU RESUR-RECT...
DIABLO, THE TRUE DEMON LORD, WILL PULVERIZE THEM!

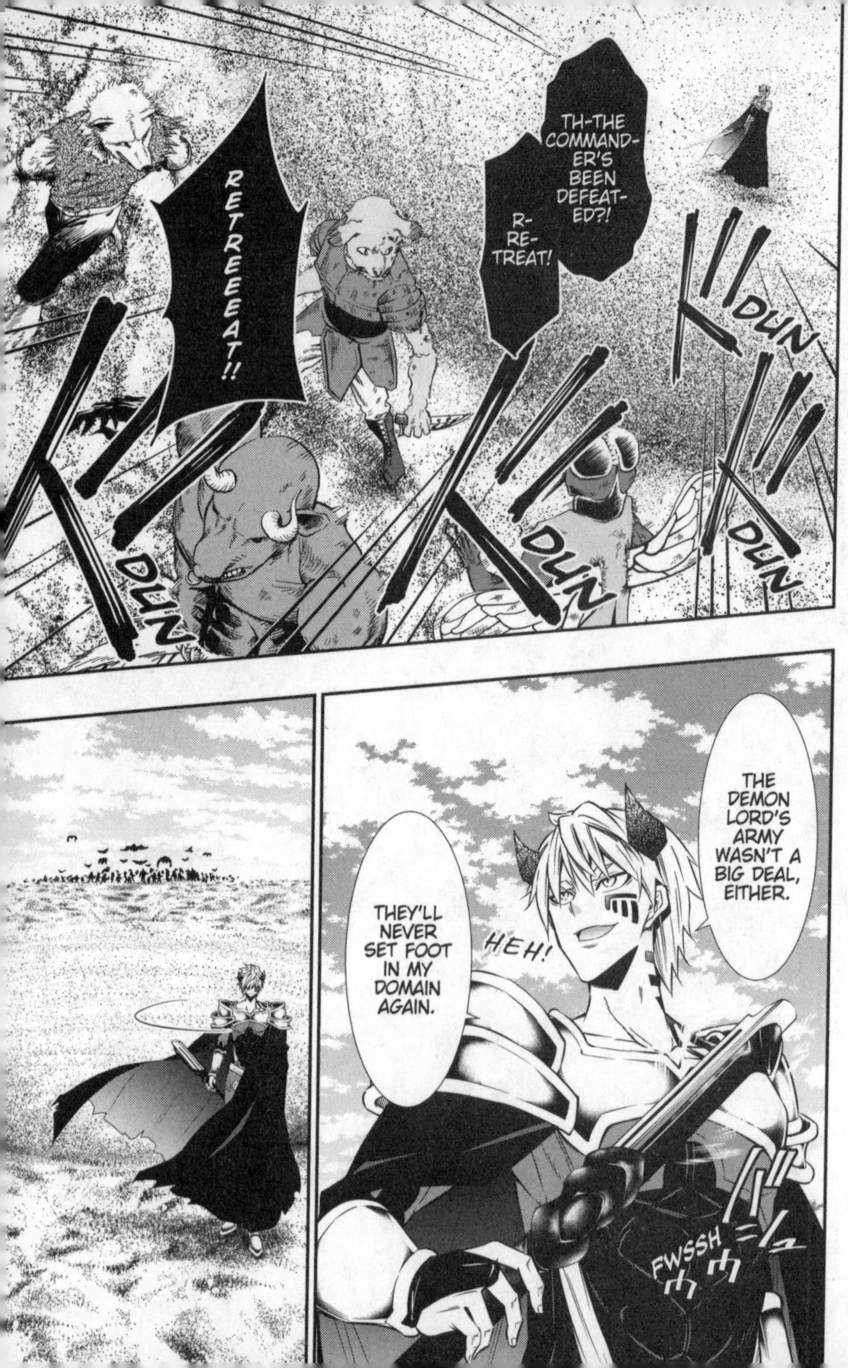
TH-THE COMMANDER'S BEEN DEFEATED?!
R-RE-TREAT!
RETREEEAT!!
DUN
DUN
DUN
DUN
THE DEMON LORD'S ARMY WASN'T A BIG DEAL, EITHER.
HEH!
THEY'LL NEVER SET FOOT IN MY DOMAIN AGAIN.
FWSSH

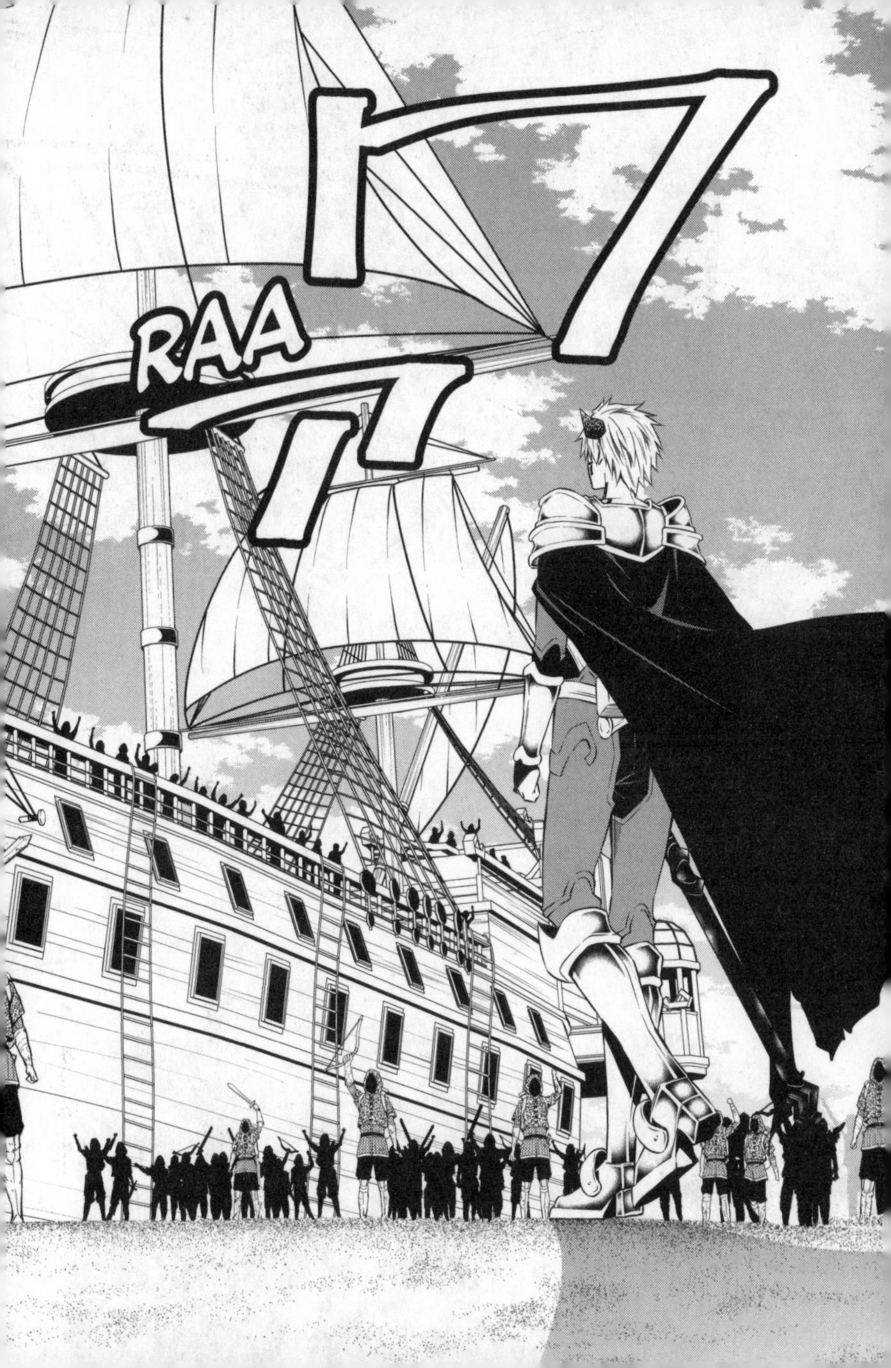
RAAA

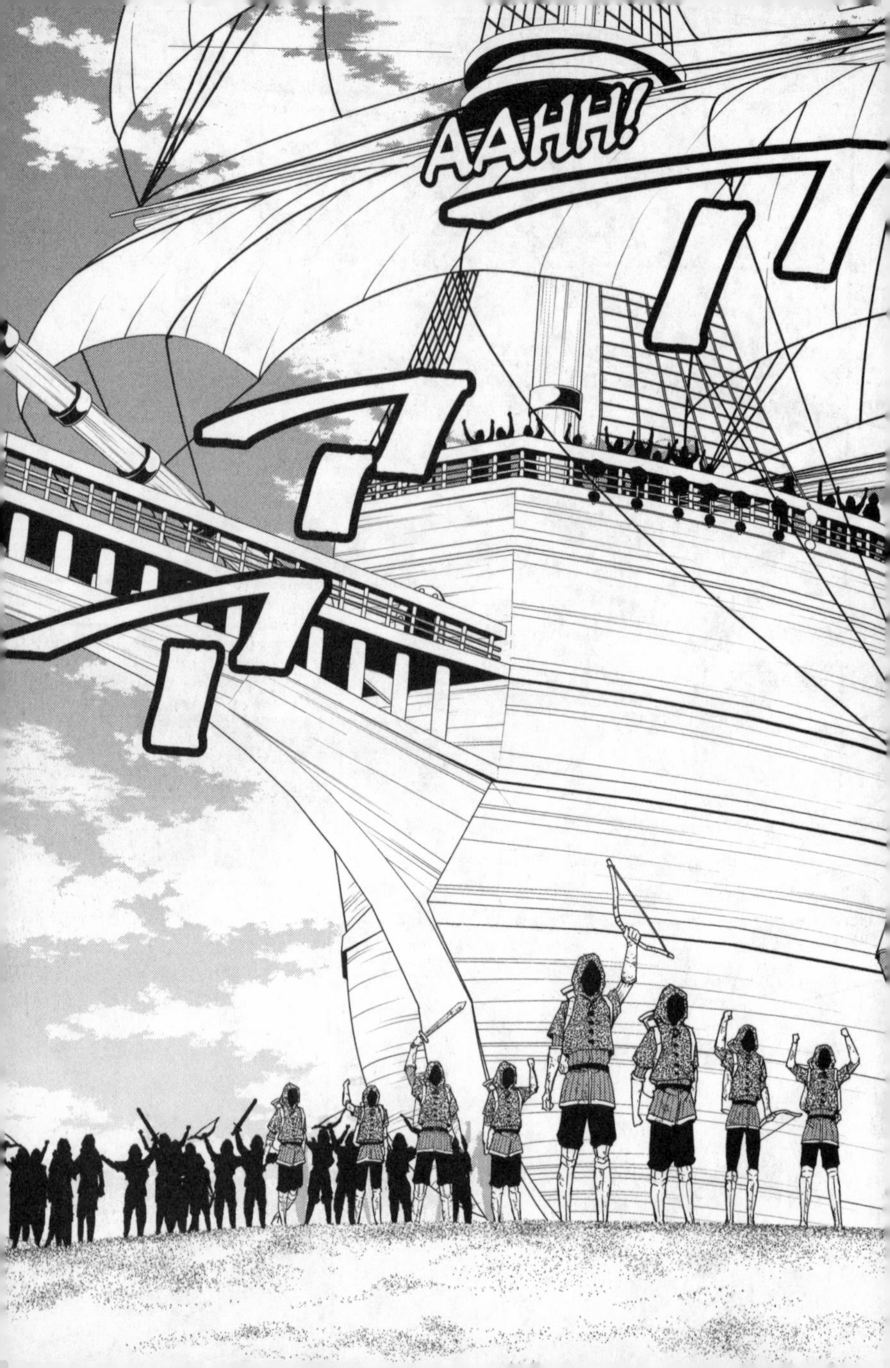
AAHH!

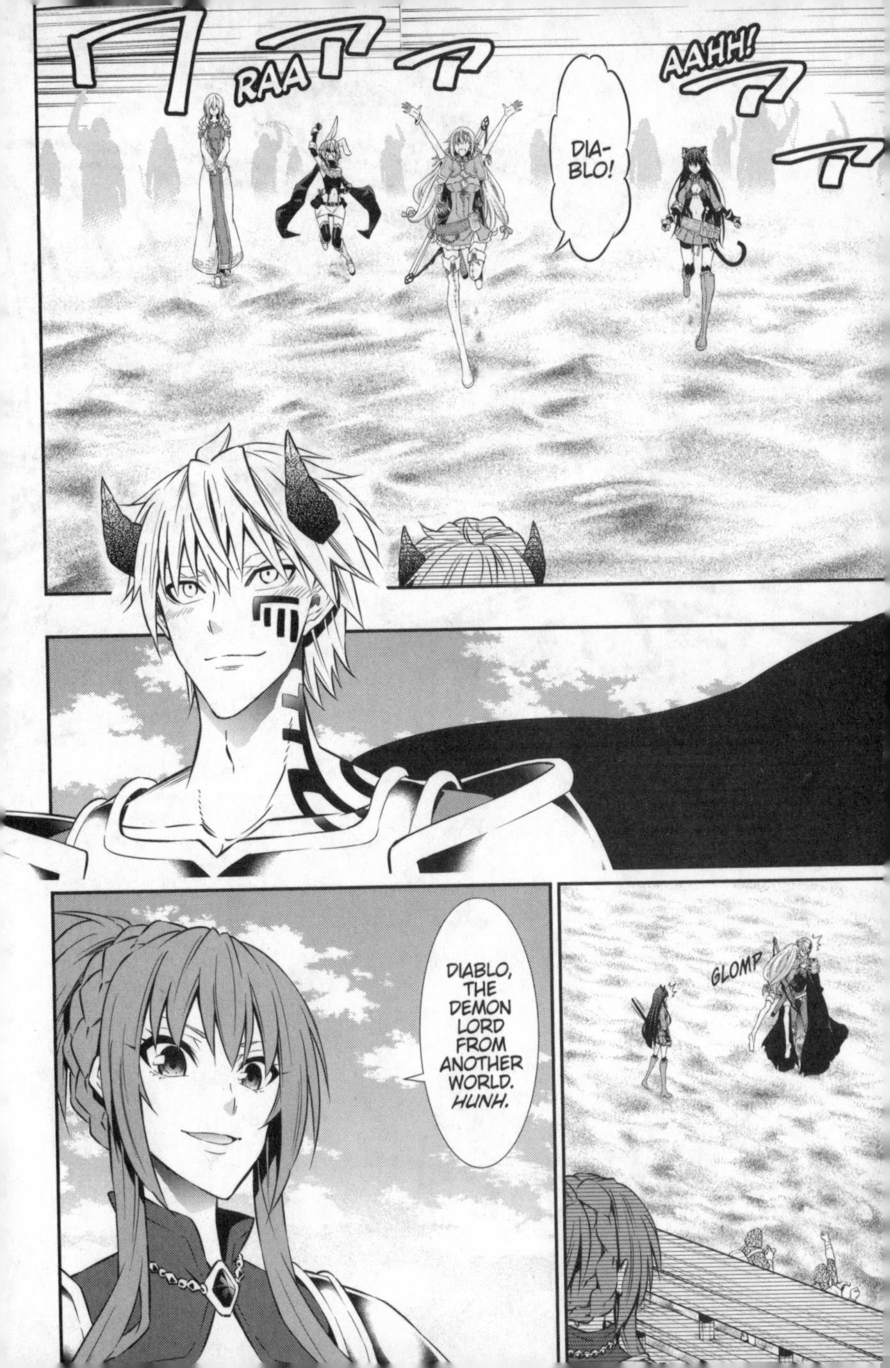
AAHH!
DIA-BLO!
RAA
GLOMP
DIABLO, THE DEMON LORD FROM ANOTHER WORLD. HUNH.

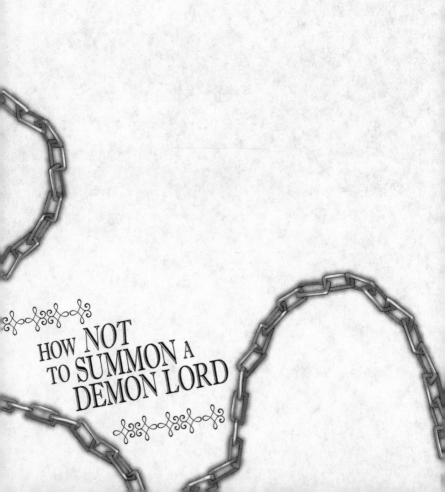

HOW NOT
TO SUMMON A
DEMON LORD

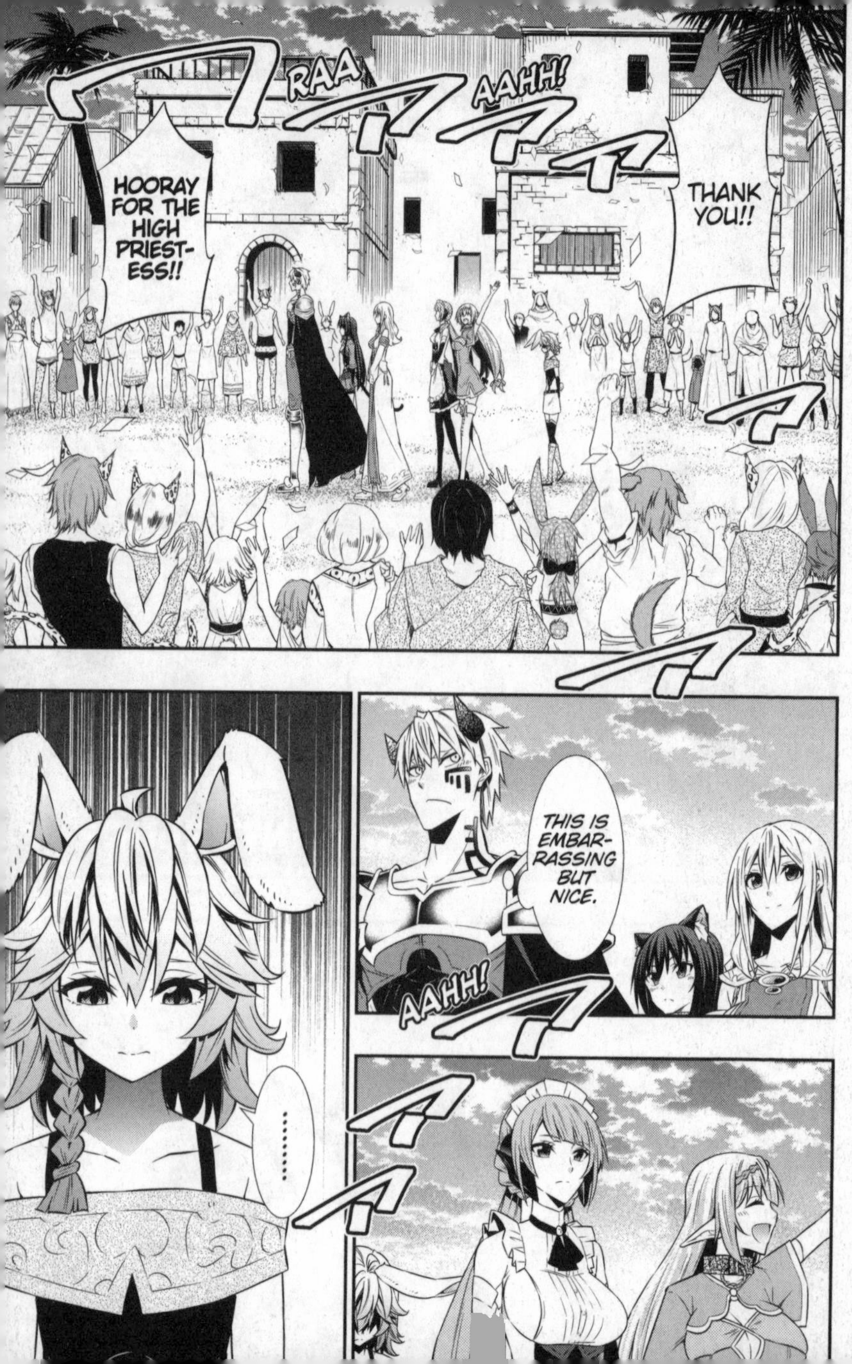
THANK YOU!!
RAA AAHH!
HOORAY FOR THE HIGH PRIEST-ESS!!
THIS IS EMBAR-RASSING BUT NICE.
AAHH!
......

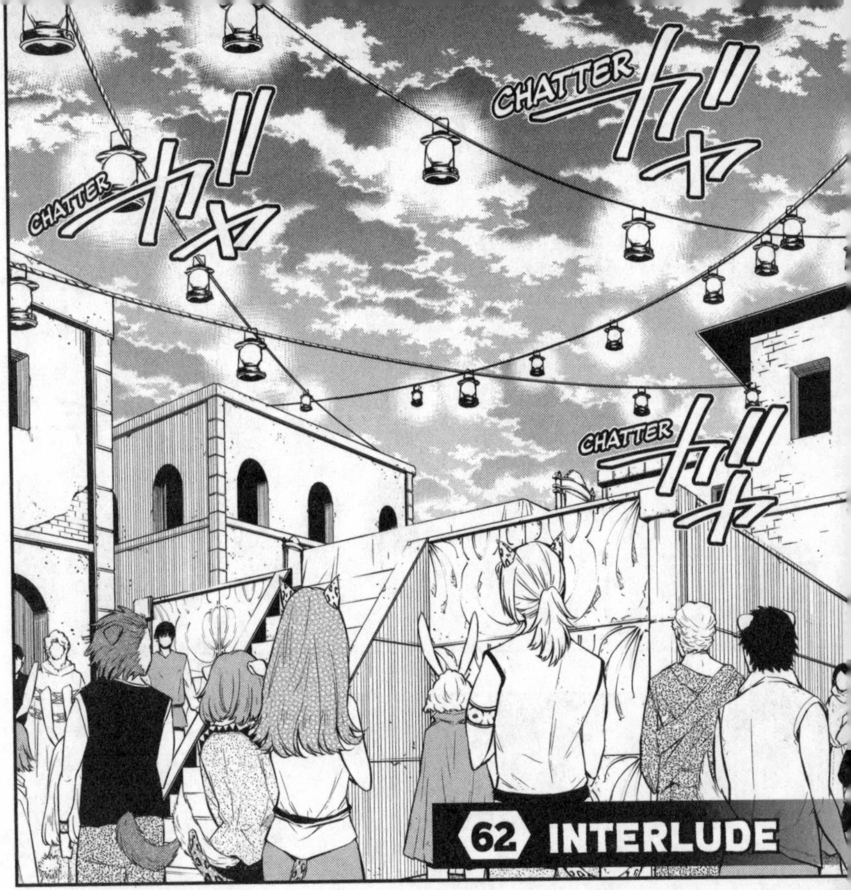
CHATTER ガヤ
CHATTER ガヤ
CHATTER ガヤ
62 INTERLUDE

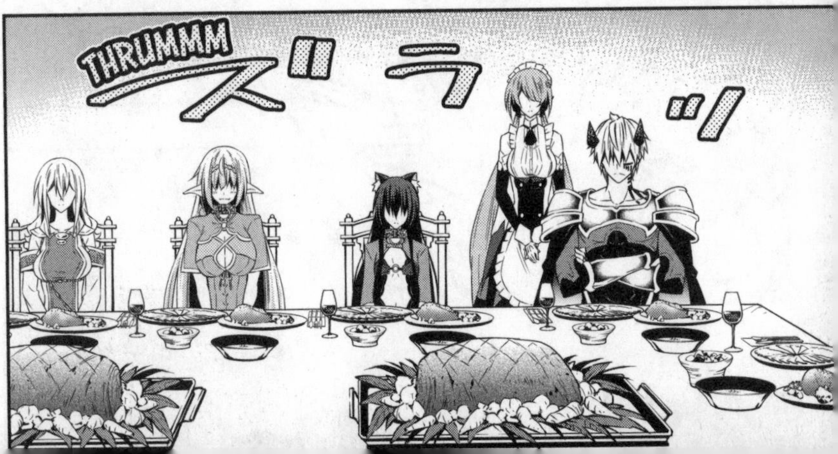
THRUMMM ズラッ

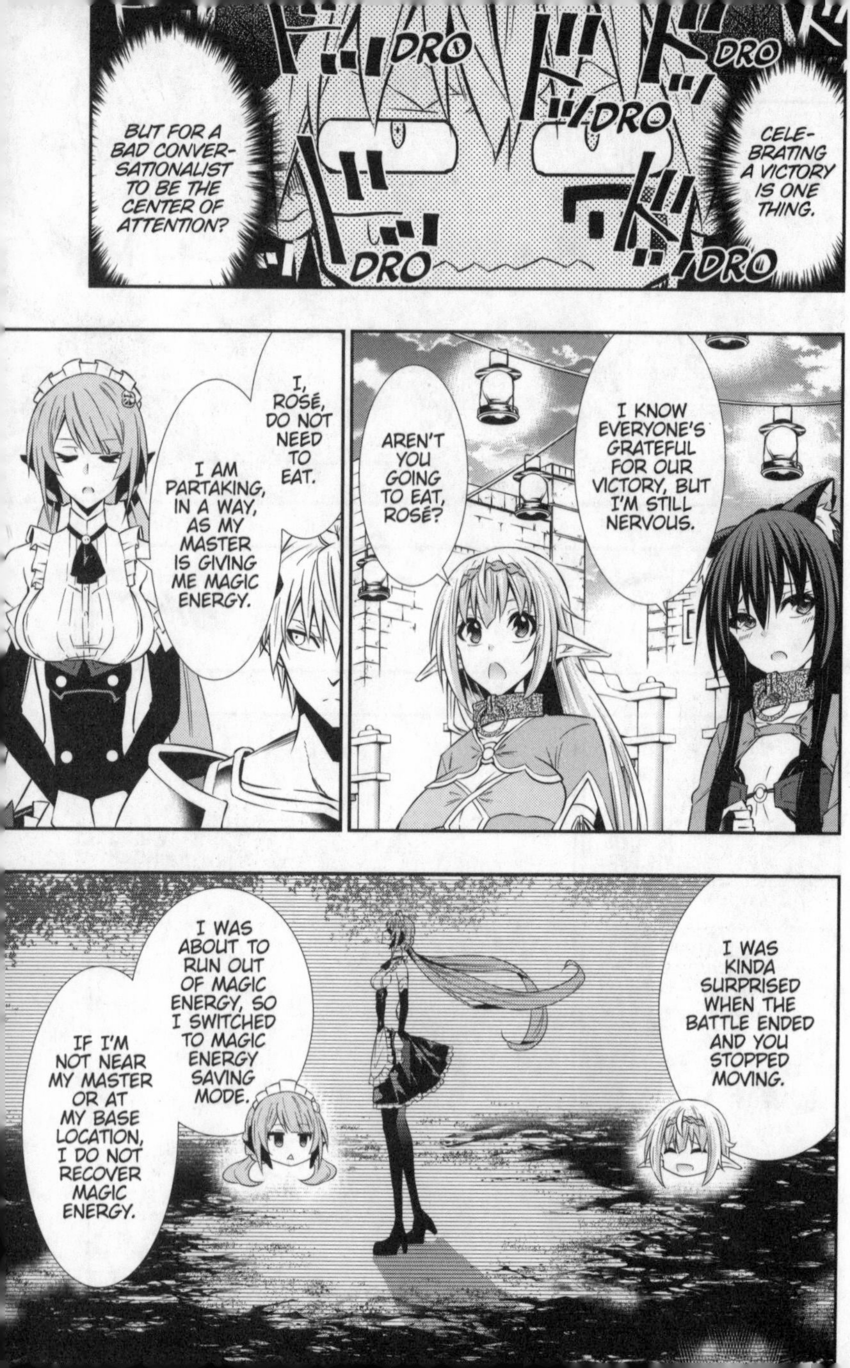
DRO
DRO
DRO
CELE-BRATING A VICTORY IS ONE THING.
BUT FOR A BAD CONVER-SATIONALIST TO BE THE CENTER OF ATTENTION?
DRO
DRO
DRO
I KNOW EVERYONE'S GRATEFUL FOR OUR VICTORY, BUT I'M STILL NERVOUS.
AREN'T YOU GOING TO EAT, ROSÉ?
I, ROSÉ, DO NOT NEED TO EAT.
I AM PARTAKING, IN A WAY, AS MY MASTER IS GIVING ME MAGIC ENERGY.
I WAS KINDA SURPRISED WHEN THE BATTLE ENDED AND YOU STOPPED MOVING.
I WAS ABOUT TO RUN OUT OF MAGIC ENERGY, SO I SWITCHED TO MAGIC ENERGY SAVING MODE.
IF I'M NOT NEAR MY MASTER OR AT MY BASE LOCATION, I DO NOT RECOVER MAGIC ENERGY.

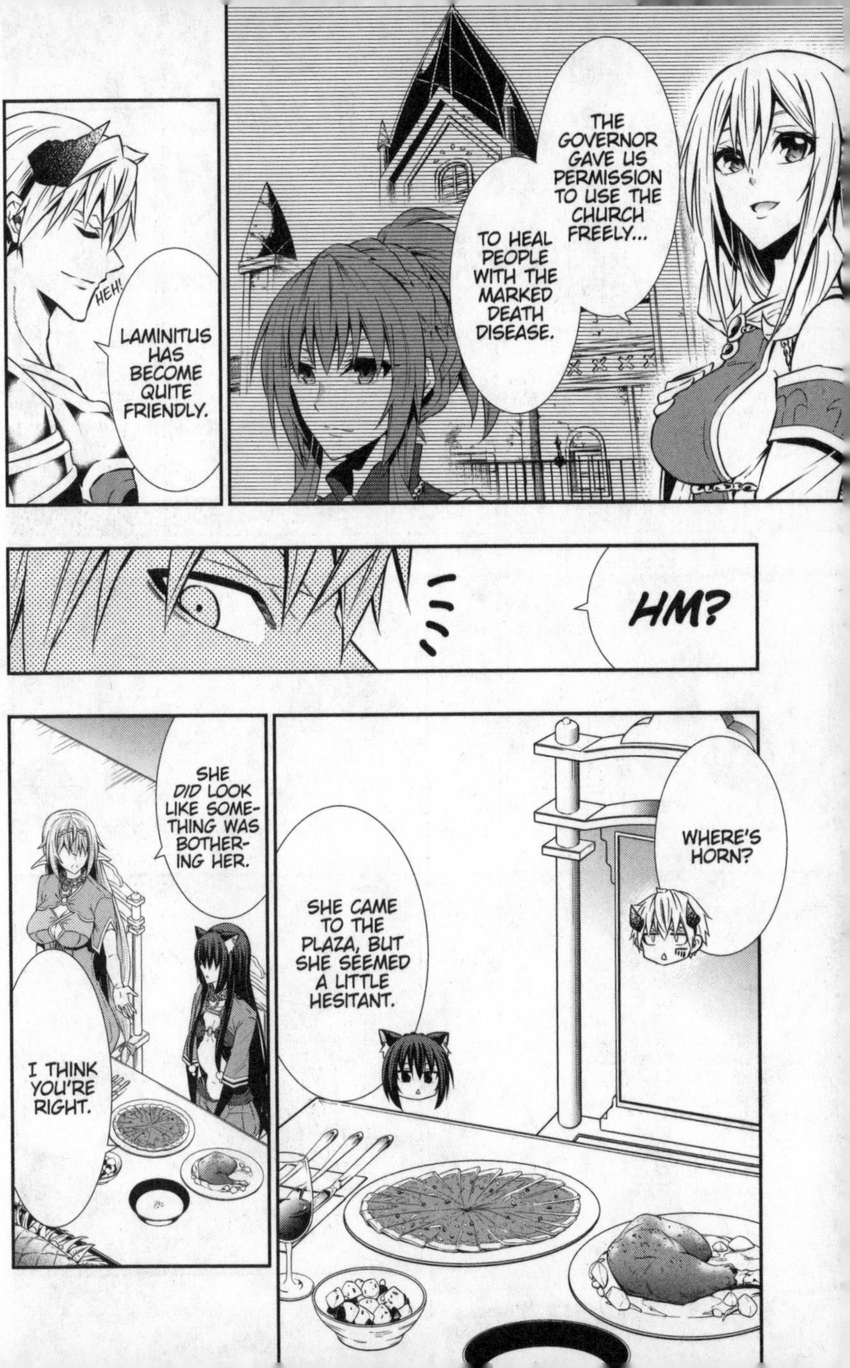
THE GOVERNOR GAVE US PERMISSION TO USE THE CHURCH FREELY...
TO HEAL PEOPLE WITH THE MARKED DEATH DISEASE.
HEH!
LAMINITUS HAS BECOME QUITE FRIENDLY.
HM?
WHERE'S HORN?
SHE CAME TO THE PLAZA, BUT SHE SEEMED A LITTLE HESITANT.
SHE *DID* LOOK LIKE SOMETHING WAS BOTHERING HER.
I THINK YOU'RE RIGHT.

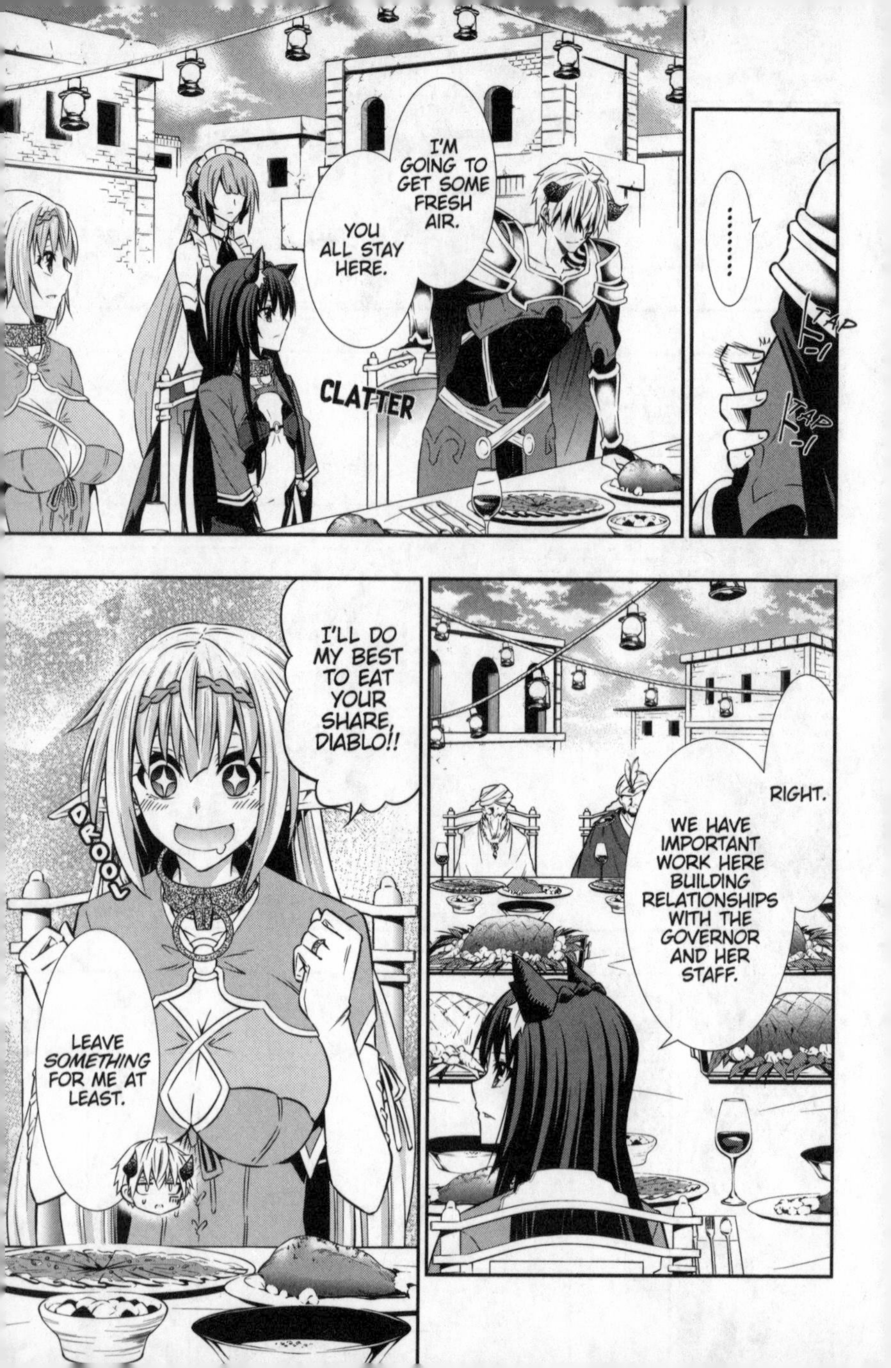
......
TAP
TAP
I'M GOING TO GET SOME FRESH AIR.
YOU ALL STAY HERE.
CLATTER
RIGHT.
WE HAVE IMPORTANT WORK HERE BUILDING RELATIONSHIPS WITH THE GOVERNOR AND HER STAFF.
I'LL DO MY BEST TO EAT YOUR SHARE, DIABLO!!
DROOL
LEAVE SOMETHING FOR ME AT LEAST.

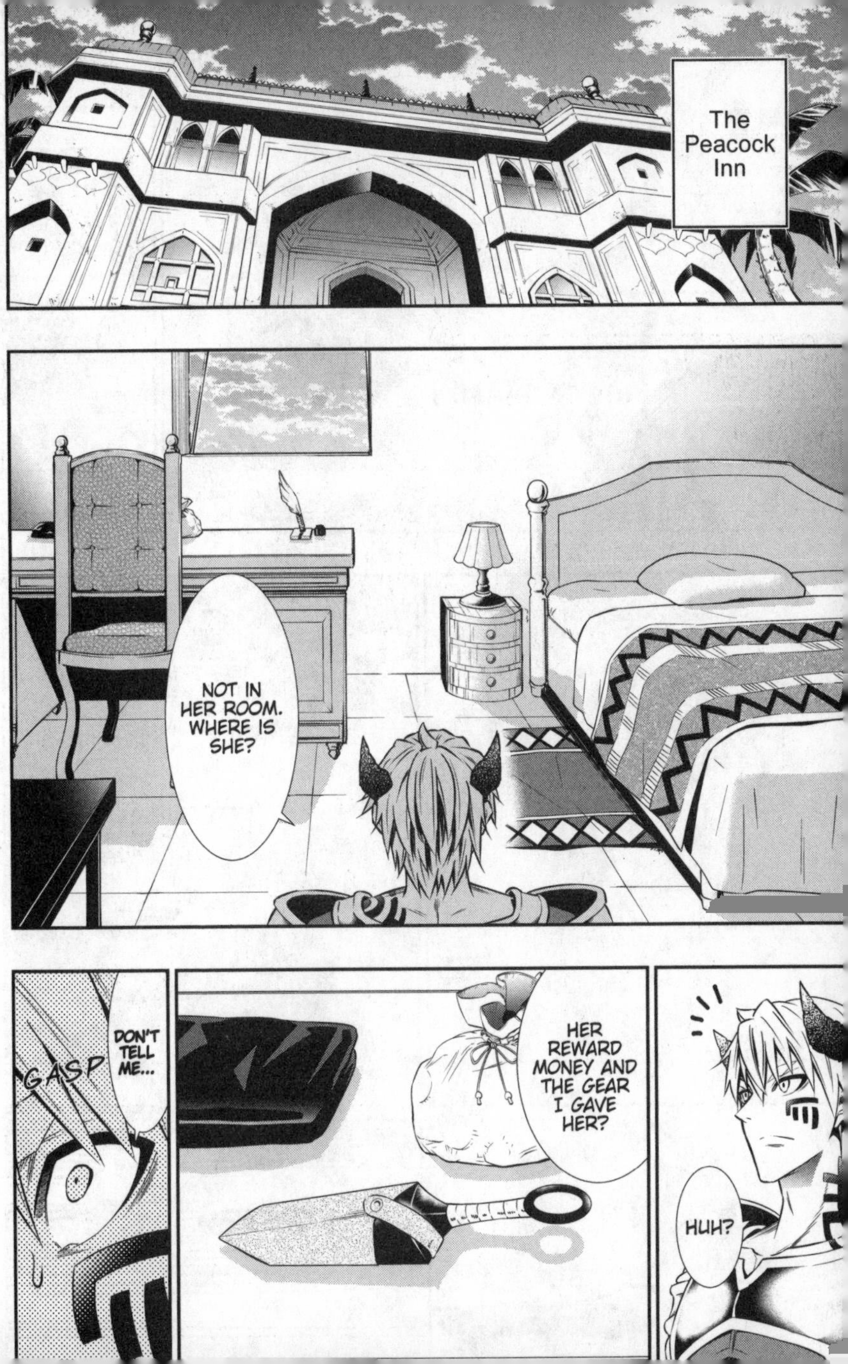
The Peacock Inn
NOT IN HER ROOM. WHERE IS SHE?
HUH?
HER REWARD MONEY AND THE GEAR I GAVE HER?
GASP
DON'T TELL ME...

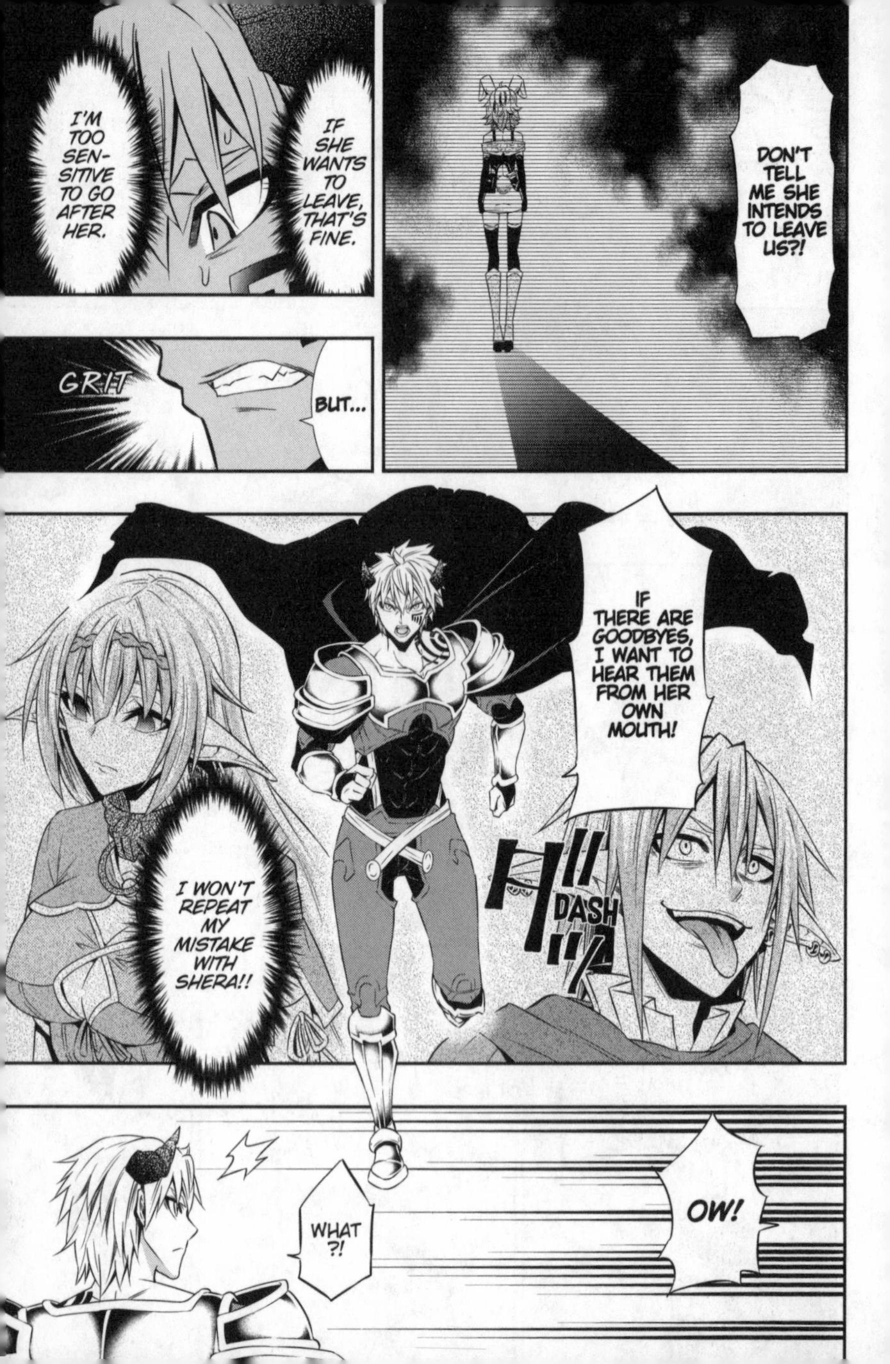

DON'T TELL ME SHE INTENDS TO LEAVE US?!
IF SHE WANTS TO LEAVE, THAT'S FINE.
I'M TOO SEN-SITIVE TO GO AFTER HER.
BUT...
GRIT
IF THERE ARE GOODBYES, I WANT TO HEAR THEM FROM HER OWN MOUTH!
DASH
I WON'T REPEAT MY MISTAKE WITH SHERA!!
OW!
WHAT?!

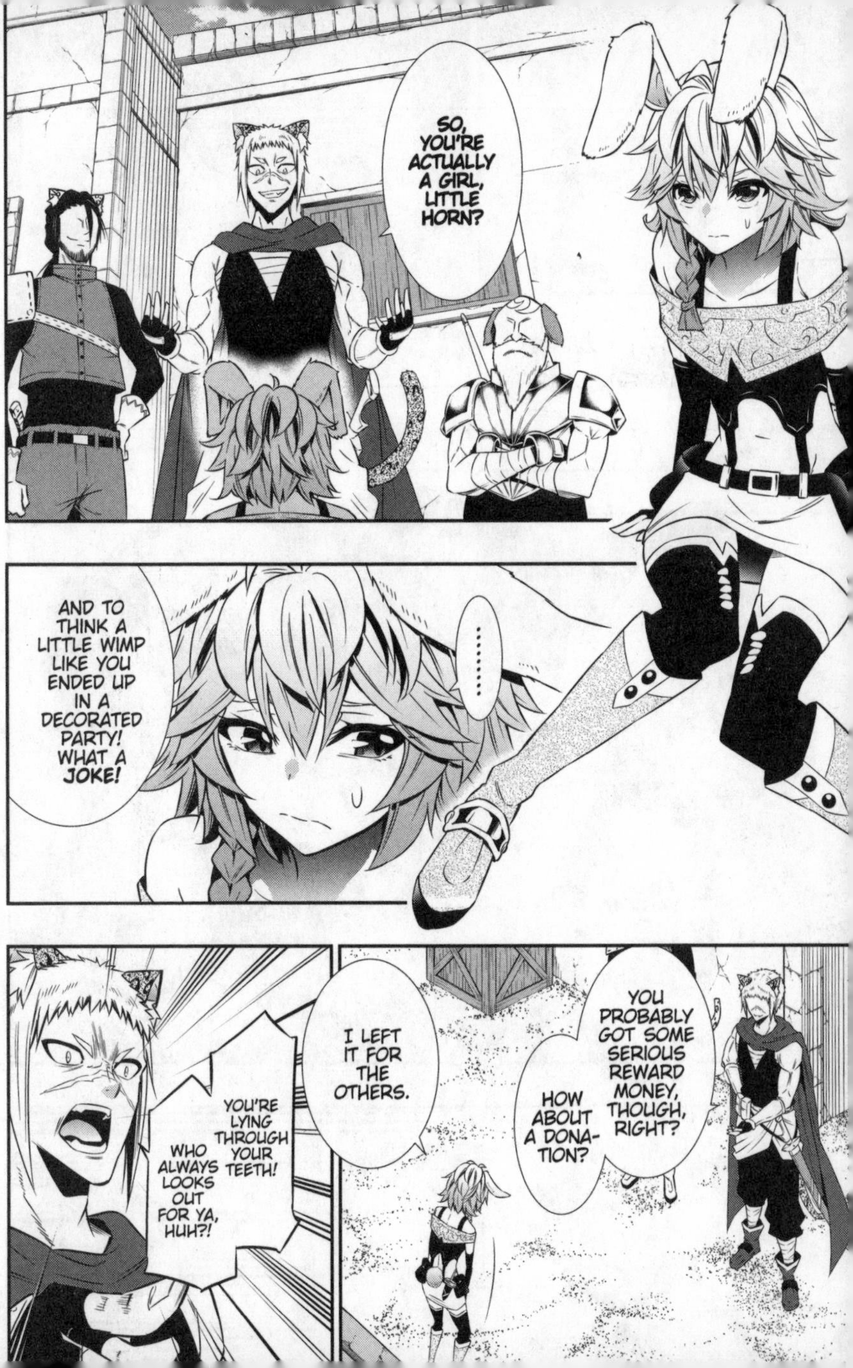
SO, YOU'RE ACTUALLY A GIRL, LITTLE HORN?
......
AND TO THINK A LITTLE WIMP LIKE YOU ENDED UP IN A DECORATED PARTY! WHAT A JOKE!
YOU PROBABLY GOT SOME SERIOUS REWARD MONEY, THOUGH, RIGHT?
HOW ABOUT A DONA-TION?
I LEFT IT FOR THE OTHERS.
YOU'RE LYING THROUGH YOUR TEETH!
WHO ALWAYS LOOKS OUT FOR YA, HUH?!

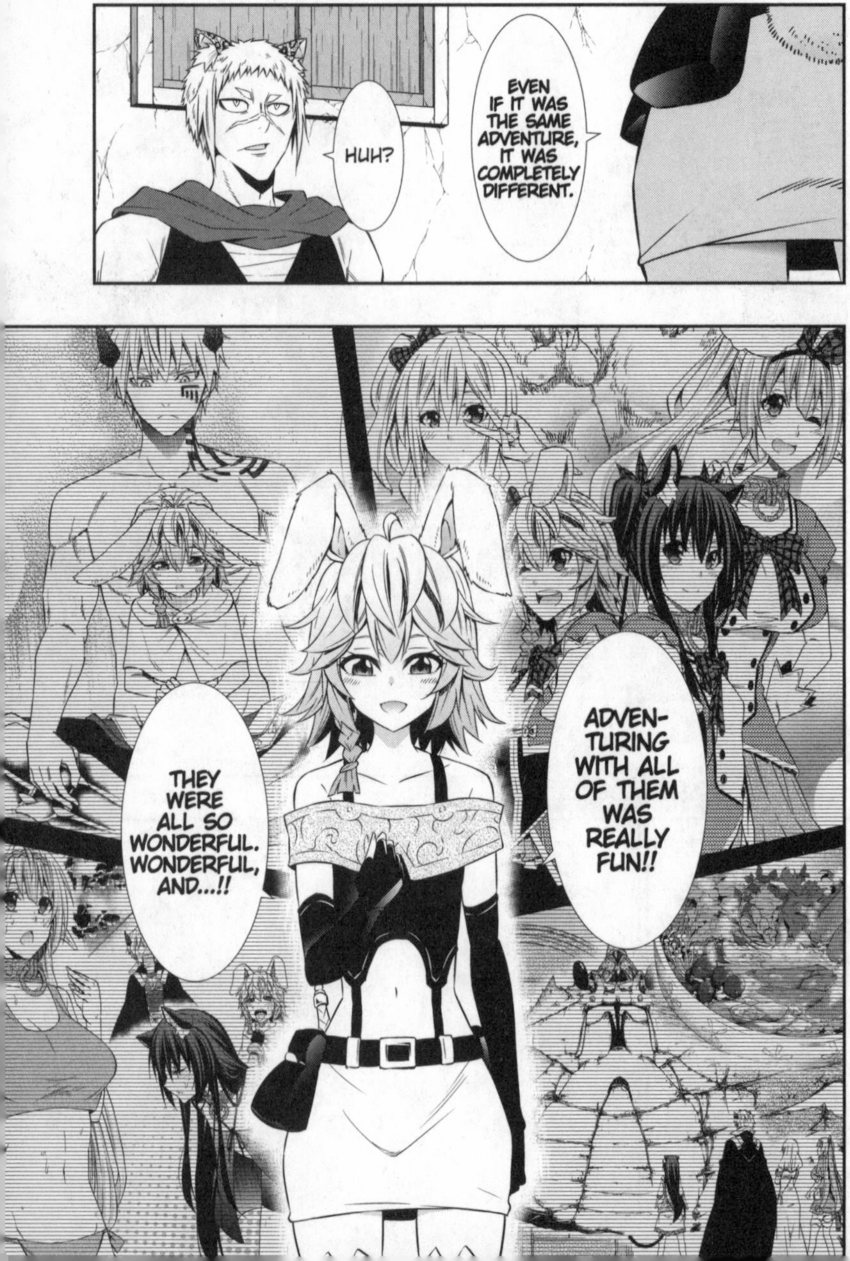
EVEN IF IT WAS THE SAME ADVENTURE, IT WAS COMPLETELY DIFFERENT.
HUH?
ADVEN-TURING WITH ALL OF THEM WAS REALLY FUN!!
THEY WERE ALL SO WONDERFUL. WONDERFUL, AND...!!

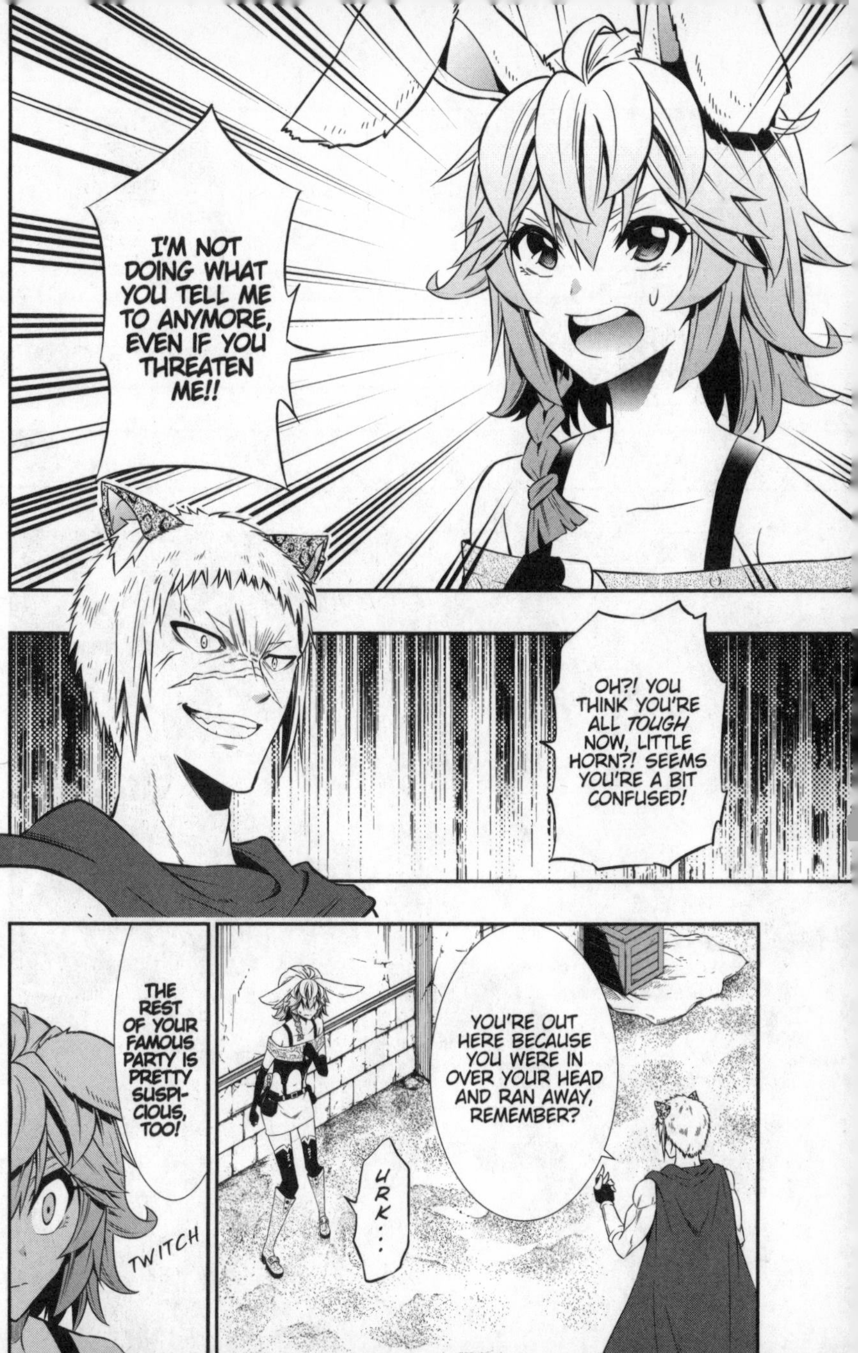
I'M NOT DOING WHAT YOU TELL ME TO ANYMORE, EVEN IF YOU THREATEN ME!!
OH?! YOU THINK YOU'RE ALL *TOUGH* NOW, LITTLE HORN?! SEEMS YOU'RE A BIT CONFUSED!
YOU'RE OUT HERE BECAUSE YOU WERE IN OVER YOUR HEAD AND RAN AWAY, REMEMBER?
URK...
THE REST OF YOUR FAMOUS PARTY IS PRETTY SUSPI-CIOUS, TOO!
TWITCH

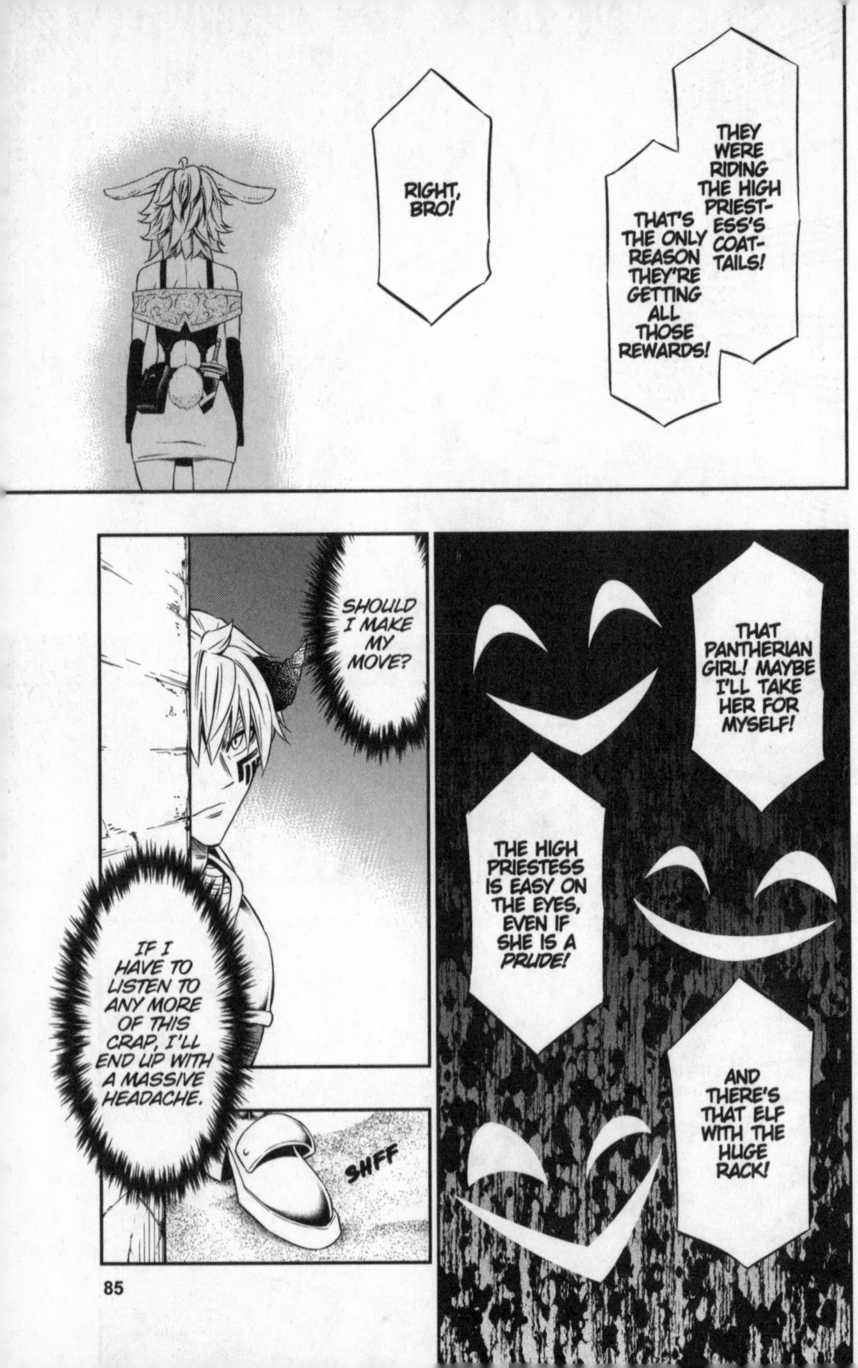
THEY WERE RIDING THE HIGH PRIEST-ESS'S COAT-TAILS!
THAT'S THE ONLY REASON THEY'RE GETTING ALL THOSE REWARDS!
RIGHT, BRO!
THAT PANTHERIAN GIRL! MAYBE I'LL TAKE HER FOR MYSELF!
THE HIGH PRIESTESS IS EASY ON THE EYES, EVEN IF SHE IS A *PRUDE!*
AND THERE'S THAT ELF WITH THE HUGE RACK!
SHOULD I MAKE MY MOVE?
IF I HAVE TO LISTEN TO ANY MORE OF THIS CRAP, I'LL END UP WITH A MASSIVE HEADACHE.
SHFF

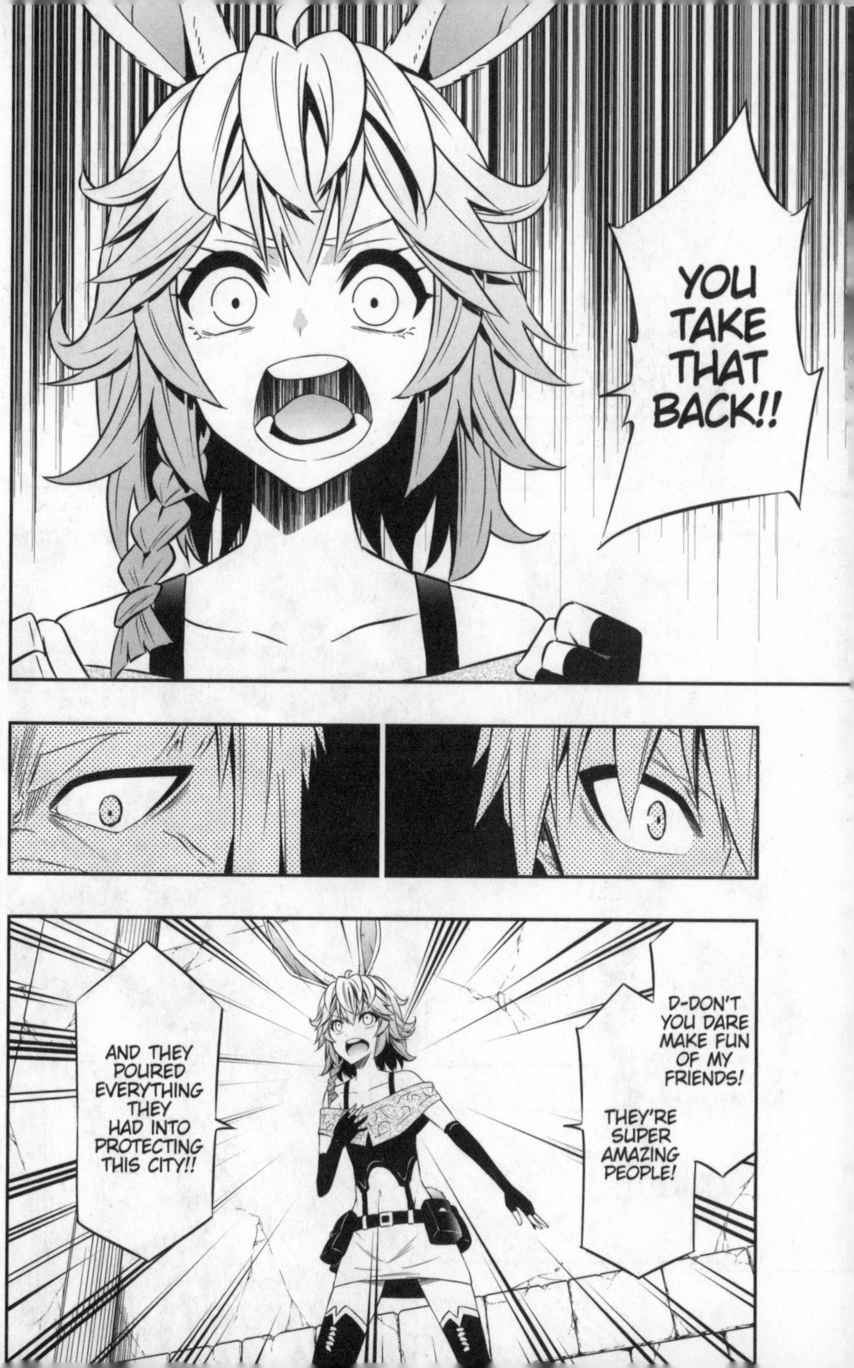
YOU TAKE THAT BACK!!
D-DON'T YOU DARE MAKE FUN OF MY FRIENDS!
THEY'RE SUPER AMAZING PEOPLE!
AND THEY POURED EVERYTHING THEY HAD INTO PROTECTING THIS CITY!!

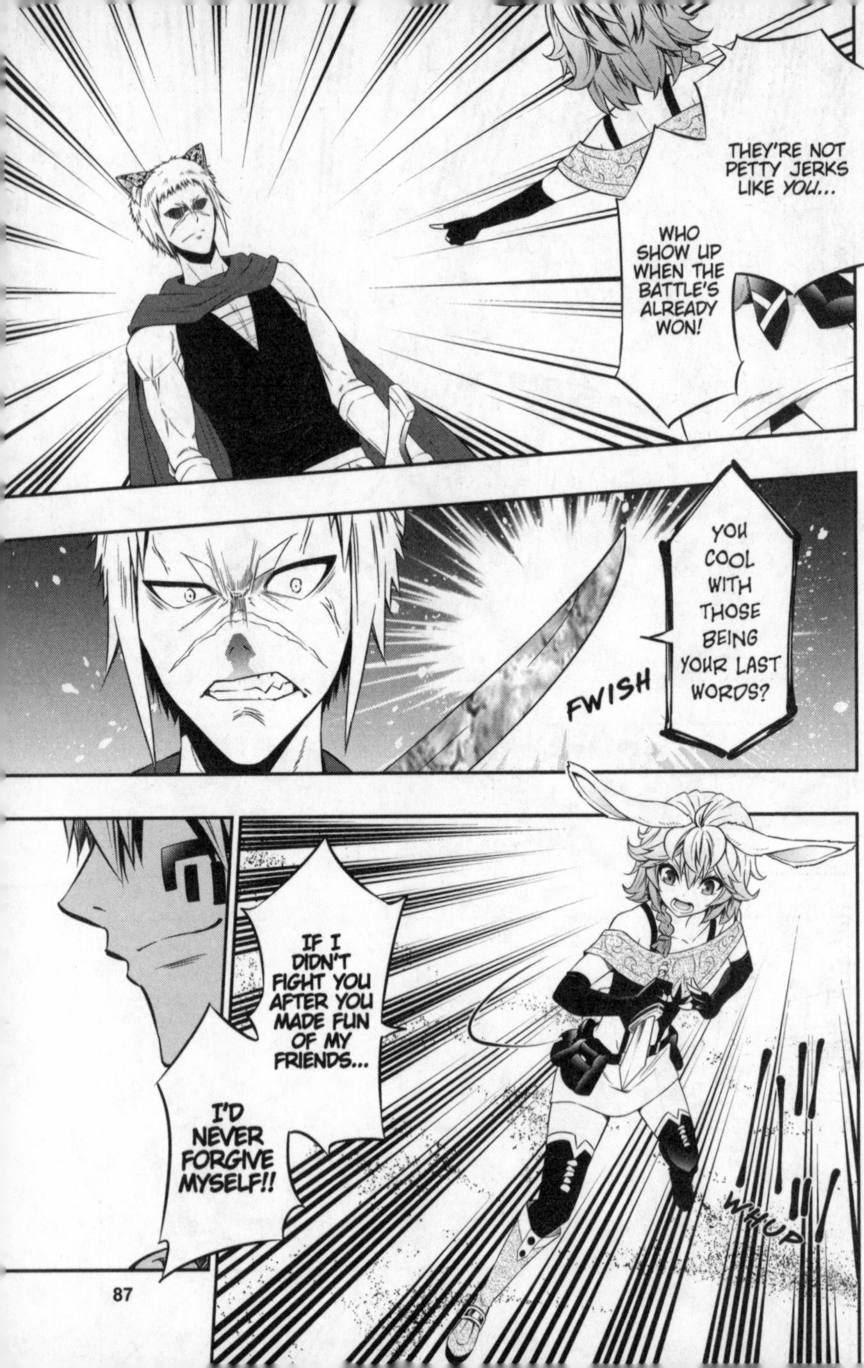
THEY'RE NOT PETTY JERKS LIKE YOU...
WHO SHOW UP WHEN THE BATTLE'S ALREADY WON!
YOU COOL WITH THOSE BEING YOUR LAST WORDS?
FWISH
IF I DIDN'T FIGHT YOU AFTER YOU MADE FUN OF MY FRIENDS...
I'D NEVER FORGIVE MYSELF!!
WHUP

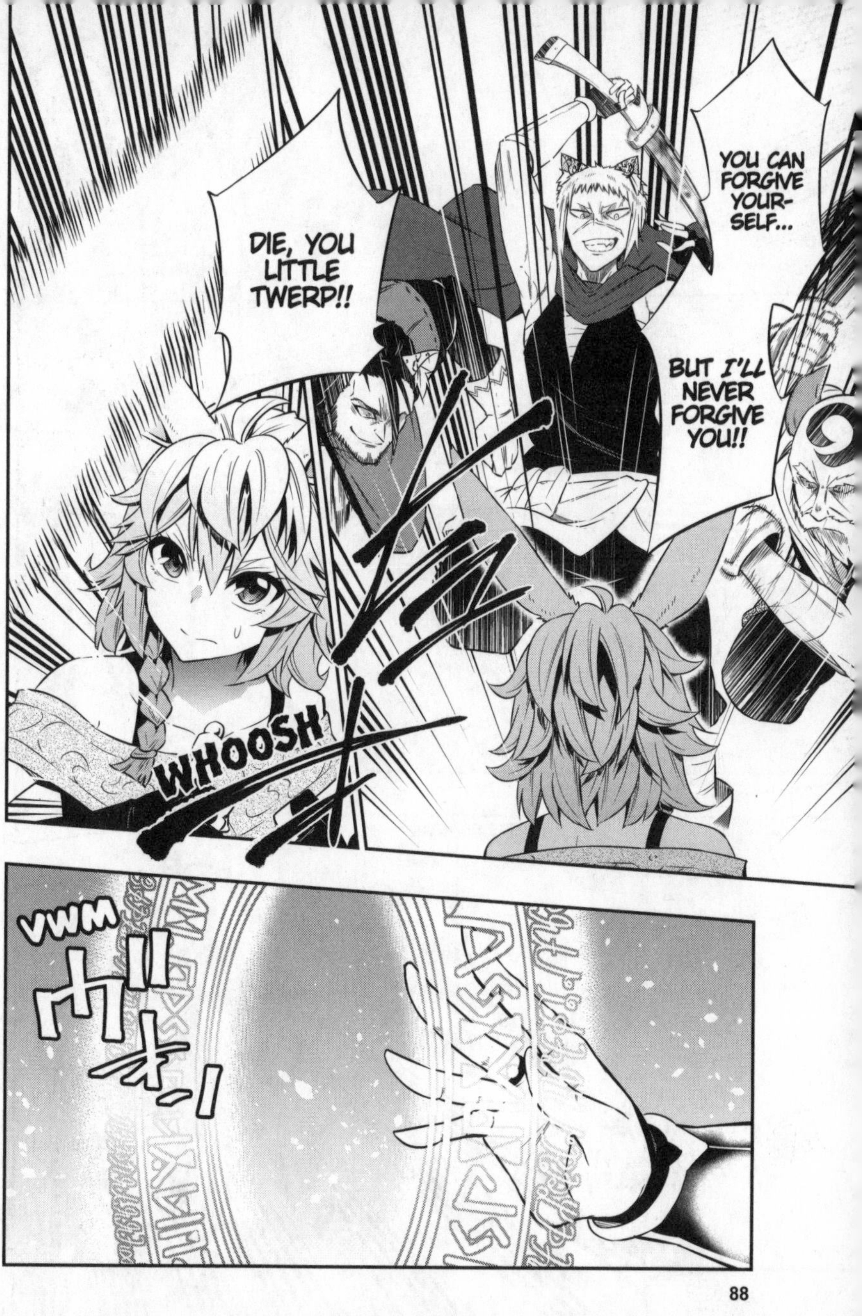
YOU CAN FORGIVE YOUR-SELF...
BUT I'LL NEVER FORGIVE YOU!!
DIE, YOU LITTLE TWERP!!
WHOOSH
VWM

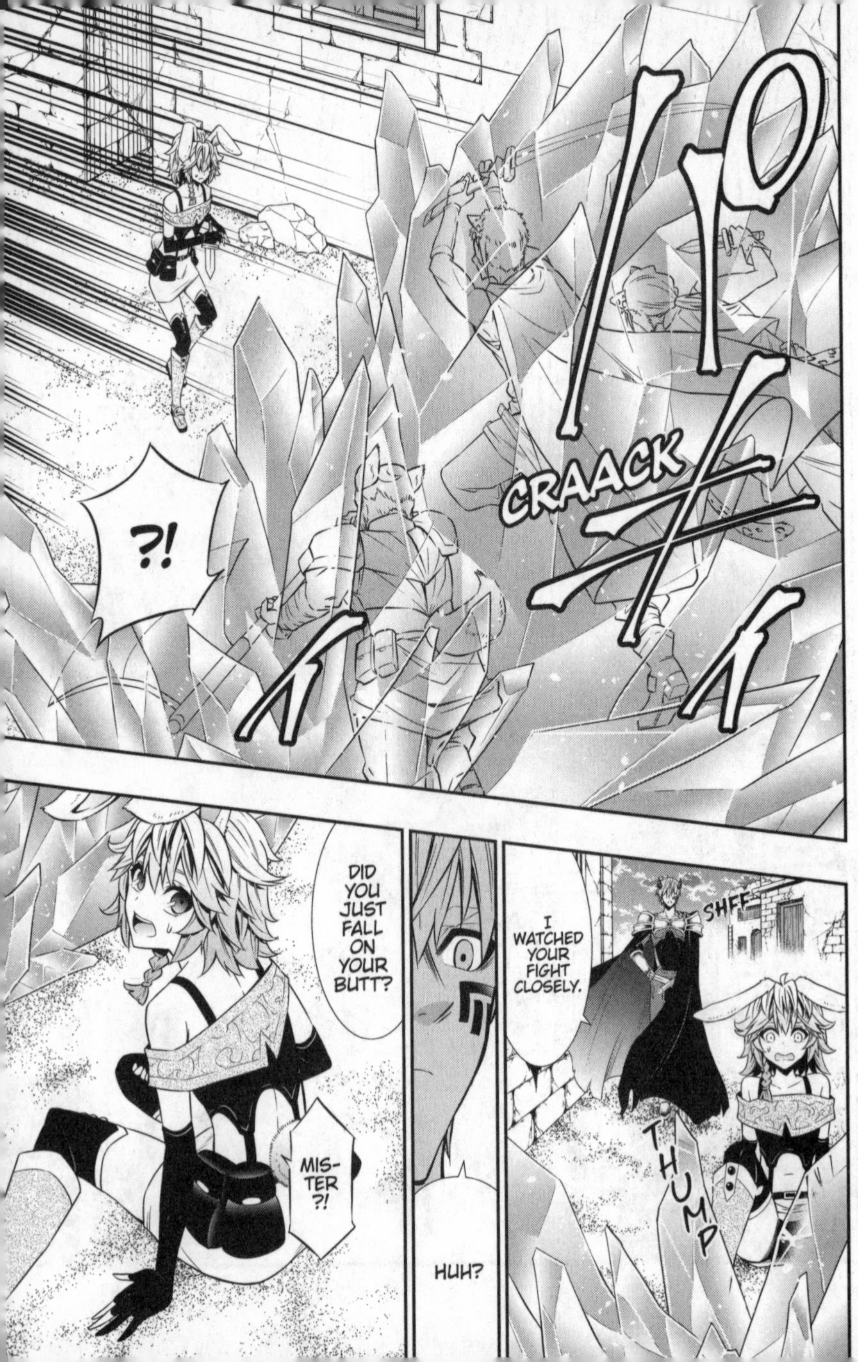
CRAACK
?!
SHFF
I WATCHED YOUR FIGHT CLOSELY.
THUMP
HUH?
DID YOU JUST FALL ON YOUR BUTT?
MISTER?!

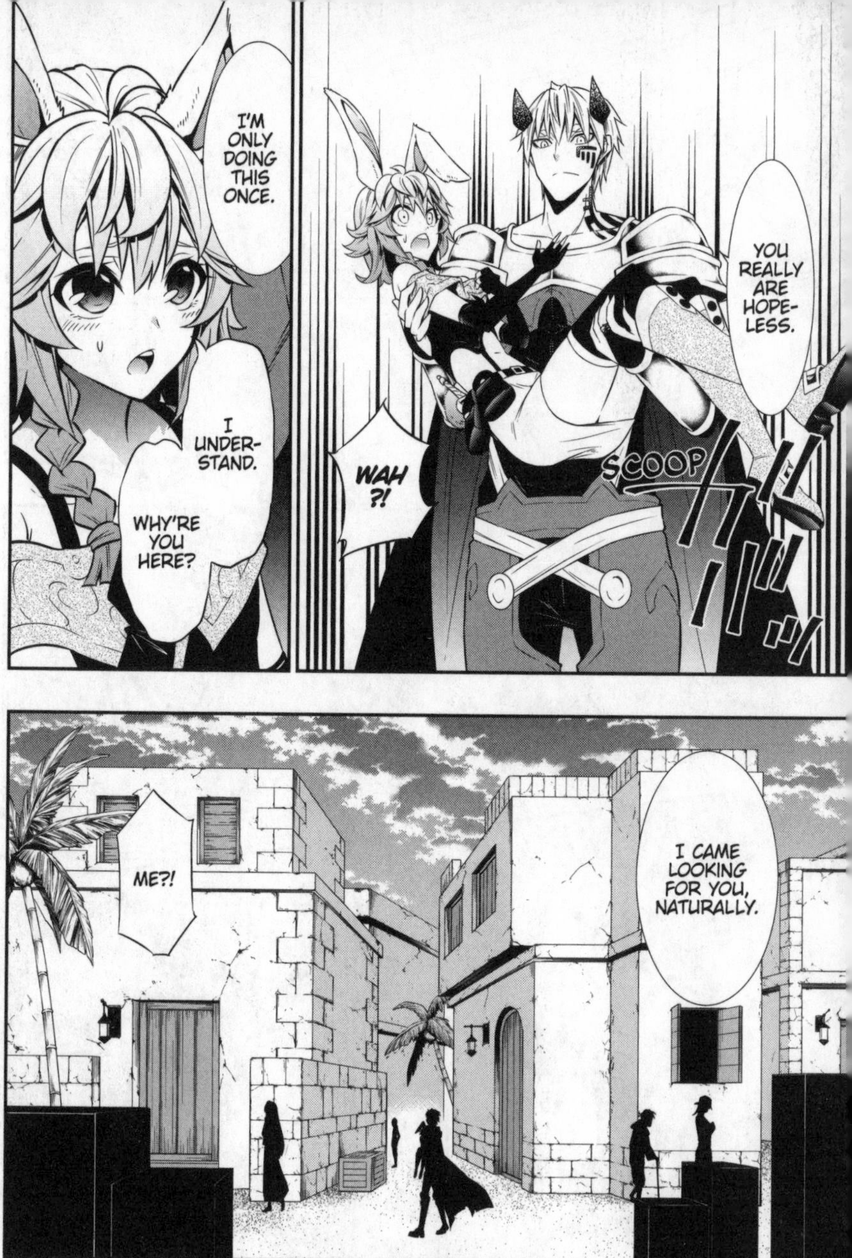
YOU REALLY ARE HOPELESS.
WAH?!
SCOOP
I'M ONLY DOING THIS ONCE.
I UNDERSTAND.
WHY'RE YOU HERE?
I CAME LOOKING FOR YOU, NATURALLY.
ME?!

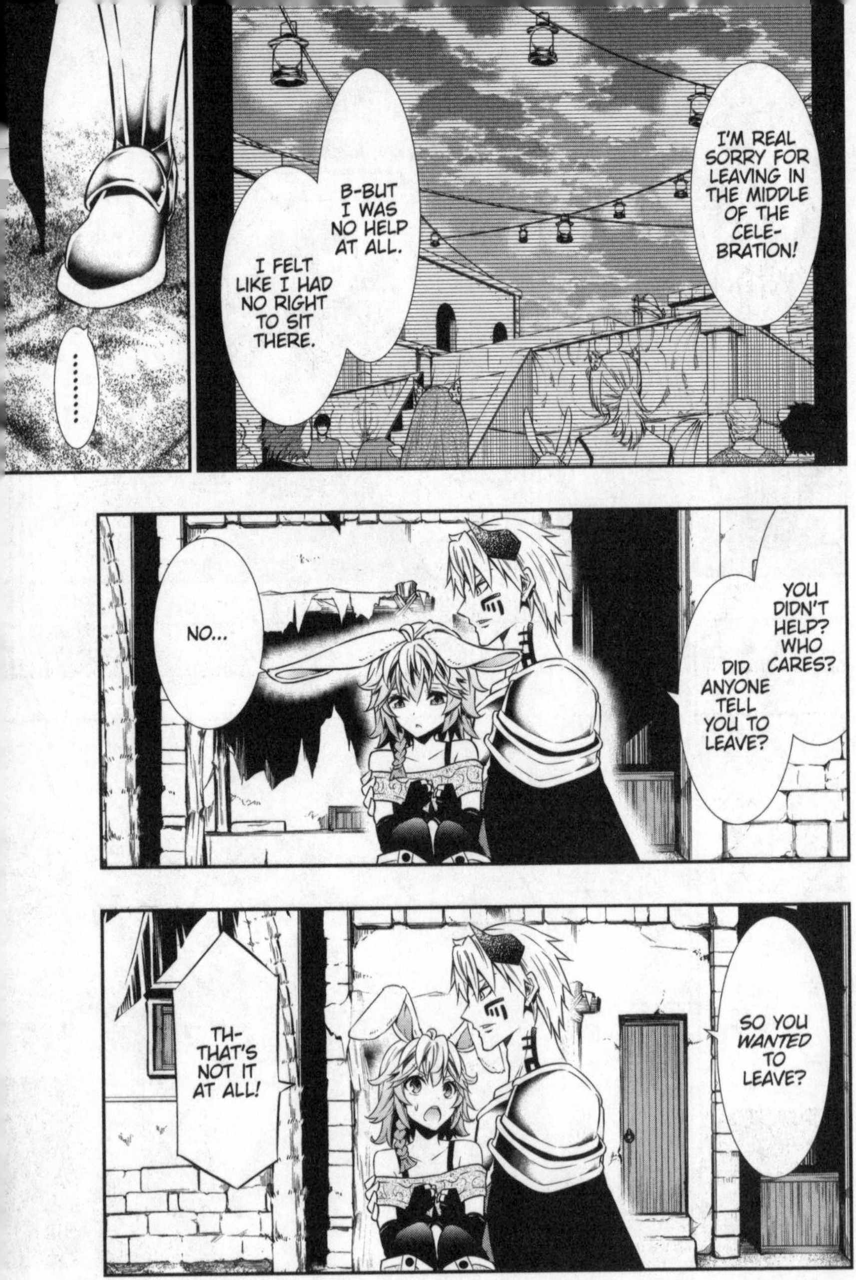
I'M REAL SORRY FOR LEAVING IN THE MIDDLE OF THE CELE-BRATION!
B-BUT I WAS NO HELP AT ALL.
I FELT LIKE I HAD NO RIGHT TO SIT THERE.
......
YOU DIDN'T HELP? WHO CARES?
DID ANYONE TELL YOU TO LEAVE?
NO...
SO YOU WANTED TO LEAVE?
TH-THAT'S NOT IT AT ALL!

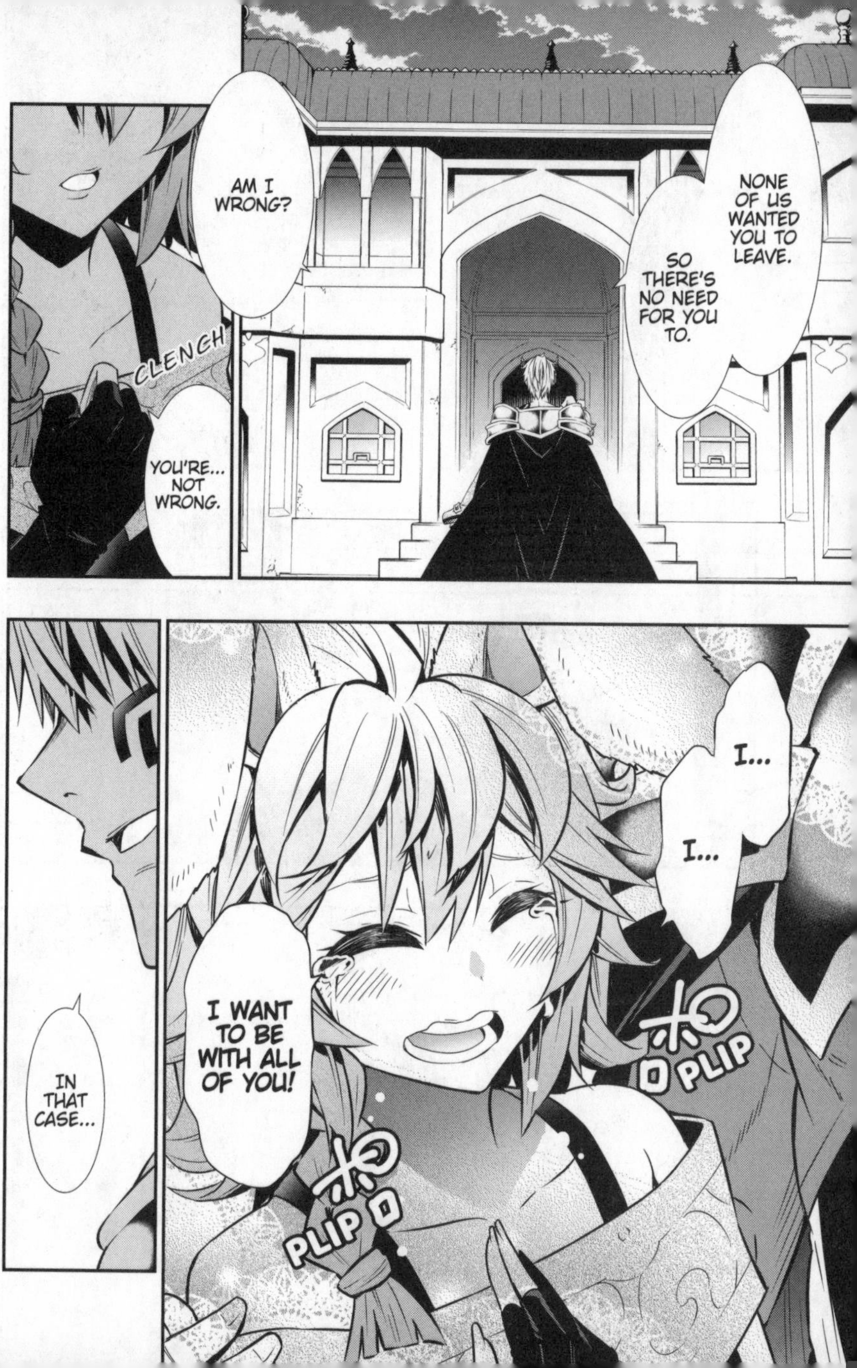
NONE OF US WANTED YOU TO LEAVE.
SO THERE'S NO NEED FOR YOU TO.
AM I WRONG?
CLENCH
YOU'RE... NOT WRONG.
I...
I...
PLIP
I WANT TO BE WITH ALL OF YOU!
PLIP
IN THAT CASE...

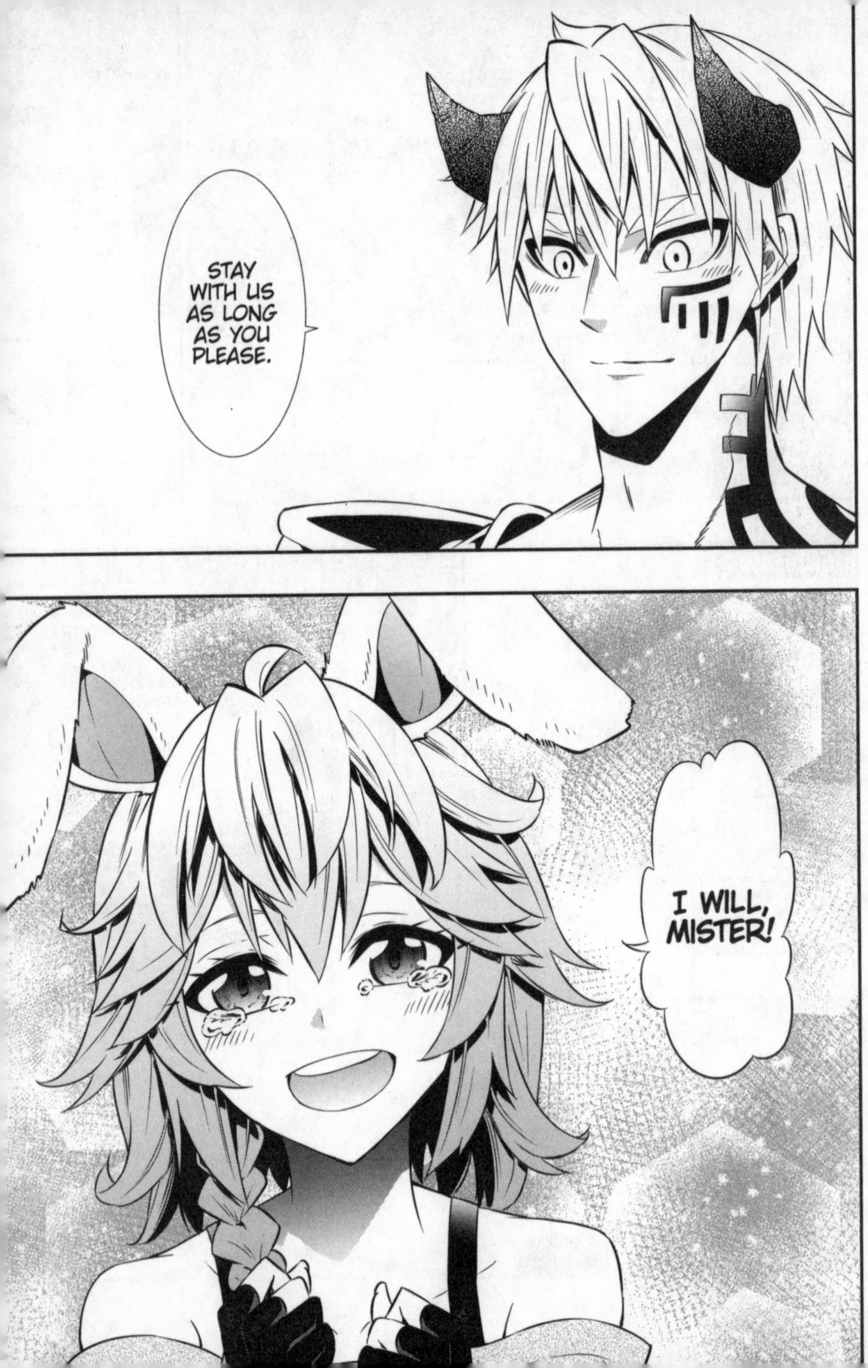
STAY WITH US AS LONG AS YOU PLEASE.
I WILL, MISTER!

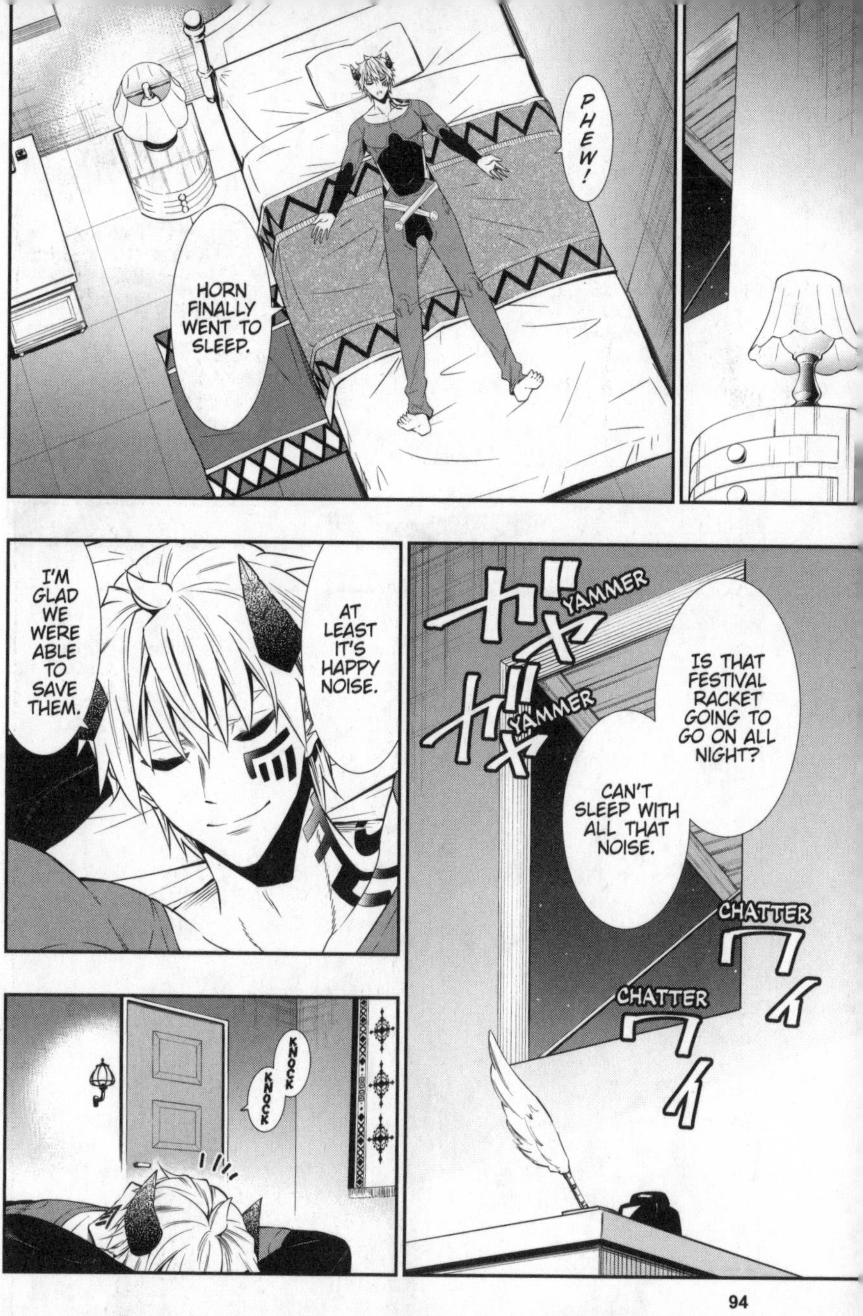
PHEW!
HORN FINALLY WENT TO SLEEP.
YAMMER
YAMMER
IS THAT FESTIVAL RACKET GOING TO GO ON ALL NIGHT?
CAN'T SLEEP WITH ALL THAT NOISE.
CHATTER
CHATTER
AT LEAST IT'S HAPPY NOISE.
I'M GLAD WE WERE ABLE TO SAVE THEM.
KNOCK
KNOCK

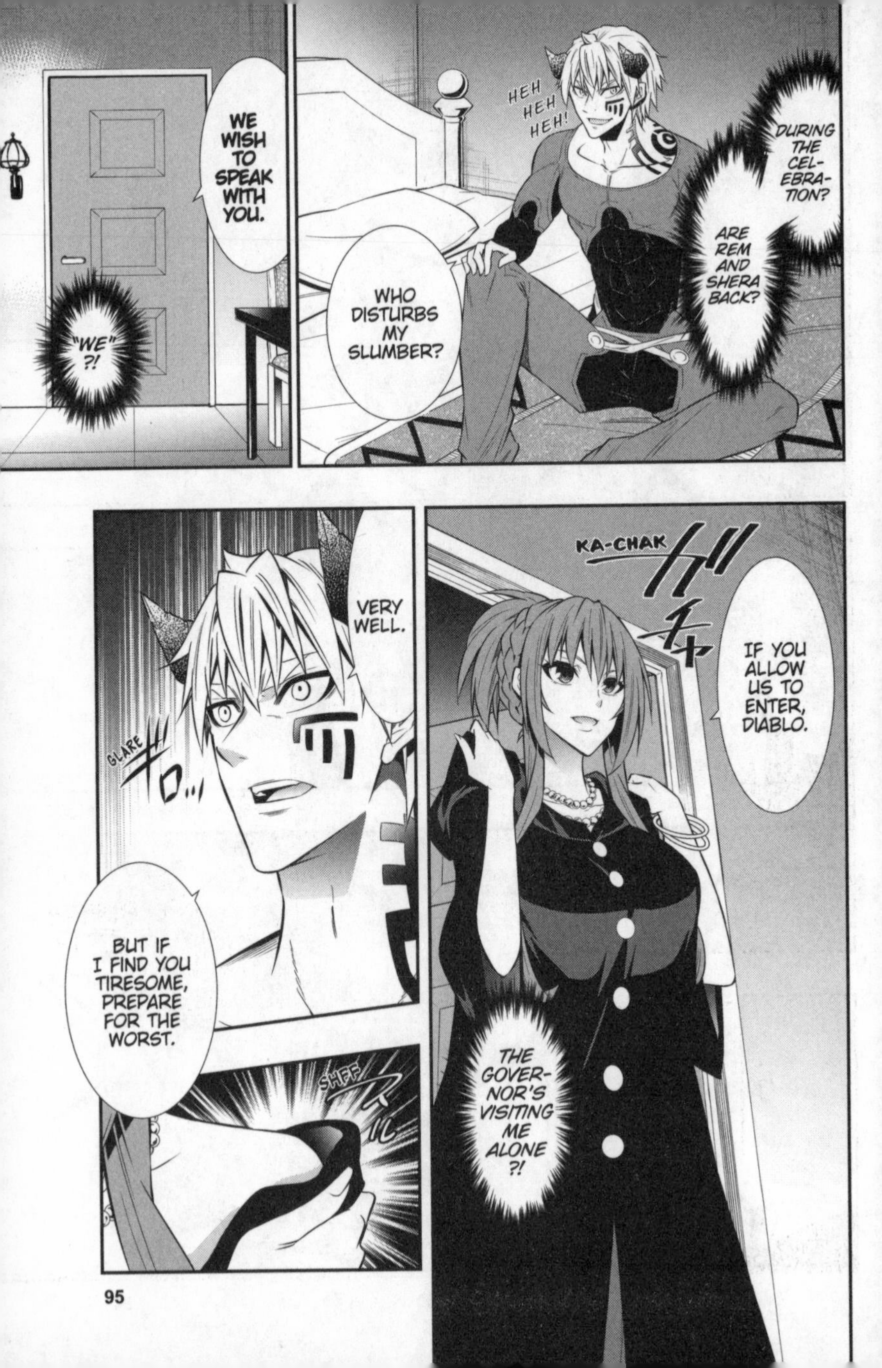
DURING THE CELEBRATION?
HEH HEH HEH!
ARE REM AND SHERA BACK?
WHO DISTURBS MY SLUMBER?
WE WISH TO SPEAK WITH YOU.
"WE"?!
KA-CHAK
IF YOU ALLOW US TO ENTER, DIABLO.
THE GOVERNOR'S VISITING ME ALONE?!
VERY WELL.
GLARE
BUT IF I FIND YOU TIRESOME, PREPARE FOR THE WORST.
SHFF

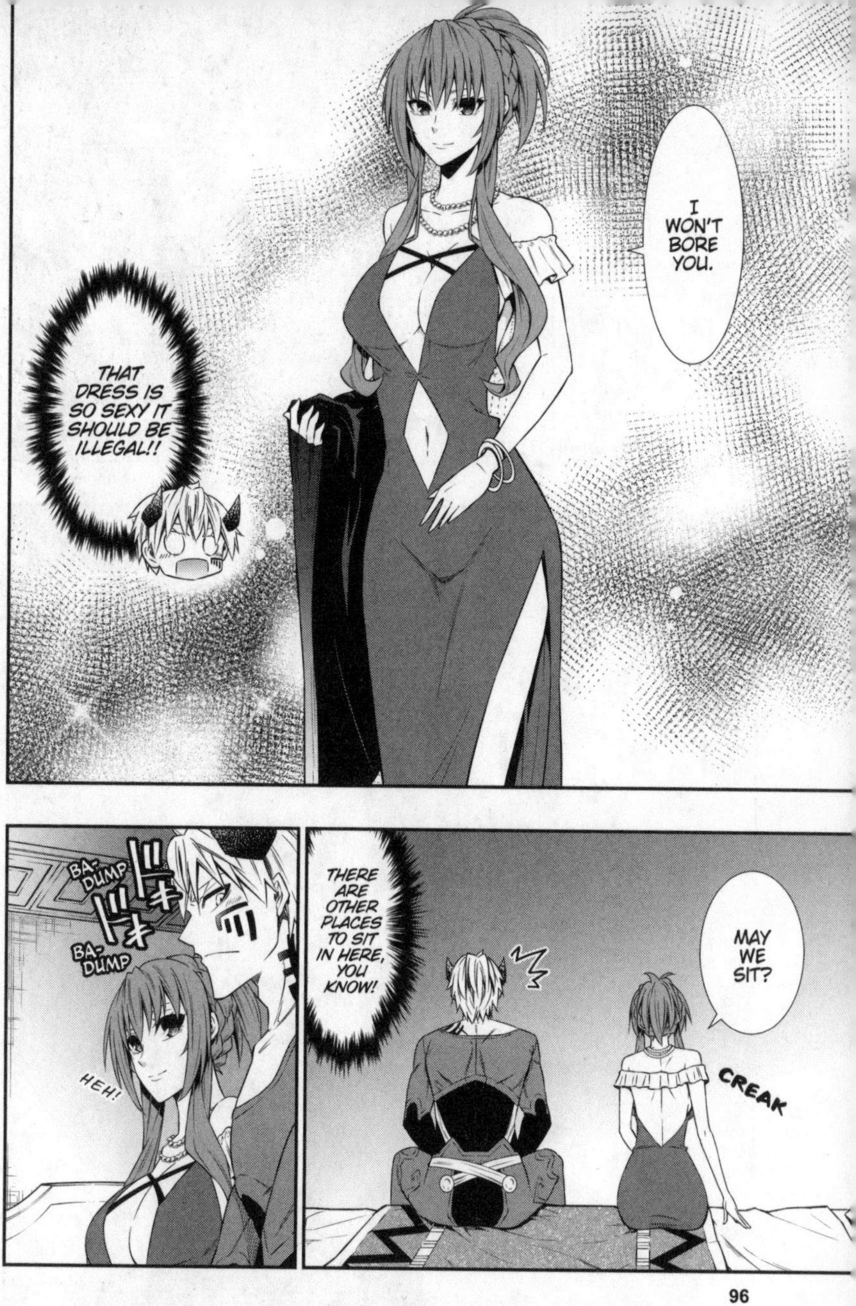
I WON'T BORE YOU.
THAT DRESS IS SO SEXY IT SHOULD BE ILLEGAL!!
MAY WE SIT?
CREAK
THERE ARE OTHER PLACES TO SIT IN HERE, YOU KNOW!
BA-DUMP ドキ
ドキ BA-DUMP
HEH!

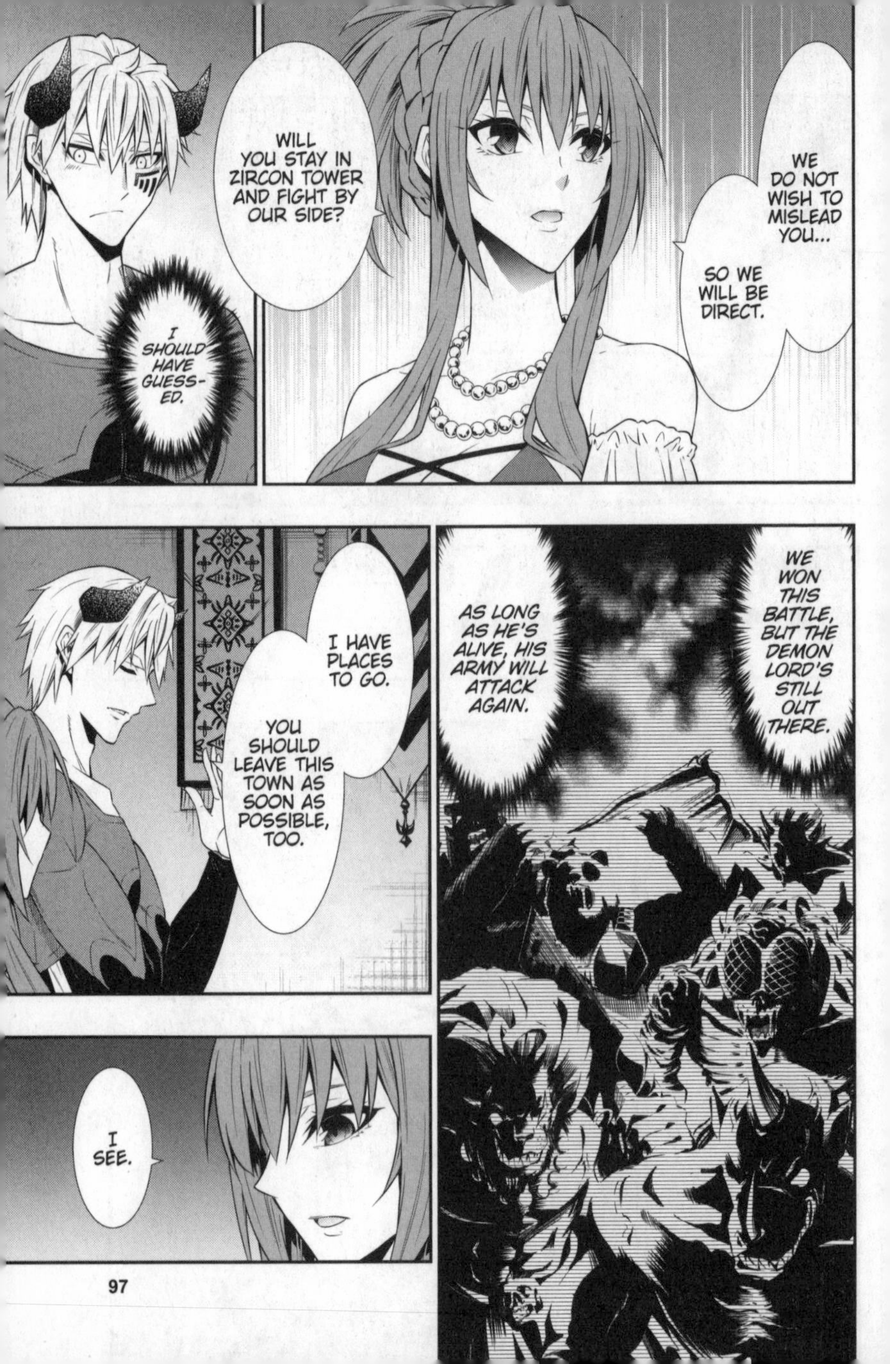
WE DO NOT WISH TO MISLEAD YOU...
SO WE WILL BE DIRECT.
WILL YOU STAY IN ZIRCON TOWER AND FIGHT BY OUR SIDE?
I SHOULD HAVE GUESS-ED.
WE WON THIS BATTLE, BUT THE DEMON LORD'S STILL OUT THERE.
AS LONG AS HE'S ALIVE, HIS ARMY WILL ATTACK AGAIN.
I HAVE PLACES TO GO.
YOU SHOULD LEAVE THIS TOWN AS SOON AS POSSIBLE, TOO.
I SEE.

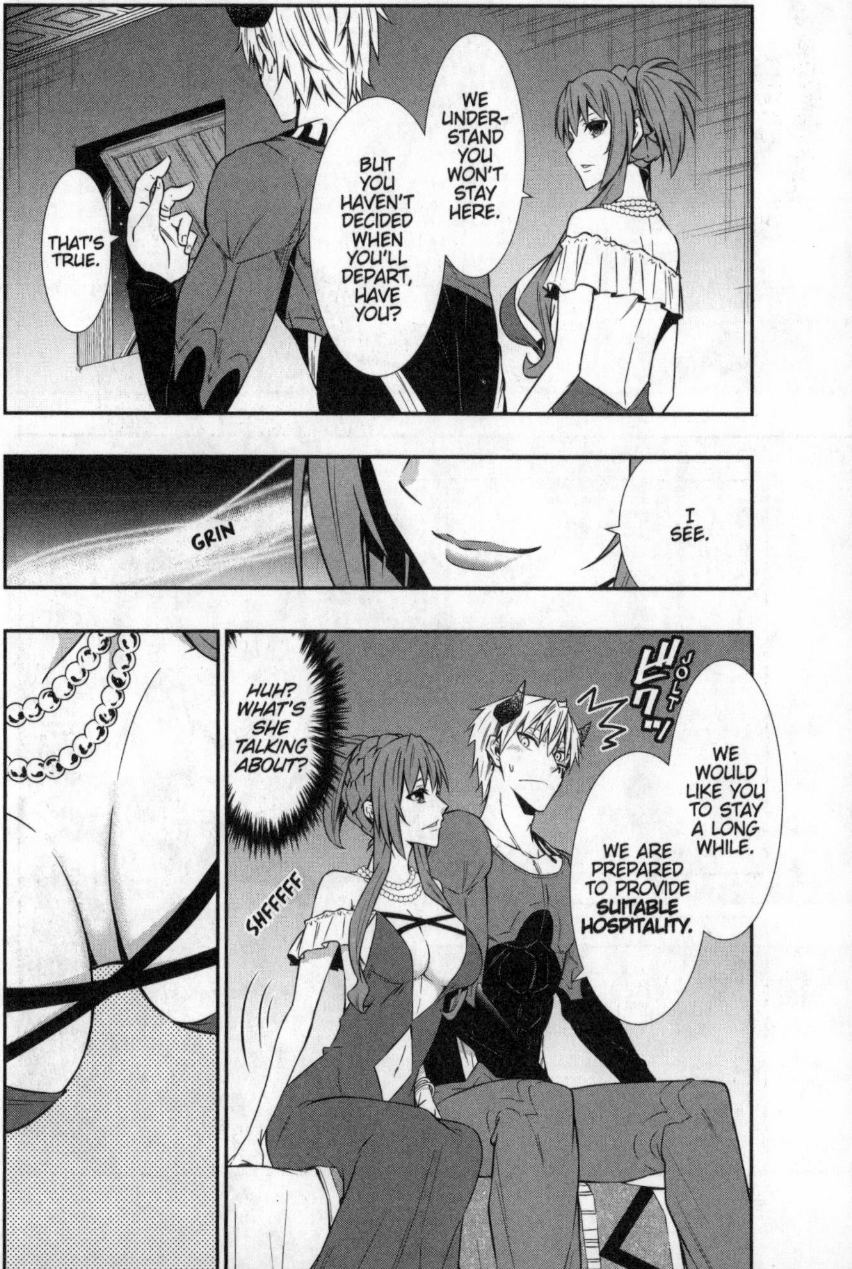
WE UNDER-STAND YOU WON'T STAY HERE.
BUT YOU HAVEN'T DECIDED WHEN YOU'LL DEPART, HAVE YOU?
THAT'S TRUE.
I SEE.
GRIN
ビクッ
JOLT
WE WOULD LIKE YOU TO STAY A LONG WHILE.
WE ARE PREPARED TO PROVIDE SUITABLE HOSPITALITY.
HUH? WHAT'S SHE TALKING ABOUT?
SHFFFFF

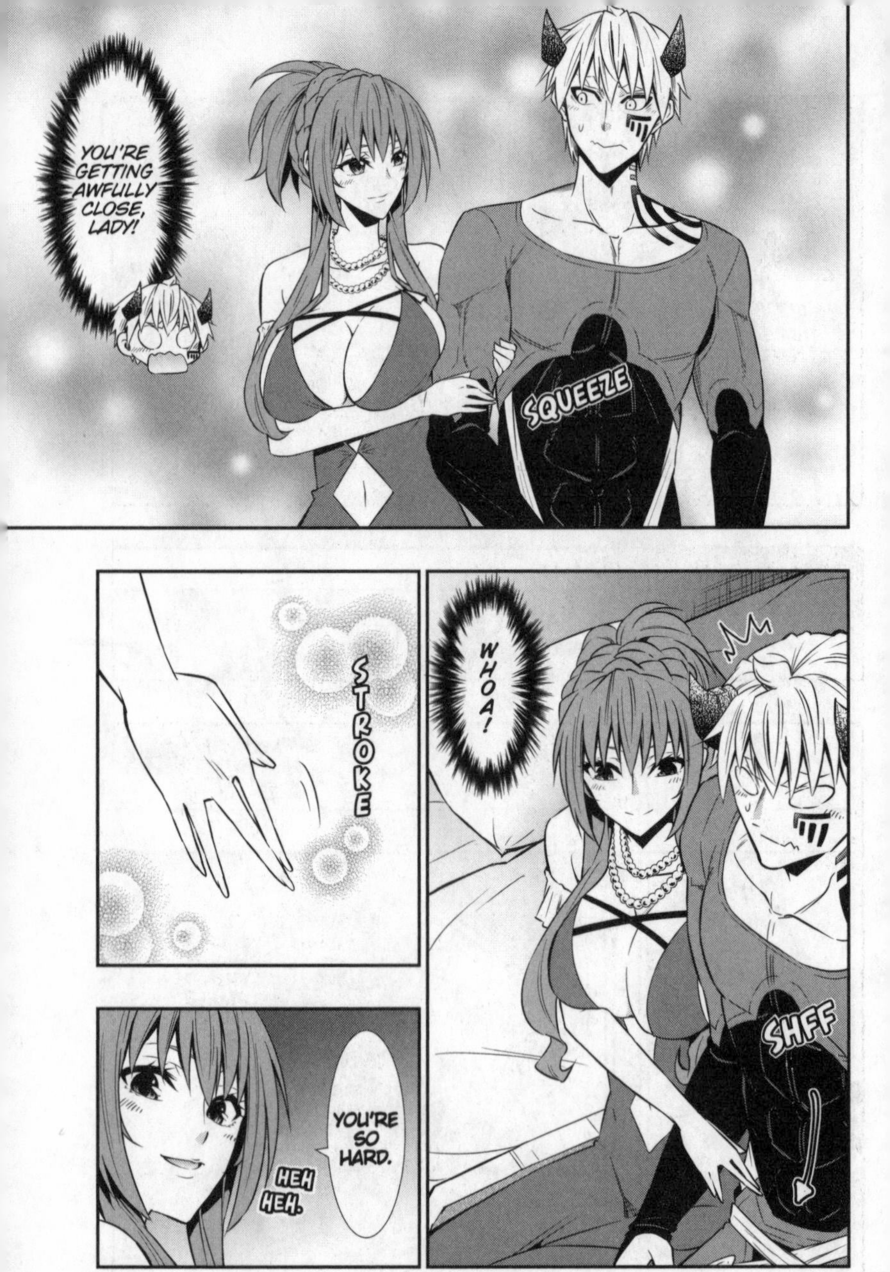
YOU'RE GETTING AWFULLY CLOSE, LADY!
SQUEEZE
WHOA!
SHFF
STROKE
YOU'RE SO HARD.
HEH HEH.

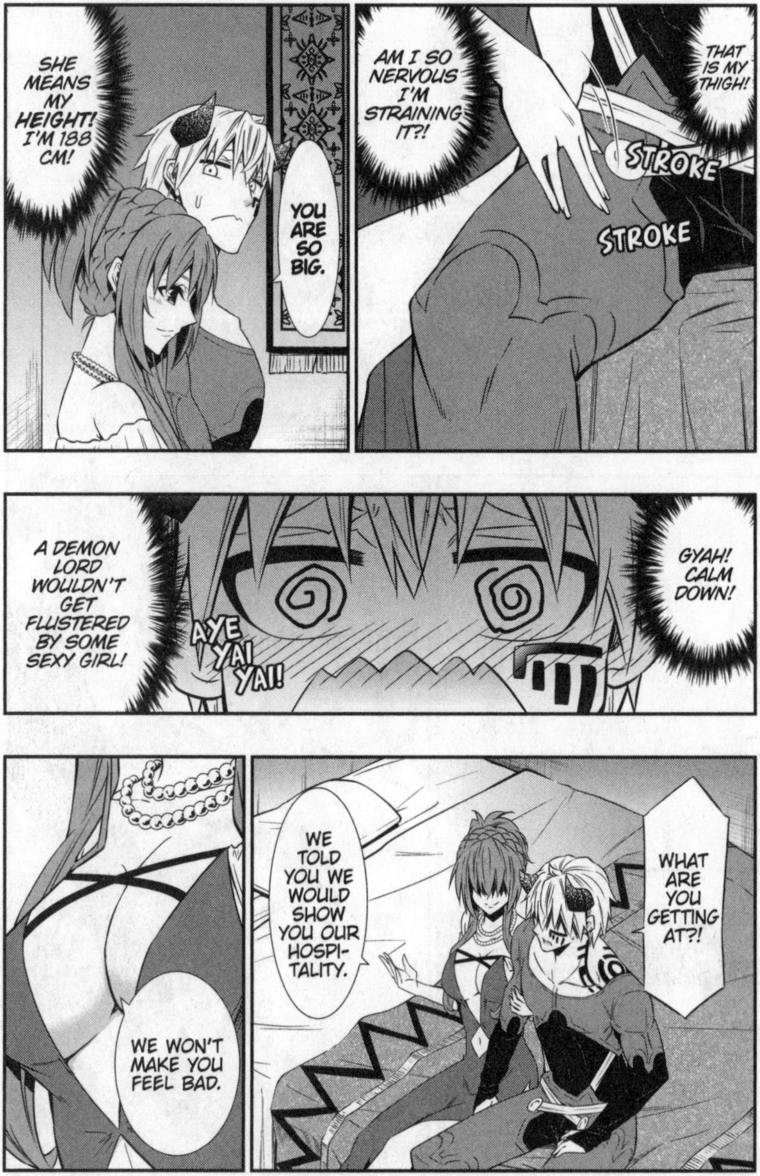
THAT IS MY THIGH!
AM I SO NERVOUS I'M STRAINING IT?!
STROKE
STROKE
YOU ARE SO BIG.
SHE MEANS MY HEIGHT! I'M 188 CM!
GYAH! CALM DOWN!
AYE YAI YAI!
A DEMON LORD WOULDN'T GET FLUSTERED BY SOME SEXY GIRL!
WHAT ARE YOU GETTING AT?!
WE TOLD YOU WE WOULD SHOW YOU OUR HOSPI-TALITY.
WE WON'T MAKE YOU FEEL BAD.

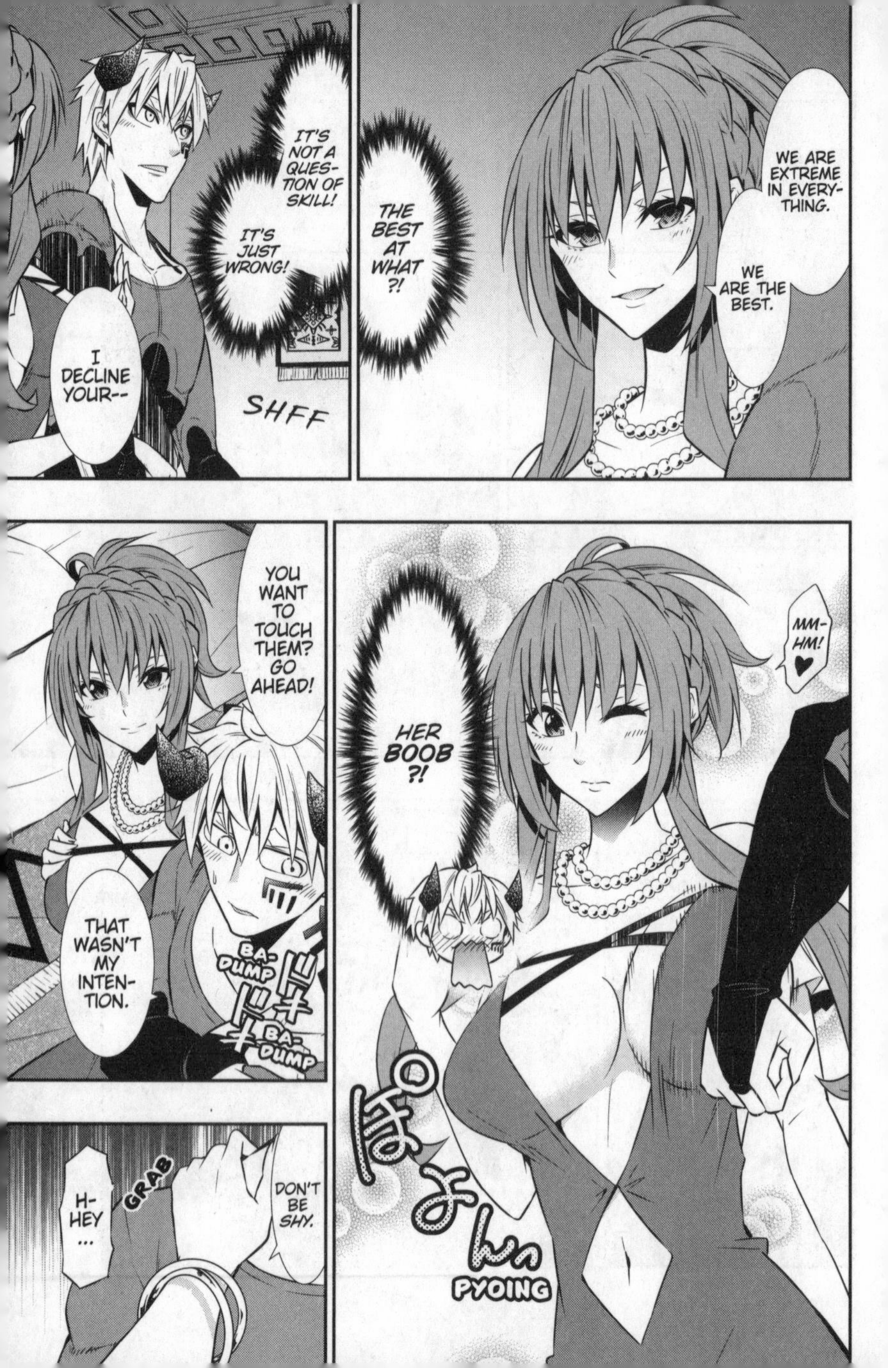

WE ARE EXTREME IN EVERY-THING.
WE ARE THE BEST.
THE BEST AT WHAT?!
IT'S NOT A QUES-TION OF SKILL!
IT'S JUST WRONG!
SHFF
I DECLINE YOUR--
MM-HM! ♥
HER BOOB?!
ぽよん
PYOING
YOU WANT TO TOUCH THEM? GO AHEAD!
THAT WASN'T MY INTEN-TION.
ドキドキ
BA-DUMP BA-DUMP
DON'T BE SHY.
GRAB
H-HEY ...

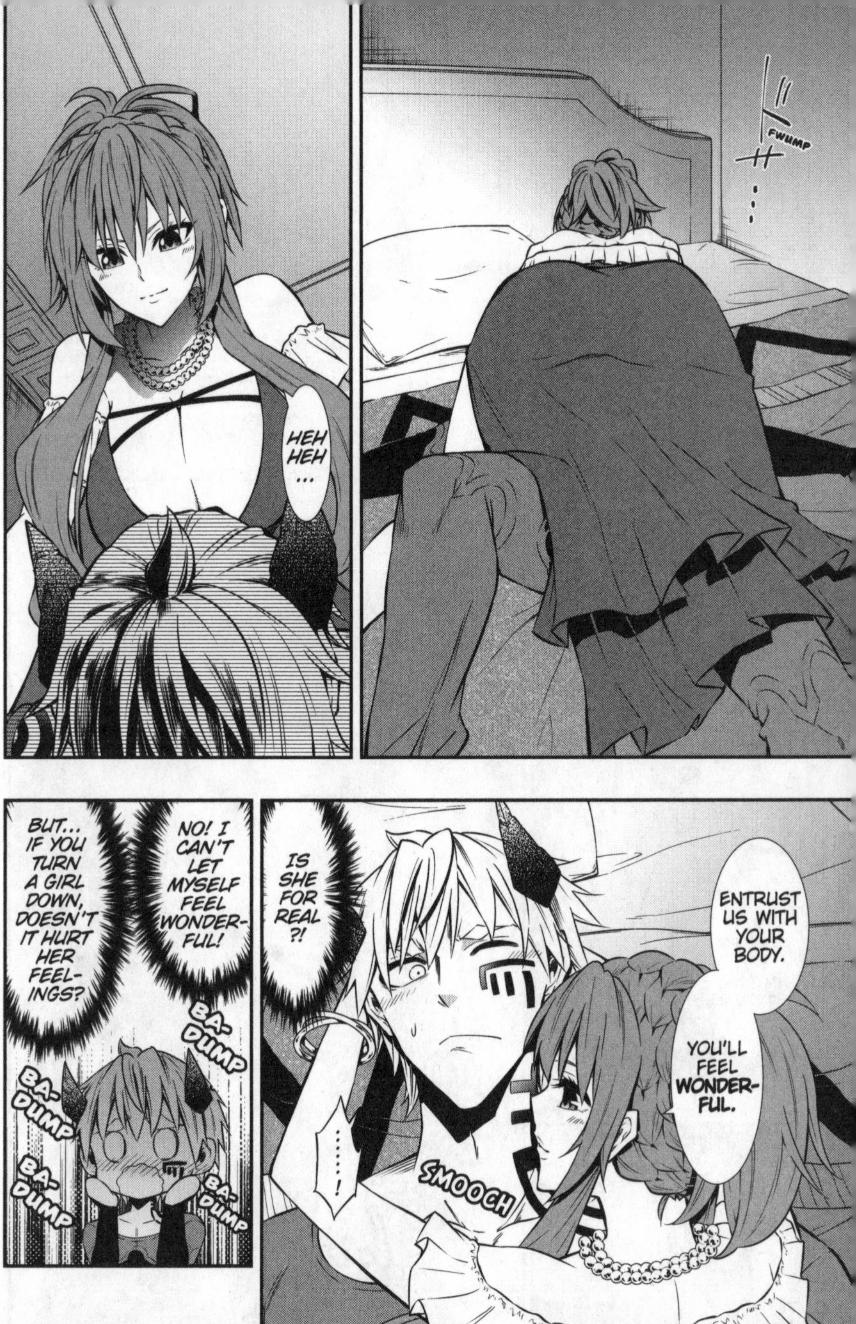
FWUMP
...
HEH HEH ...
ENTRUST US WITH YOUR BODY.
YOU'LL FEEL WONDERFUL.
SMOOCH
......!
IS SHE FOR REAL?!
NO! I CAN'T LET MYSELF FEEL WONDERFUL!
BUT... IF YOU TURN A GIRL DOWN, DOESN'T IT HURT HER FEELINGS?
BA-DUMP
BA-DUMP
BA-DUMP
BA-DUMP

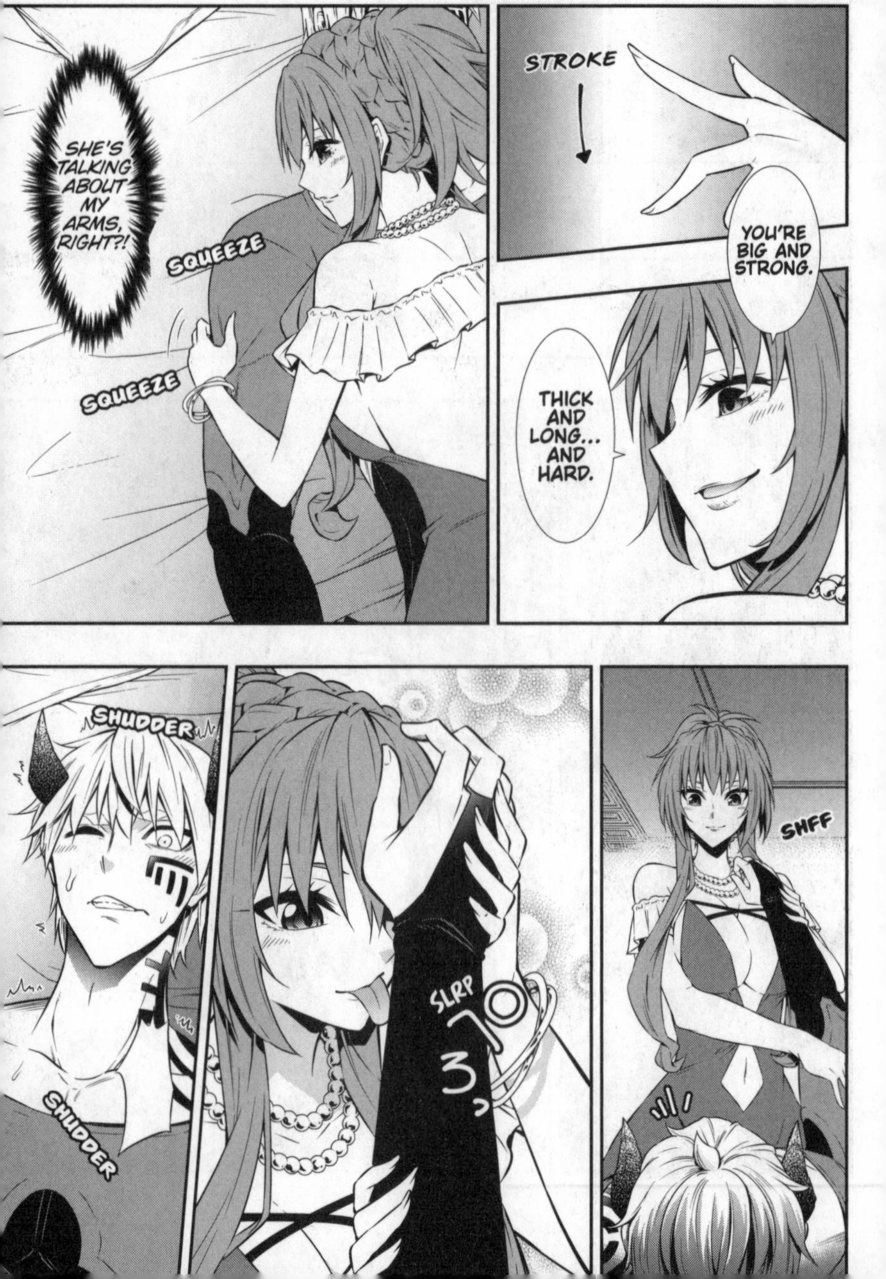
STROKE
YOU'RE BIG AND STRONG.
THICK AND LONG... AND HARD.
SHE'S TALKING ABOUT MY ARMS, RIGHT?!
SQUEEZE
SQUEEZE
SHFF
SLRP
SHUDDER
SHUDDER

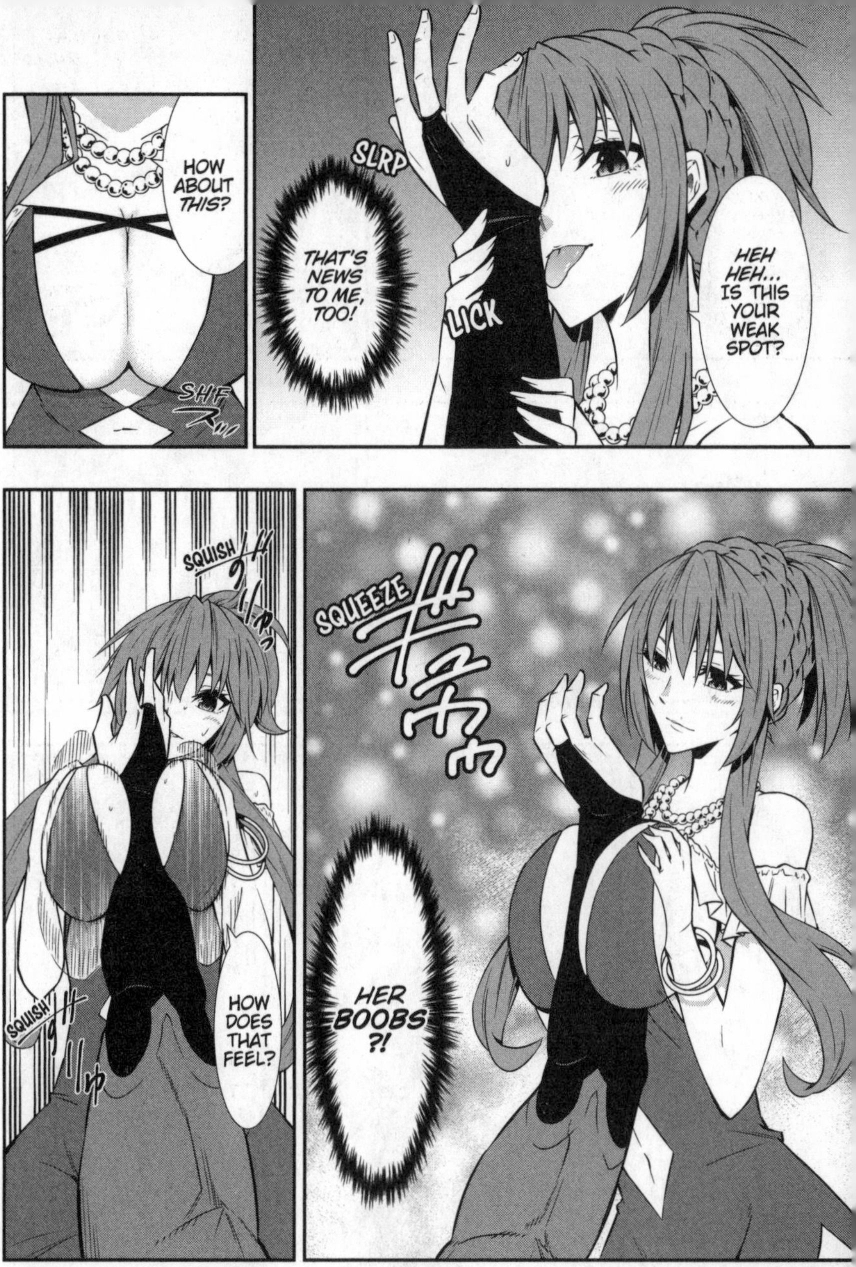
HEH HEH... IS THIS YOUR WEAK SPOT?
SLRP
THAT'S NEWS TO ME, TOO!
LICK
HOW ABOUT THIS?
SHF
SQUEEZE
HER BOOBS?!
SQUISH
HOW DOES THAT FEEL?
SQUISH

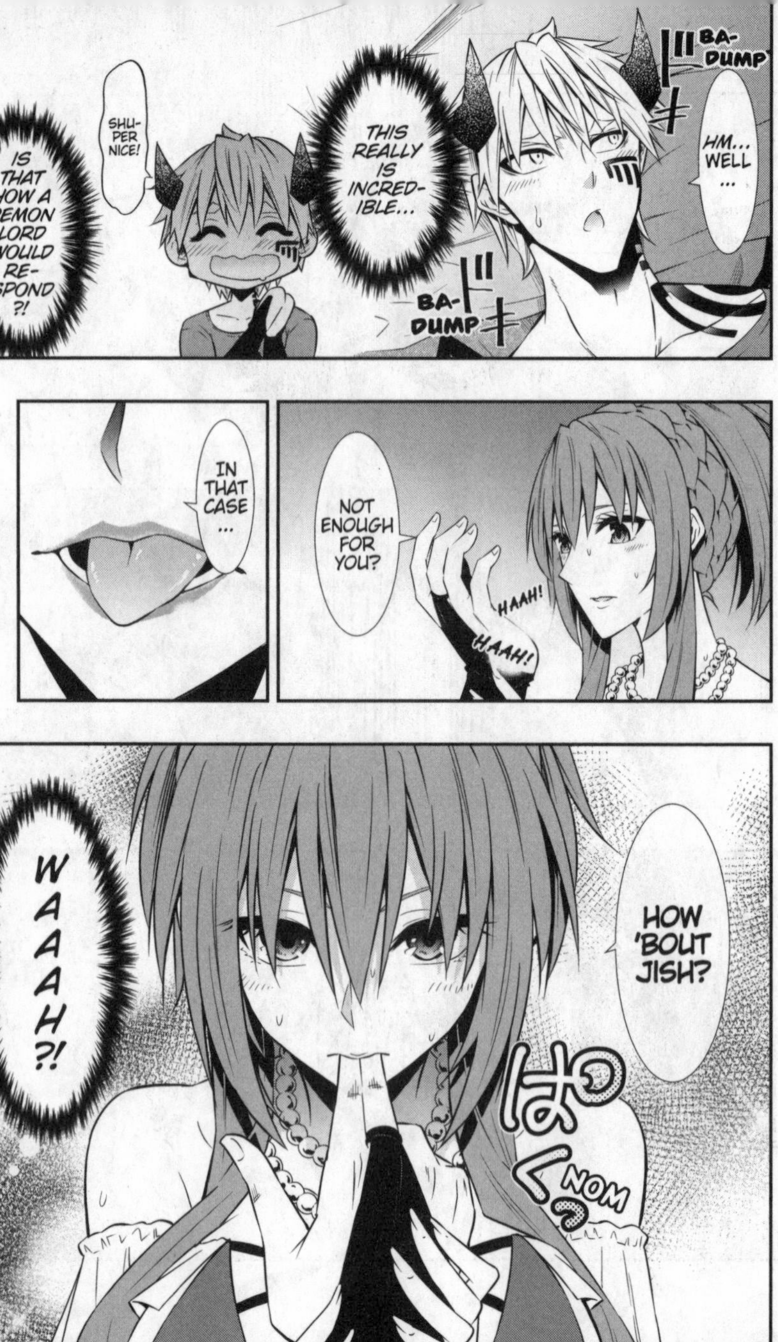
BA-DUMP
HM... WELL ...
THIS REALLY IS INCREDIBLE...
BA-DUMP
SHU-PER NICE!
IS THAT HOW A DEMON LORD WOULD RE-SPOND?!
NOT ENOUGH FOR YOU?
HAAH!
HAAH!
IN THAT CASE ...
HOW 'BOUT JISH?
NOM
WAAAAH?!

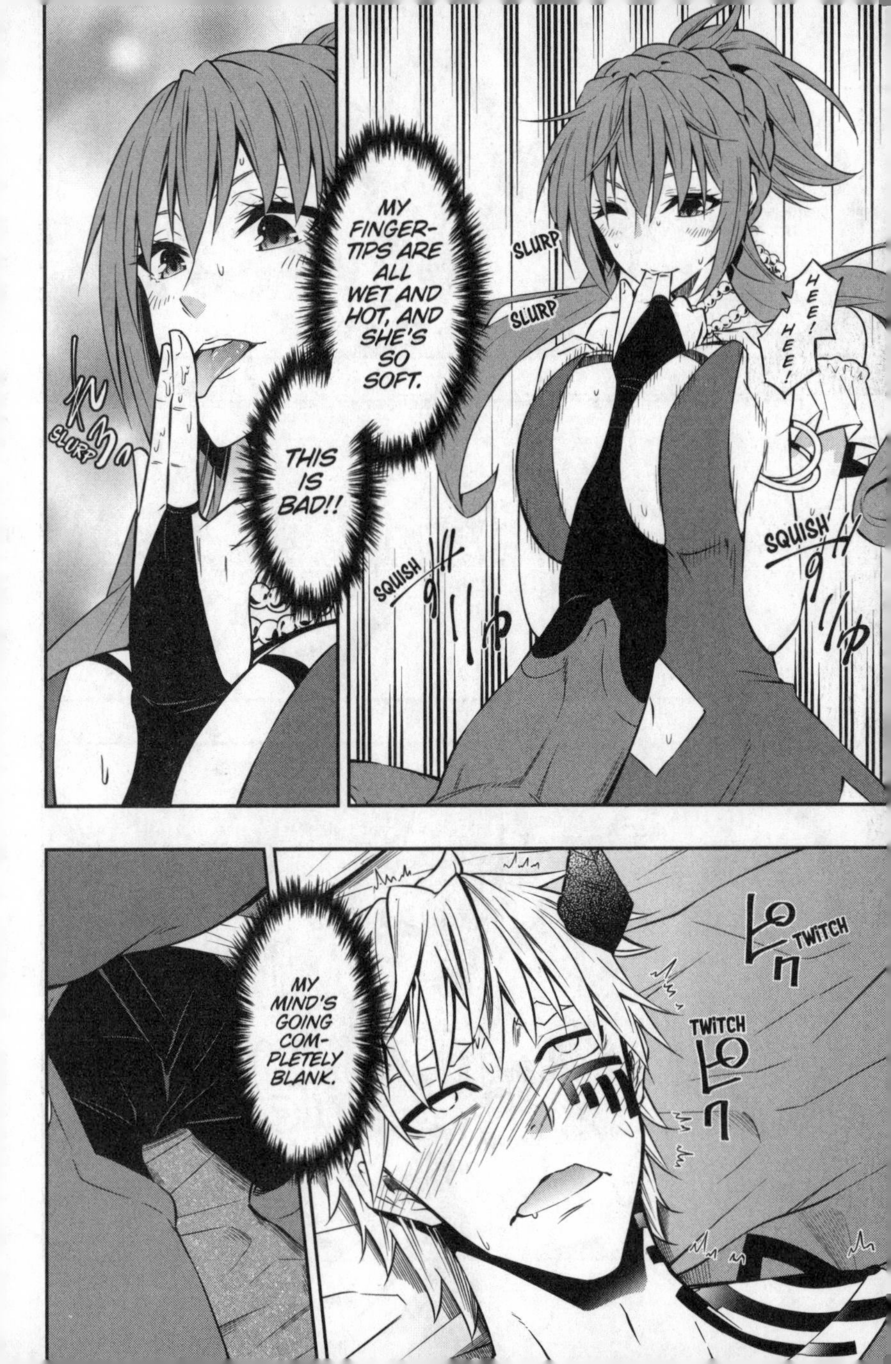
HEE! HEE!
SLURP
SLURP
SQUISH
SQUISH
MY FINGER-TIPS ARE ALL WET AND HOT, AND SHE'S SO SOFT.
THIS IS BAD!!
SLURP
TWITCH
TWITCH
MY MIND'S GOING COM-PLETELY BLANK.

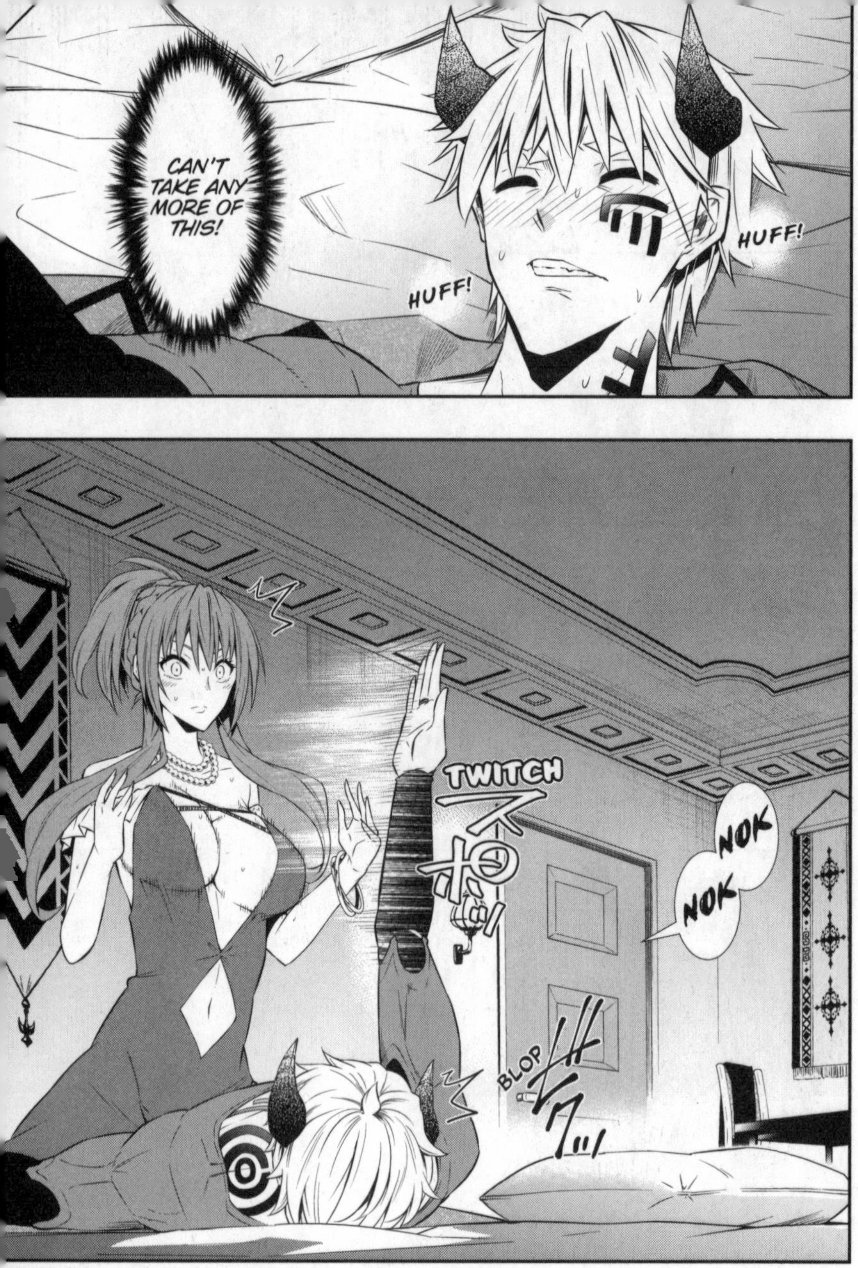
HUFF!
CAN'T TAKE ANY MORE OF THIS!
HUFF!
NOK NOK
TWITCH
BLOP

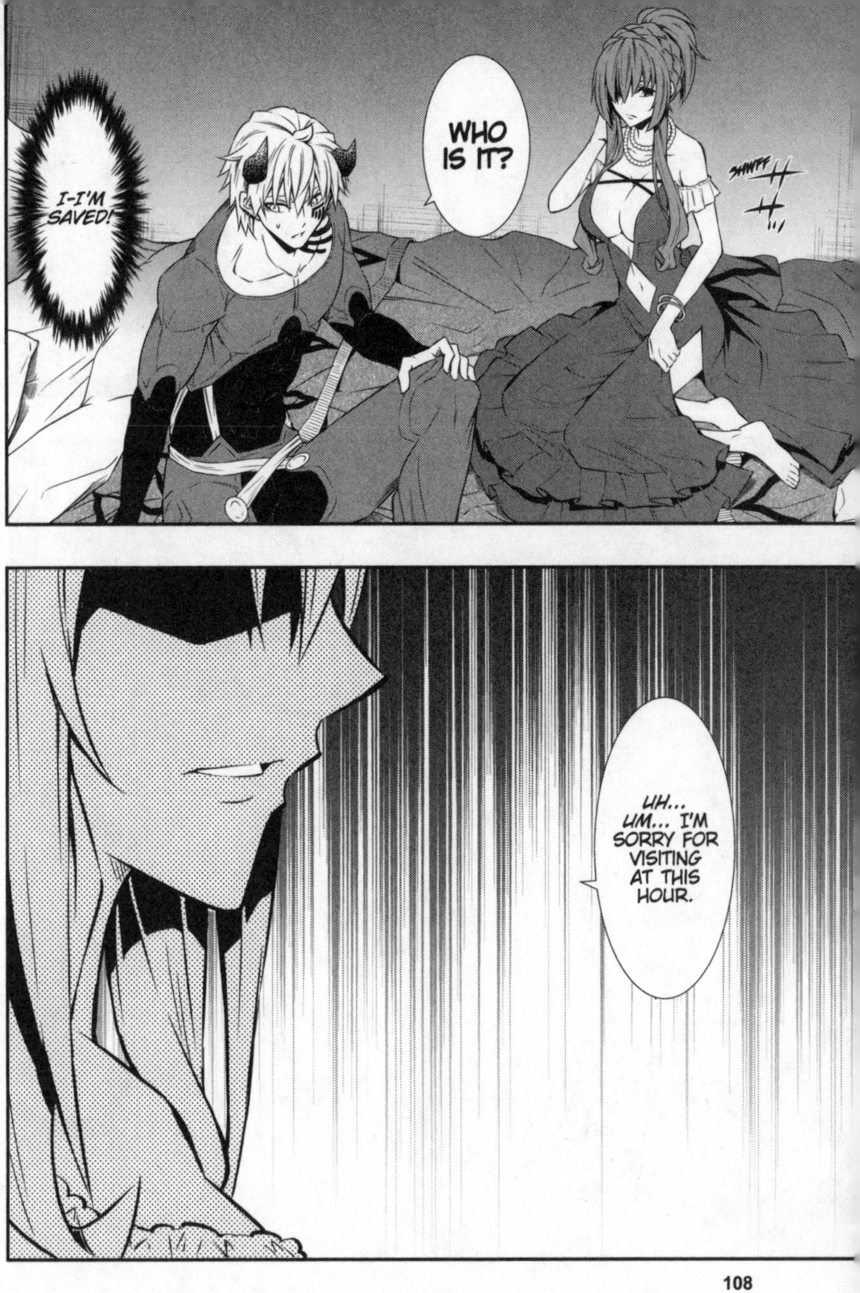
SHWFF
WHO IS IT?
I-I'M SAVED!
UH... UM... I'M SORRY FOR VISITING AT THIS HOUR.

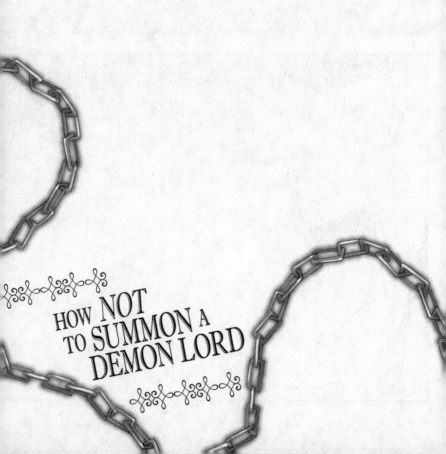

HOW NOT TO SUMMON A DEMON LORD

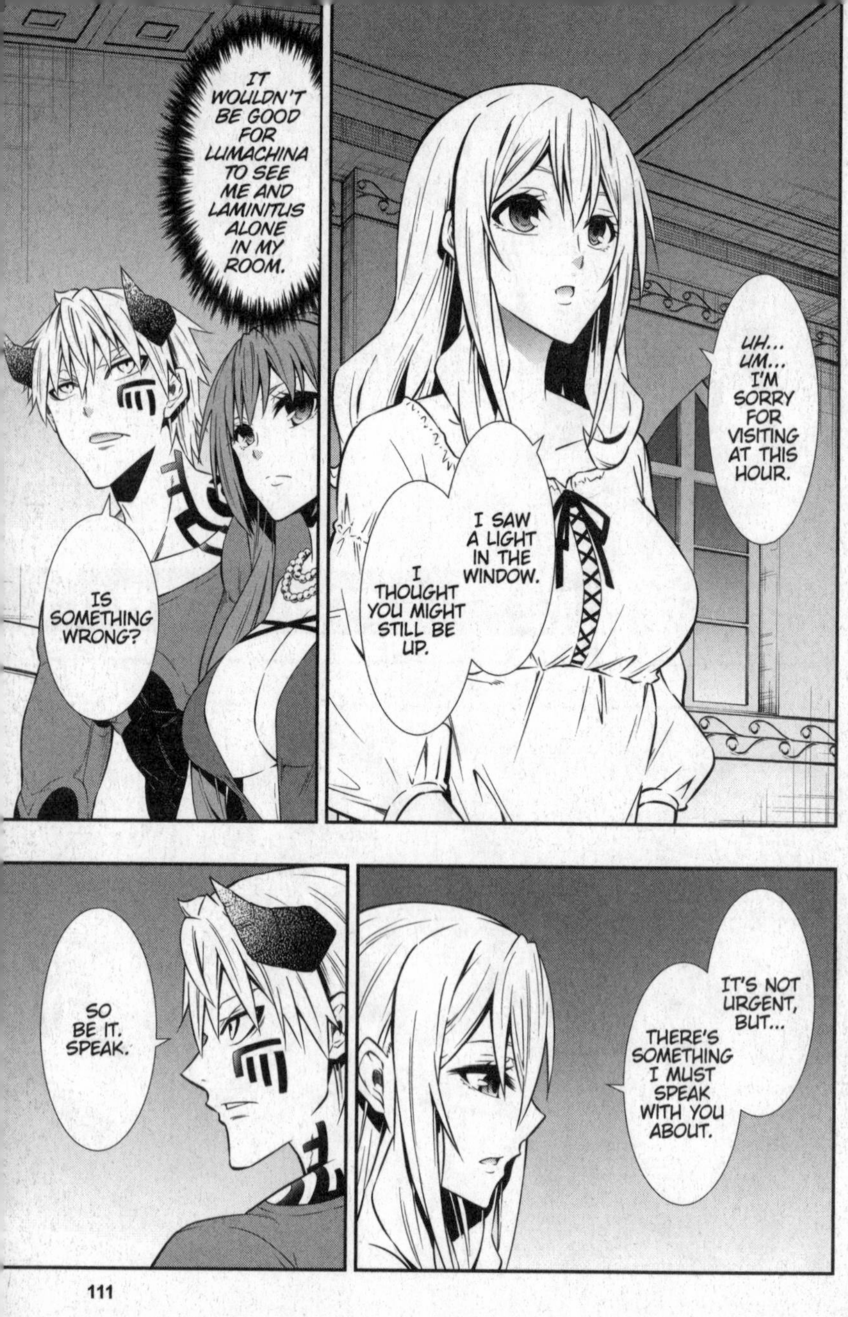
UH... UM... I'M SORRY FOR VISITING AT THIS HOUR.
I SAW A LIGHT IN THE WINDOW.
I THOUGHT YOU MIGHT STILL BE UP.
IT WOULDN'T BE GOOD FOR LUMACHINA TO SEE ME AND LAMINITUS ALONE IN MY ROOM.
IS SOMETHING WRONG?
IT'S NOT URGENT, BUT...
THERE'S SOMETHING I MUST SPEAK WITH YOU ABOUT.
SO BE IT. SPEAK.

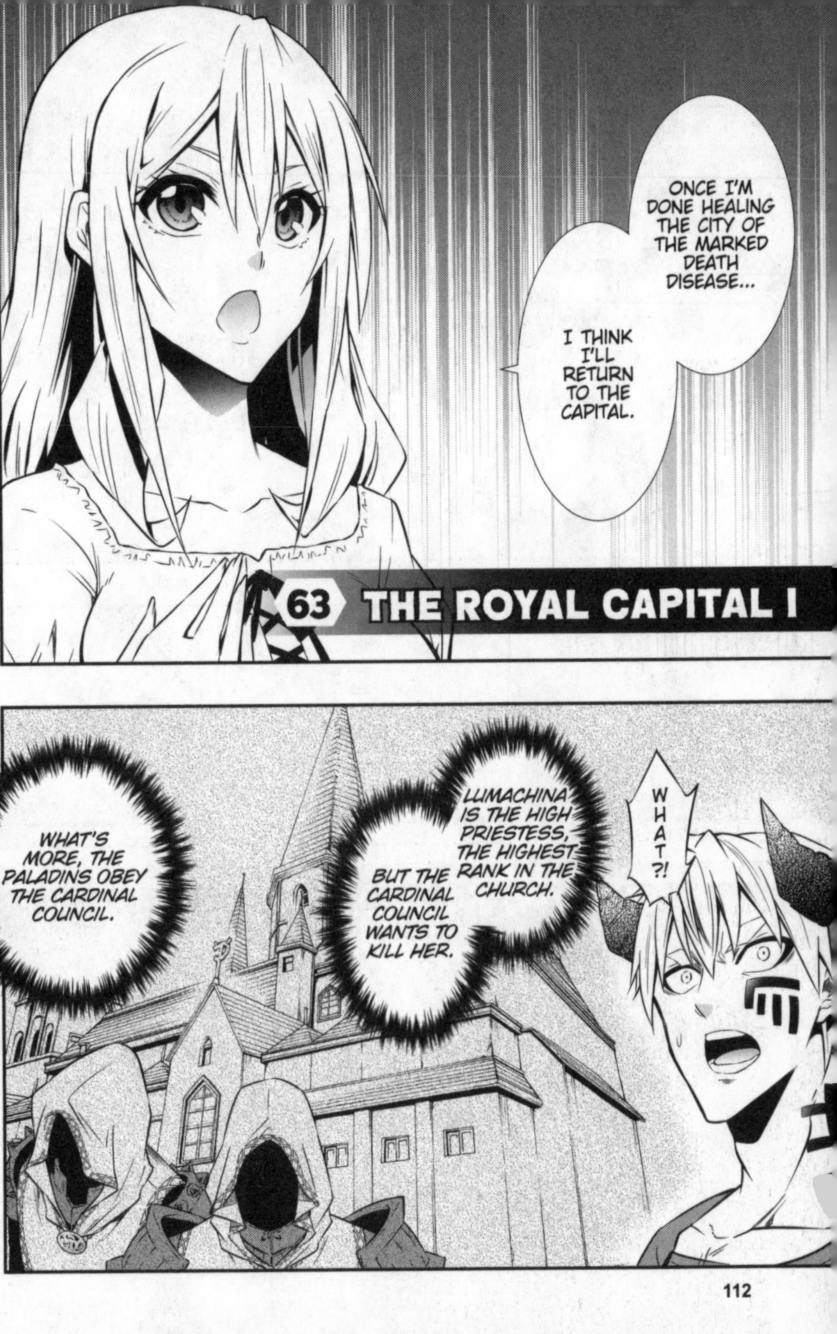
ONCE I'M DONE HEALING THE CITY OF THE MARKED DEATH DISEASE...
I THINK I'LL RETURN TO THE CAPITAL.
63 THE ROYAL CAPITAL I
WHAT?!
LUMACHINA IS THE HIGH PRIESTESS, THE HIGHEST RANK IN THE CHURCH.
BUT THE CARDINAL COUNCIL WANTS TO KILL HER.
WHAT'S MORE, THE PALADINS OBEY THE CARDINAL COUNCIL.

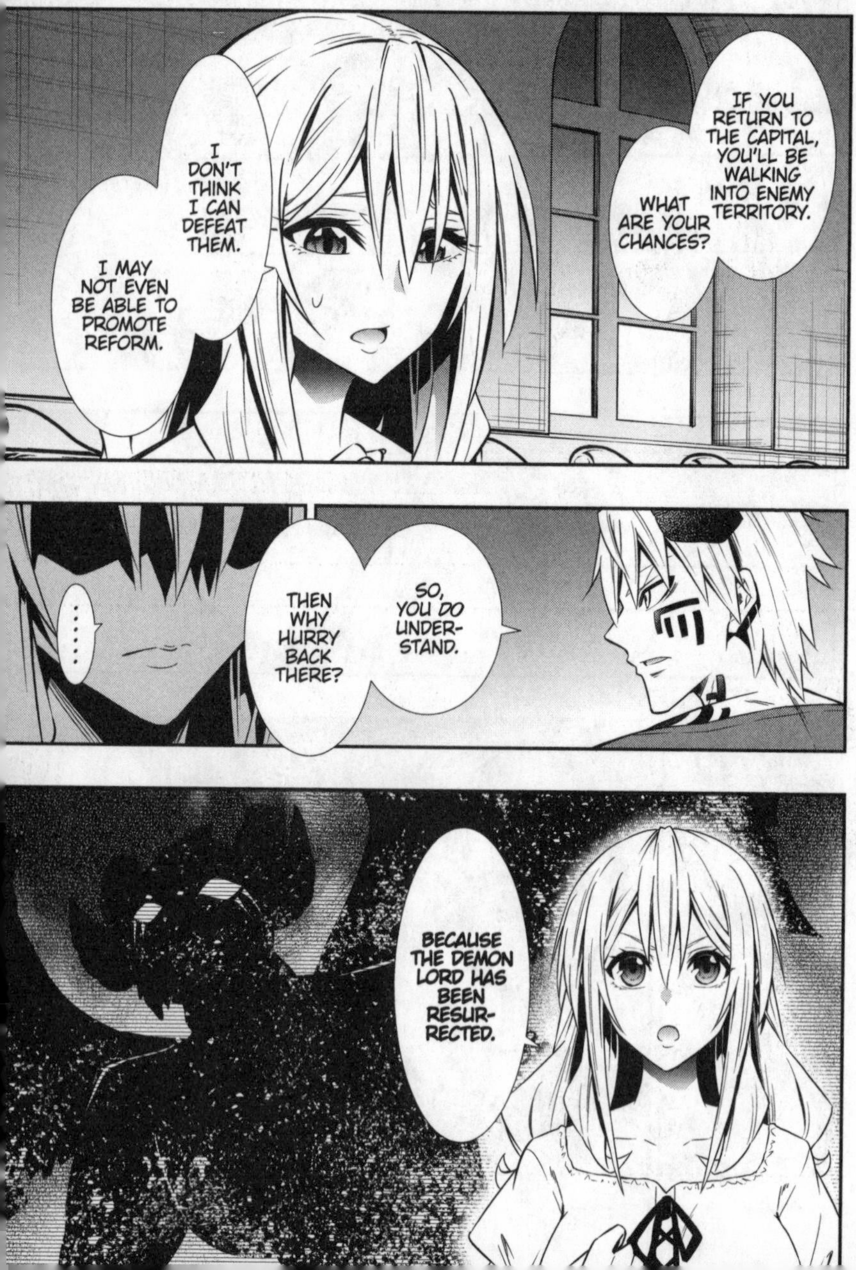
IF YOU RETURN TO THE CAPITAL, YOU'LL BE WALKING INTO ENEMY TERRITORY.
WHAT ARE YOUR CHANCES?
I DON'T THINK I CAN DEFEAT THEM.
I MAY NOT EVEN BE ABLE TO PROMOTE REFORM.
SO, YOU *DO* UNDER-STAND.
THEN WHY HURRY BACK THERE?
......
BECAUSE THE DEMON LORD HAS BEEN RESUR-RECTED.

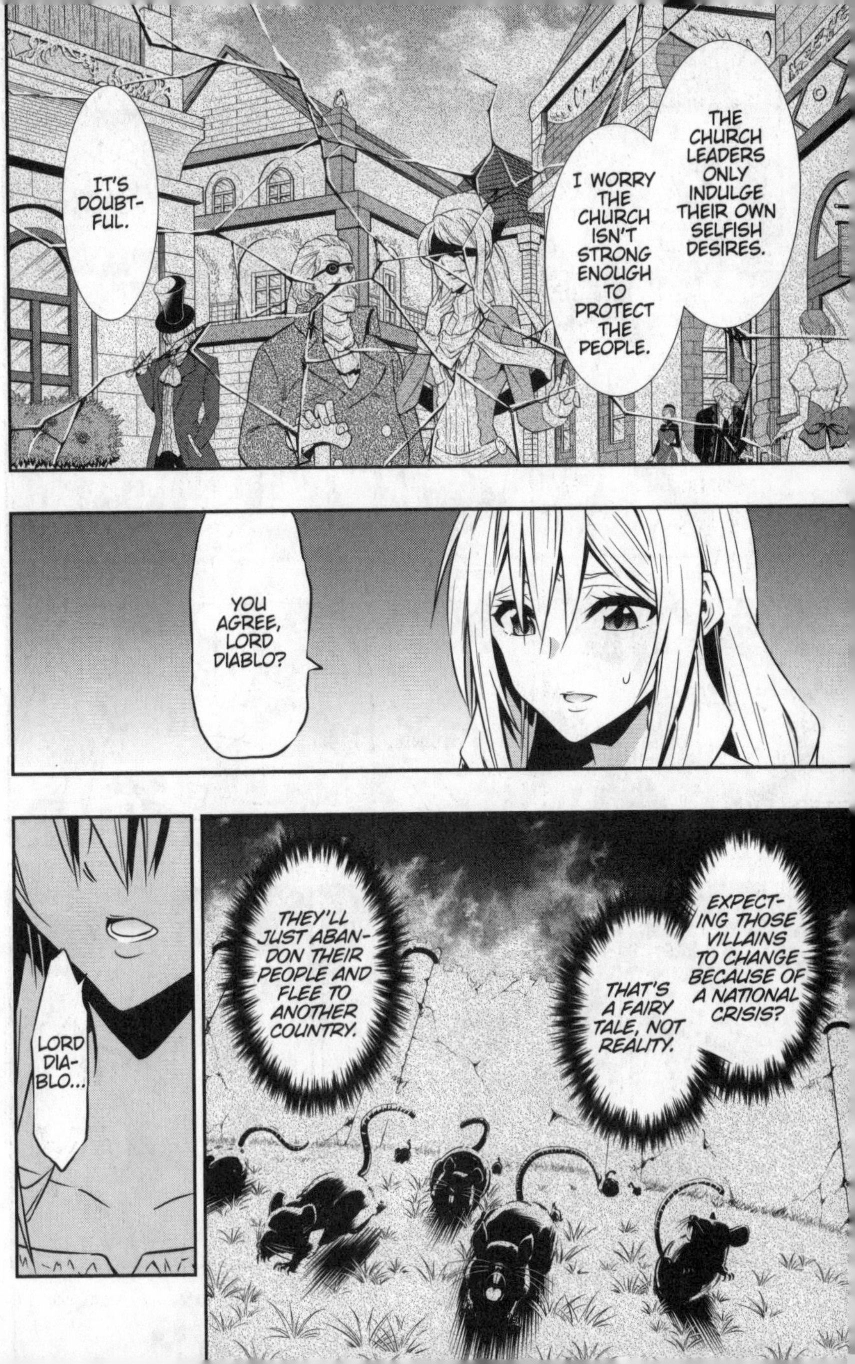
THE CHURCH LEADERS ONLY INDULGE THEIR OWN SELFISH DESIRES.
I WORRY THE CHURCH ISN'T STRONG ENOUGH TO PROTECT THE PEOPLE.
IT'S DOUBT-FUL.
YOU AGREE, LORD DIABLO?
EXPECT-ING THOSE VILLAINS TO CHANGE BECAUSE OF A NATIONAL CRISIS?
THAT'S A FAIRY TALE, NOT REALITY.
THEY'LL JUST ABAN-DON THEIR PEOPLE AND FLEE TO ANOTHER COUNTRY.
LORD DIA-BLO...

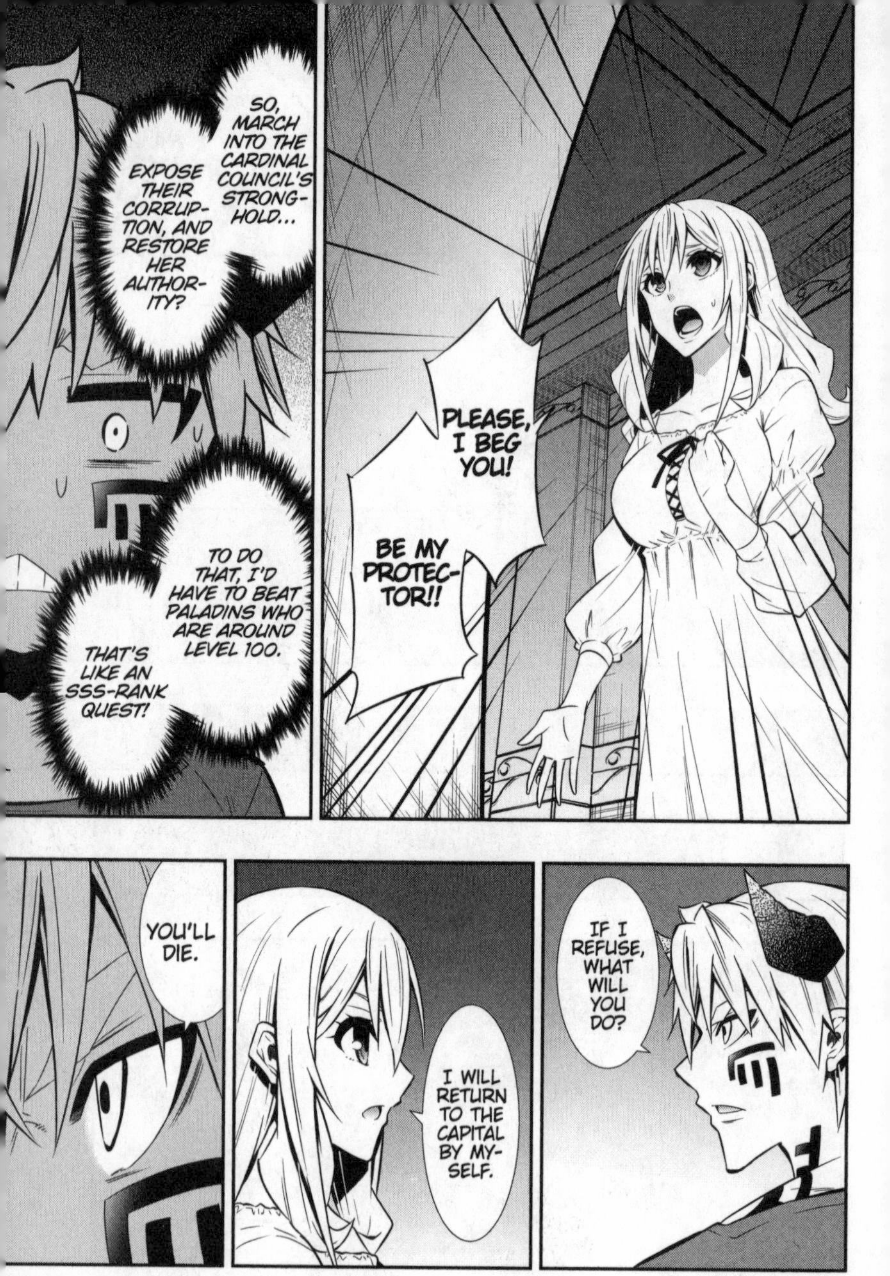
PLEASE, I BEG YOU!
BE MY PROTECTOR!!
SO, MARCH INTO THE CARDINAL COUNCIL'S STRONGHOLD...
EXPOSE THEIR CORRUPTION, AND RESTORE HER AUTHORITY?
TO DO THAT, I'D HAVE TO BEAT PALADINS WHO ARE AROUND LEVEL 100.
THAT'S LIKE AN SSS-RANK QUEST!
IF I REFUSE, WHAT WILL YOU DO?
I WILL RETURN TO THE CAPITAL BY MYSELF.
YOU'LL DIE.

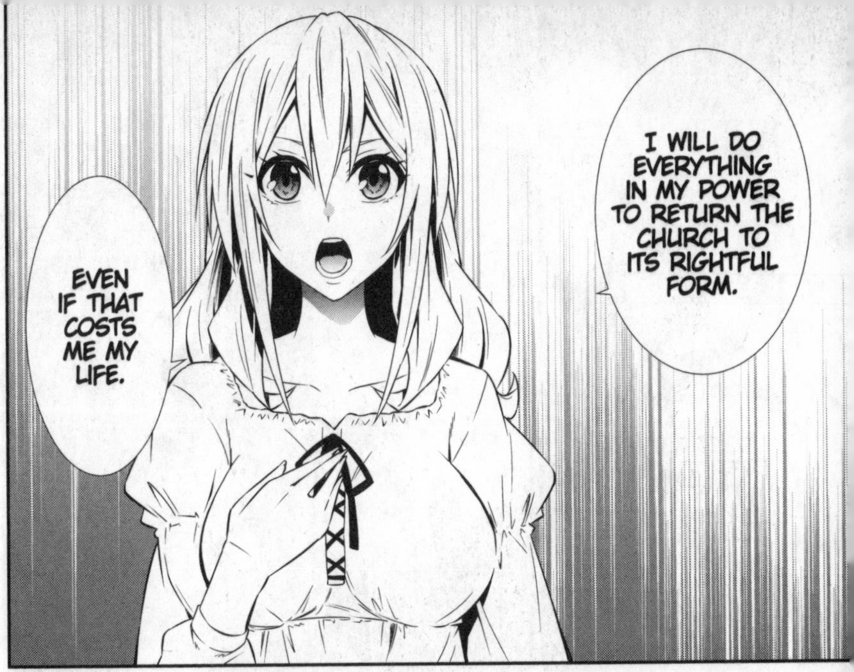
I WILL DO EVERYTHING IN MY POWER TO RETURN THE CHURCH TO ITS RIGHTFUL FORM.
EVEN IF THAT COSTS ME MY LIFE.
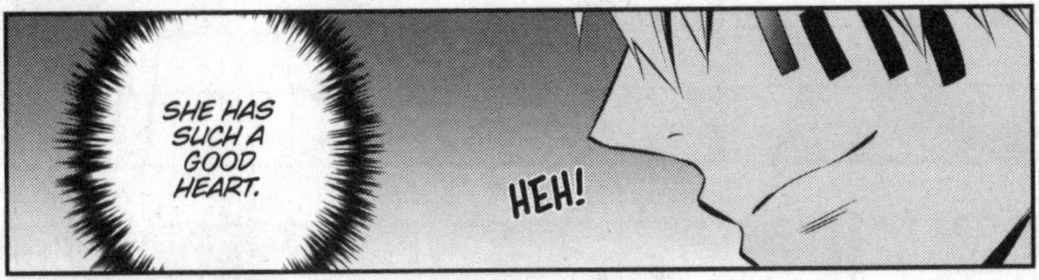
HEH!
SHE HAS SUCH A GOOD HEART.
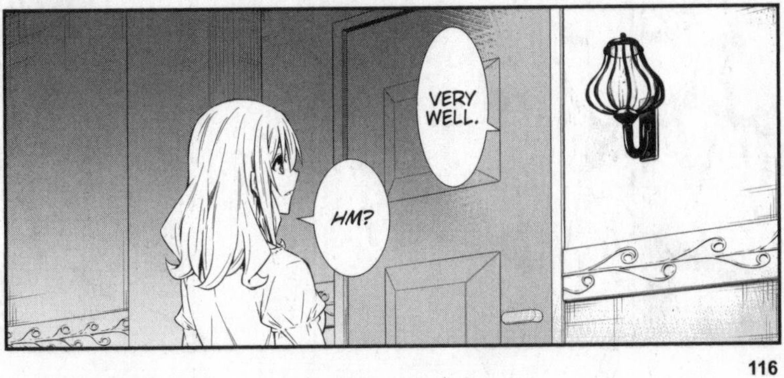
VERY WELL.
HM?

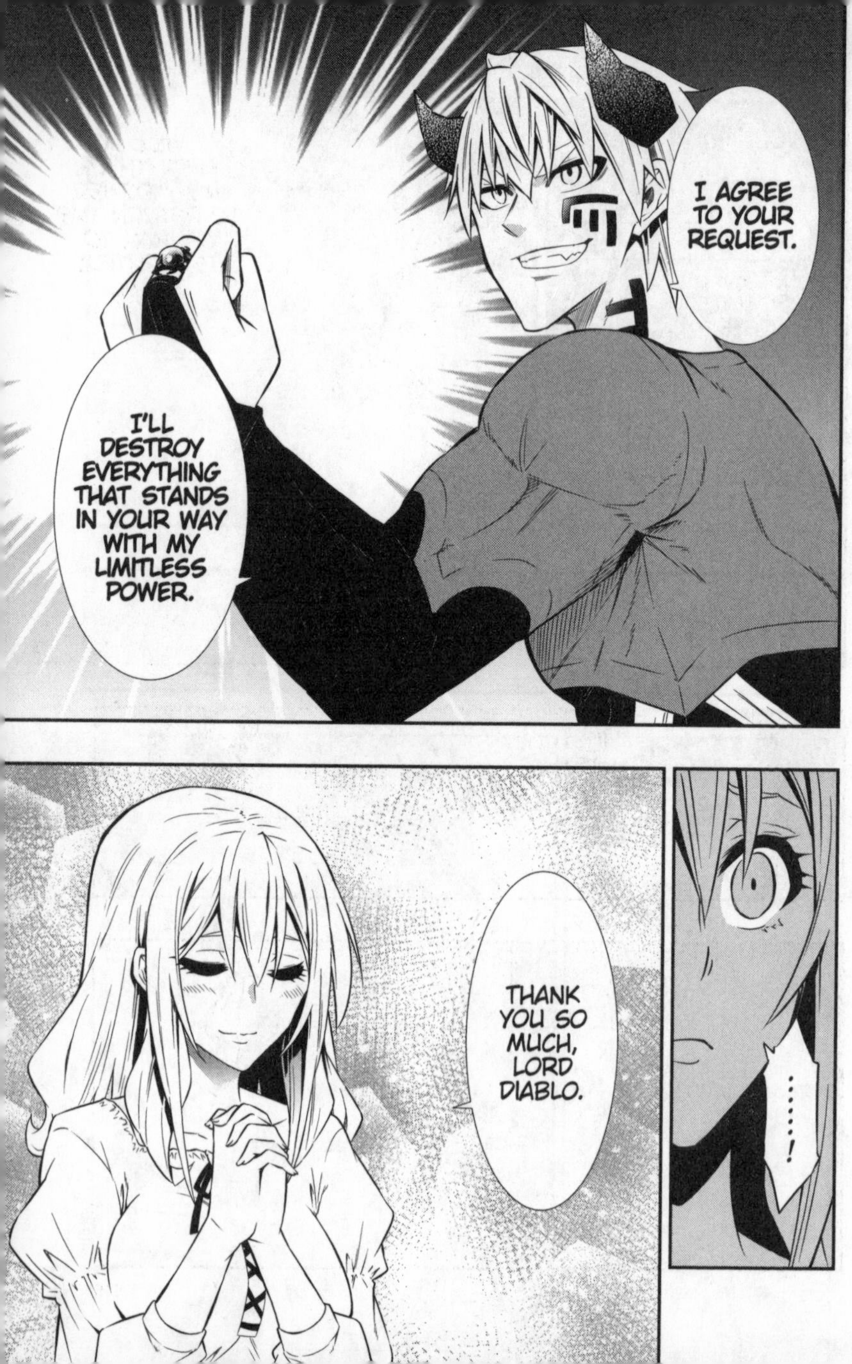
I AGREE TO YOUR REQUEST.
I'LL DESTROY EVERYTHING THAT STANDS IN YOUR WAY WITH MY LIMITLESS POWER.
......!
THANK YOU SO MUCH, LORD DIABLO.

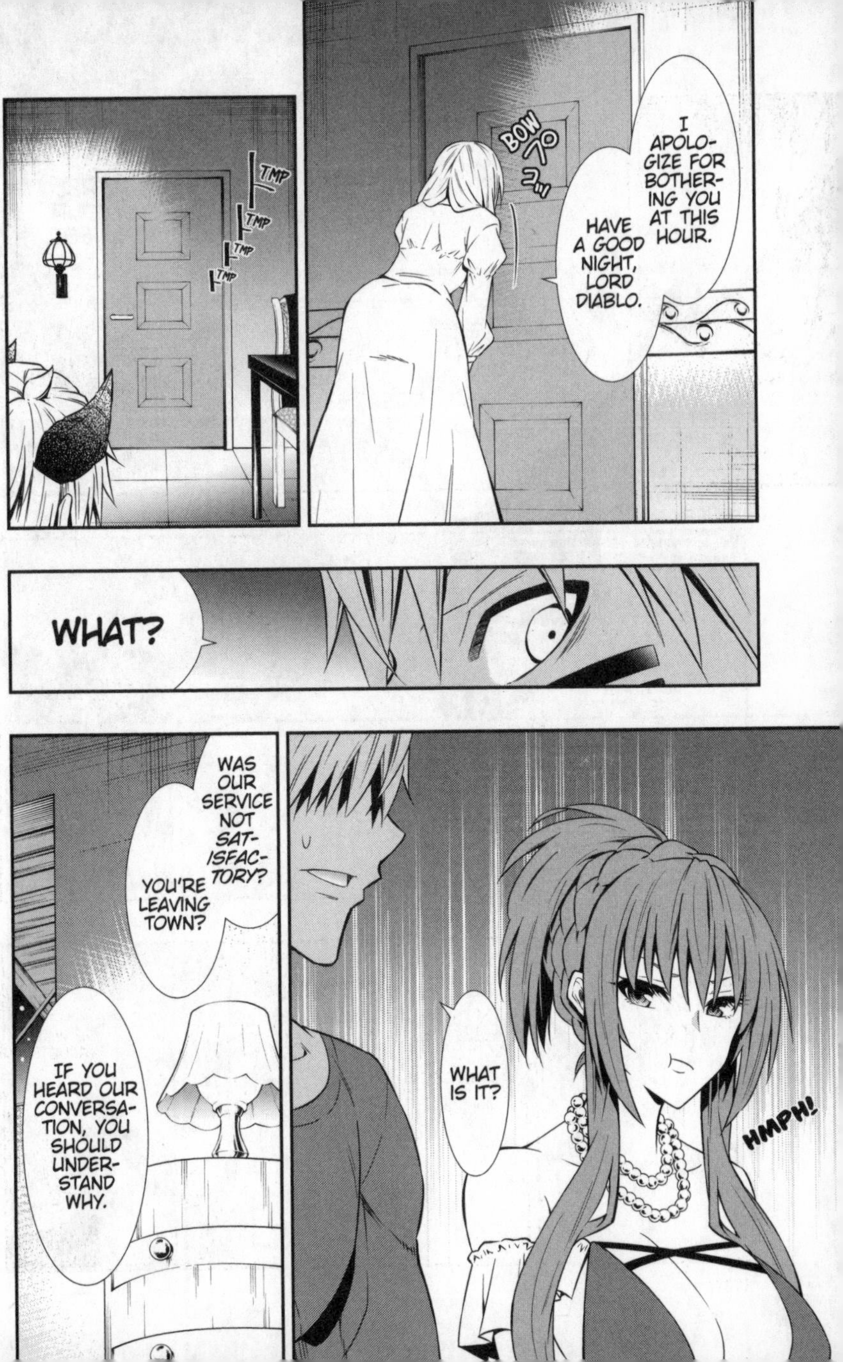
BOW
I APOLOGIZE FOR BOTHERING YOU AT THIS HOUR.
HAVE A GOOD NIGHT, LORD DIABLO.
TMP
TMP
TMP
TMP
WHAT?
HMPH!
WHAT IS IT?
WAS OUR SERVICE NOT SATISFACTORY?
YOU'RE LEAVING TOWN?
IF YOU HEARD OUR CONVERSATION, YOU SHOULD UNDERSTAND WHY.

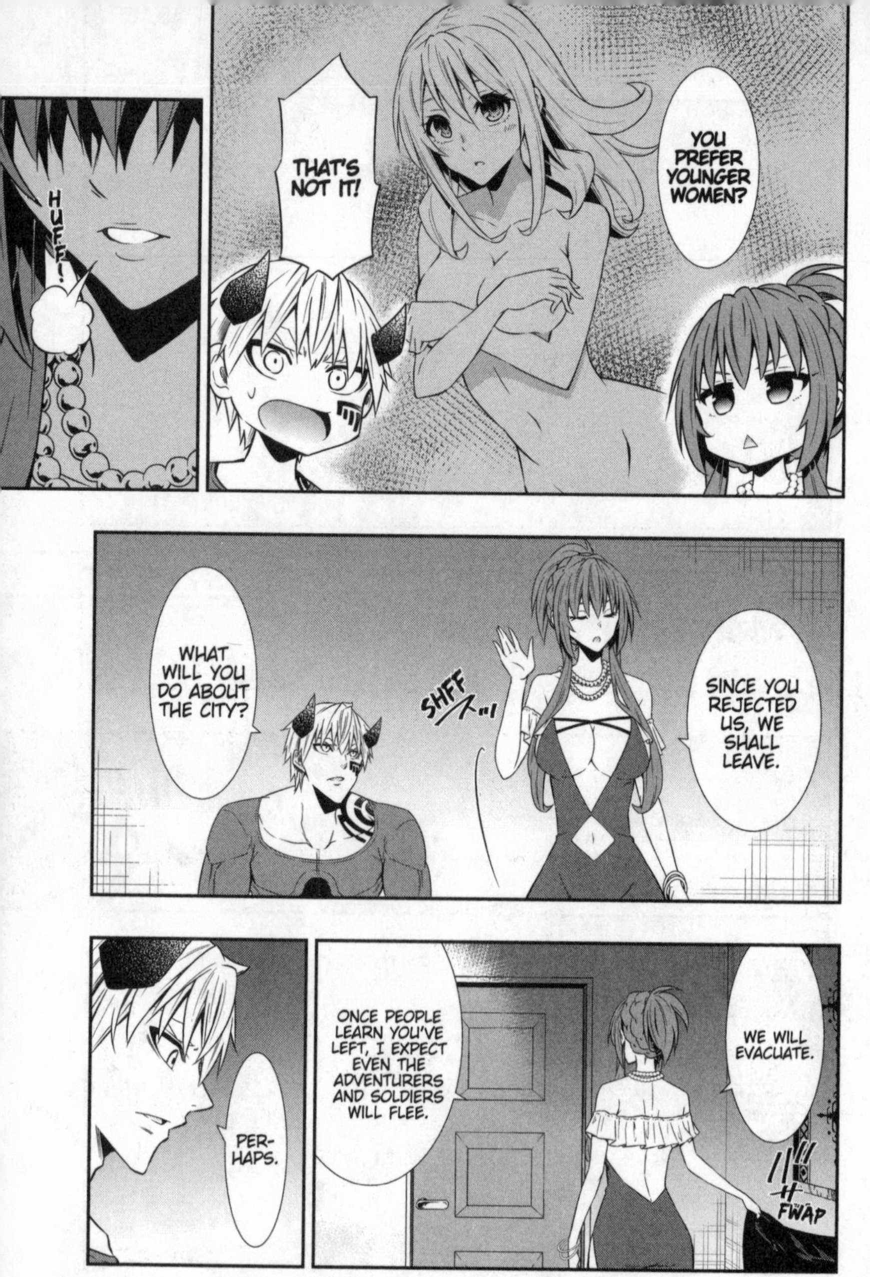
YOU PREFER YOUNGER WOMEN?
THAT'S NOT IT!
HUFF!
SINCE YOU REJECTED US, WE SHALL LEAVE.
SHFF
WHAT WILL YOU DO ABOUT THE CITY?
WE WILL EVACUATE.
ONCE PEOPLE LEARN YOU'VE LEFT, I EXPECT EVEN THE ADVENTURERS AND SOLDIERS WILL FLEE.
FWAP
PER-HAPS.

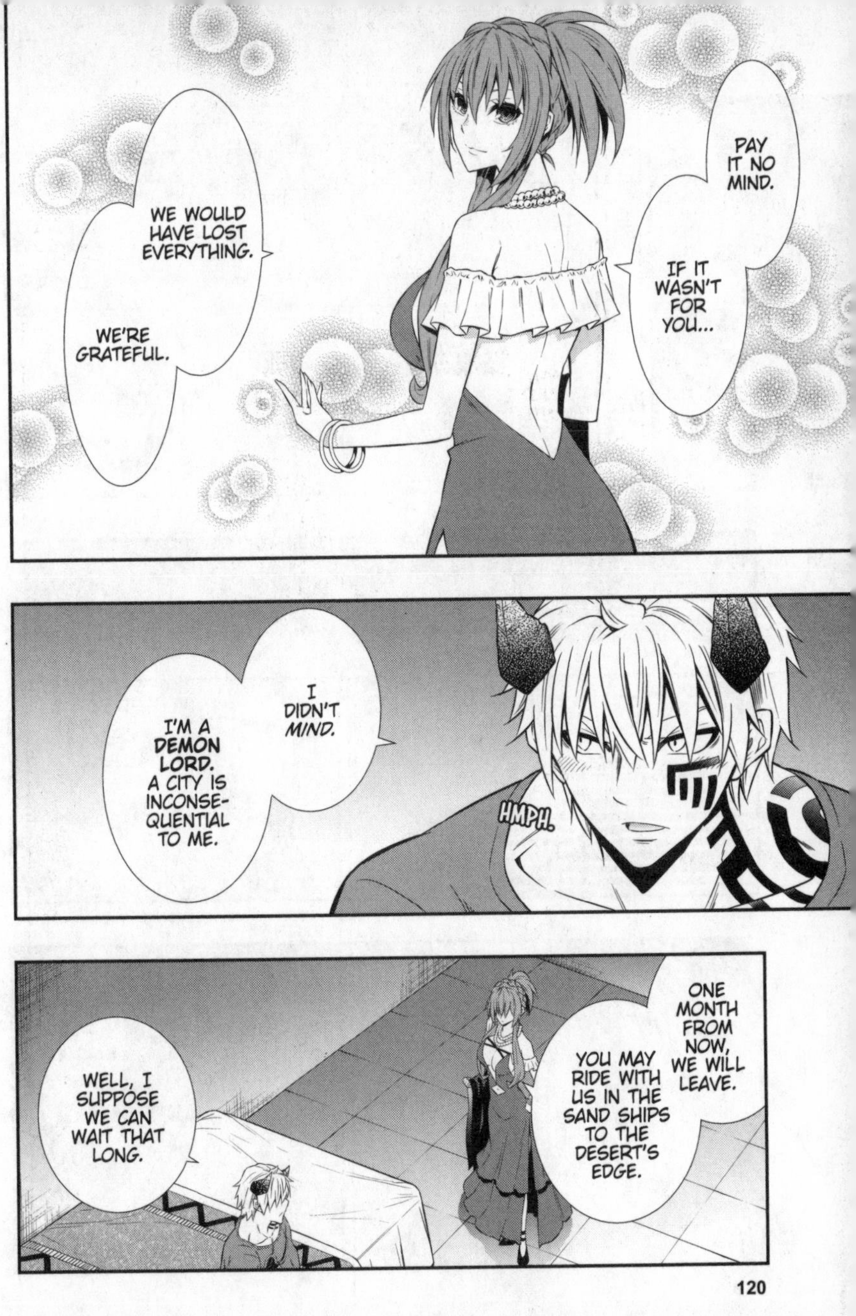
PAY IT NO MIND.
IF IT WASN'T FOR YOU...
WE WOULD HAVE LOST EVERYTHING.
WE'RE GRATEFUL.
I DIDN'T MIND.
I'M A DEMON LORD. A CITY IS INCONSEQUENTIAL TO ME.
HMPH.
ONE MONTH FROM NOW, WE WILL LEAVE.
YOU MAY RIDE WITH US IN THE SAND SHIPS TO THE DESERT'S EDGE.
WELL, I SUPPOSE WE CAN WAIT THAT LONG.

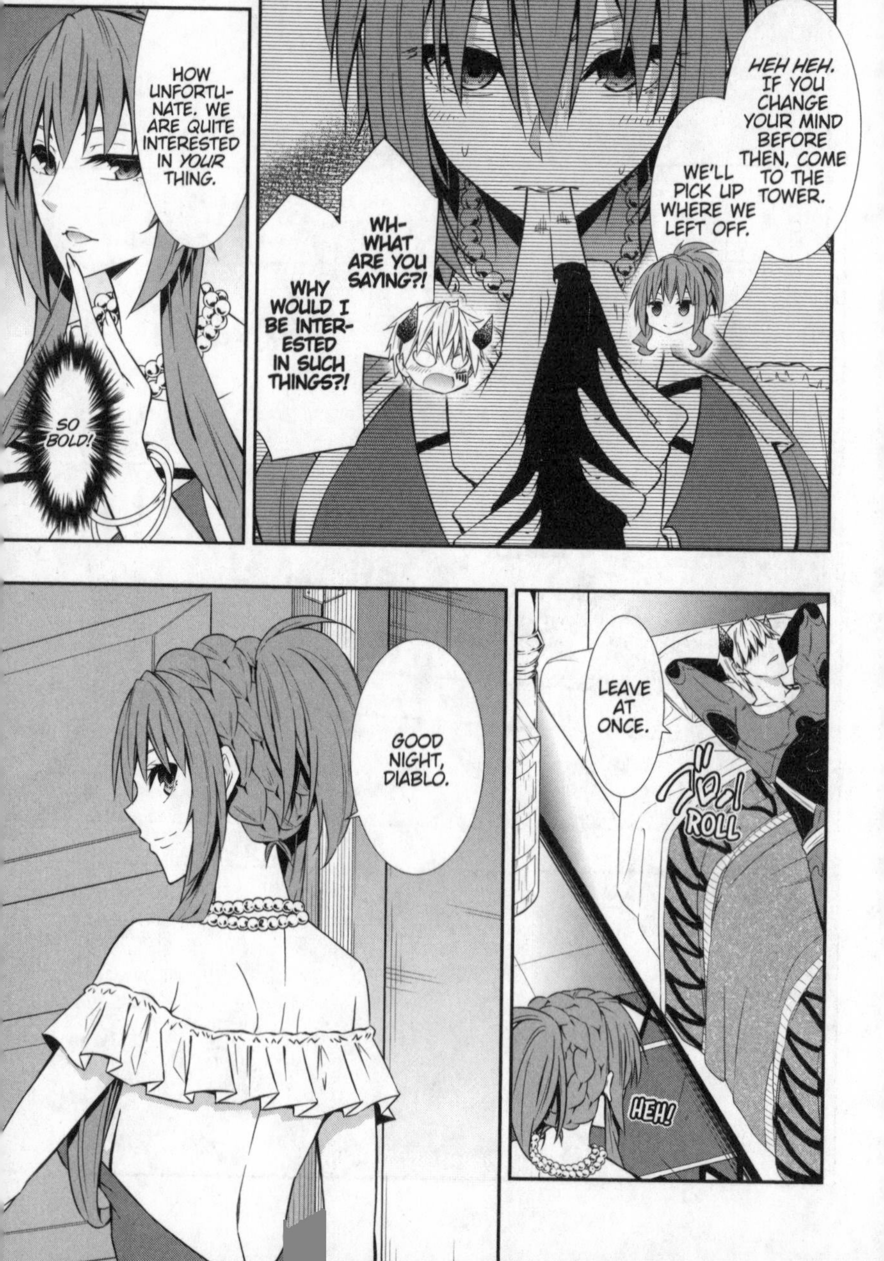
HEH HEH. IF YOU CHANGE YOUR MIND BEFORE THEN, COME TO THE TOWER.
WE'LL PICK UP WHERE WE LEFT OFF.
WH-WHAT ARE YOU SAYING?!
WHY WOULD I BE INTERESTED IN SUCH THINGS?!
HOW UNFORTUNATE. WE ARE QUITE INTERESTED IN *YOUR* THING.
SO BOLD!
LEAVE AT ONCE.
ROLL
HEH!
GOOD NIGHT, DIABLO.

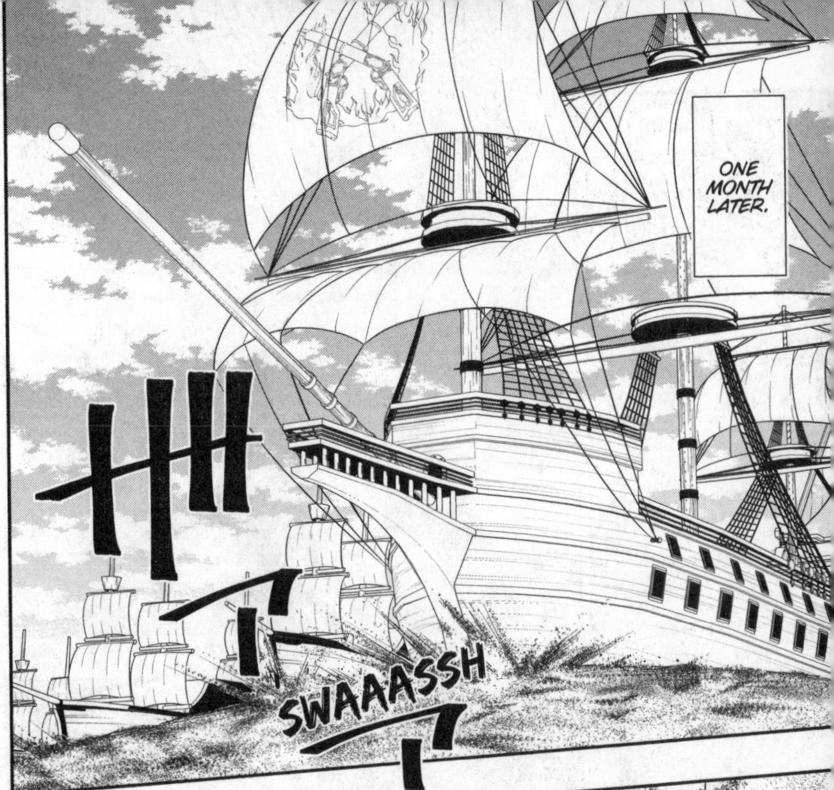
ONE MONTH LATER.
SWAAASSH
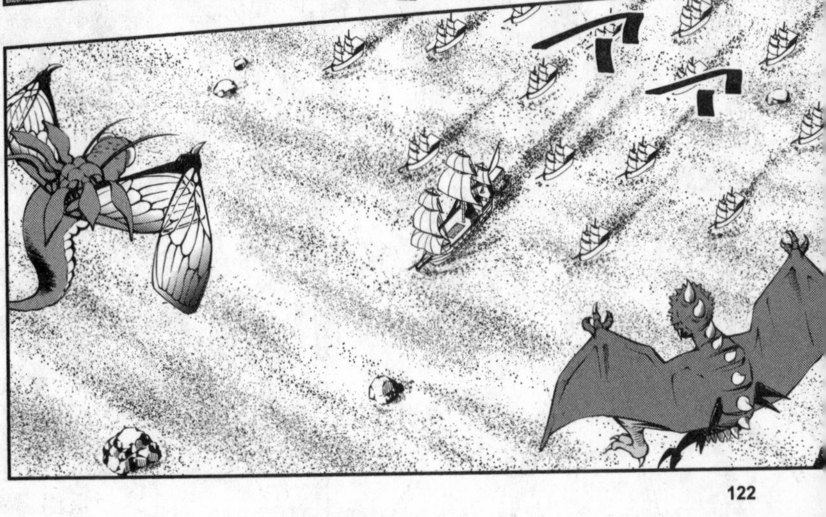

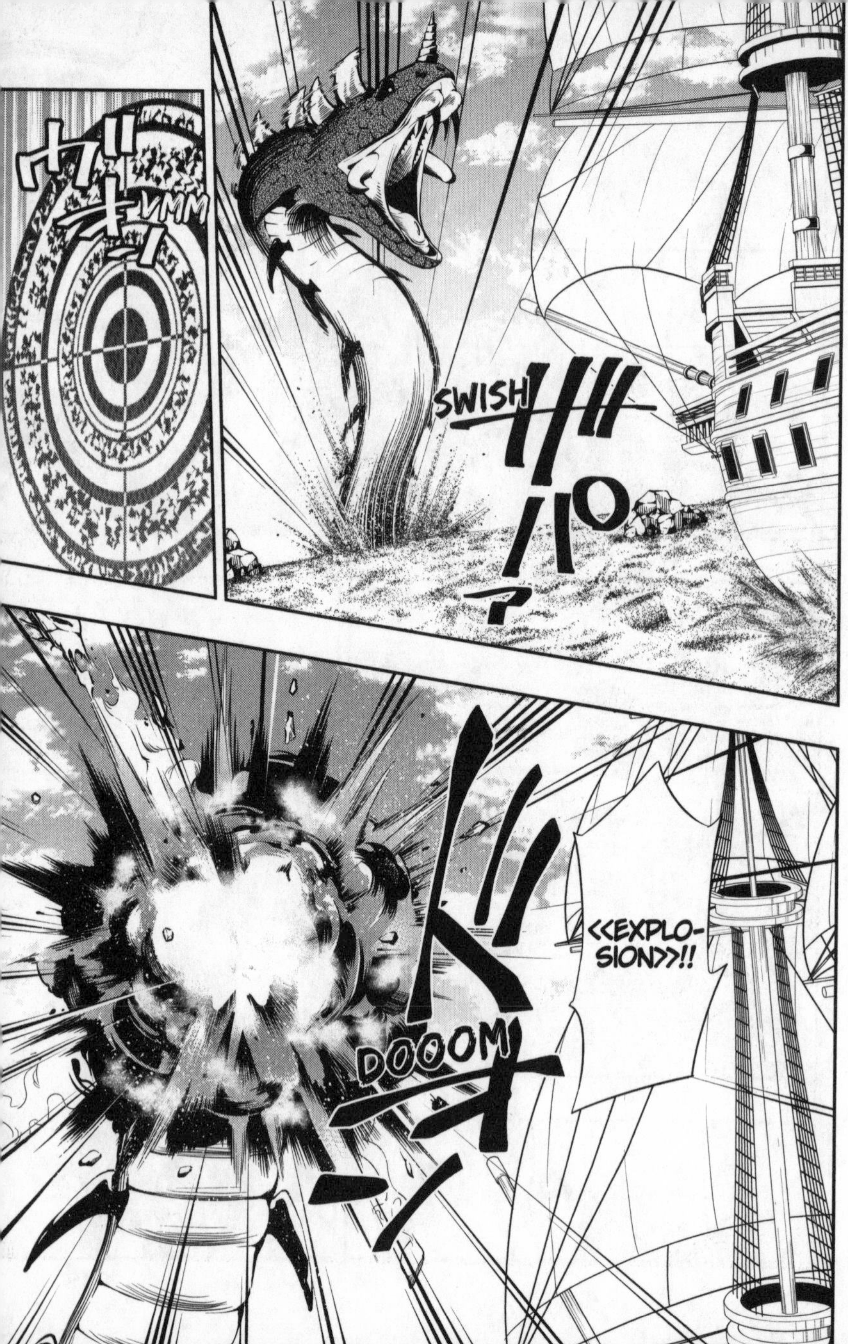
SWISH
VMM
<<EXPLOSION>>!!
DOOOM

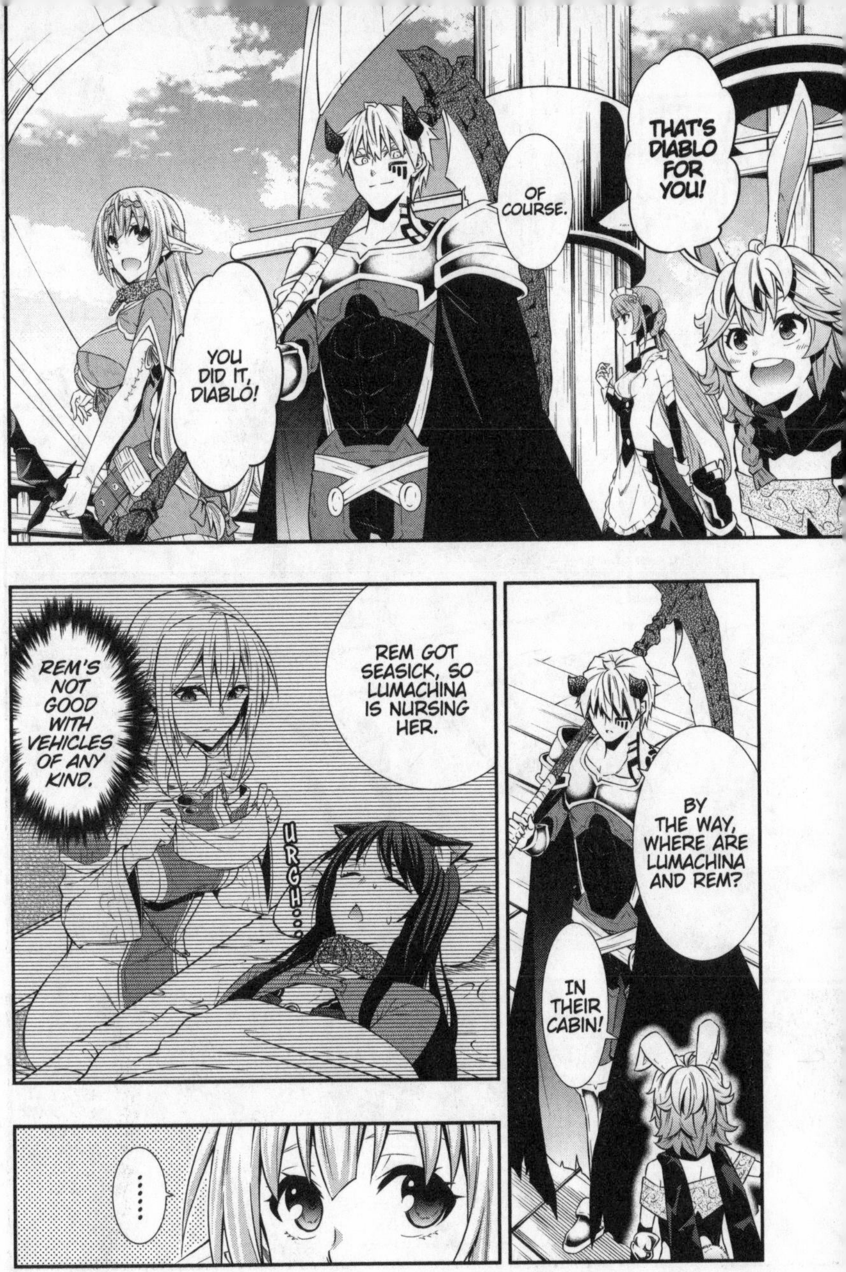
THAT'S DIABLO FOR YOU!
OF COURSE.
YOU DID IT, DIABLO!
BY THE WAY, WHERE ARE LUMACHINA AND REM?
IN THEIR CABIN!
REM GOT SEASICK, SO LUMACHINA IS NURSING HER.
URGH...
REM'S NOT GOOD WITH VEHICLES OF ANY KIND.
......

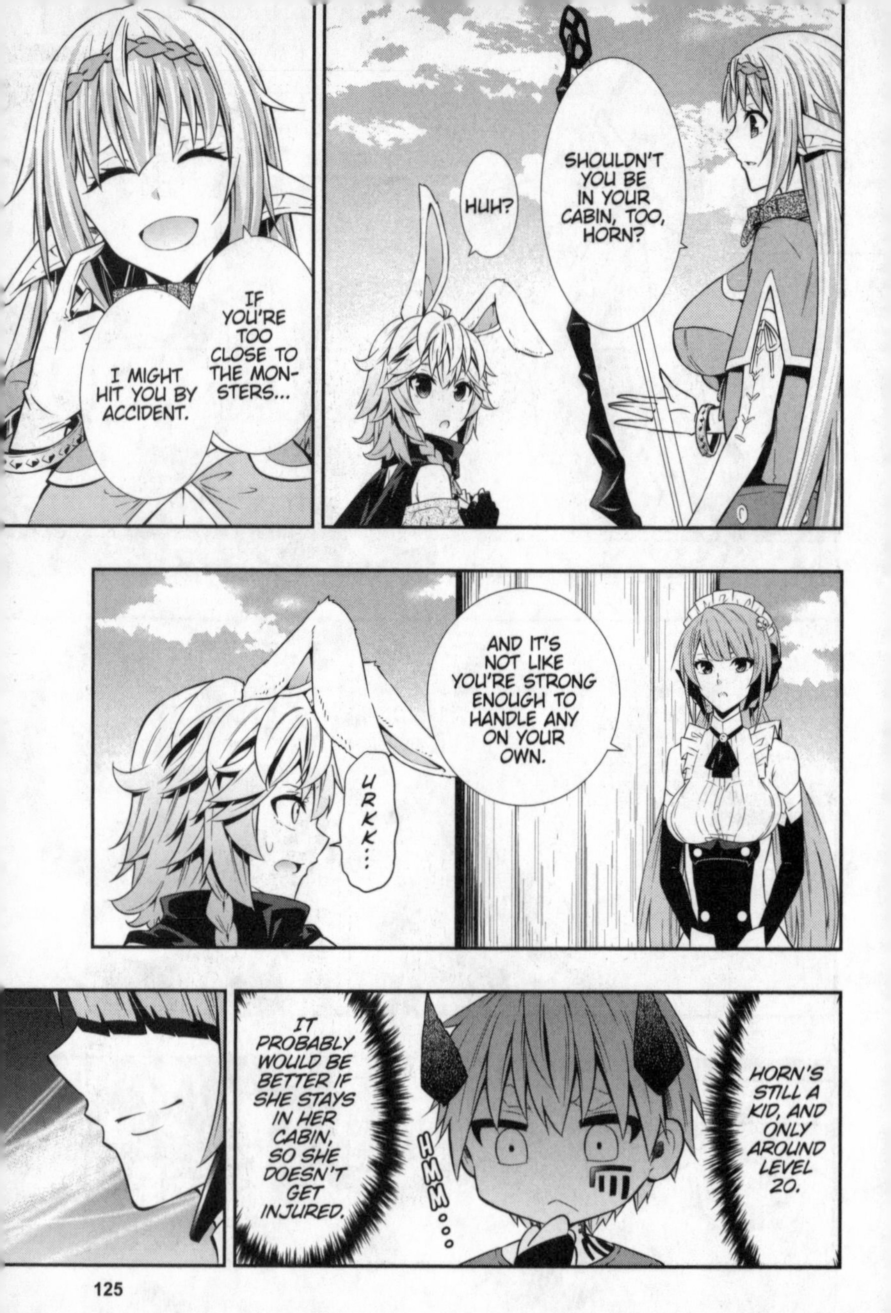
SHOULDN'T YOU BE IN YOUR CABIN, TOO, HORN?
HUH?
IF YOU'RE TOO CLOSE TO THE MON-STERS...
I MIGHT HIT YOU BY ACCIDENT.
AND IT'S NOT LIKE YOU'RE STRONG ENOUGH TO HANDLE ANY ON YOUR OWN.
URKK...
HORN'S STILL A KID, AND ONLY AROUND LEVEL 20.
HMM...
IT PROBABLY WOULD BE BETTER IF SHE STAYS IN HER CABIN, SO SHE DOESN'T GET INJURED.

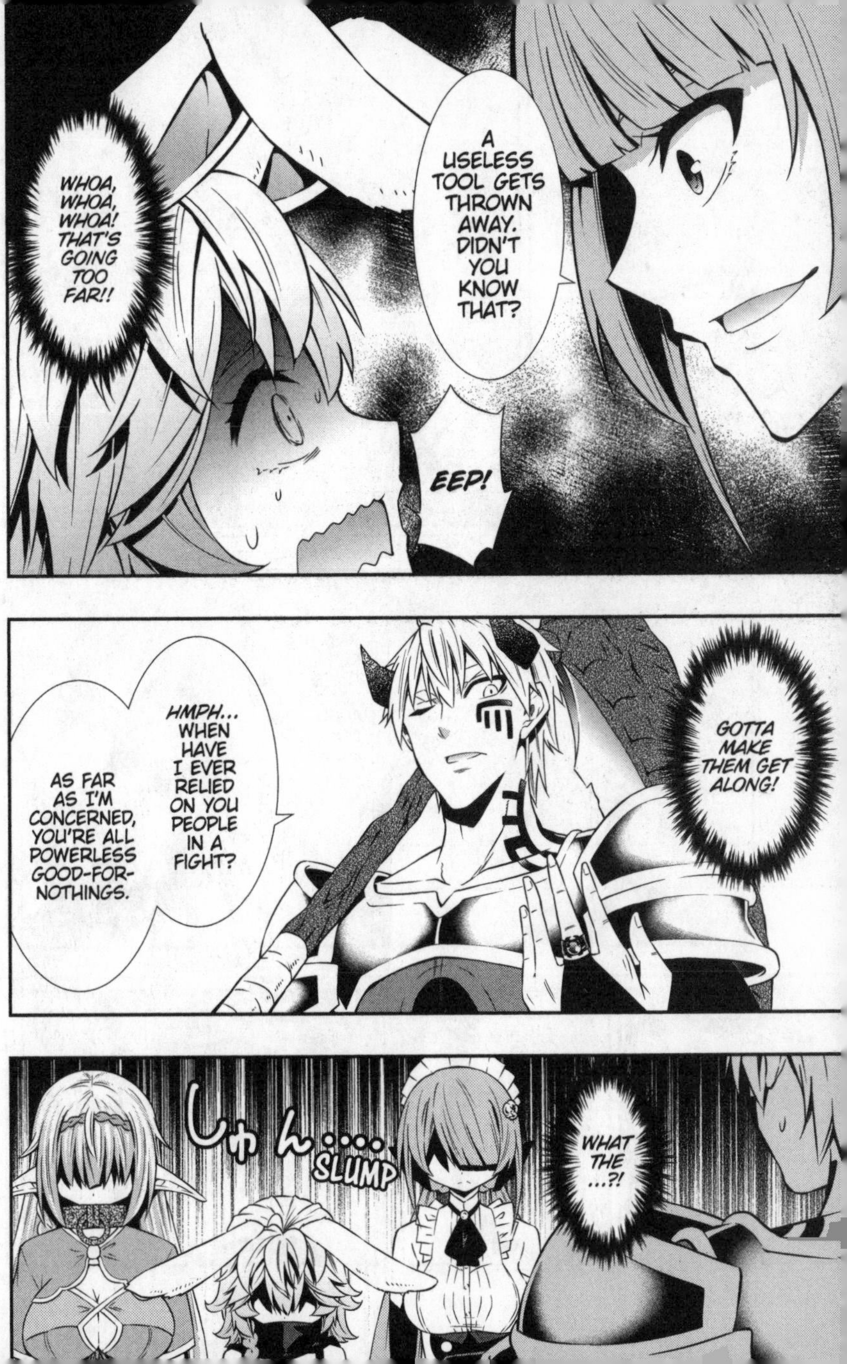
A USELESS TOOL GETS THROWN AWAY. DIDN'T YOU KNOW THAT?
WHOA, WHOA, WHOA! THAT'S GOING TOO FAR!!
EEP!
GOTTA MAKE THEM GET ALONG!
HMPH... WHEN HAVE I EVER RELIED ON YOU PEOPLE IN A FIGHT?
AS FAR AS I'M CONCERNED, YOU'RE ALL POWERLESS GOOD-FOR-NOTHINGS.
WHAT THE ...?!
しゅん....
SLUMP

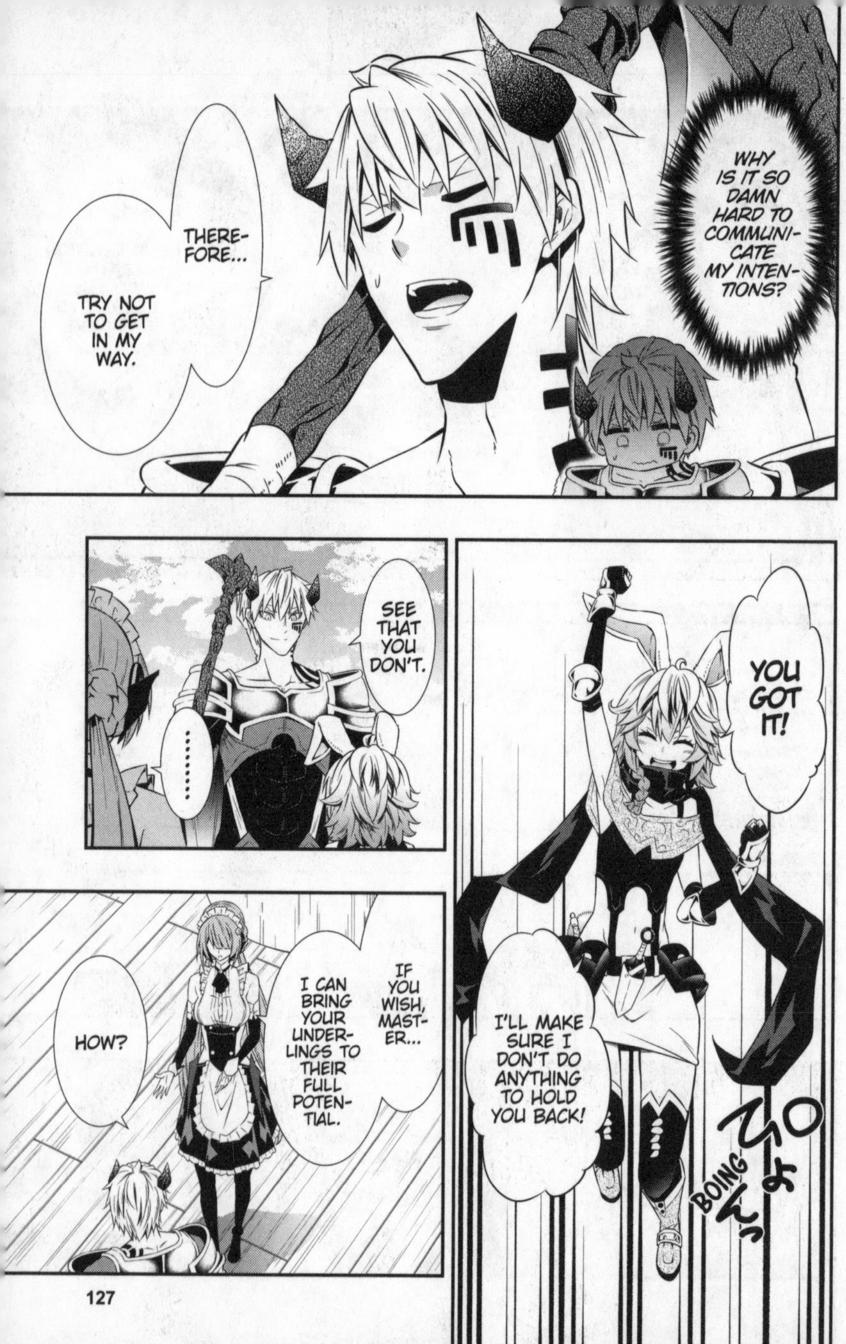
WHY IS IT SO DAMN HARD TO COMMUNICATE MY INTENTIONS?
THEREFORE...
TRY NOT TO GET IN MY WAY.
YOU GOT IT!
I'LL MAKE SURE I DON'T DO ANYTHING TO HOLD YOU BACK!
BOING
SEE THAT YOU DON'T.
......
IF YOU WISH, MASTER...
I CAN BRING YOUR UNDERLINGS TO THEIR FULL POTENTIAL.
HOW?

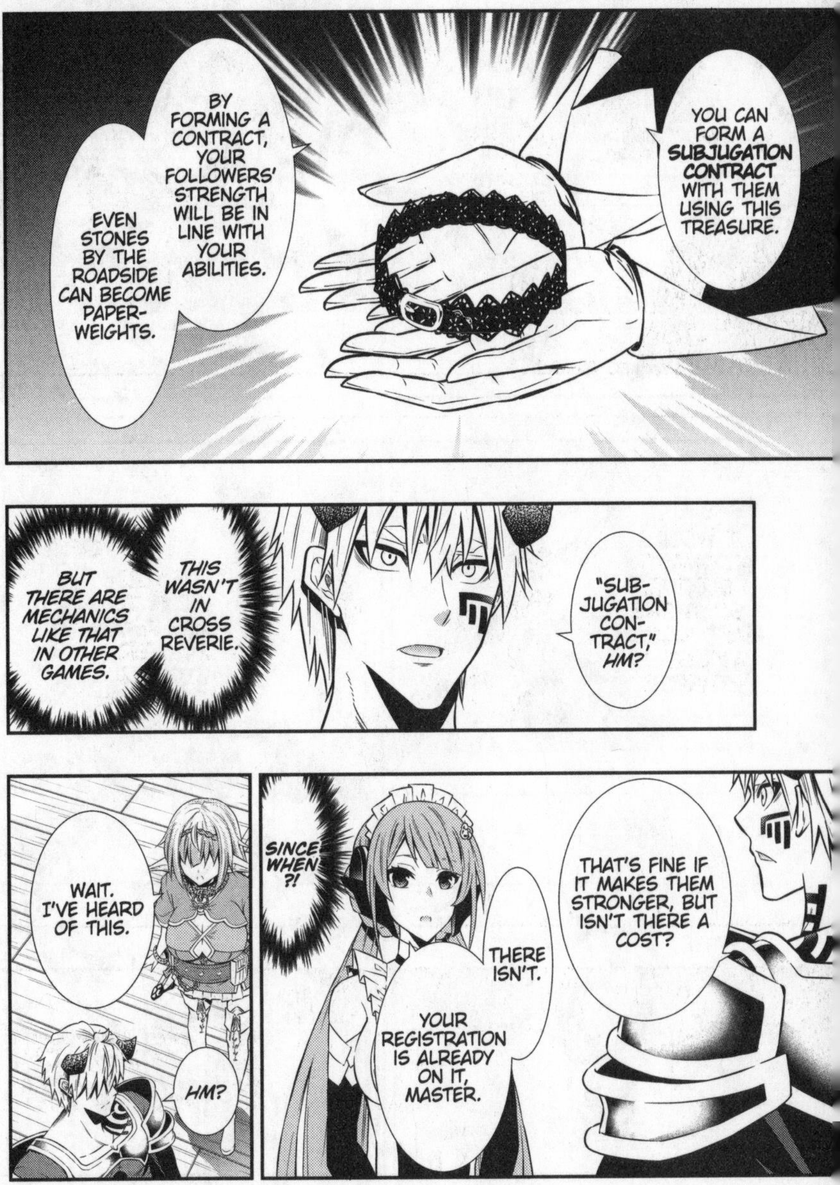
YOU CAN FORM A SUBJUGATION CONTRACT WITH THEM USING THIS TREASURE.
BY FORMING A CONTRACT, YOUR FOLLOWERS' STRENGTH WILL BE IN LINE WITH YOUR ABILITIES.
EVEN STONES BY THE ROADSIDE CAN BECOME PAPER-WEIGHTS.
"SUB-JUGATION CON-TRACT," HM?
THIS WASN'T IN CROSS REVERIE.
BUT THERE ARE MECHANICS LIKE THAT IN OTHER GAMES.
THAT'S FINE IF IT MAKES THEM STRONGER, BUT ISN'T THERE A COST?
THERE ISN'T.
YOUR REGISTRATION IS ALREADY ON IT, MASTER.
SINCE WHEN?!
WAIT. I'VE HEARD OF THIS.
HM?

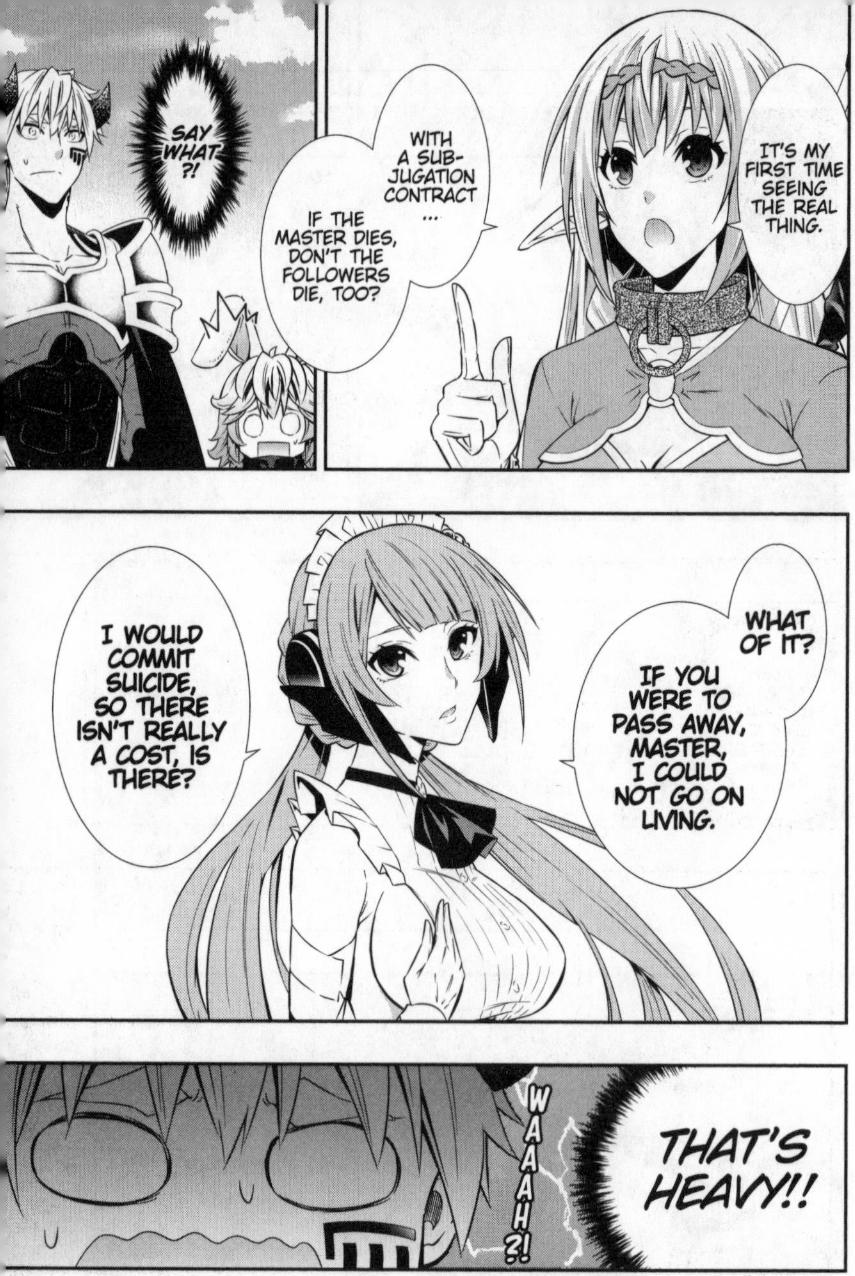
IT'S MY FIRST TIME SEEING THE REAL THING.
WITH A SUB-JUGATION CONTRACT ...
IF THE MASTER DIES, DON'T THE FOLLOWERS DIE, TOO?
SAY WHAT ?!
WHAT OF IT?
IF YOU WERE TO PASS AWAY, MASTER, I COULD NOT GO ON LIVING.
I WOULD COMMIT SUICIDE, SO THERE ISN'T REALLY A COST, IS THERE?
THAT'S HEAVY!!
WAAAAH?!

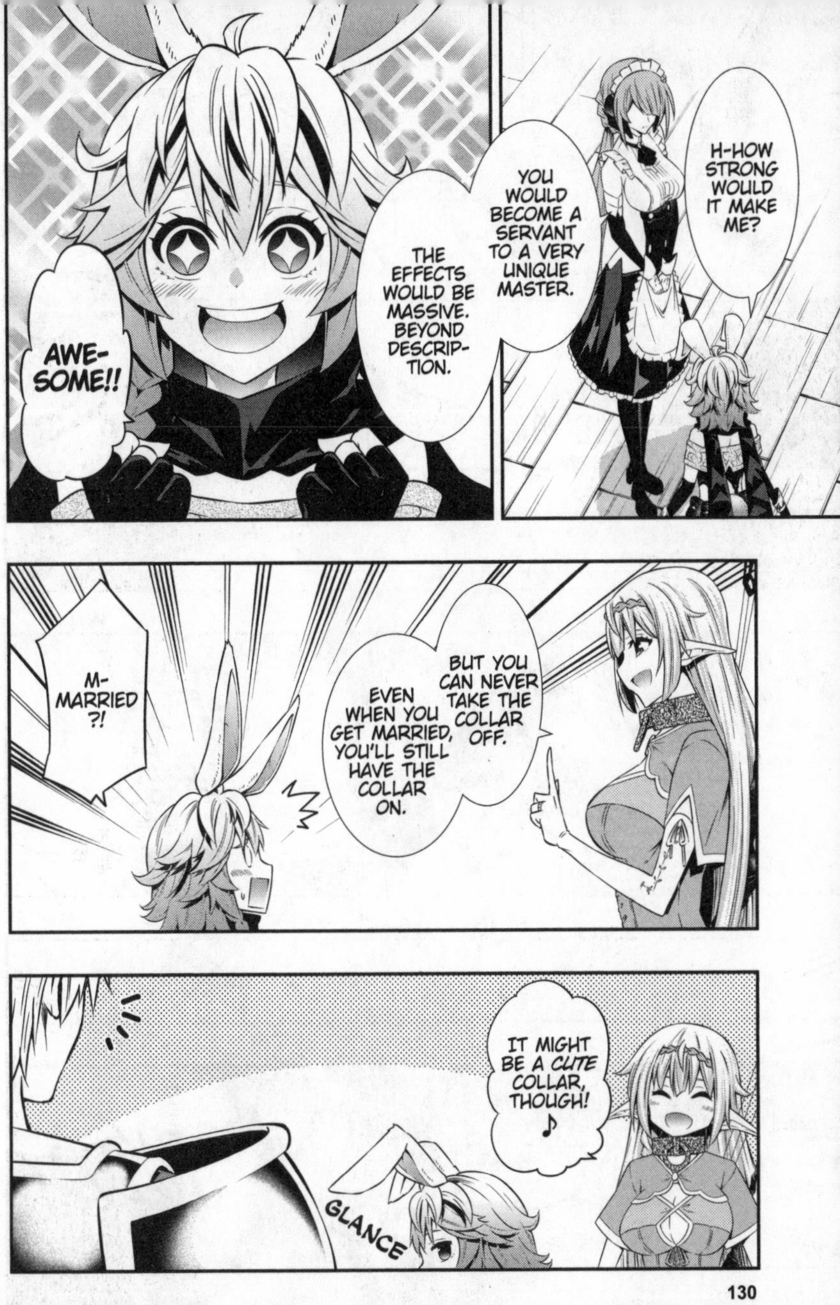
H-HOW STRONG WOULD IT MAKE ME?
YOU WOULD BECOME A SERVANT TO A VERY UNIQUE MASTER.
THE EFFECTS WOULD BE MASSIVE. BEYOND DESCRIP-TION.
AWE-SOME!!
BUT YOU CAN NEVER TAKE THE COLLAR OFF.
EVEN WHEN YOU GET MARRIED, YOU'LL STILL HAVE THE COLLAR ON.
M-MARRIED?!
IT MIGHT BE A *CUTE* COLLAR, THOUGH! ♪
GLANCE

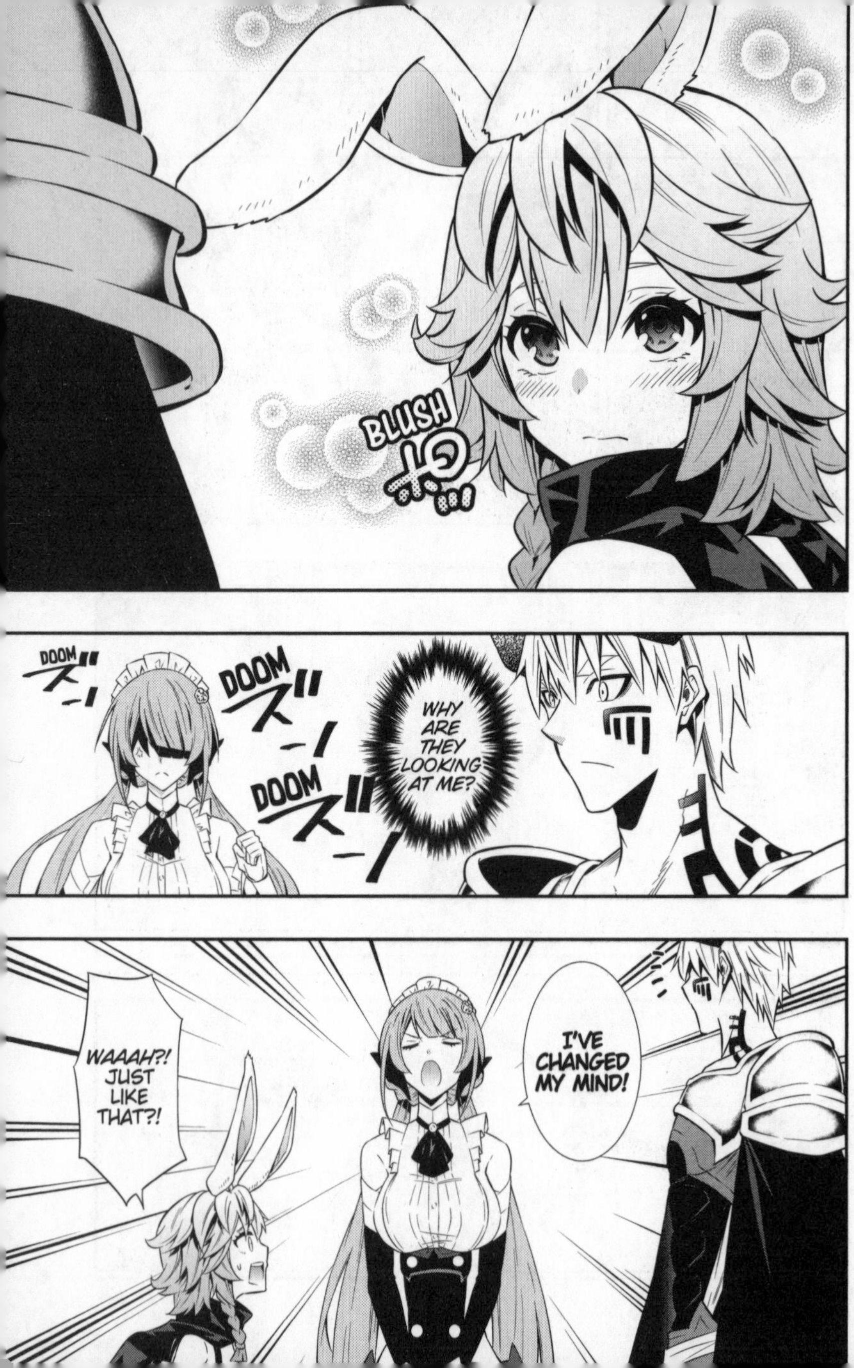
BLUSH
WHY ARE THEY LOOKING AT ME?
DOOM
DOOM
DOOM
I'VE CHANGED MY MIND!
WAAAH?! JUST LIKE THAT?!

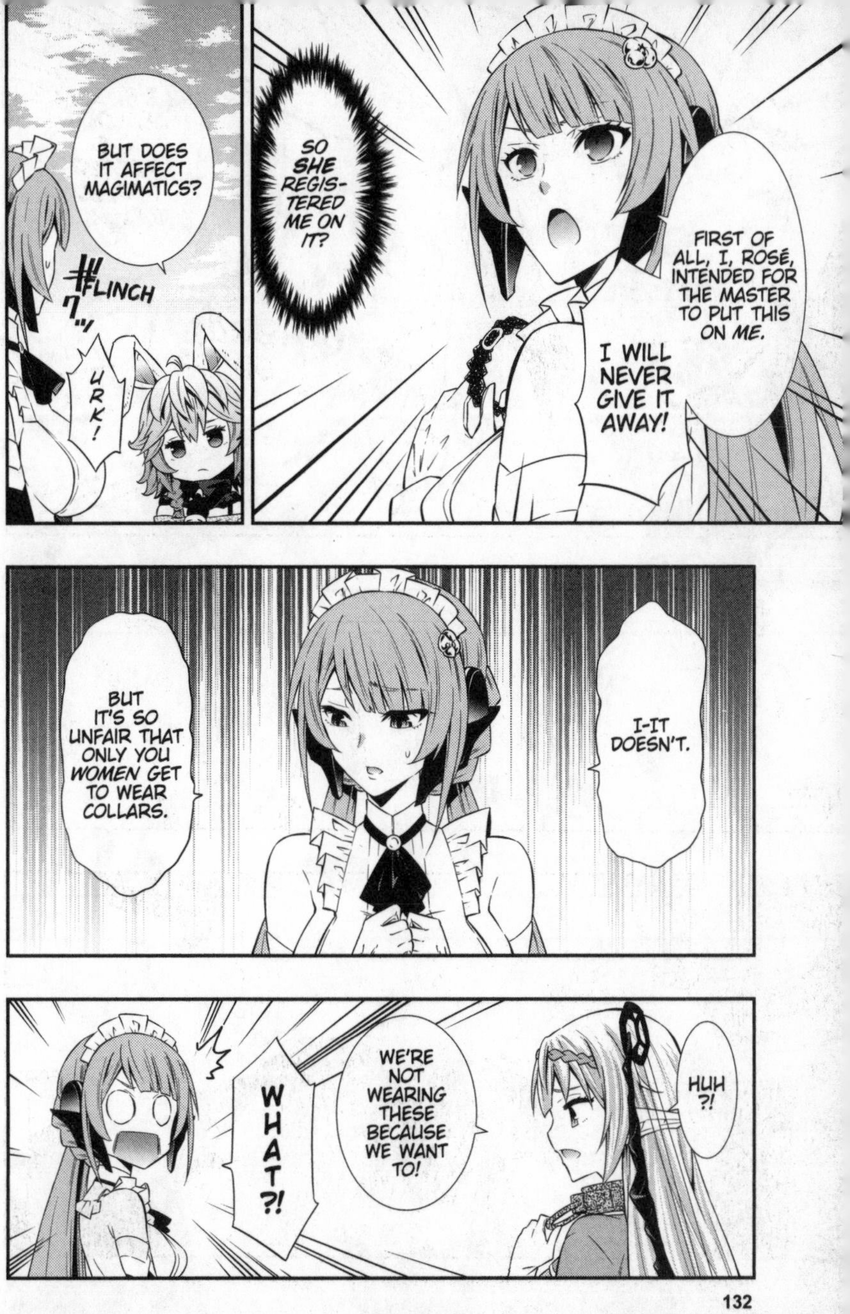
FIRST OF ALL, I, ROSÉ, INTENDED FOR THE MASTER TO PUT THIS ON ME.
I WILL NEVER GIVE IT AWAY!
SO SHE REGISTERED ME ON IT?
BUT DOES IT AFFECT MAGIMATICS?
FLINCH
URK!
I-IT DOESN'T.
BUT IT'S SO UNFAIR THAT ONLY YOU WOMEN GET TO WEAR COLLARS.
HUH?!
WE'RE NOT WEARING THESE BECAUSE WE WANT TO!
WHAT?!

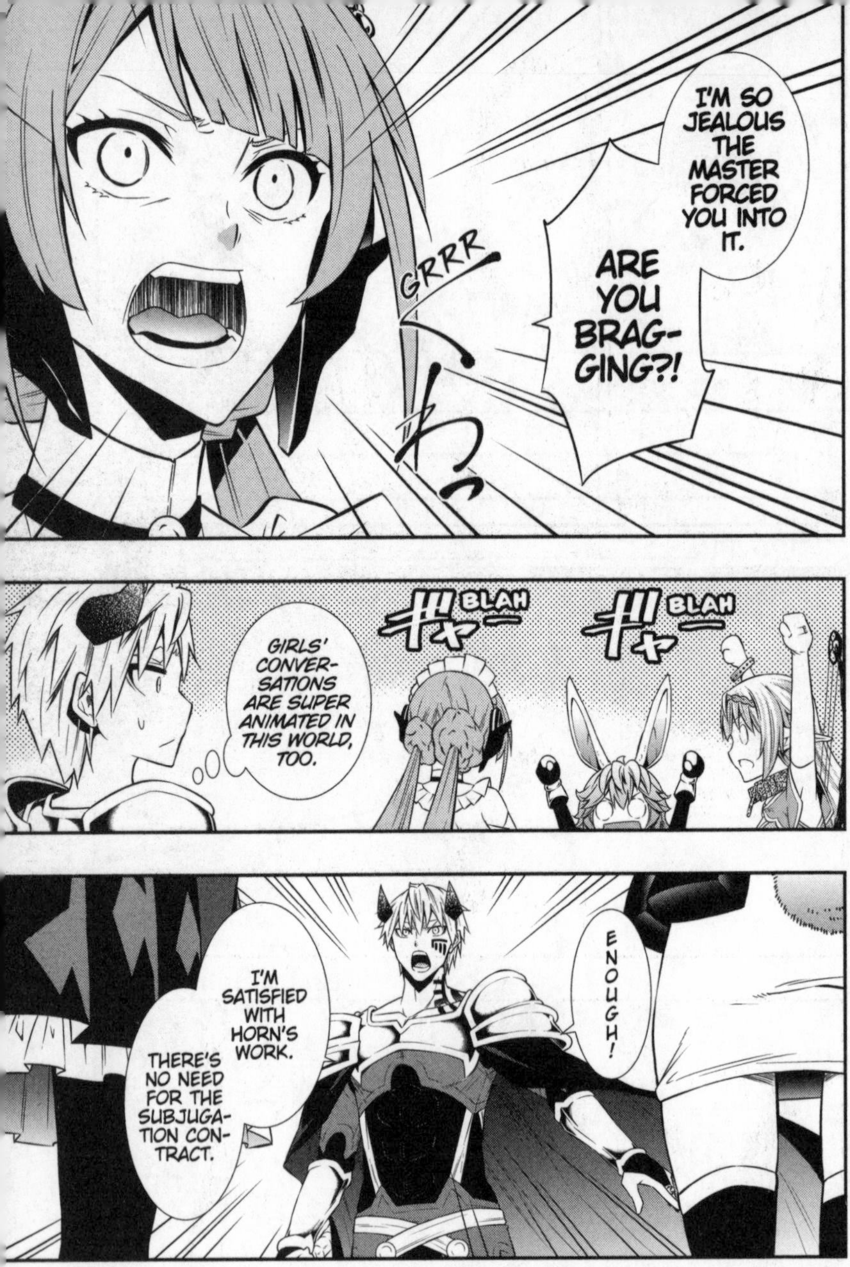
I'M SO JEALOUS THE MASTER FORCED YOU INTO IT.
ARE YOU BRAG-GING?!
GRRR
BLAH
BLAH
GIRLS' CONVER-SATIONS ARE SUPER ANIMATED IN THIS WORLD, TOO.
ENOUGH!
I'M SATISFIED WITH HORN'S WORK.
THERE'S NO NEED FOR THE SUBJUGA-TION CON-TRACT.

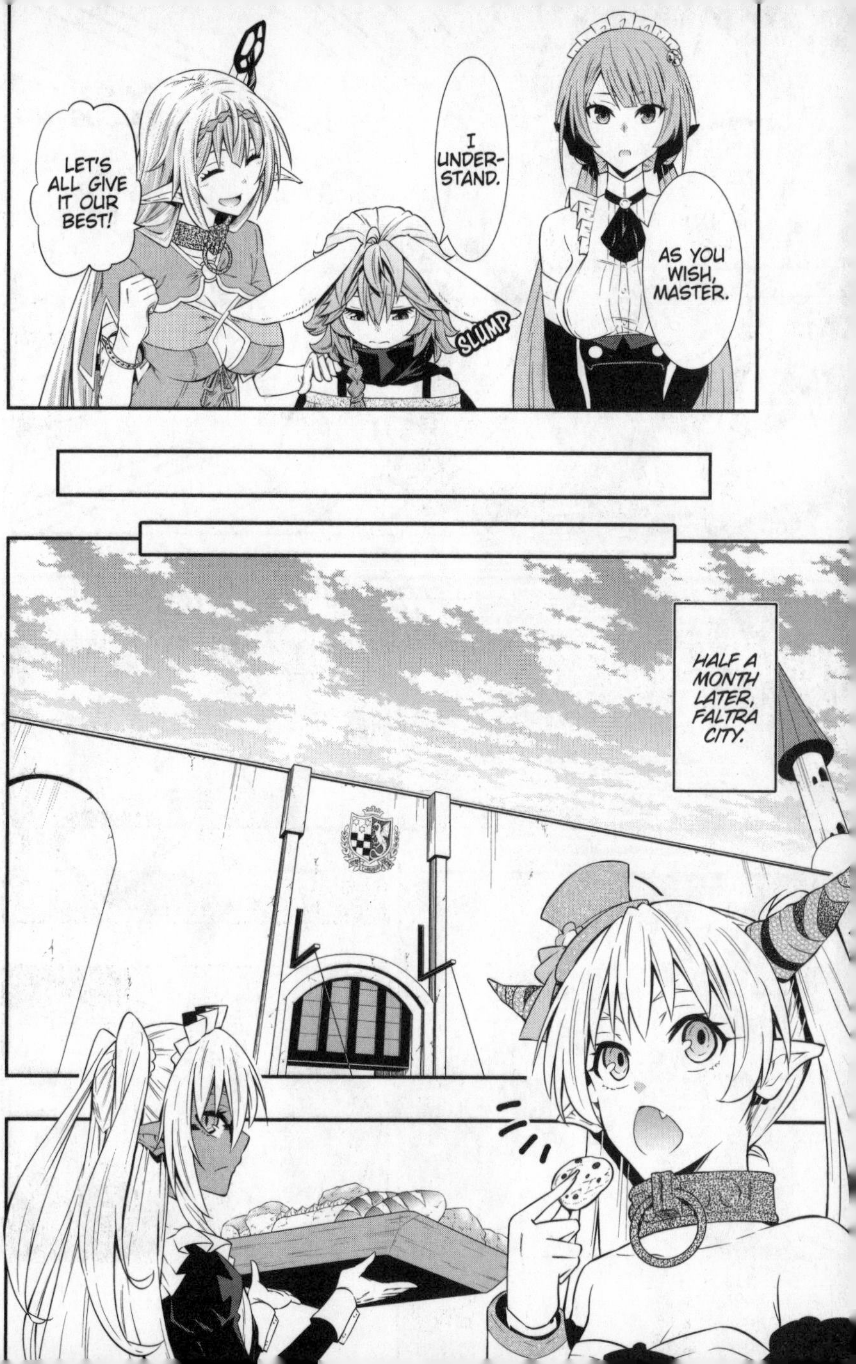
AS YOU WISH, MASTER.
I UNDER-STAND.
SLUMP
LET'S ALL GIVE IT OUR BEST!
HALF A MONTH LATER, FALTRA CITY.

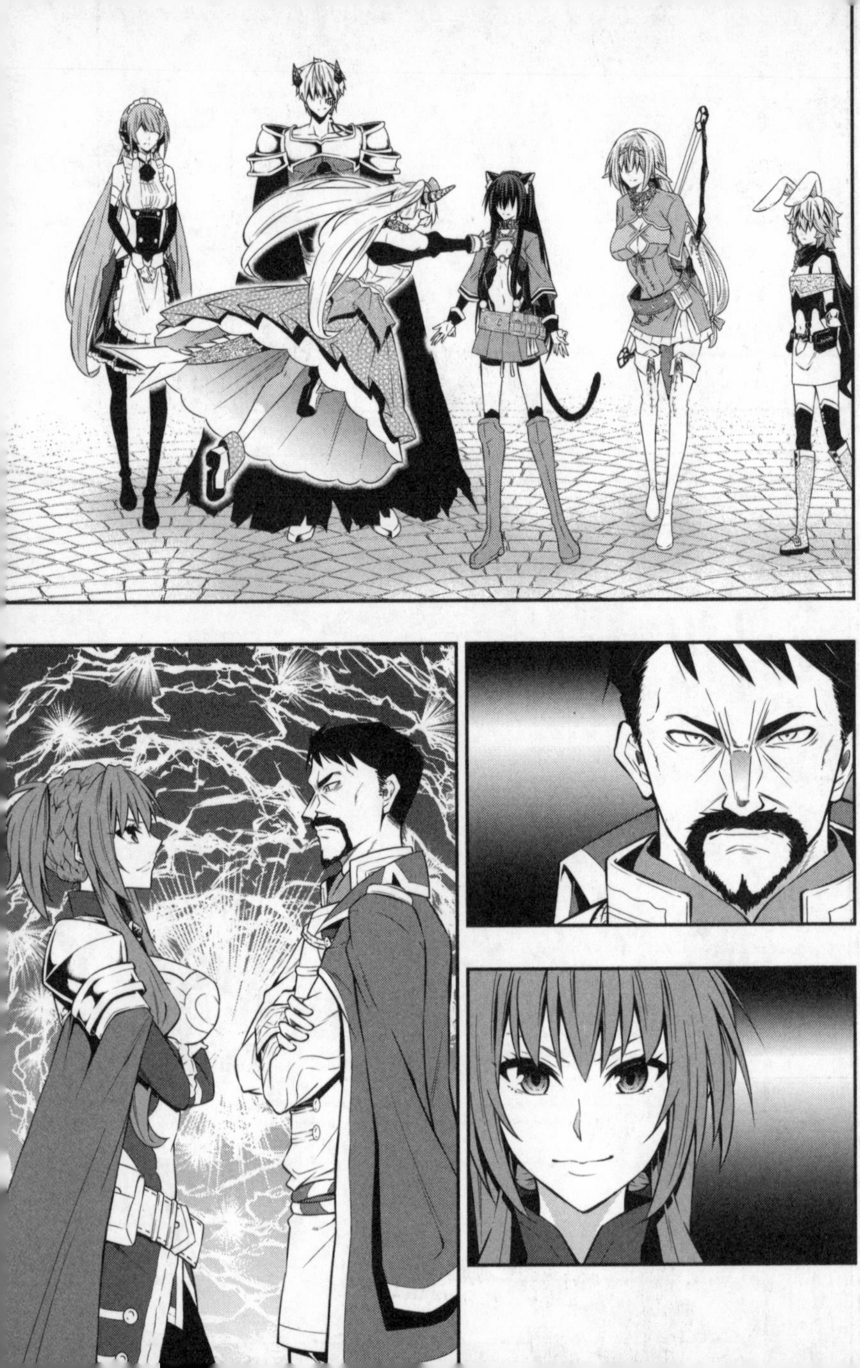

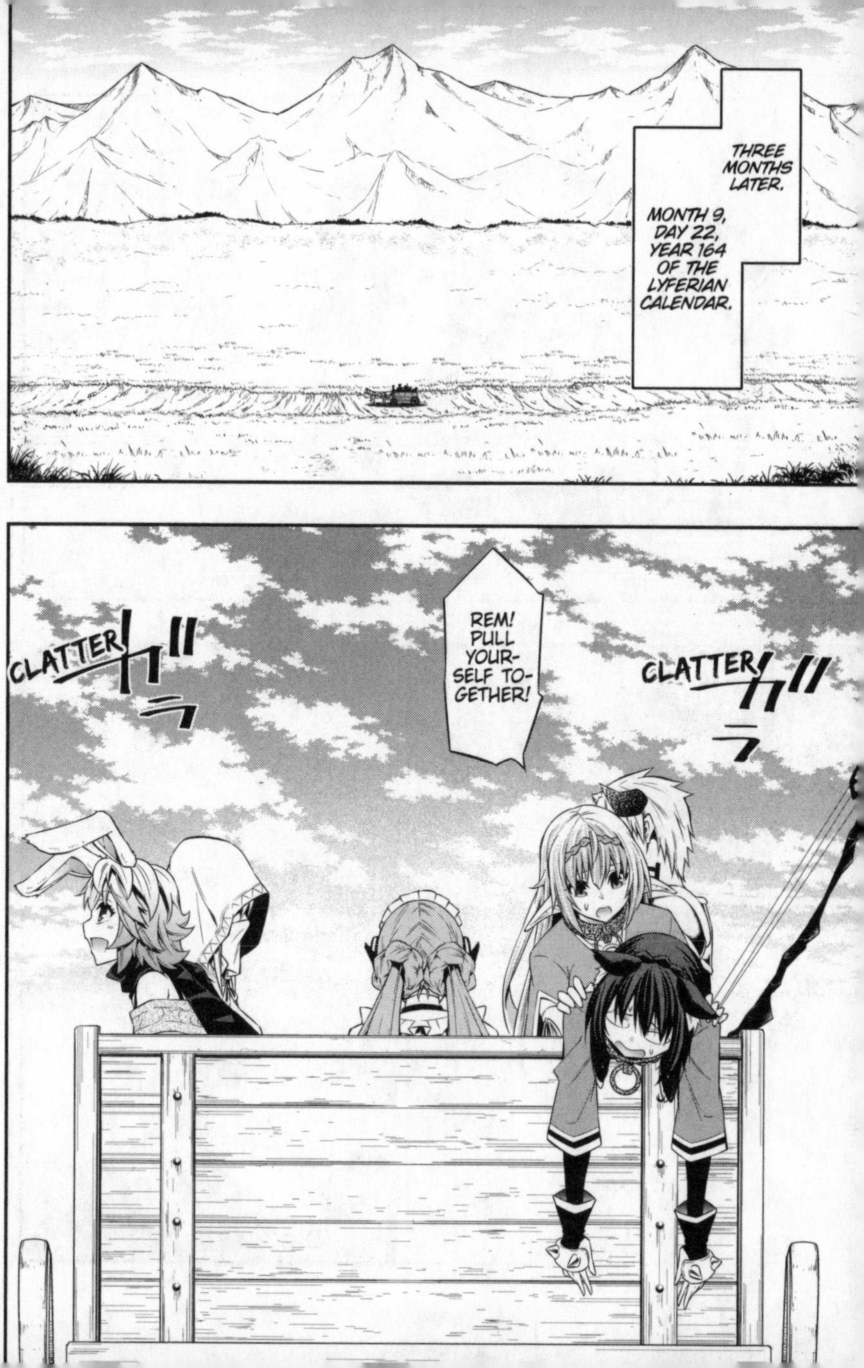
THREE MONTHS LATER.
MONTH 9, DAY 22, YEAR 164 OF THE LYFERIAN CALENDAR.
CLATTER
REM! PULL YOUR-SELF TO-GETHER!
CLATTER

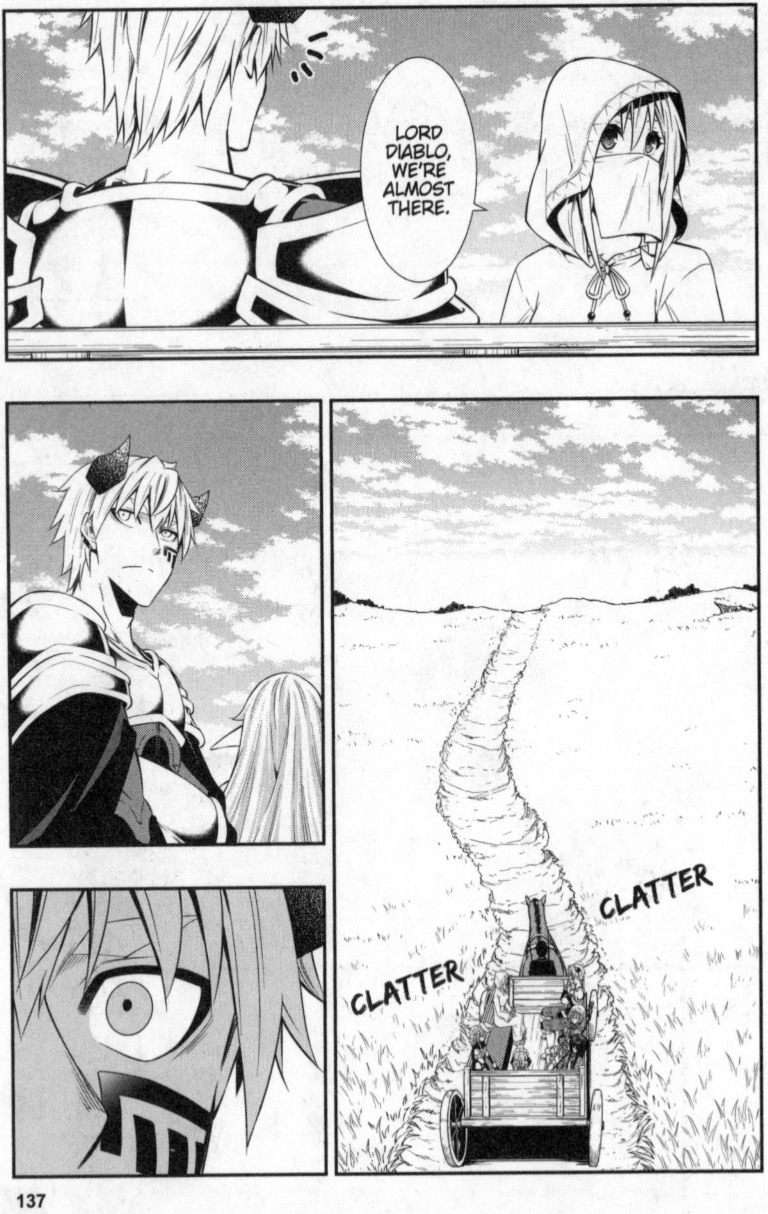
LORD DIABLO, WE'RE ALMOST THERE.
CLATTER
CLATTER

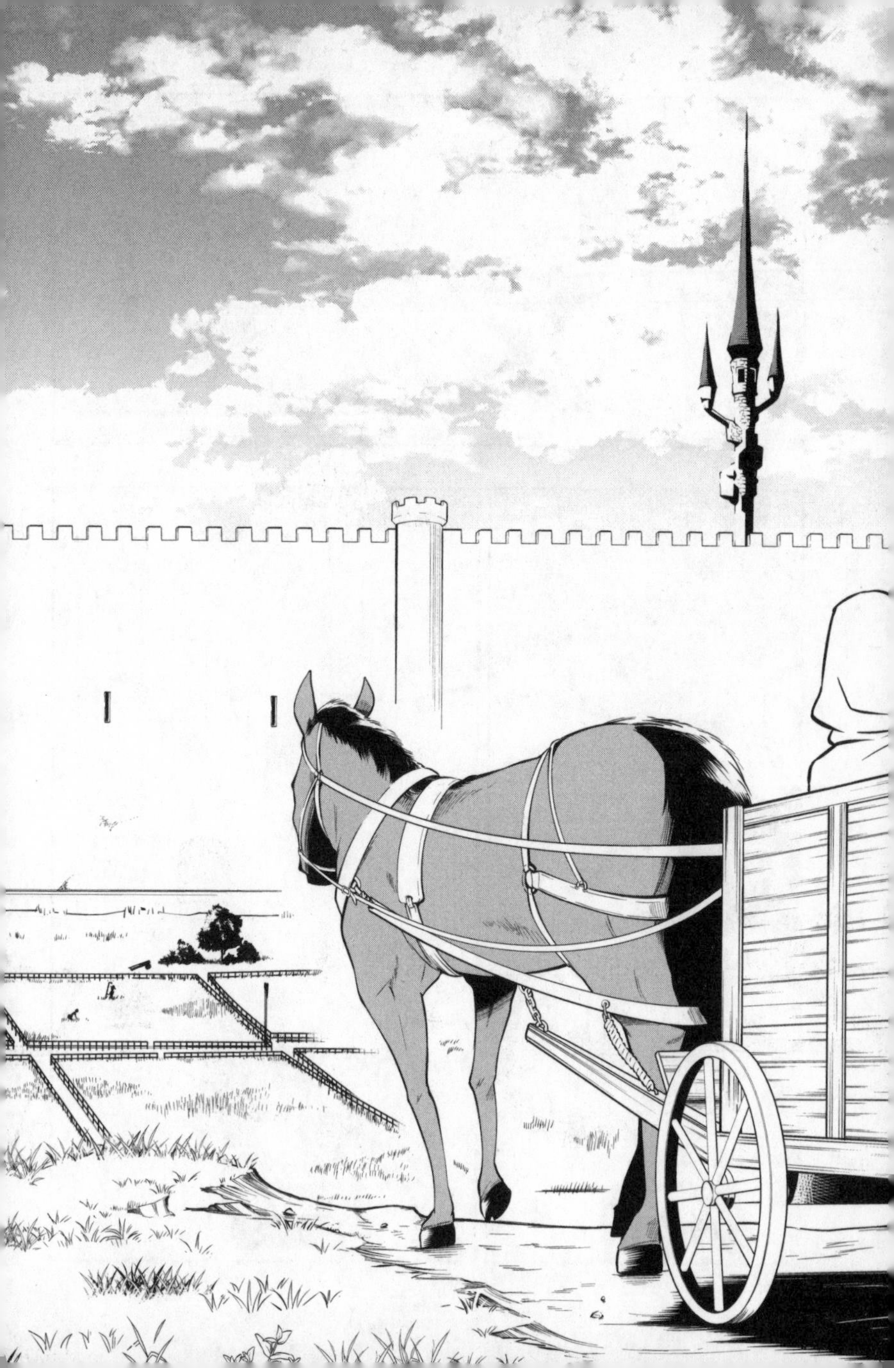

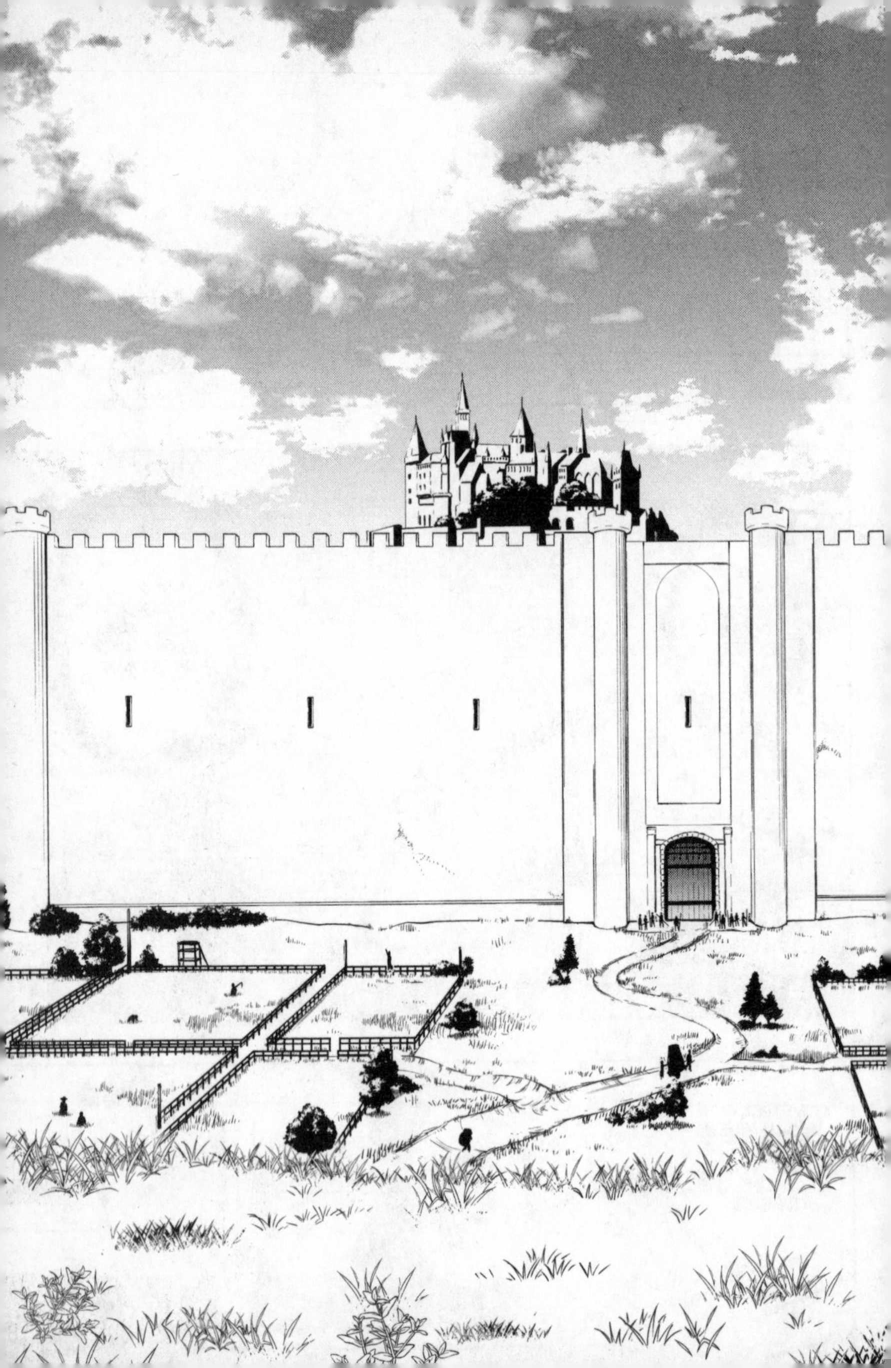

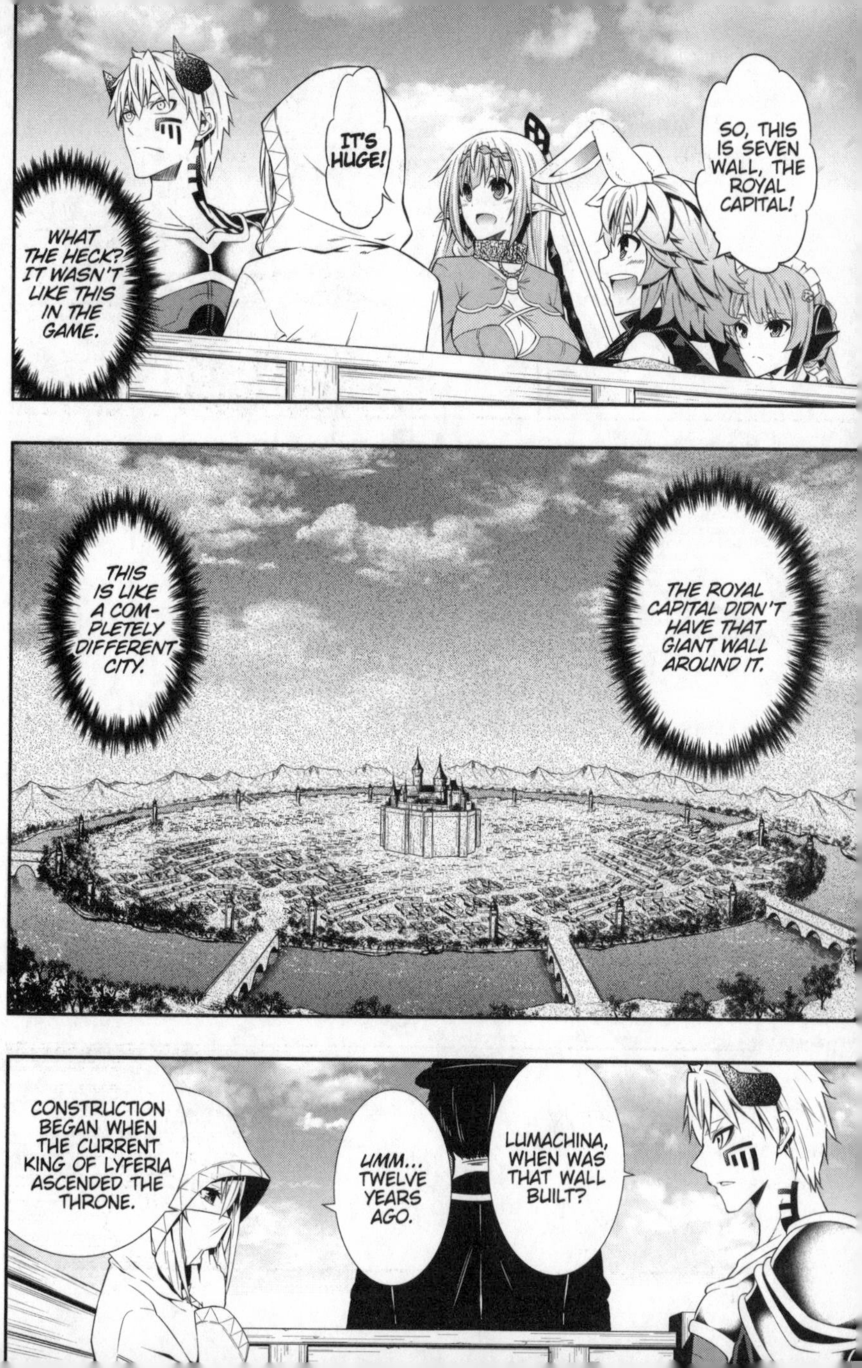
SO, THIS IS SEVEN WALL, THE ROYAL CAPITAL!
IT'S HUGE!
WHAT THE HECK? IT WASN'T LIKE THIS IN THE GAME.
THE ROYAL CAPITAL DIDN'T HAVE THAT GIANT WALL AROUND IT.
THIS IS LIKE A COM-PLETELY DIFFERENT CITY.
LUMACHINA, WHEN WAS THAT WALL BUILT?
UMM... TWELVE YEARS AGO.
CONSTRUCTION BEGAN WHEN THE CURRENT KING OF LYFERIA ASCENDED THE THRONE.

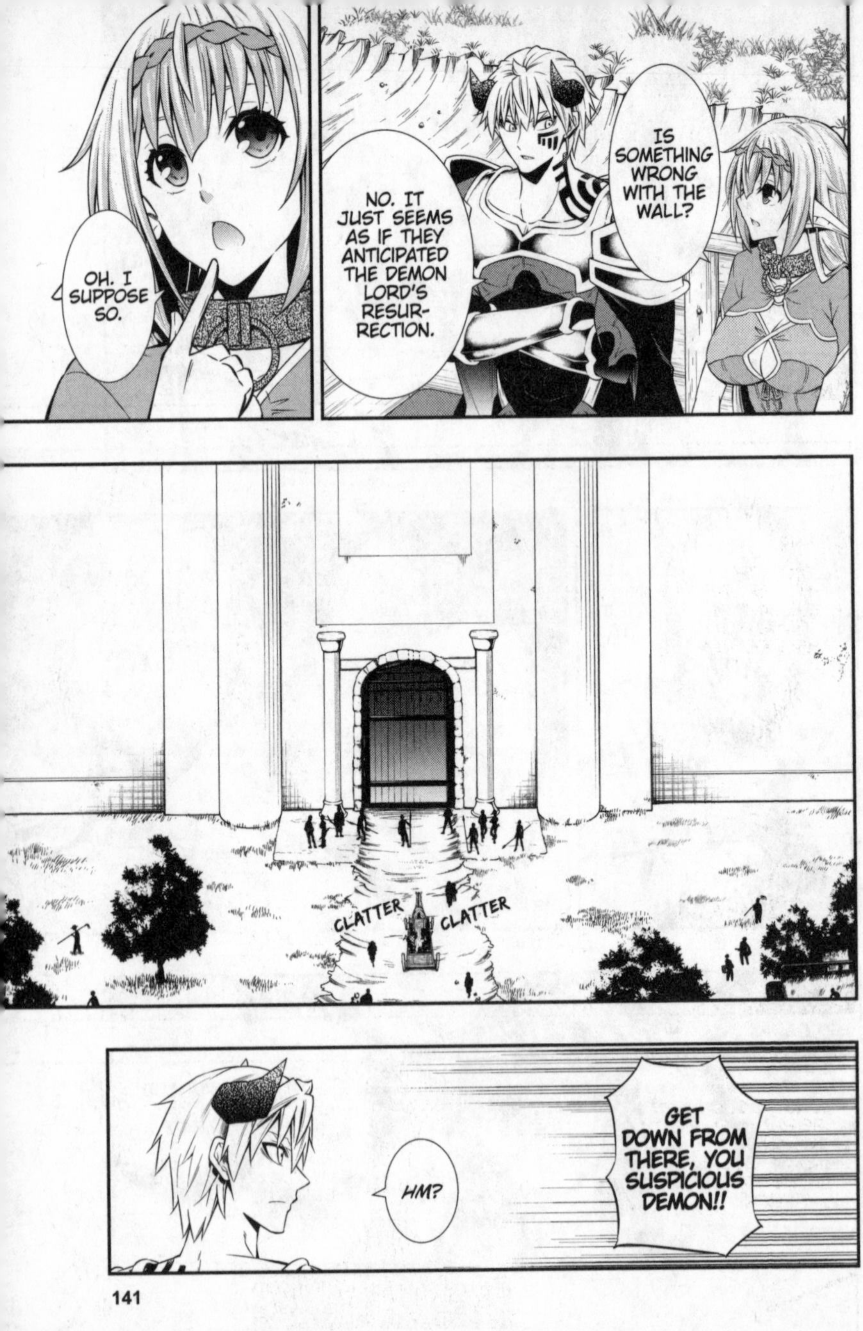
IS SOMETHING WRONG WITH THE WALL?
NO. IT JUST SEEMS AS IF THEY ANTICIPATED THE DEMON LORD'S RESUR-RECTION.
OH. I SUPPOSE SO.
CLATTER CLATTER
GET DOWN FROM THERE, YOU SUSPICIOUS DEMON!!
HM?

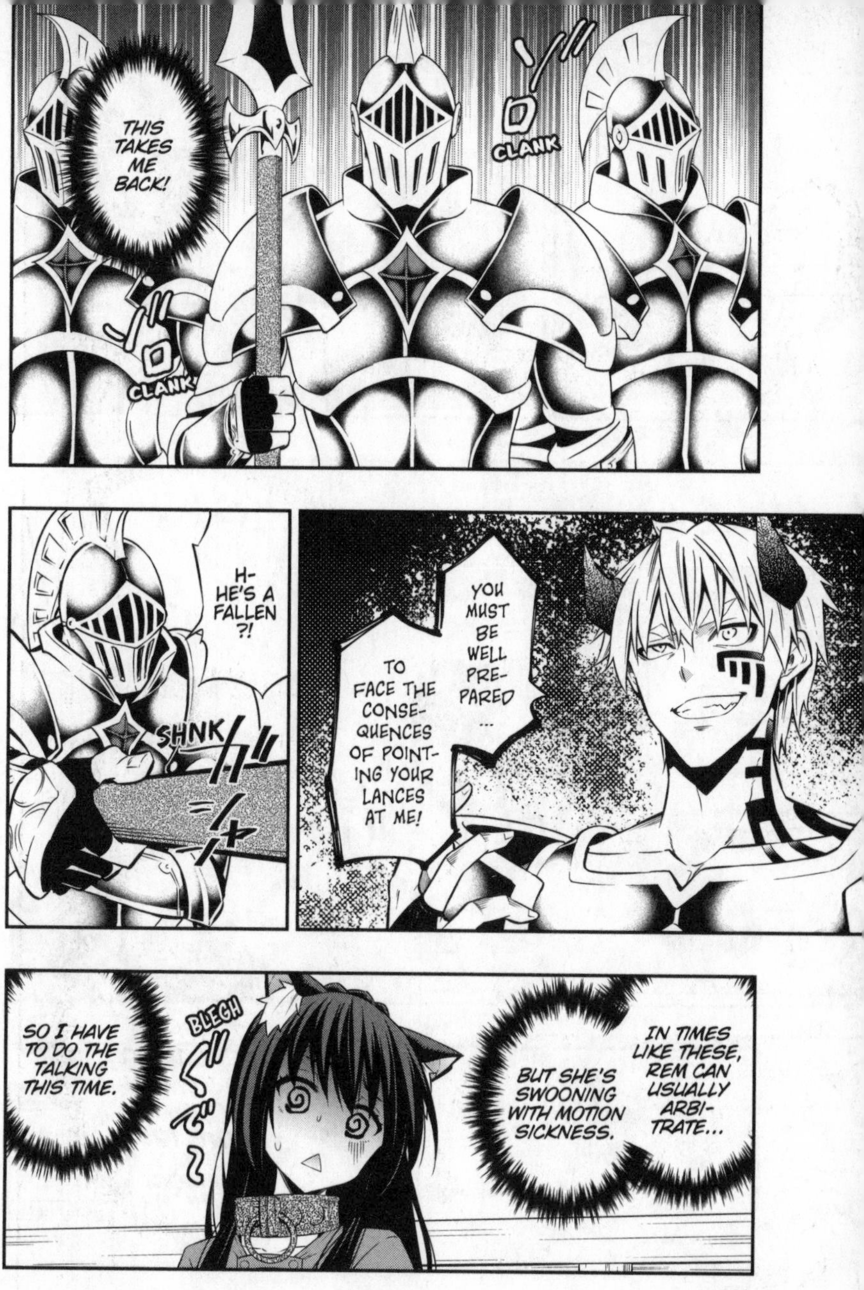
CLANK
THIS TAKES ME BACK!
CLANK
YOU MUST BE WELL PREPARED...
TO FACE THE CONSEQUENCES OF POINTING YOUR LANCES AT ME!
H-HE'S A FALLEN?!
SHNK
IN TIMES LIKE THESE, REM CAN USUALLY ARBITRATE...
BUT SHE'S SWOONING WITH MOTION SICKNESS.
BLEGH
SO I HAVE TO DO THE TALKING THIS TIME.

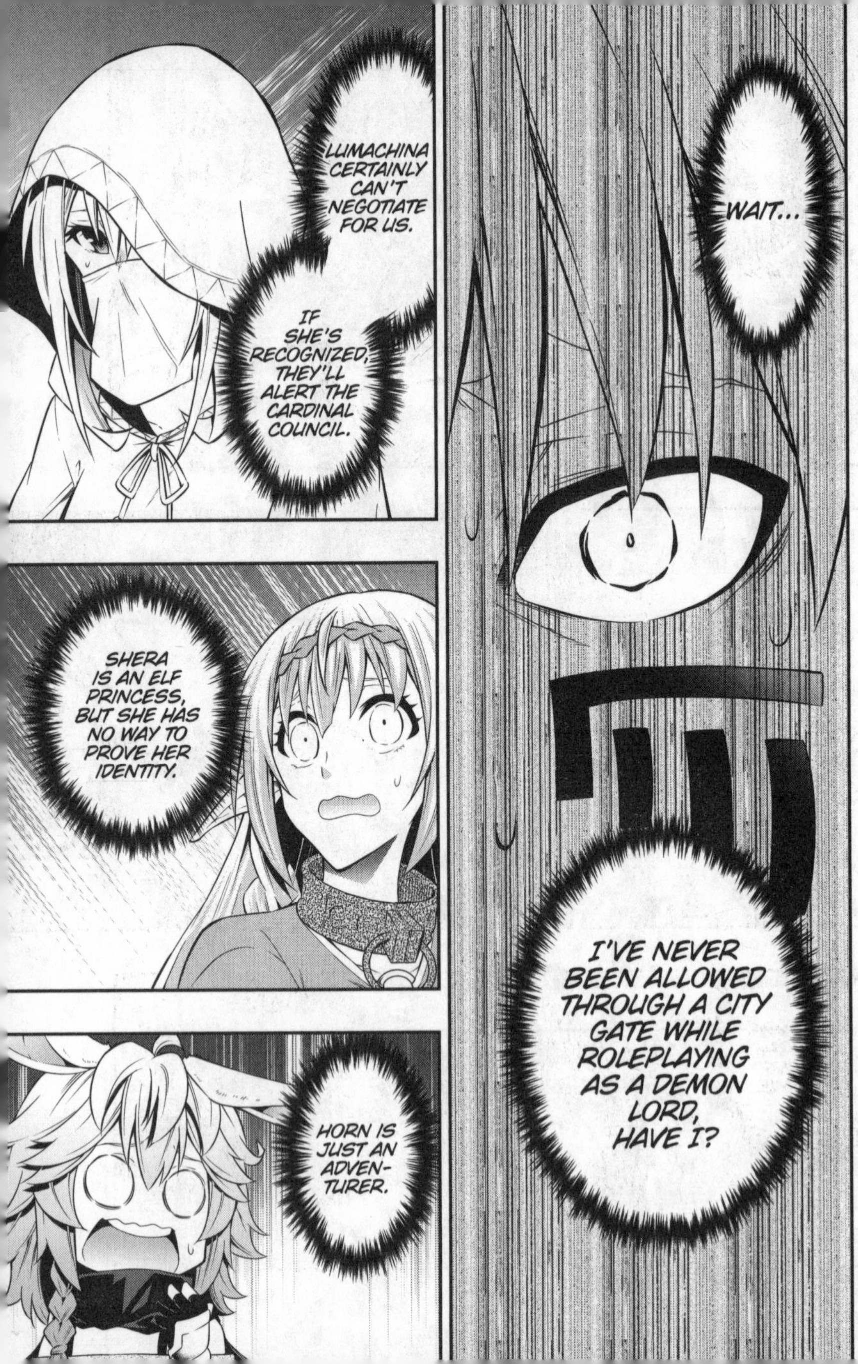
WAIT...
I'VE NEVER BEEN ALLOWED THROUGH A CITY GATE WHILE ROLEPLAYING AS A DEMON LORD, HAVE I?
LUMACHINA CERTAINLY CAN'T NEGOTIATE FOR US.
IF SHE'S RECOGNIZED, THEY'LL ALERT THE CARDINAL COUNCIL.
SHERA IS AN ELF PRINCESS, BUT SHE HAS NO WAY TO PROVE HER IDENTITY.
HORN IS JUST AN ADVEN-TURER.

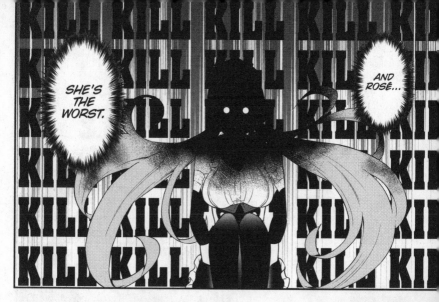

SHE'S THE WORST.

AND ROSE...

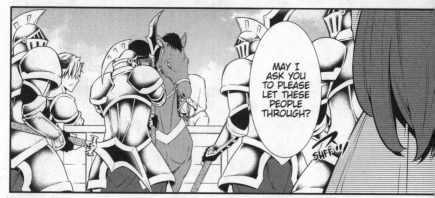

MAY I ASK YOU TO PLEASE LET THESE PEOPLE THROUGH?

SHFF!!

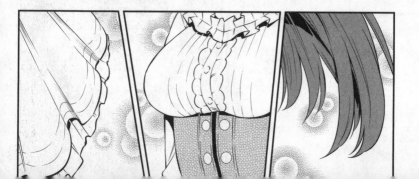

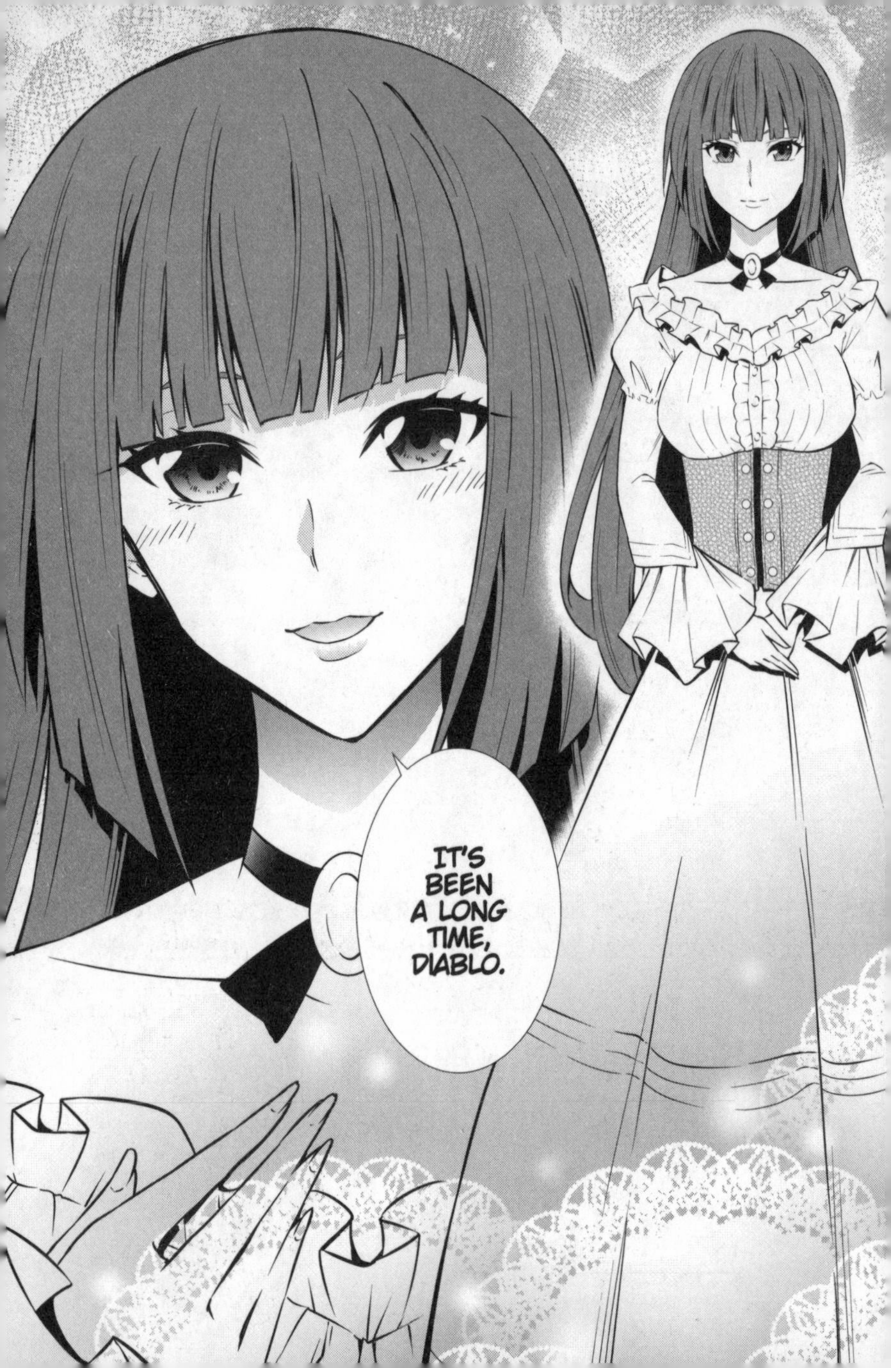
IT'S BEEN A LONG TIME, DIABLO.

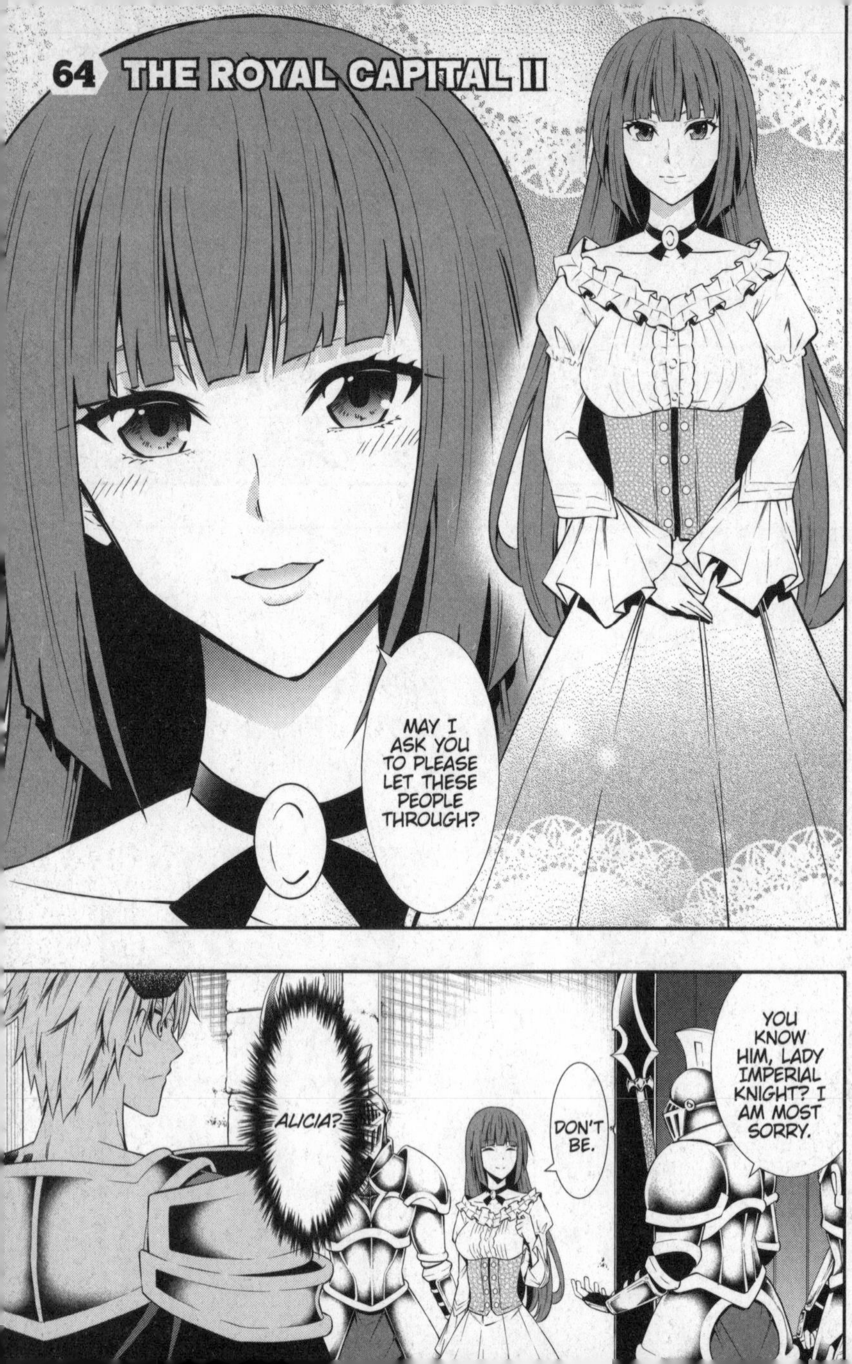
64 THE ROYAL CAPITAL II
MAY I ASK YOU TO PLEASE LET THESE PEOPLE THROUGH?
YOU KNOW HIM, LADY IMPERIAL KNIGHT? I AM MOST SORRY.
DON'T BE.
ALICIA?

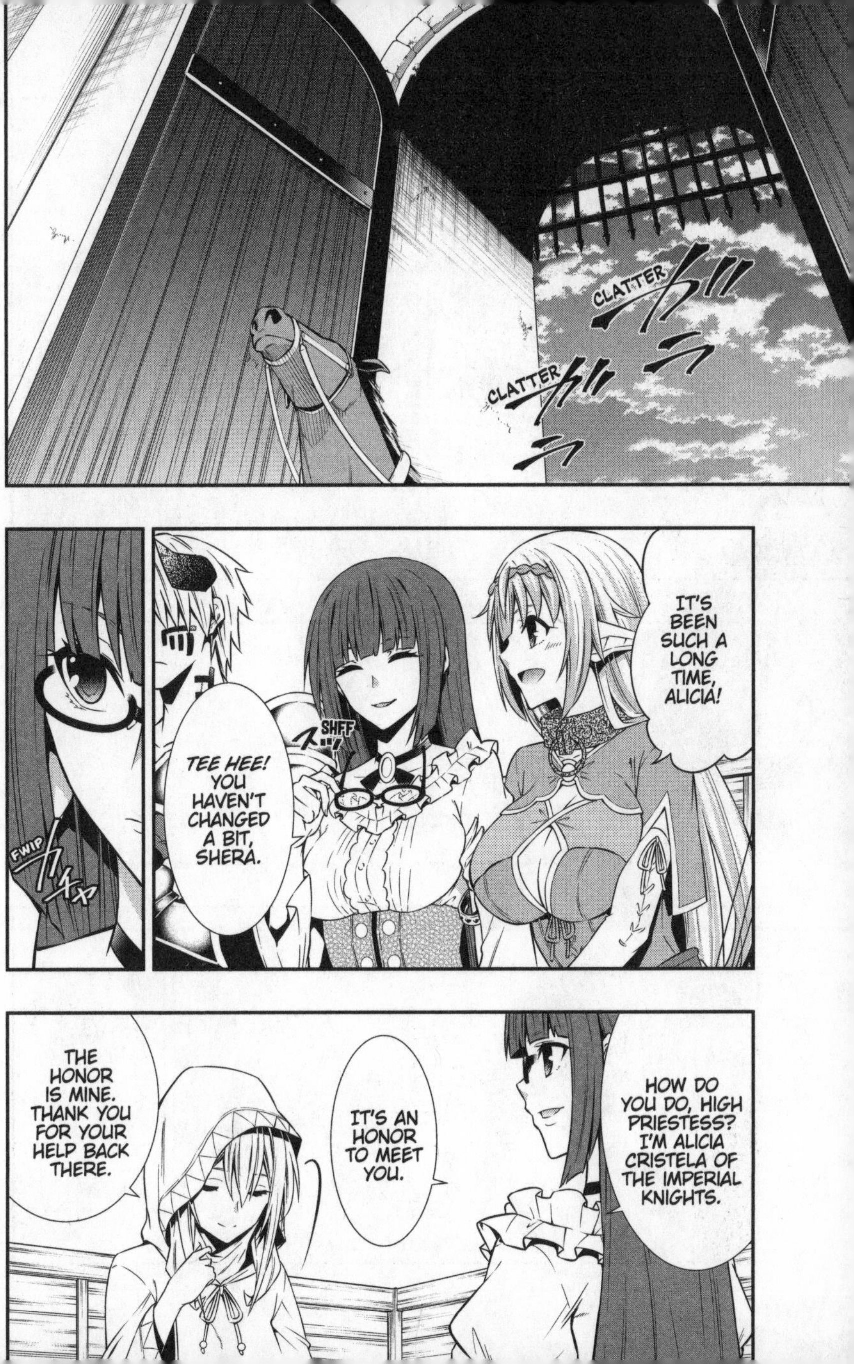
CLATTER
CLATTER
IT'S BEEN SUCH A LONG TIME, ALICIA!
SHFF
TEE HEE! YOU HAVEN'T CHANGED A BIT, SHERA.
FWIP
HOW DO YOU DO, HIGH PRIESTESS? I'M ALICIA CRISTELA OF THE IMPERIAL KNIGHTS.
IT'S AN HONOR TO MEET YOU.
THE HONOR IS MINE. THANK YOU FOR YOUR HELP BACK THERE.

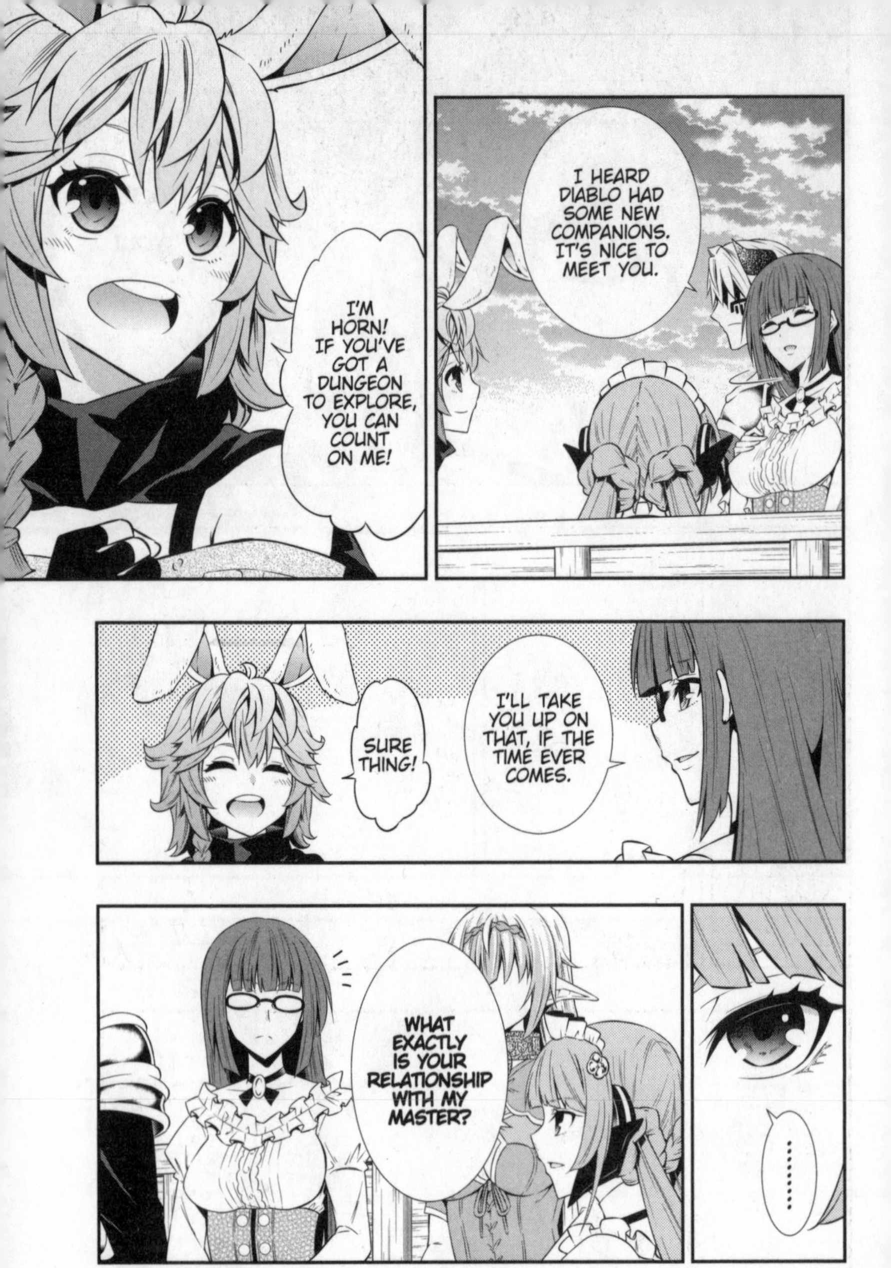
I HEARD DIABLO HAD SOME NEW COMPANIONS. IT'S NICE TO MEET YOU.
I'M HORN! IF YOU'VE GOT A DUNGEON TO EXPLORE, YOU CAN COUNT ON ME!
I'LL TAKE YOU UP ON THAT, IF THE TIME EVER COMES.
SURE THING!
......
WHAT EXACTLY IS YOUR RELATIONSHIP WITH MY MASTER?

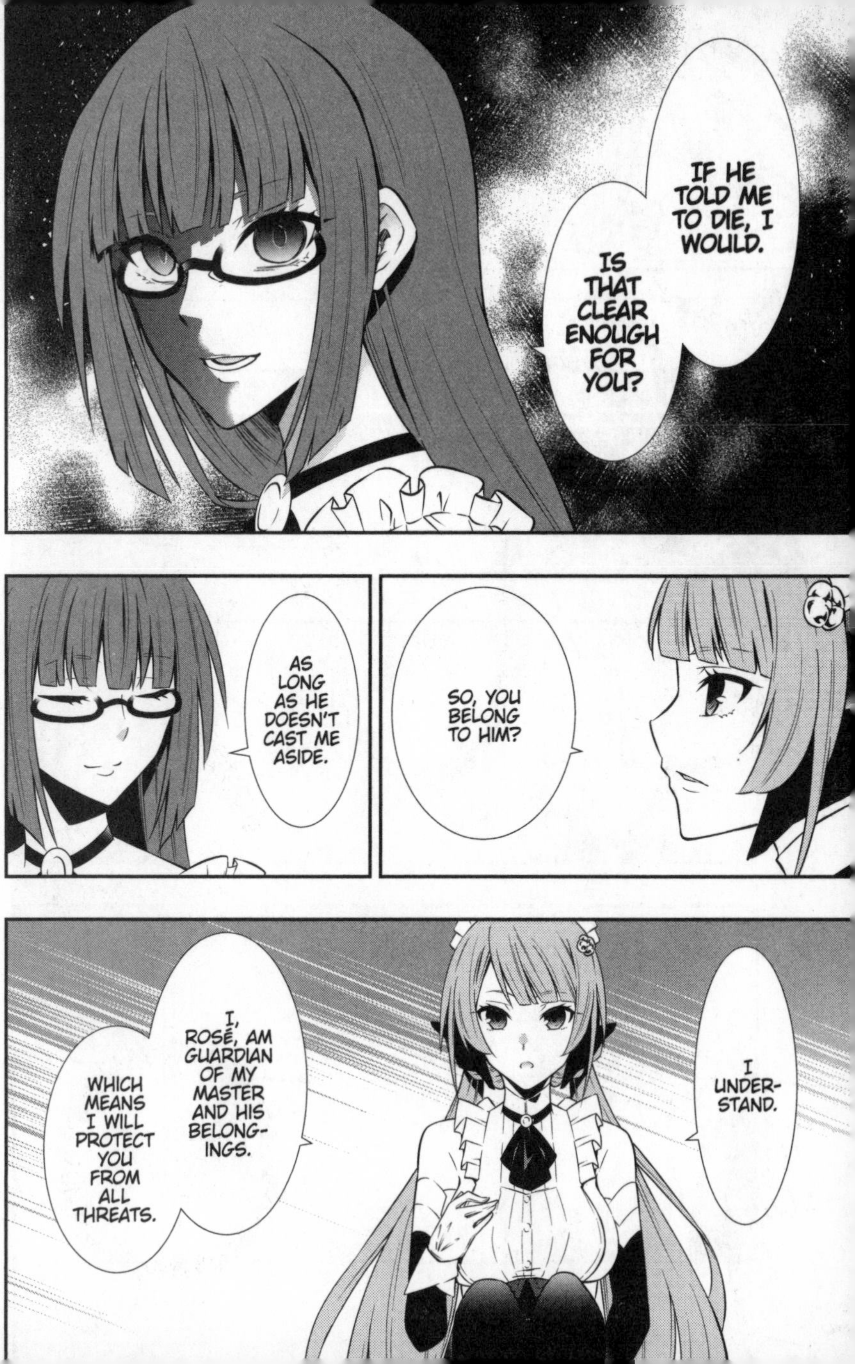
IF HE TOLD ME TO DIE, I WOULD.
IS THAT CLEAR ENOUGH FOR YOU?
SO, YOU BELONG TO HIM?
AS LONG AS HE DOESN'T CAST ME ASIDE.
I UNDERSTAND.
I, ROSÉ, AM GUARDIAN OF MY MASTER AND HIS BELONGINGS.
WHICH MEANS I WILL PROTECT YOU FROM ALL THREATS.

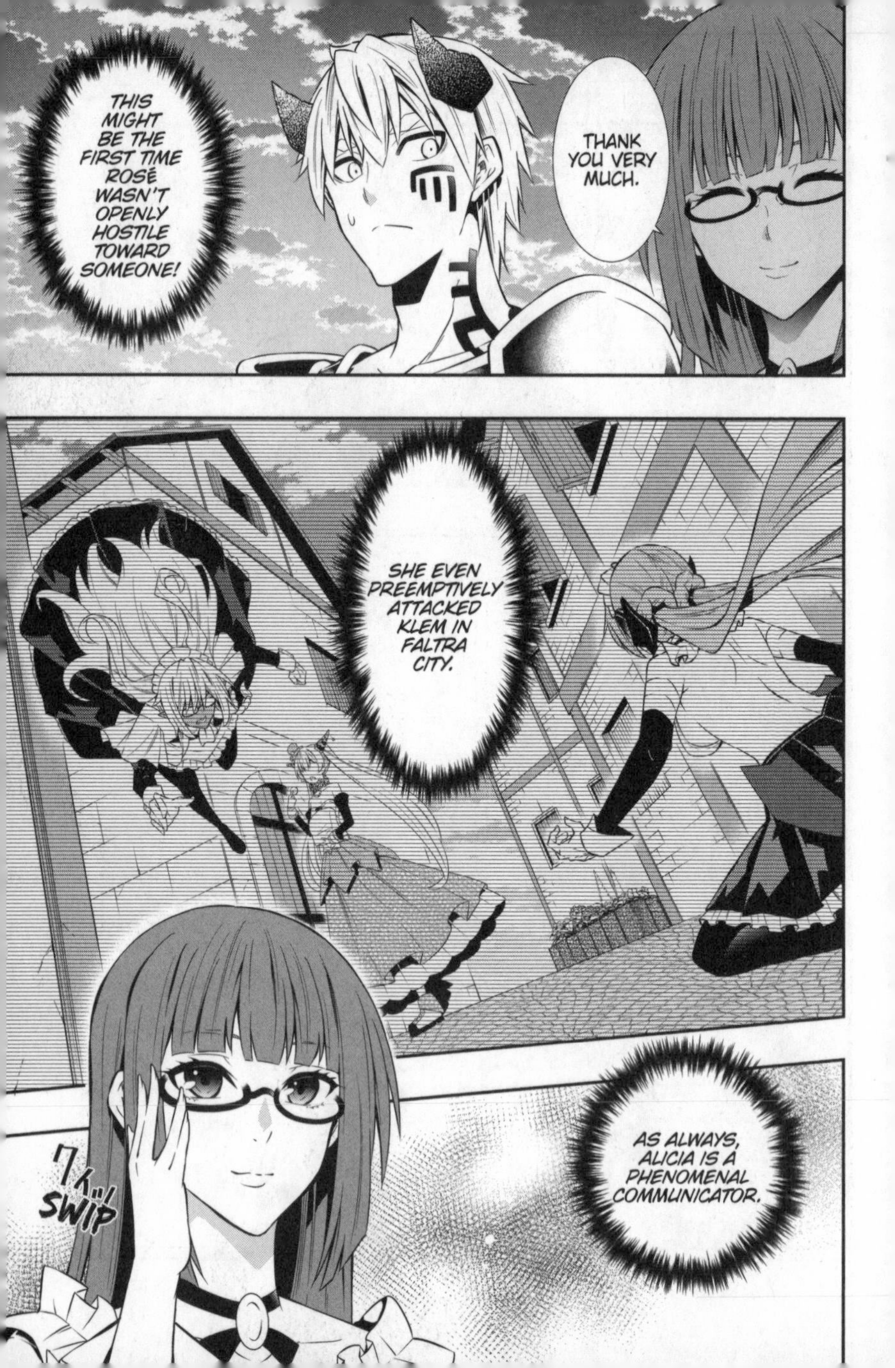
THANK YOU VERY MUCH.
THIS MIGHT BE THE FIRST TIME ROSÉ WASN'T OPENLY HOSTILE TOWARD SOMEONE!
SHE EVEN PREEMPTIVELY ATTACKED KLEM IN FALTRA CITY.
AS ALWAYS, ALICIA IS A PHENOMENAL COMMUNICATOR.
SWIP

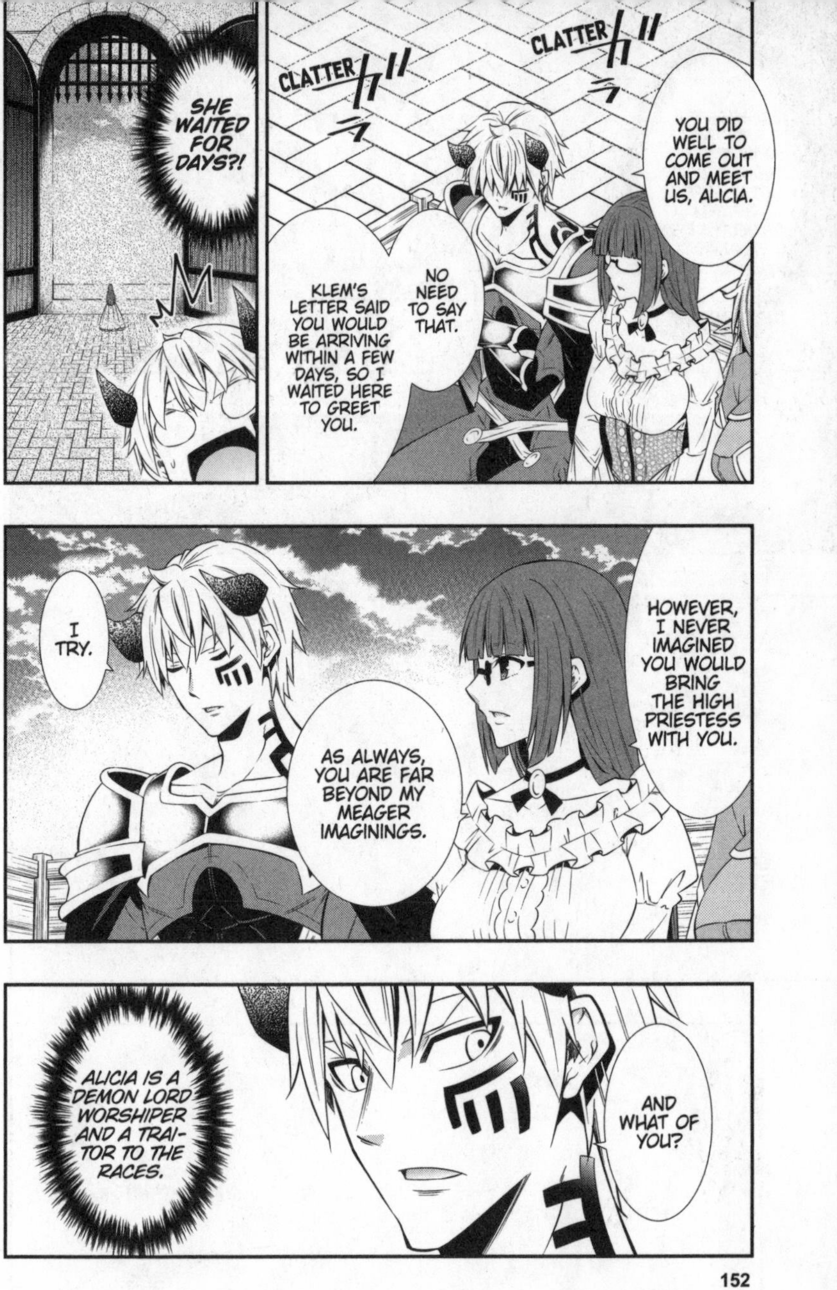
CLATTER
CLATTER
YOU DID WELL TO COME OUT AND MEET US, ALICIA.
NO NEED TO SAY THAT.
KLEM'S LETTER SAID YOU WOULD BE ARRIVING WITHIN A FEW DAYS, SO I WAITED HERE TO GREET YOU.
SHE WAITED FOR DAYS?!
HOWEVER, I NEVER IMAGINED YOU WOULD BRING THE HIGH PRIESTESS WITH YOU.
AS ALWAYS, YOU ARE FAR BEYOND MY MEAGER IMAGININGS.
I TRY.
AND WHAT OF YOU?
ALICIA IS A DEMON LORD WORSHIPER AND A TRAITOR TO THE RACES.

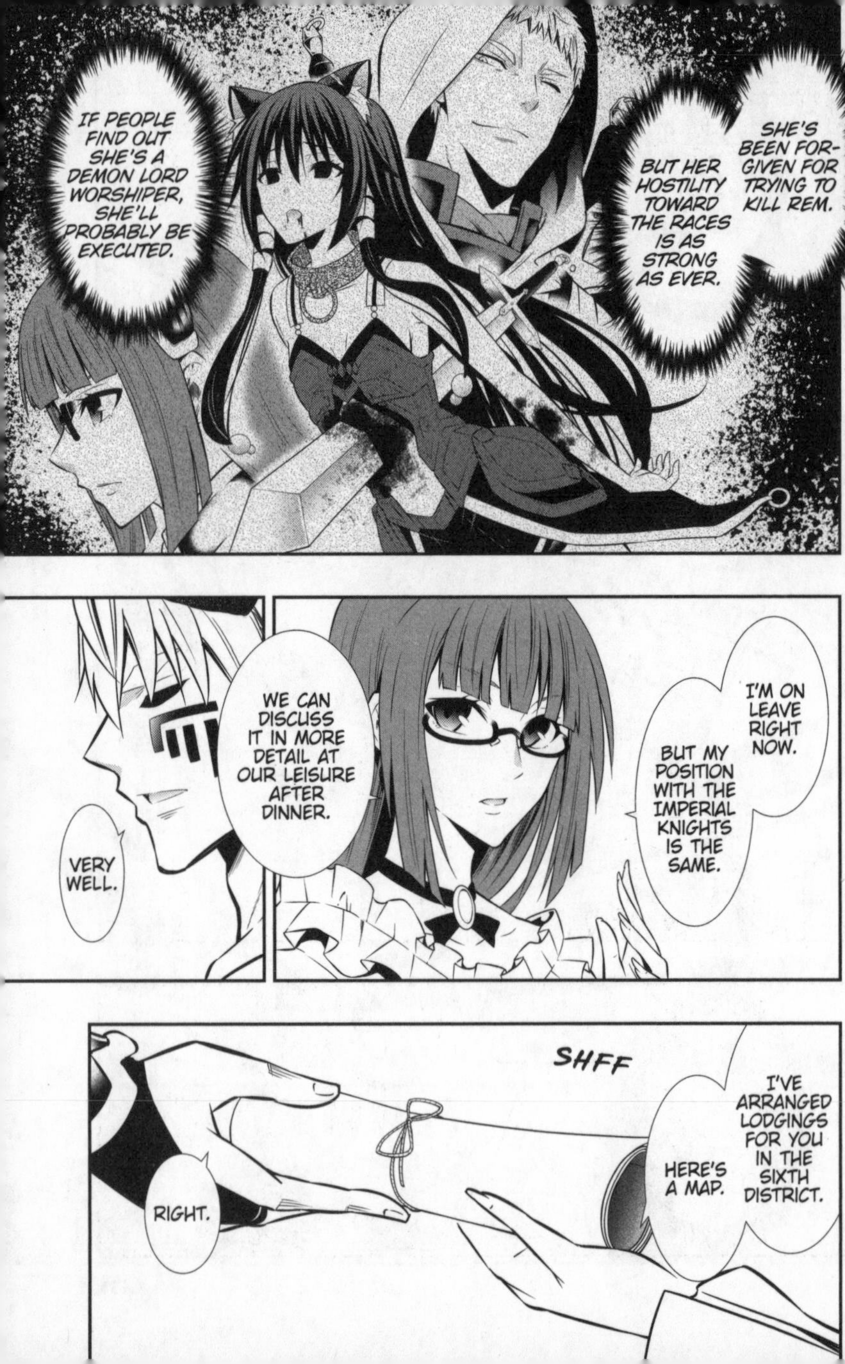
SHE'S BEEN FORGIVEN FOR TRYING TO KILL REM.
BUT HER HOSTILITY TOWARD THE RACES IS AS STRONG AS EVER.
IF PEOPLE FIND OUT SHE'S A DEMON LORD WORSHIPER, SHE'LL PROBABLY BE EXECUTED.
I'M ON LEAVE RIGHT NOW.
BUT MY POSITION WITH THE IMPERIAL KNIGHTS IS THE SAME.
WE CAN DISCUSS IT IN MORE DETAIL AT OUR LEISURE AFTER DINNER.
VERY WELL.
SHFF
I'VE ARRANGED LODGINGS FOR YOU IN THE SIXTH DISTRICT.
HERE'S A MAP.
RIGHT.

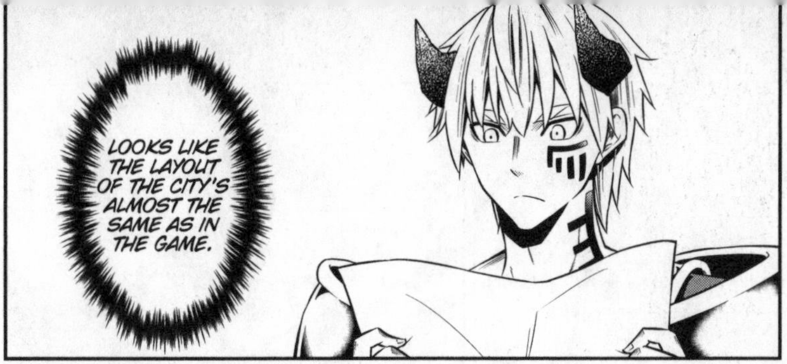
LOOKS LIKE THE LAYOUT OF THE CITY'S ALMOST THE SAME AS IN THE GAME.

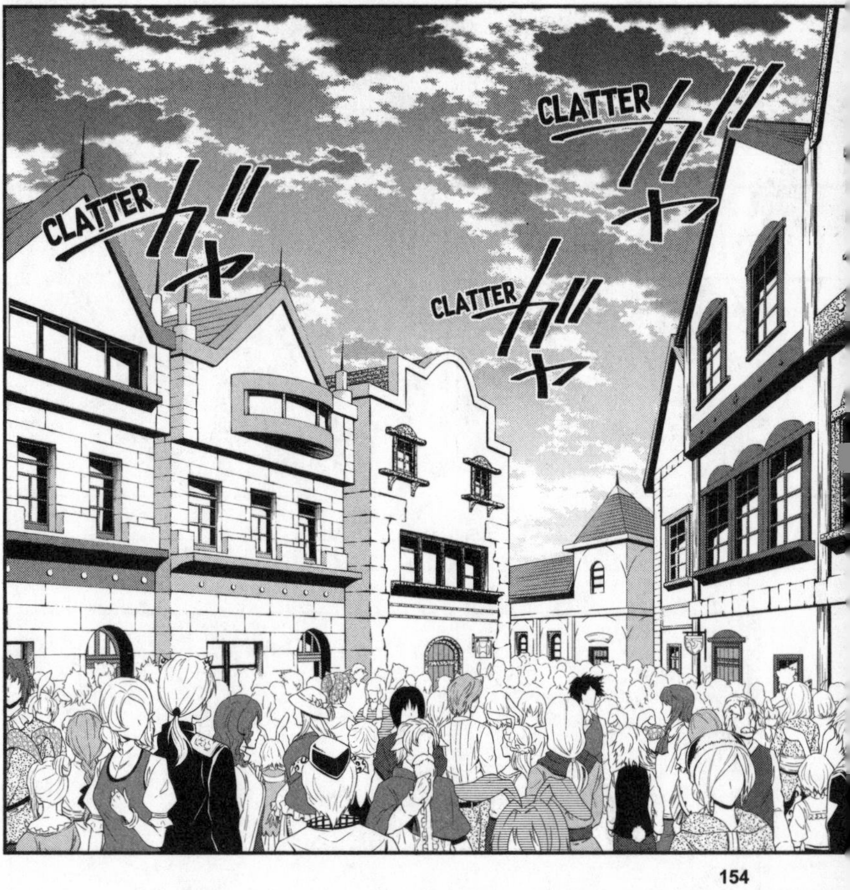
CLATTER
ガヤ
CLATTER
ガヤ
CLATTER
ガヤ

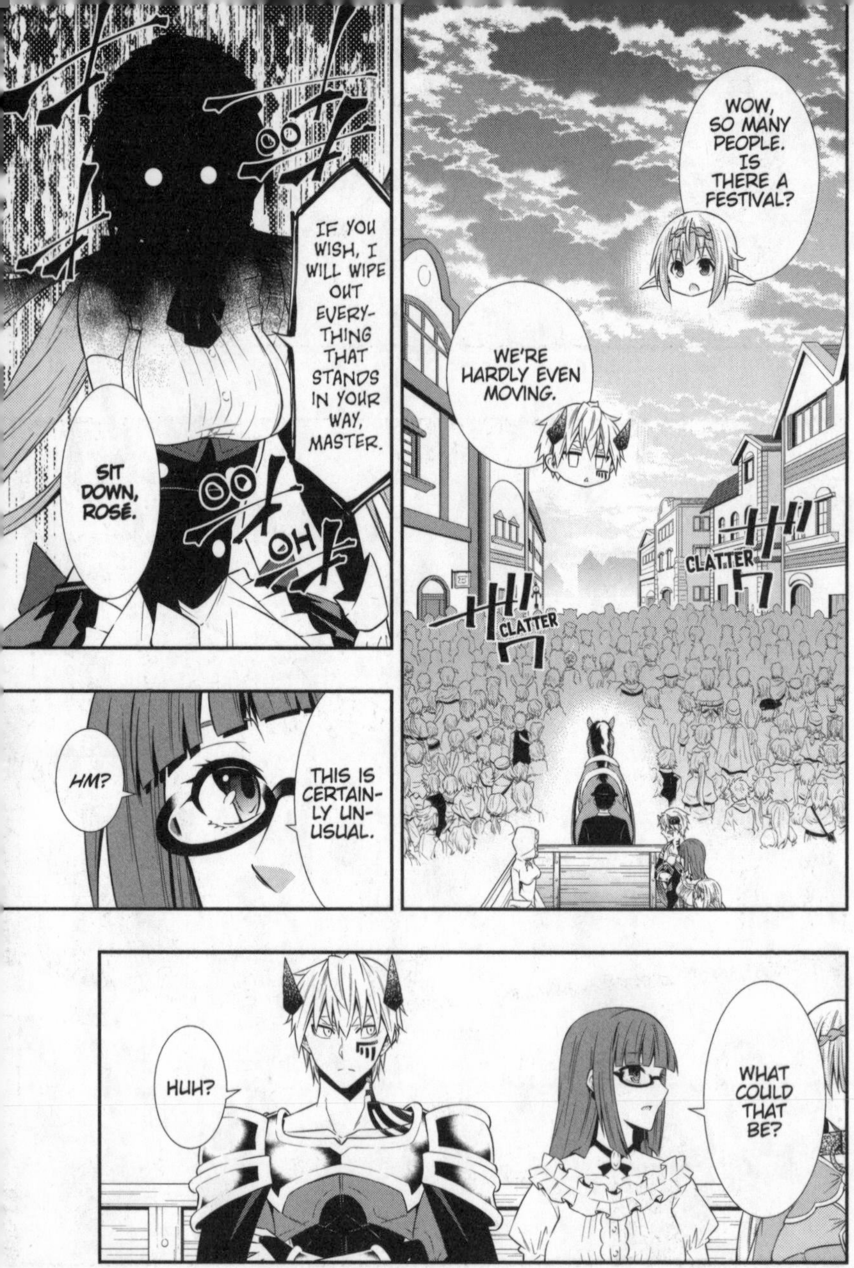
WOW, SO MANY PEOPLE. IS THERE A FESTIVAL?
WE'RE HARDLY EVEN MOVING.
CLATTER
CLATTER
IF YOU WISH, I WILL WIPE OUT EVERY-THING THAT STANDS IN YOUR WAY, MASTER.
OH
SIT DOWN, ROSE.
THIS IS CERTAIN-LY UN-USUAL.
HM?
WHAT COULD THAT BE?
HUH?

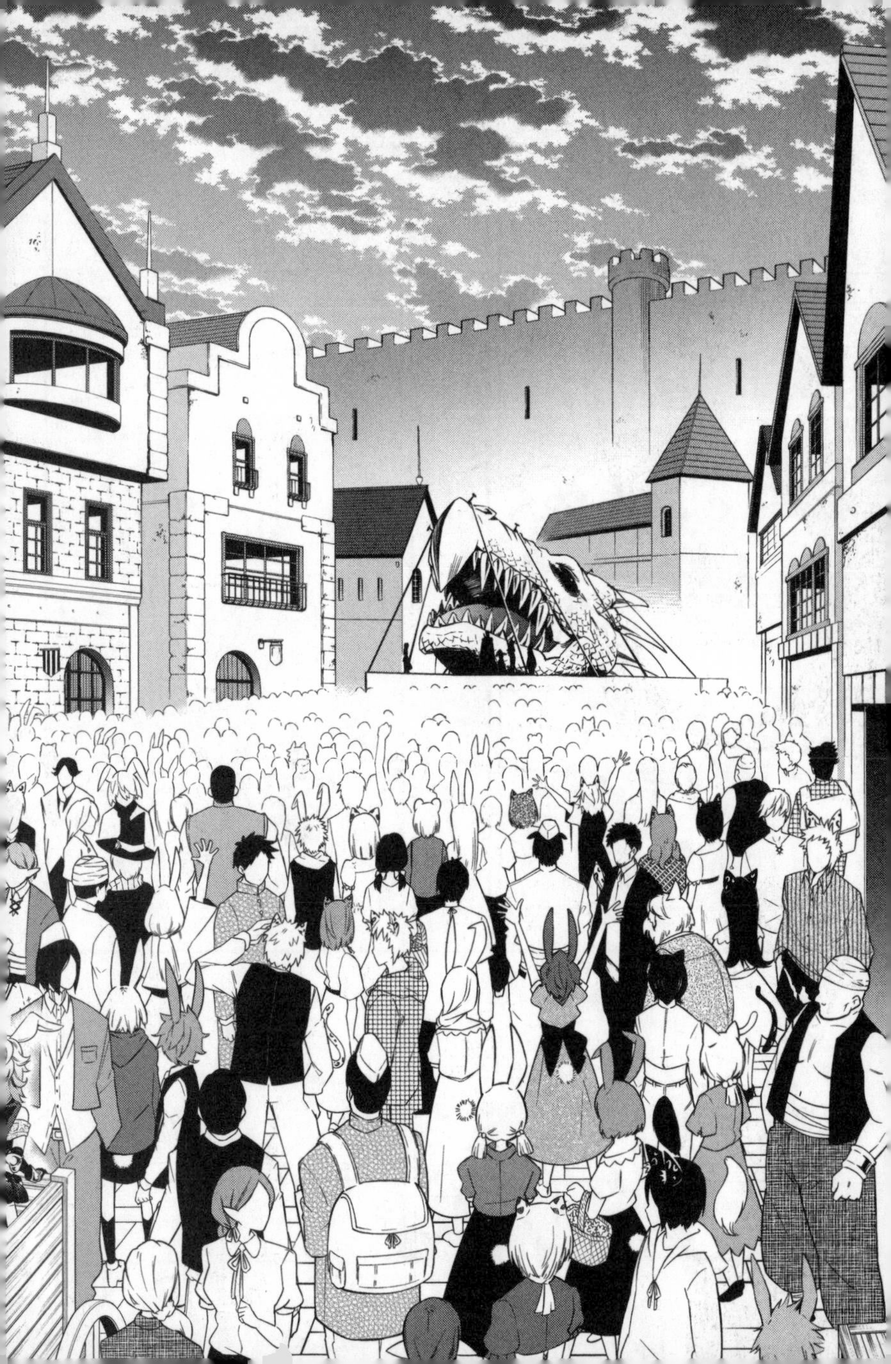

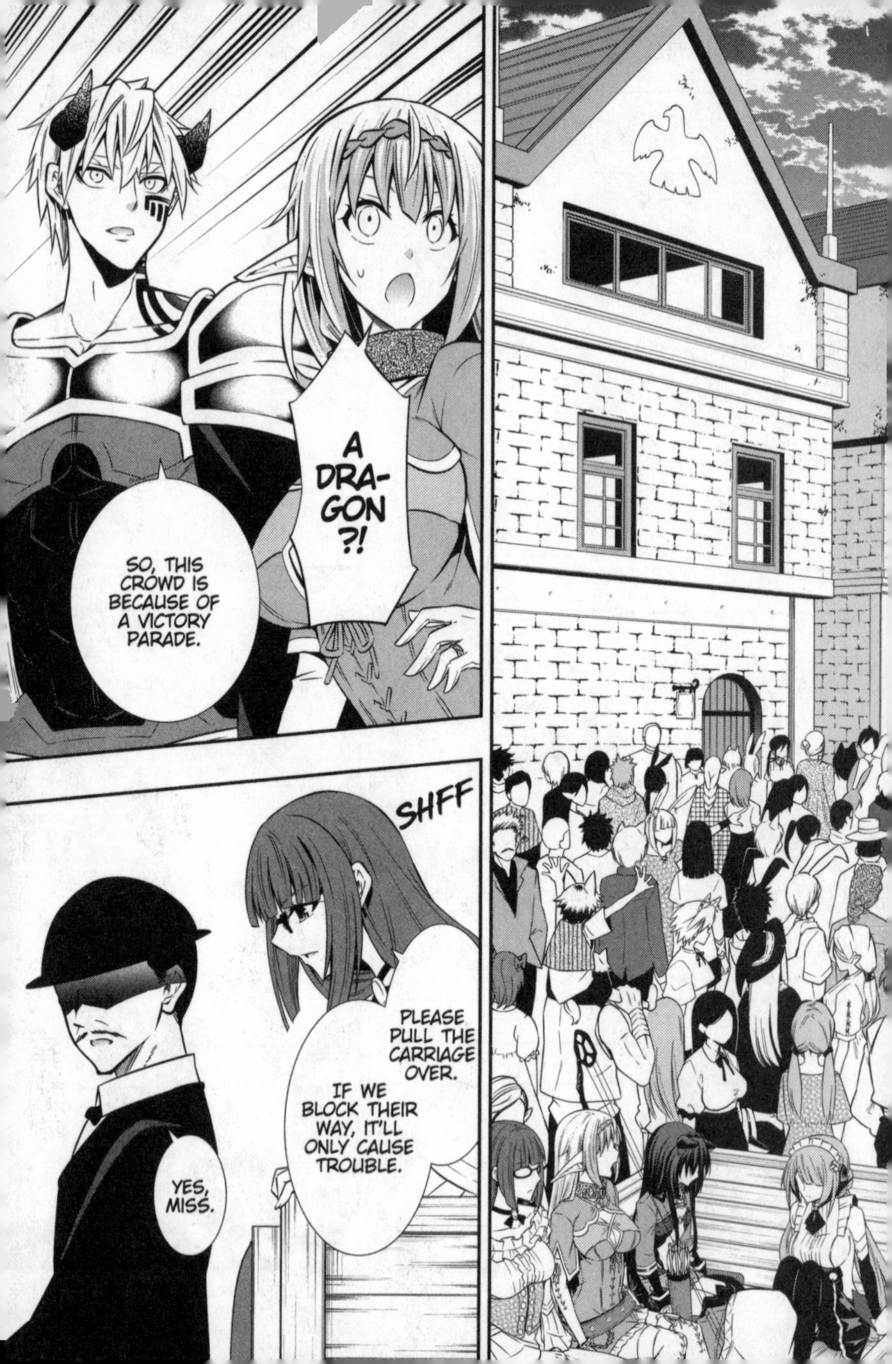
A DRA-GON?!
SO, THIS CROWD IS BECAUSE OF A VICTORY PARADE.
SHFF
PLEASE PULL THE CARRIAGE OVER.
IF WE BLOCK THEIR WAY, IT'LL ONLY CAUSE TROUBLE.
YES, MISS.

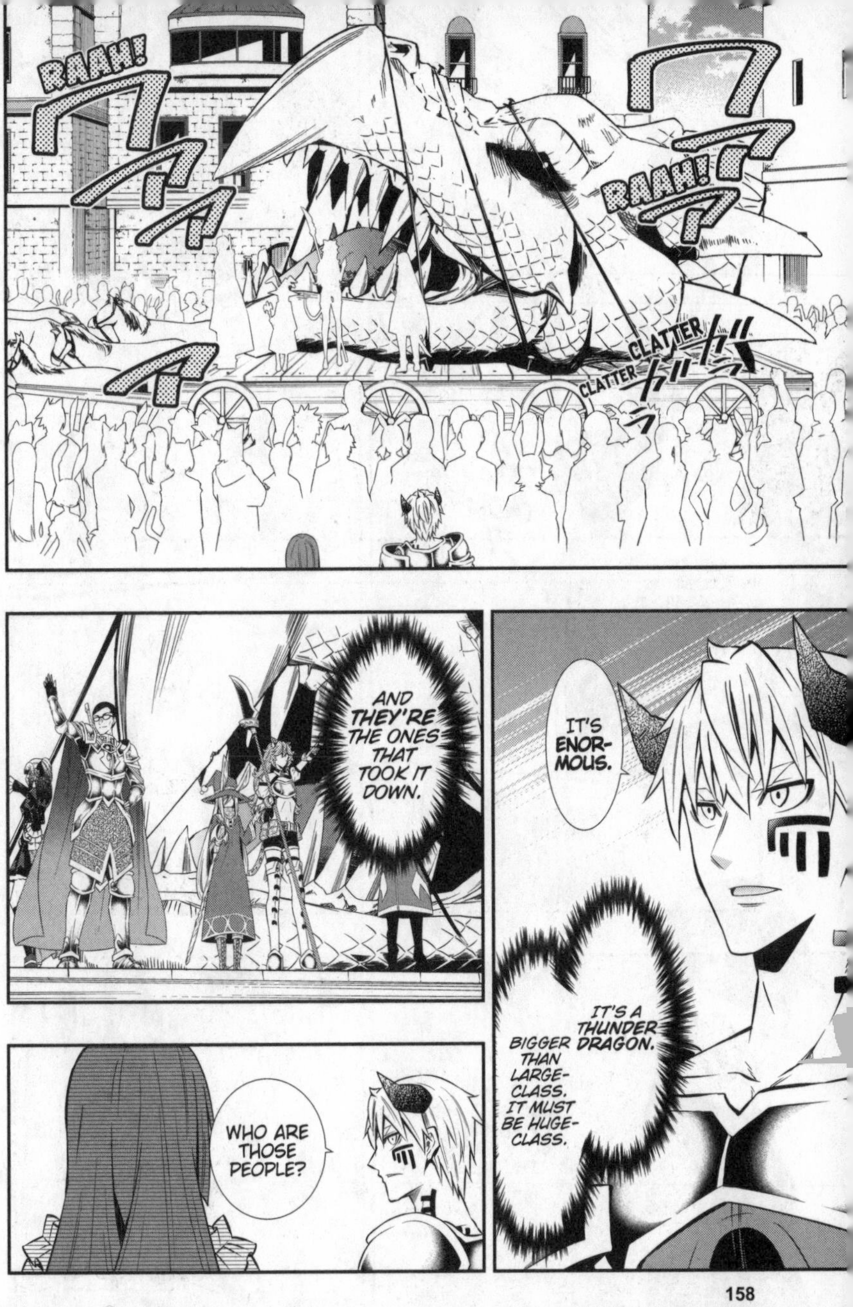
RAAH!
RAAH!
CLATTER CLATTER
IT'S ENORMOUS.
IT'S A THUNDER DRAGON.
BIGGER THAN LARGE-CLASS. IT MUST BE HUGE-CLASS.
AND THEY'RE THE ONES THAT TOOK IT DOWN.
WHO ARE THOSE PEOPLE?

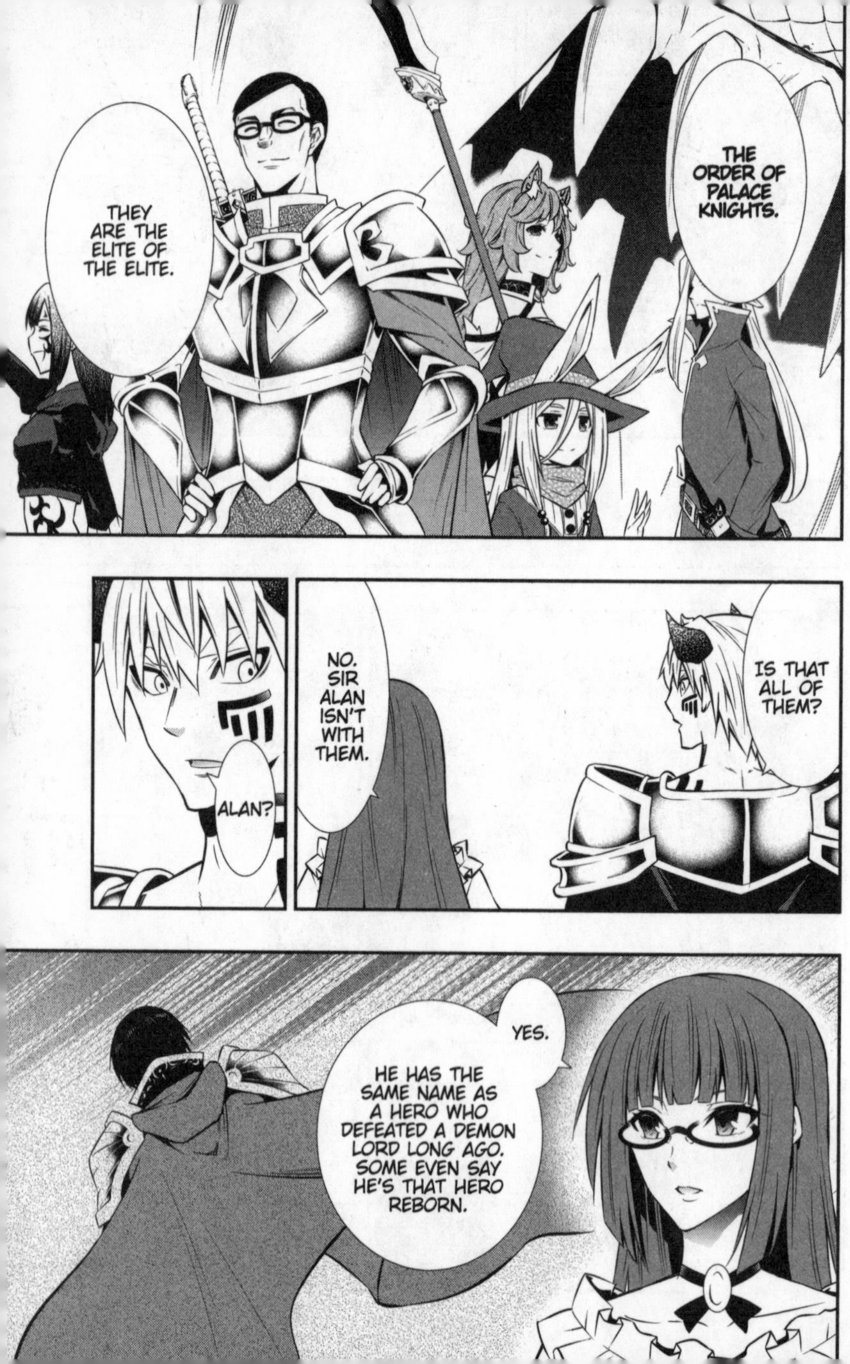
THE ORDER OF PALACE KNIGHTS.
THEY ARE THE ELITE OF THE ELITE.
IS THAT ALL OF THEM?
NO. SIR ALAN ISN'T WITH THEM.
ALAN?
YES.
HE HAS THE SAME NAME AS A HERO WHO DEFEATED A DEMON LORD LONG AGO. SOME EVEN SAY HE'S THAT HERO REBORN.

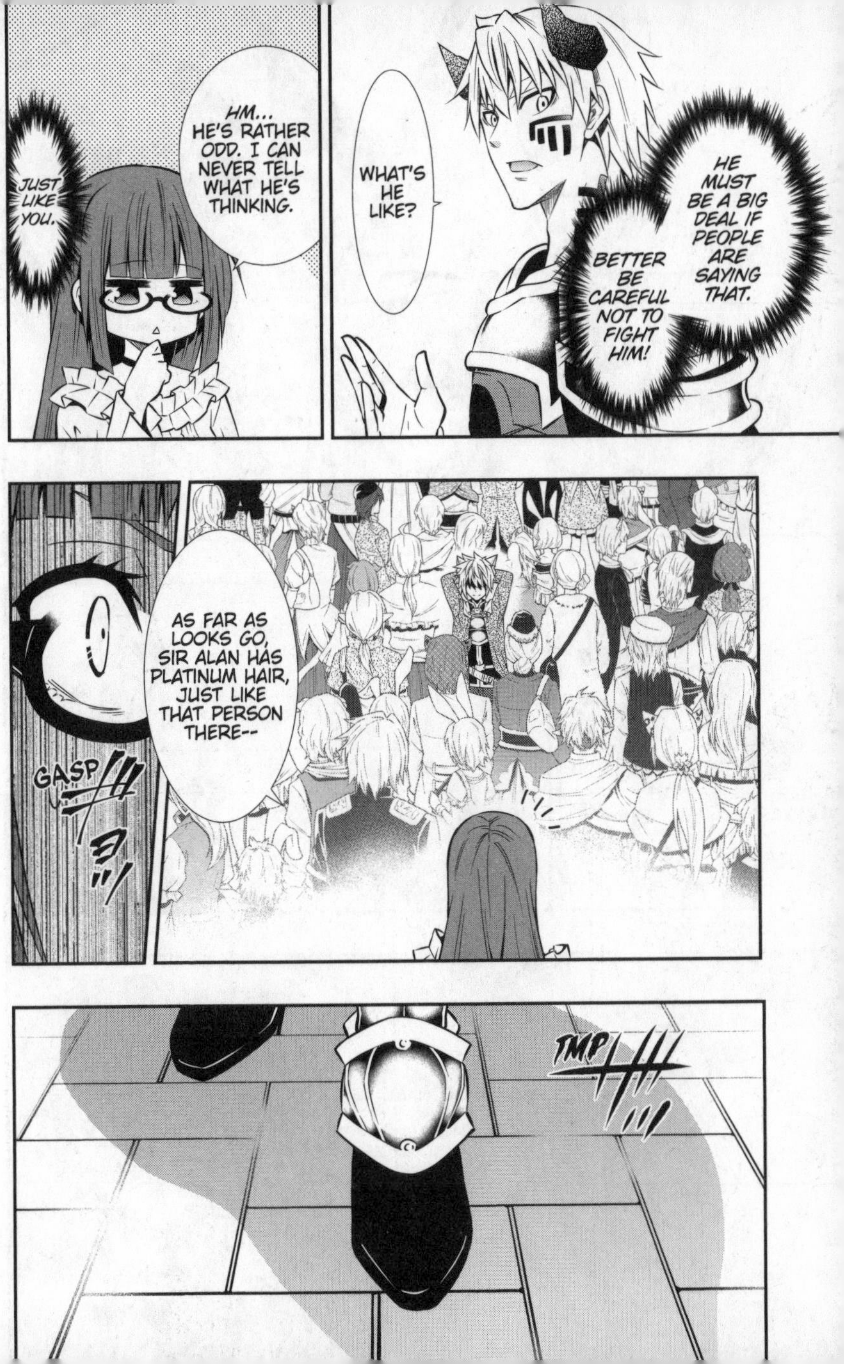
WHAT'S HE LIKE?
HE MUST BE A BIG DEAL IF PEOPLE ARE SAYING THAT.
BETTER BE CAREFUL NOT TO FIGHT HIM!
HM... HE'S RATHER ODD. I CAN NEVER TELL WHAT HE'S THINKING.
JUST LIKE YOU.
AS FAR AS LOOKS GO, SIR ALAN HAS PLATINUM HAIR, JUST LIKE THAT PERSON THERE--
GASP
TMP

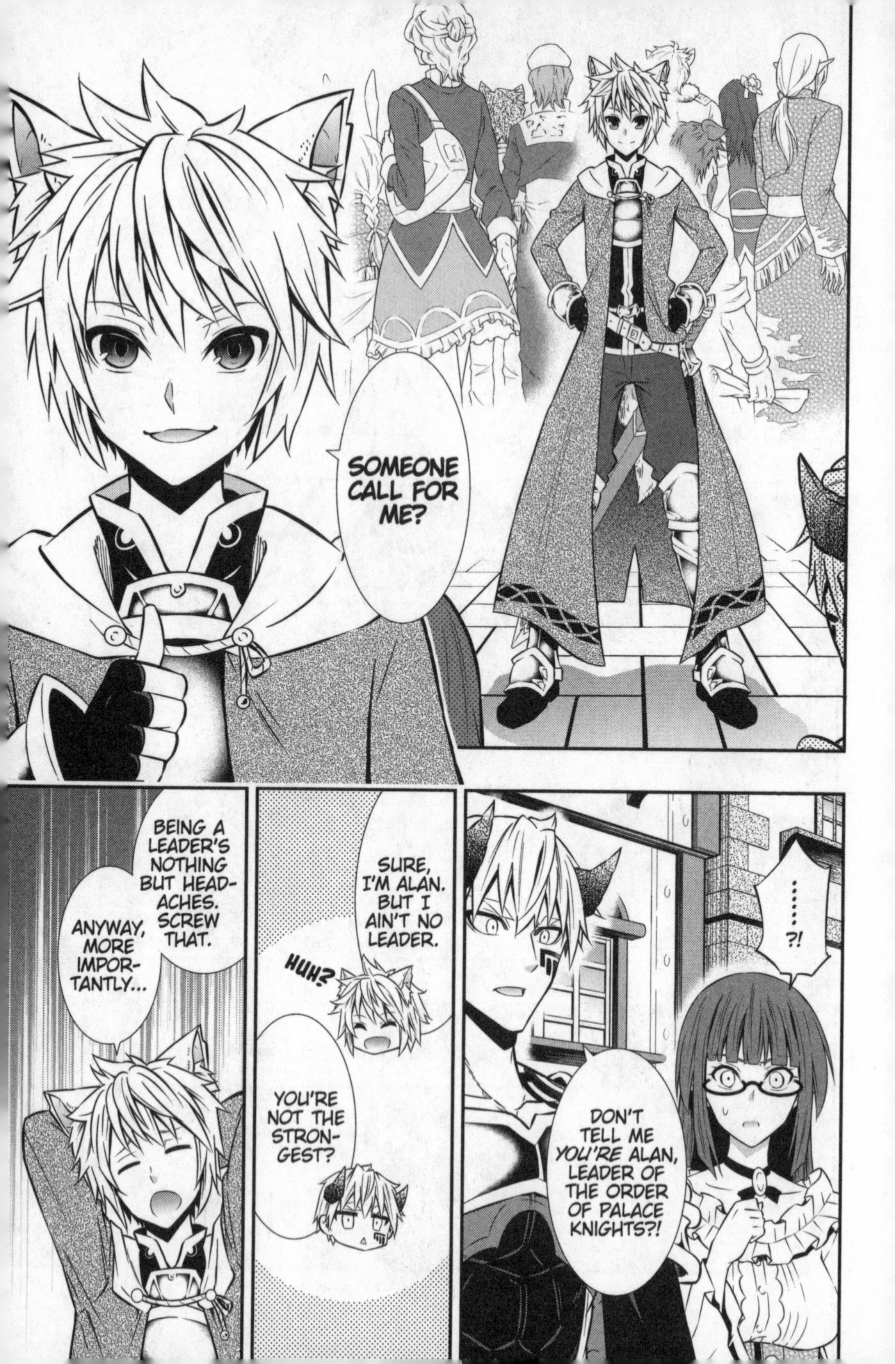
SOMEONE CALL FOR ME?
......?!
DON'T TELL ME YOU'RE ALAN, LEADER OF THE ORDER OF PALACE KNIGHTS?!
SURE, I'M ALAN. BUT I AIN'T NO LEADER.
HUH?
YOU'RE NOT THE STRONGEST?
BEING A LEADER'S NOTHING BUT HEADACHES. SCREW THAT.
ANYWAY, MORE IMPORTANTLY...

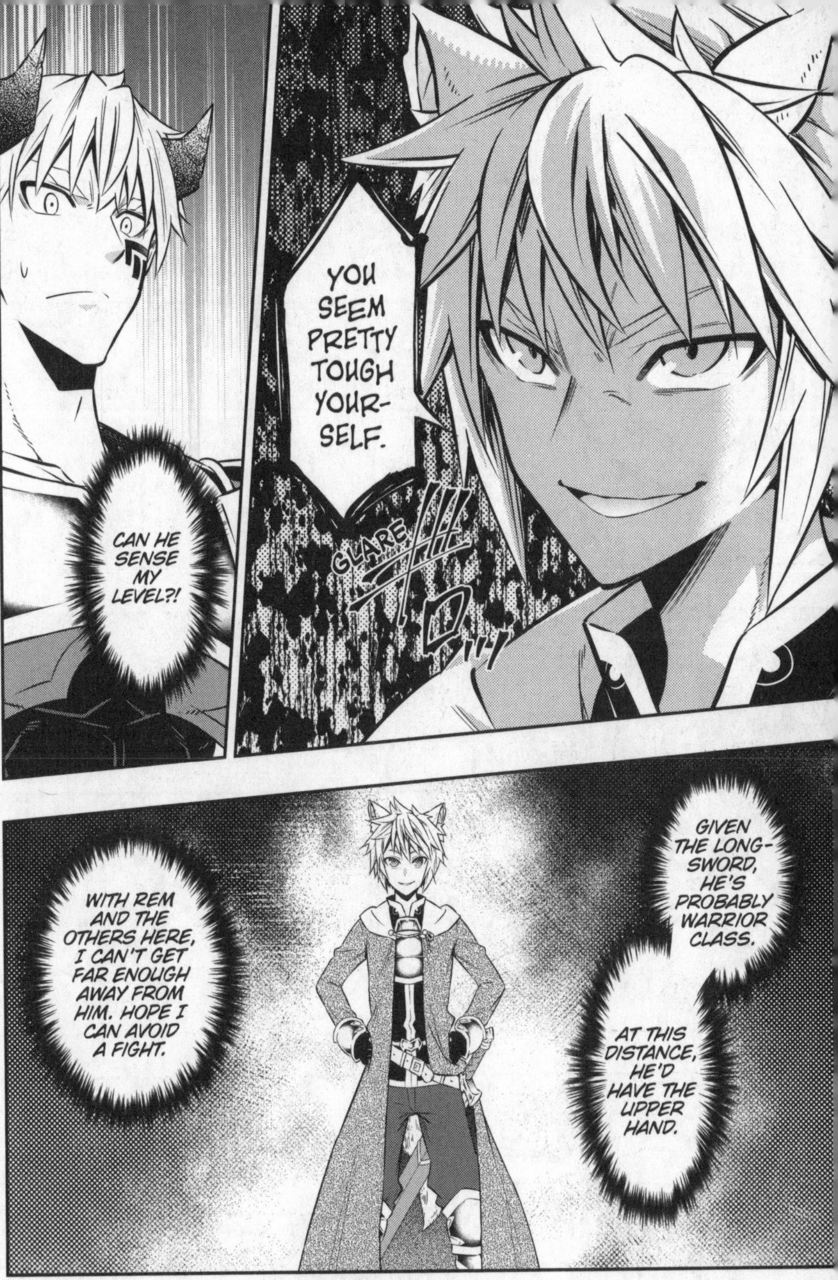
YOU SEEM PRETTY TOUGH YOURSELF.
GLARE
CAN HE SENSE MY LEVEL?!
GIVEN THE LONGSWORD, HE'S PROBABLY WARRIOR CLASS.
AT THIS DISTANCE, HE'D HAVE THE UPPER HAND.
WITH REM AND THE OTHERS HERE, I CAN'T GET FAR ENOUGH AWAY FROM HIM. HOPE I CAN AVOID A FIGHT.

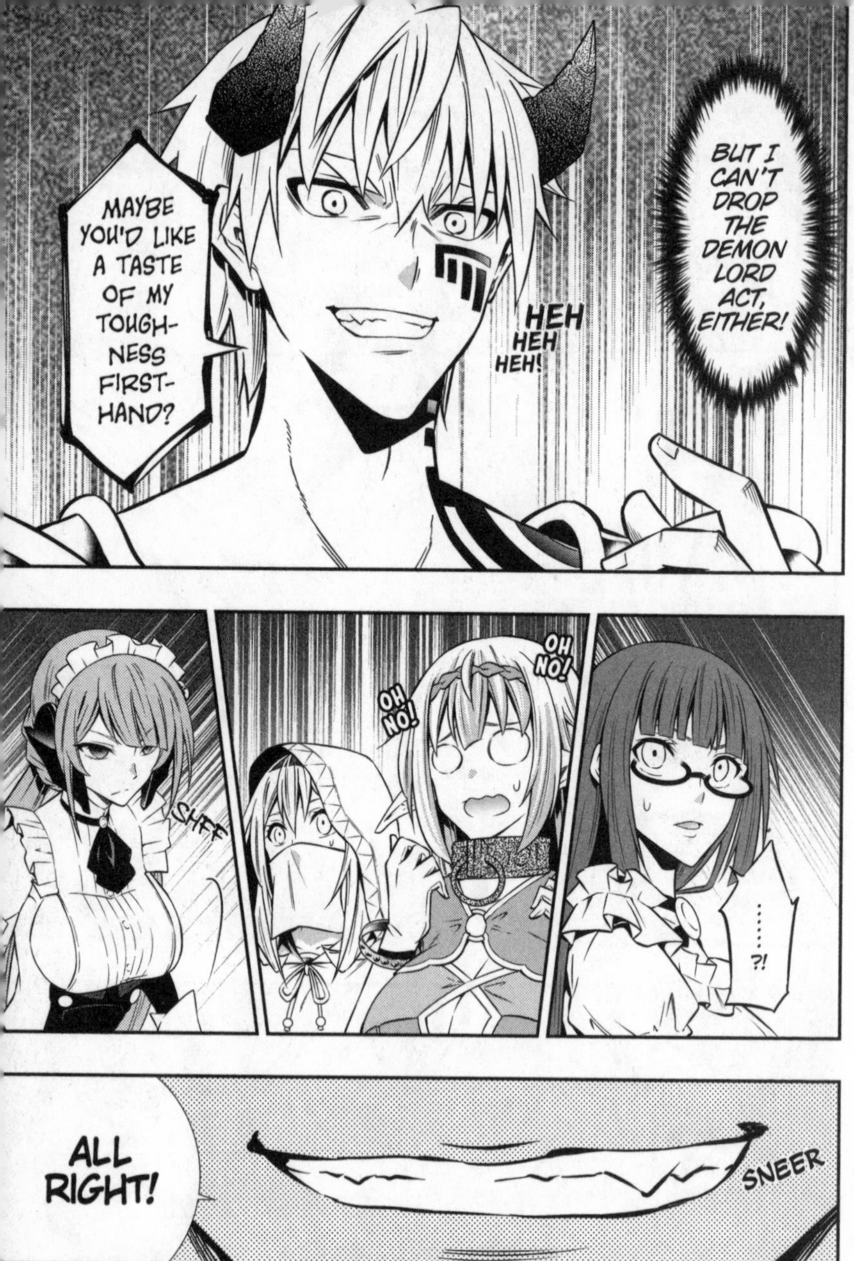
BUT I CAN'T DROP THE DEMON LORD ACT, EITHER!
HEH HEH HEH!
MAYBE YOU'D LIKE A TASTE OF MY TOUGH-NESS FIRST-HAND?
......?!
OH NO!
OH NO!
SHFF
SNEER
ALL RIGHT!

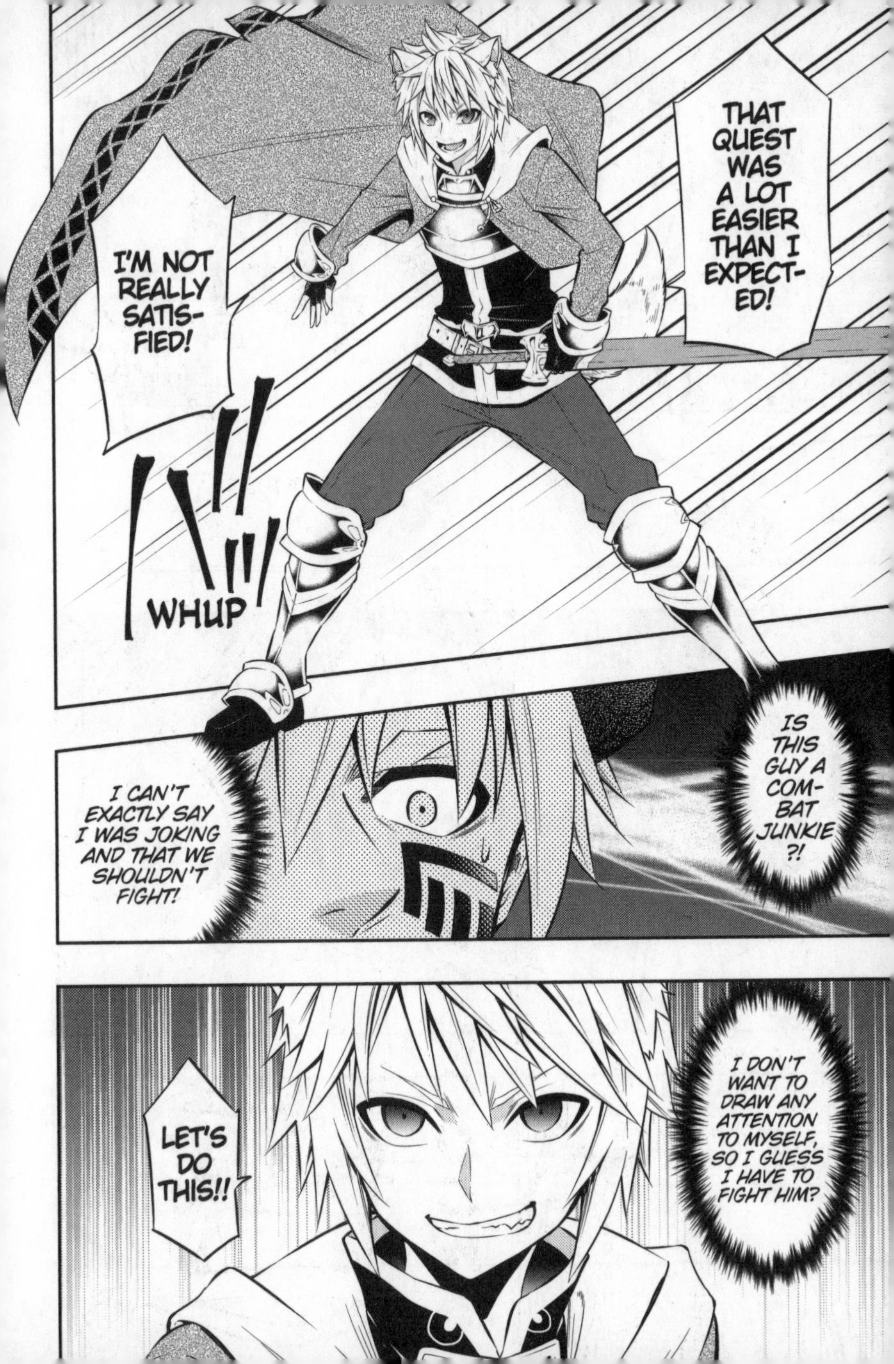
THAT QUEST WAS A LOT EASIER THAN I EXPECTED!
I'M NOT REALLY SATISFIED!
WHUP
IS THIS GUY A COMBAT JUNKIE?!
I CAN'T EXACTLY SAY I WAS JOKING AND THAT WE SHOULDN'T FIGHT!
I DON'T WANT TO DRAW ANY ATTENTION TO MYSELF, SO I GUESS I HAVE TO FIGHT HIM?
LET'S DO THIS!!

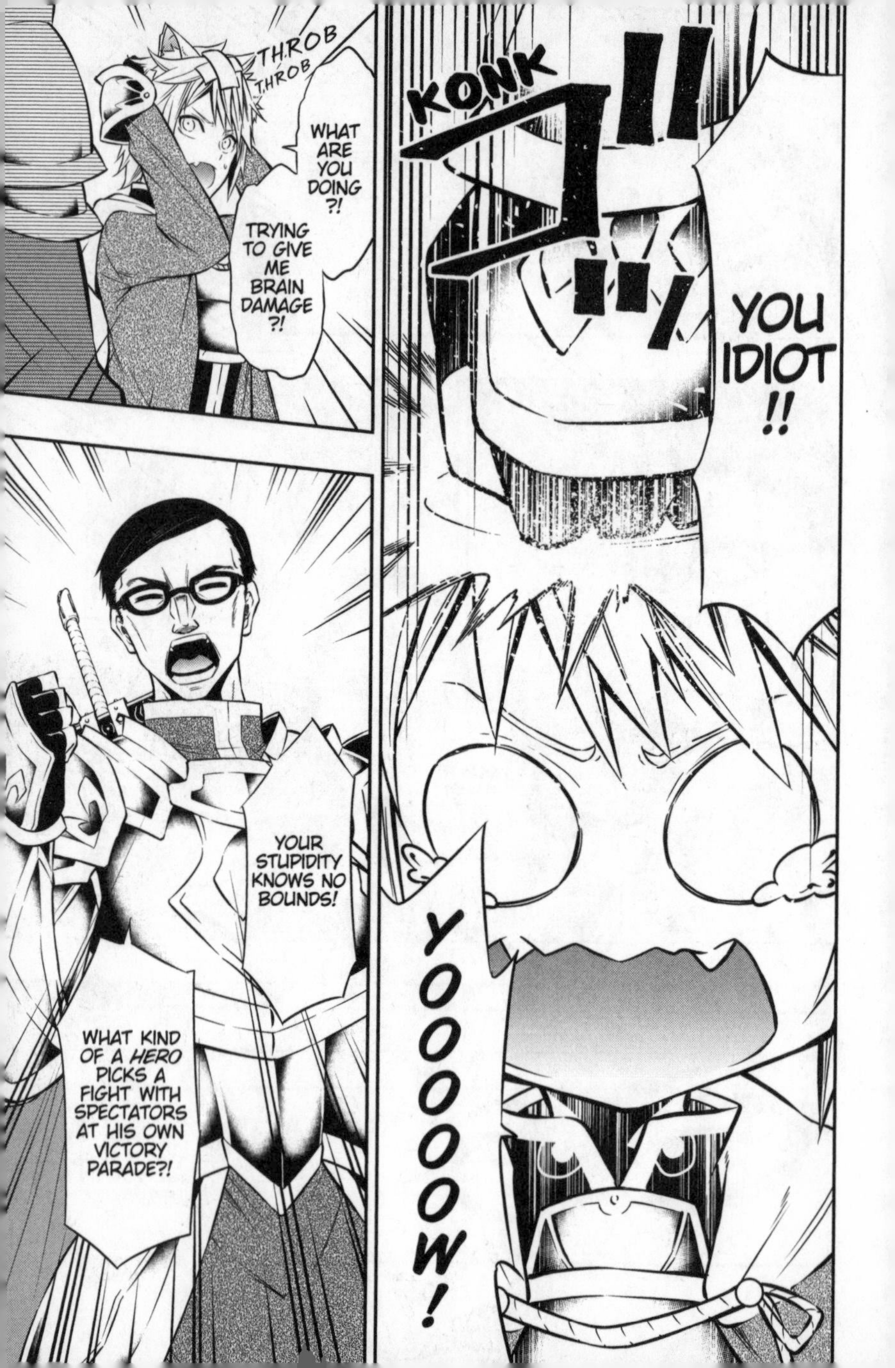
KONK
YOU IDIOT!!
YOOOOOW!
THROB THROB
WHAT ARE YOU DOING?!
TRYING TO GIVE ME BRAIN DAMAGE?!
YOUR STUPIDITY KNOWS NO BOUNDS!
WHAT KIND OF A *HERO* PICKS A FIGHT WITH SPECTATORS AT HIS OWN VICTORY PARADE?!

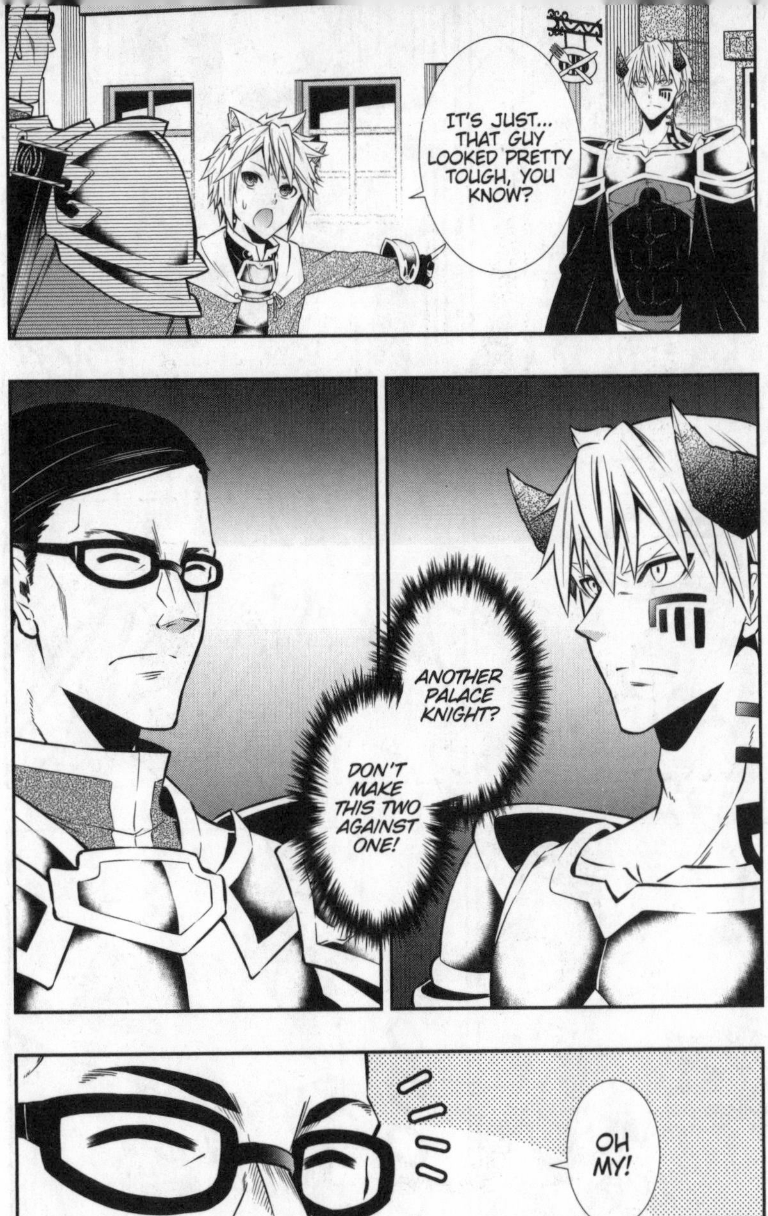
IT'S JUST... THAT GUY LOOKED PRETTY TOUGH, YOU KNOW?
ANOTHER PALACE KNIGHT?
DON'T MAKE THIS TWO AGAINST ONE!
OH MY!

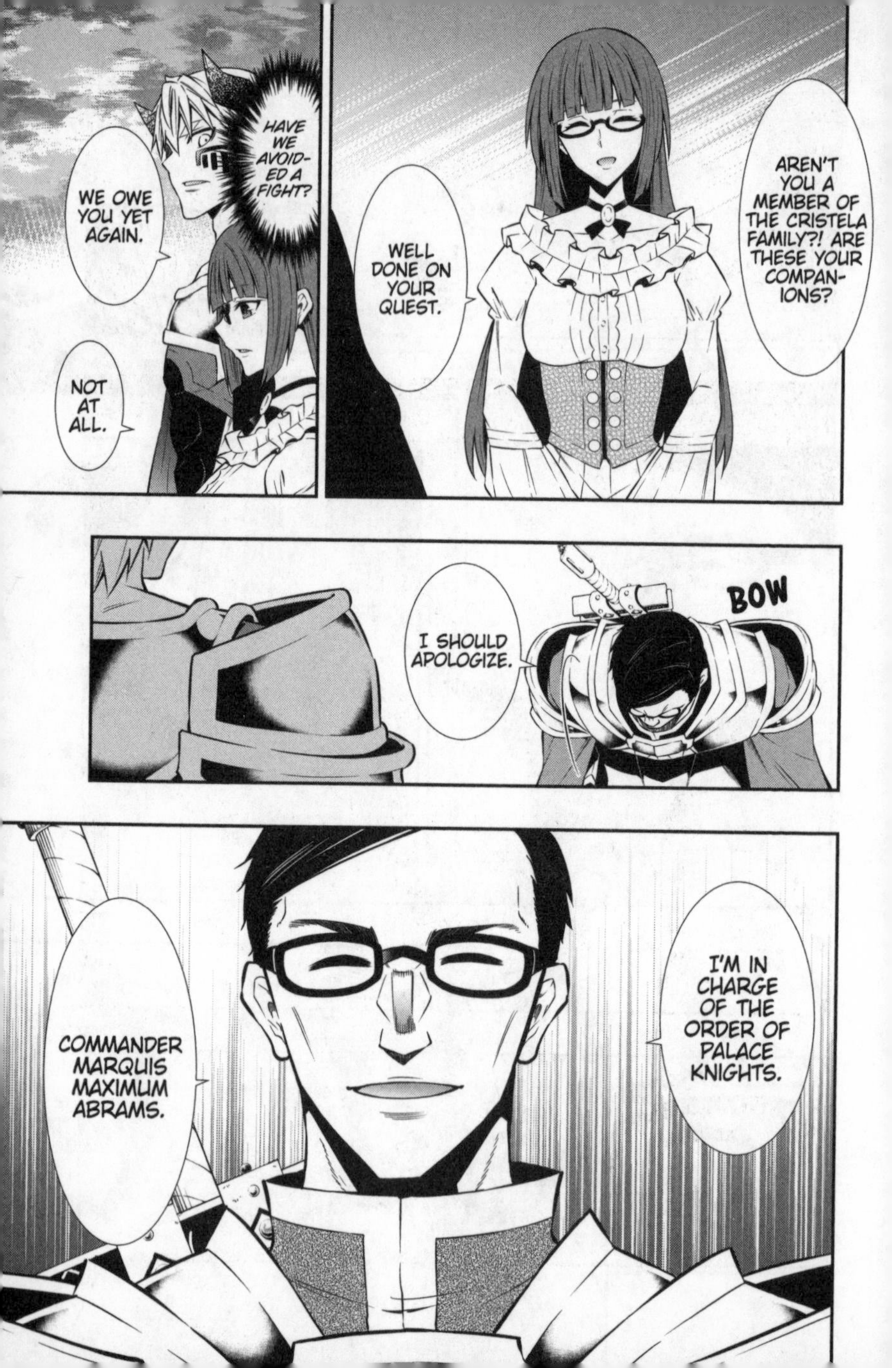
AREN'T YOU A MEMBER OF THE CRISTELA FAMILY?! ARE THESE YOUR COMPANIONS?
WELL DONE ON YOUR QUEST.
HAVE WE AVOIDED A FIGHT?
WE OWE YOU YET AGAIN.
NOT AT ALL.
BOW
I SHOULD APOLOGIZE.
I'M IN CHARGE OF THE ORDER OF PALACE KNIGHTS.
COMMANDER MARQUIS MAXIMUM ABRAMS.

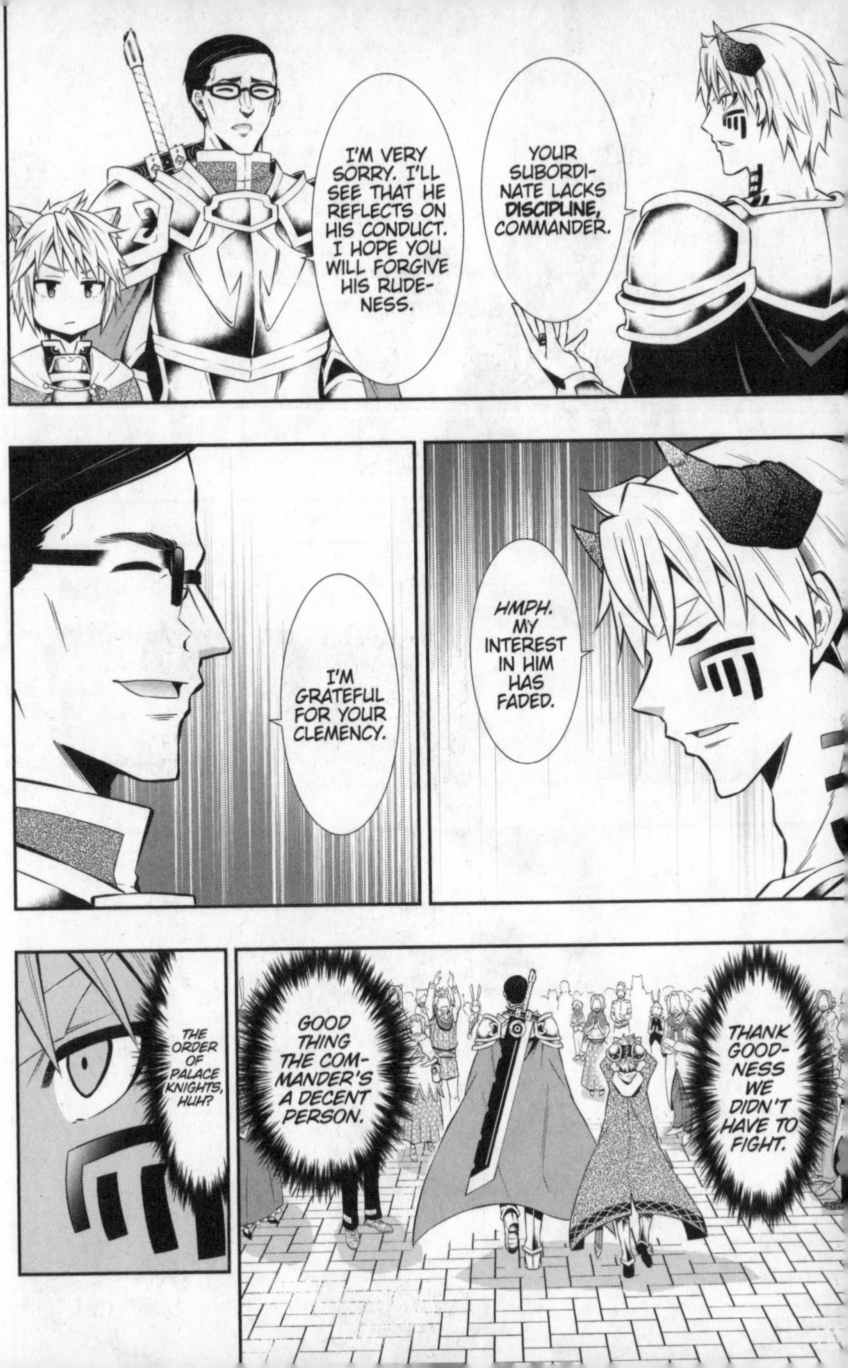
YOUR SUBORDINATE LACKS **DISCIPLINE**, COMMANDER.
I'M VERY SORRY. I'LL SEE THAT HE REFLECTS ON HIS CONDUCT. I HOPE YOU WILL FORGIVE HIS RUDENESS.
HMPH. MY INTEREST IN HIM HAS FADED.
I'M GRATEFUL FOR YOUR CLEMENCY.
THANK GOODNESS WE DIDN'T HAVE TO FIGHT.
GOOD THING THE COMMANDER'S A DECENT PERSON.
THE ORDER OF PALACE KNIGHTS, HUH?

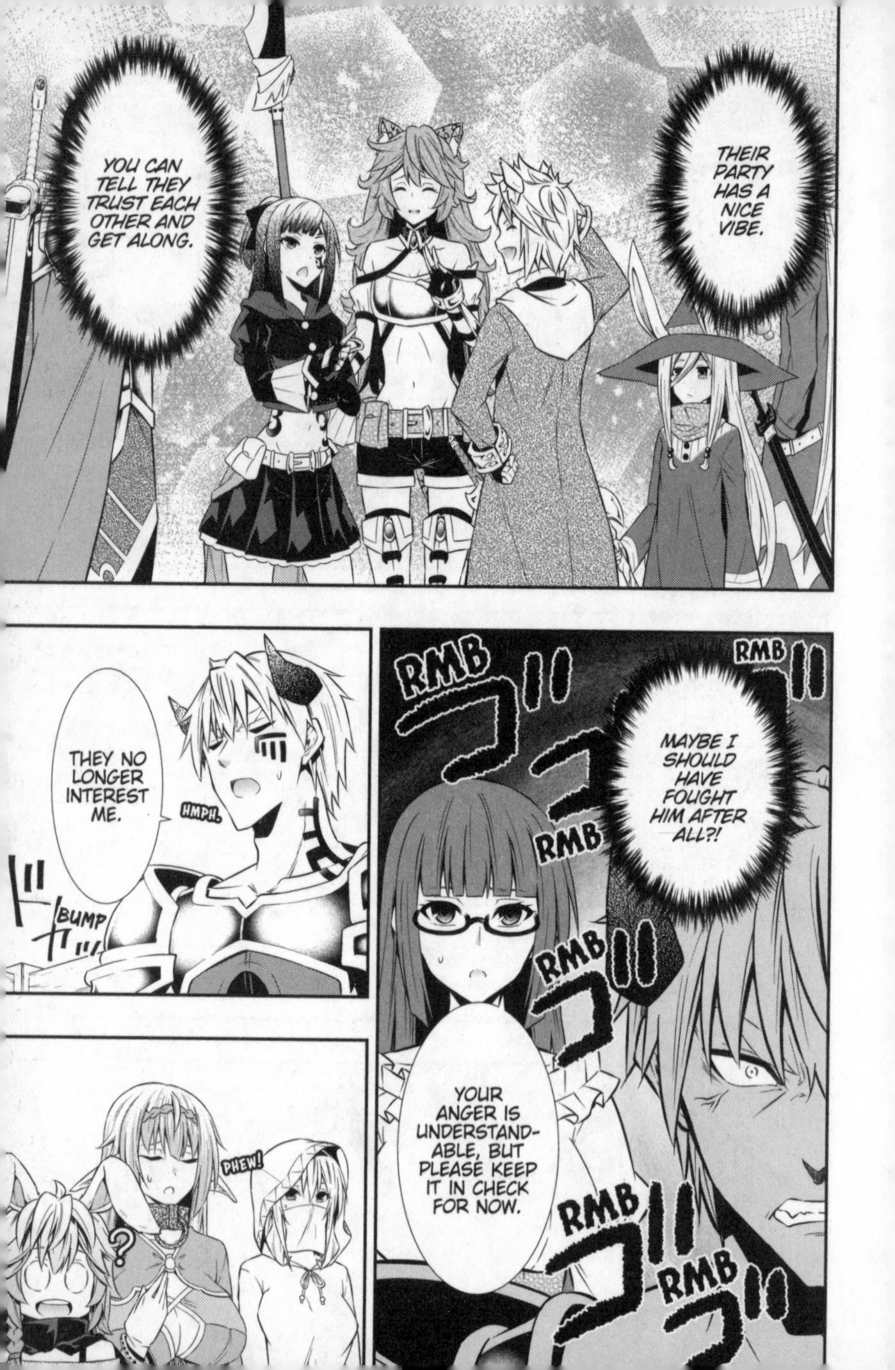
THEIR PARTY HAS A NICE VIBE.
YOU CAN TELL THEY TRUST EACH OTHER AND GET ALONG.
RMB
RMB
MAYBE I SHOULD HAVE FOUGHT HIM AFTER ALL?!
RMB
RMB
YOUR ANGER IS UNDERSTAND-ABLE, BUT PLEASE KEEP IT IN CHECK FOR NOW.
RMB
RMB
THEY NO LONGER INTEREST ME.
HMPH.
BUMP
PHEW!

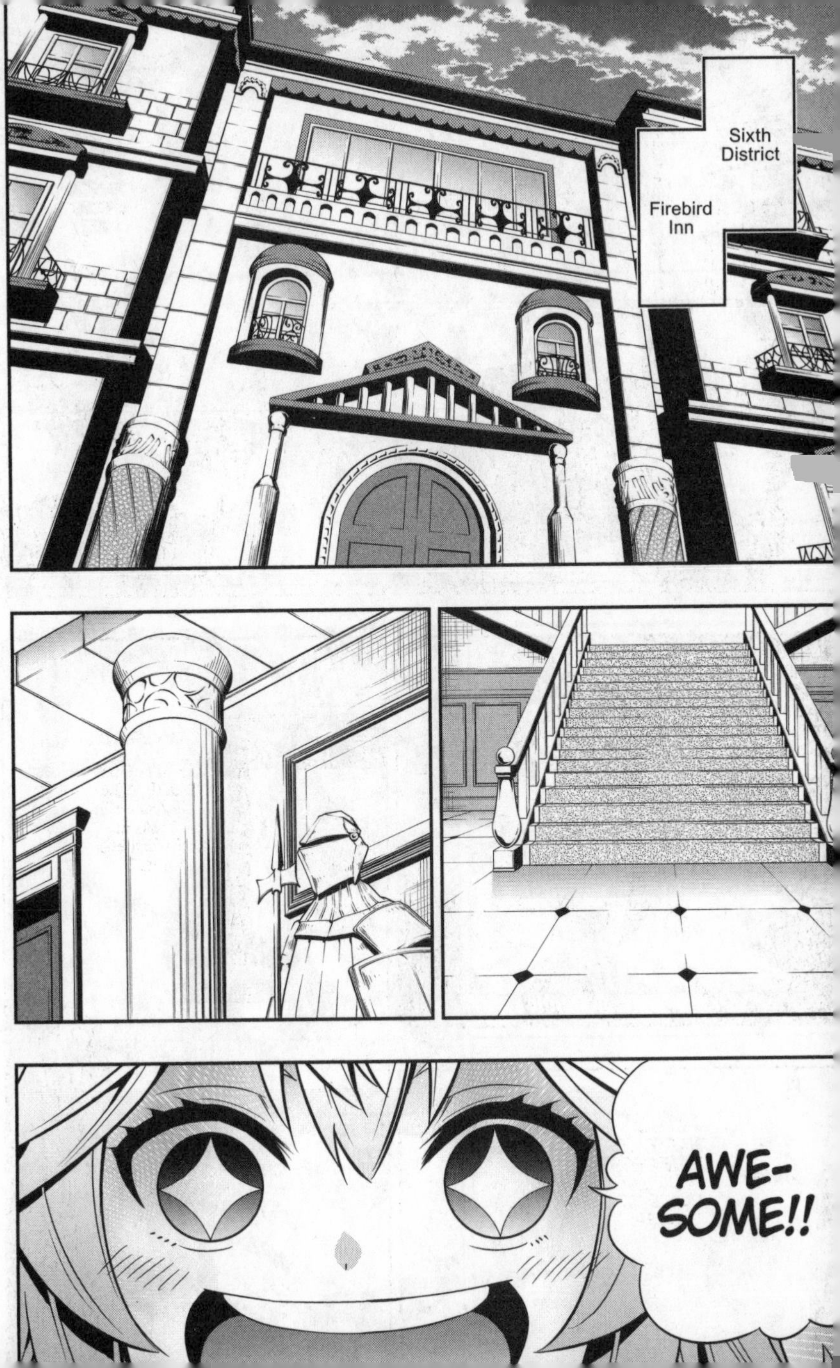
Sixth District
Firebird Inn
AWE-SOME!!

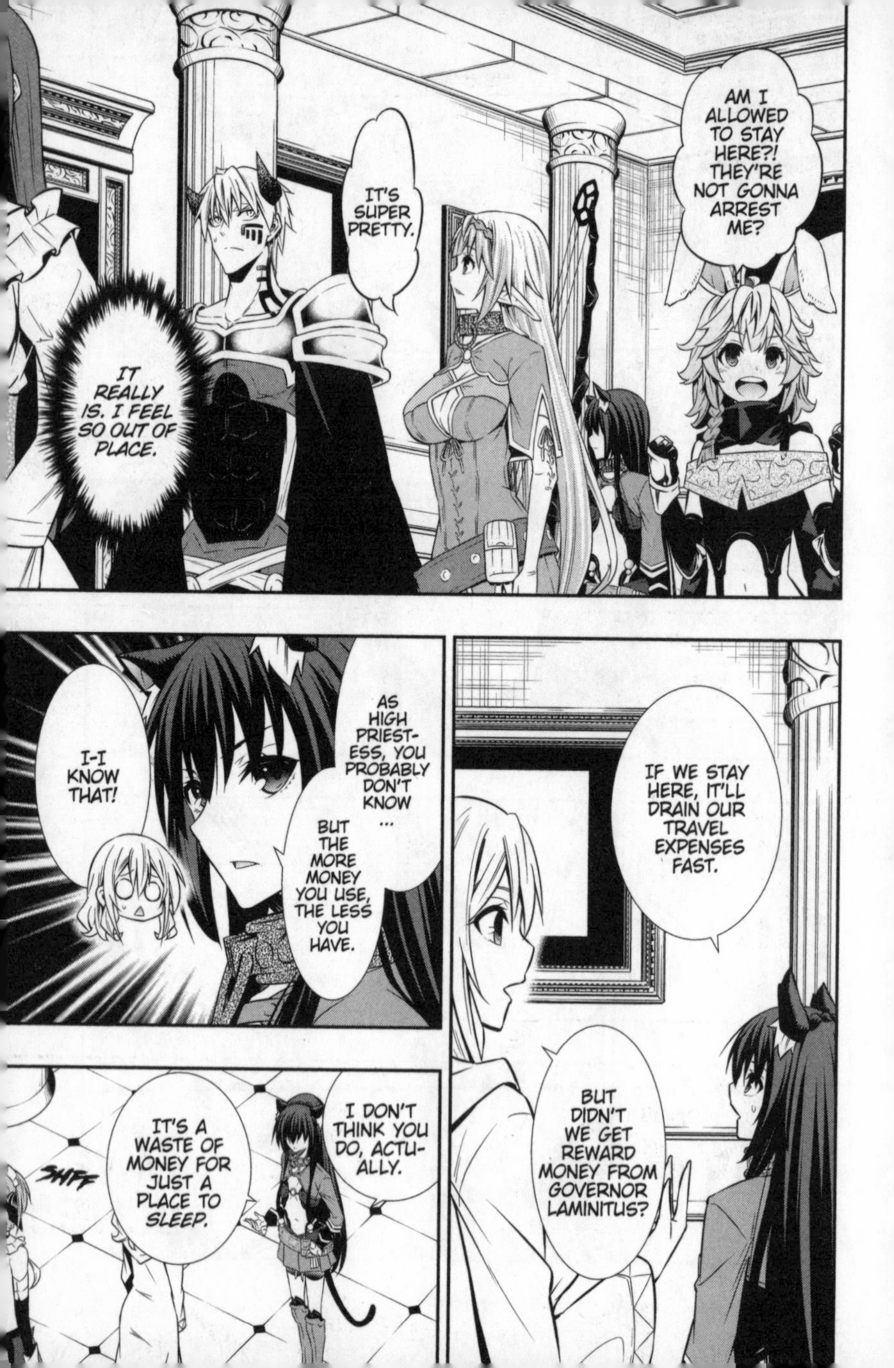
AM I ALLOWED TO STAY HERE?! THEY'RE NOT GONNA ARREST ME?
IT'S SUPER PRETTY.
IT REALLY IS. I FEEL SO OUT OF PLACE.
IF WE STAY HERE, IT'LL DRAIN OUR TRAVEL EXPENSES FAST.
BUT DIDN'T WE GET REWARD MONEY FROM GOVERNOR LAMINITUS?
AS HIGH PRIEST-ESS, YOU PROBABLY DON'T KNOW ...
BUT THE MORE MONEY YOU USE, THE LESS YOU HAVE.
I-I KNOW THAT!
I DON'T THINK YOU DO, ACTU-ALLY.
IT'S A WASTE OF MONEY FOR JUST A PLACE TO SLEEP.
SHFF

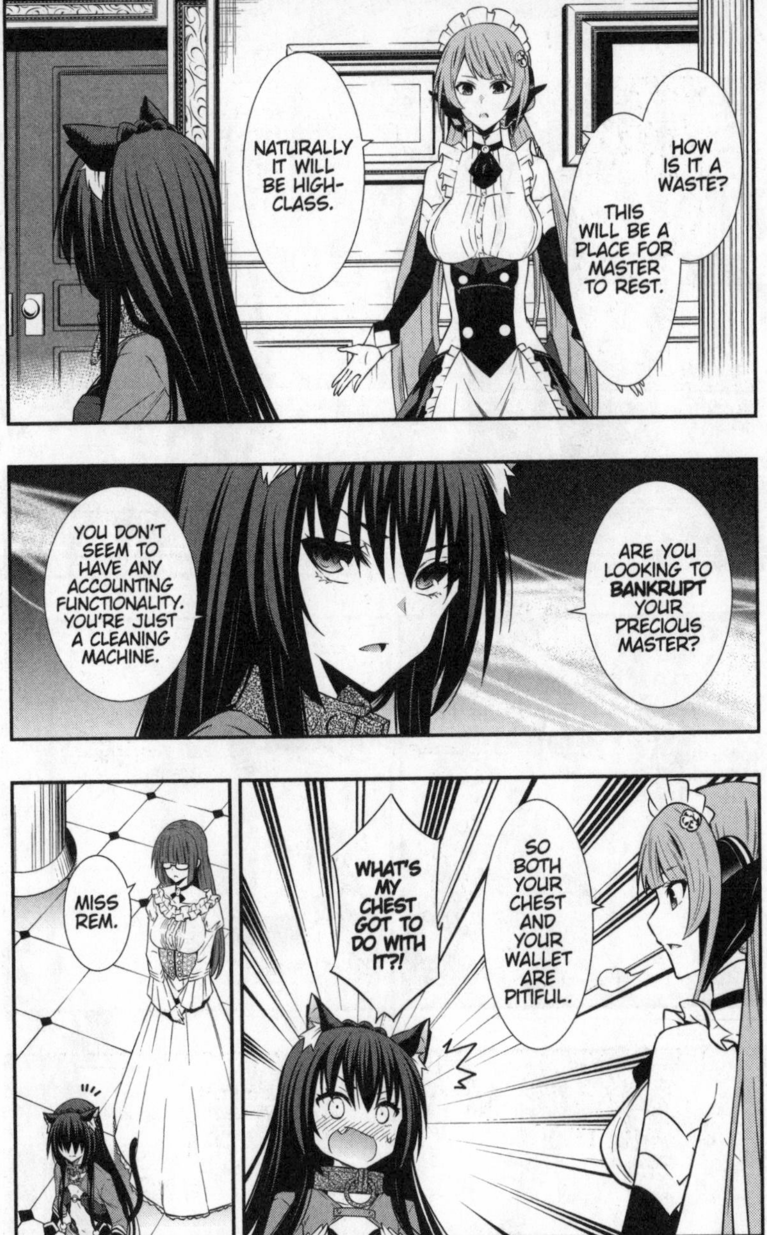
HOW IS IT A WASTE?
THIS WILL BE A PLACE FOR MASTER TO REST.
NATURALLY IT WILL BE HIGH-CLASS.
ARE YOU LOOKING TO BANKRUPT YOUR PRECIOUS MASTER?
YOU DON'T SEEM TO HAVE ANY ACCOUNTING FUNCTIONALITY. YOU'RE JUST A CLEANING MACHINE.
SO BOTH YOUR CHEST AND YOUR WALLET ARE PITIFUL.
WHAT'S MY CHEST GOT TO DO WITH IT?!
MISS REM.

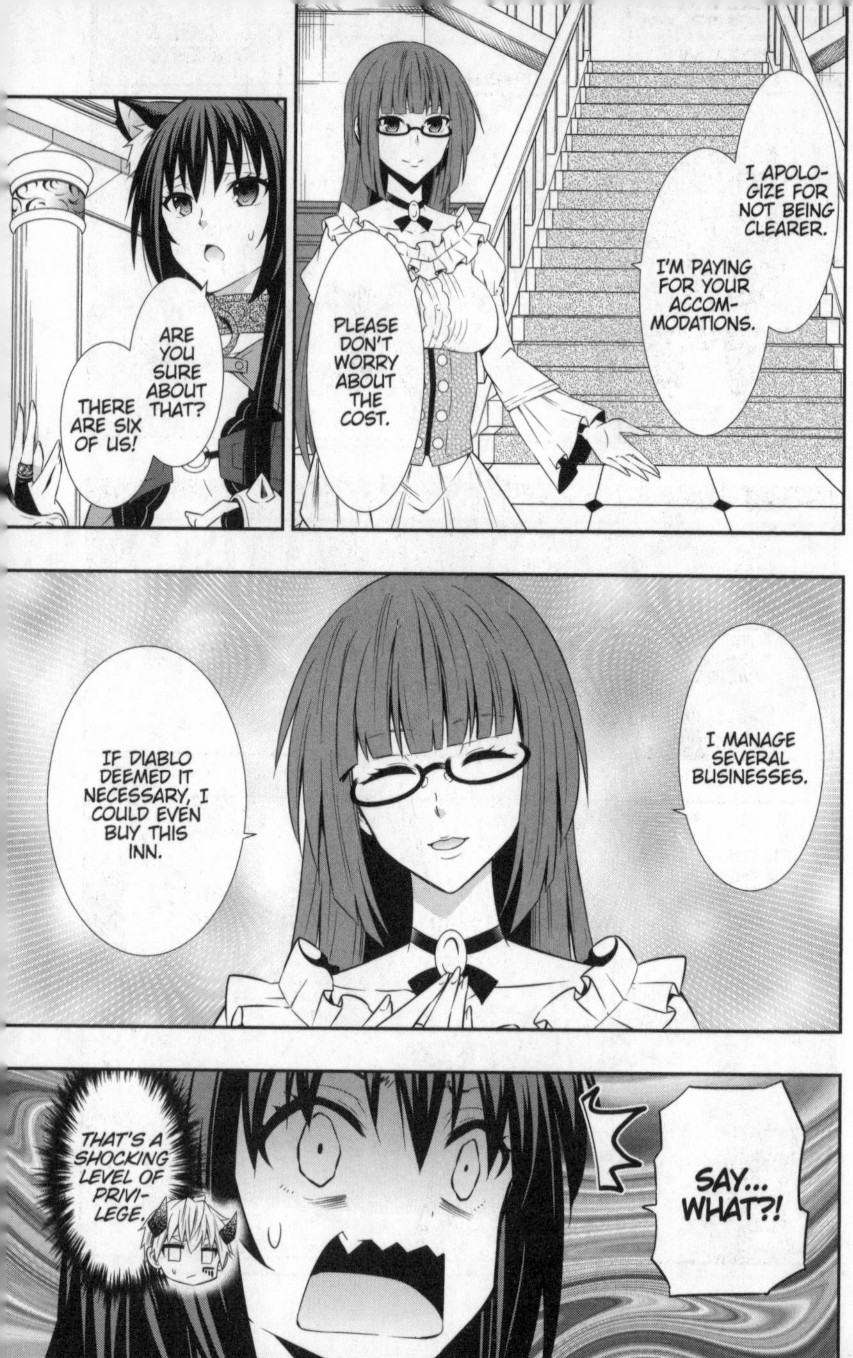
I APOLOGIZE FOR NOT BEING CLEARER.
I'M PAYING FOR YOUR ACCOMMODATIONS.
PLEASE DON'T WORRY ABOUT THE COST.
ARE YOU SURE ABOUT THAT?
THERE ARE SIX OF US!
I MANAGE SEVERAL BUSINESSES.
IF DIABLO DEEMED IT NECESSARY, I COULD EVEN BUY THIS INN.
SAY... WHAT?!
THAT'S A SHOCKING LEVEL OF PRIVILEGE.

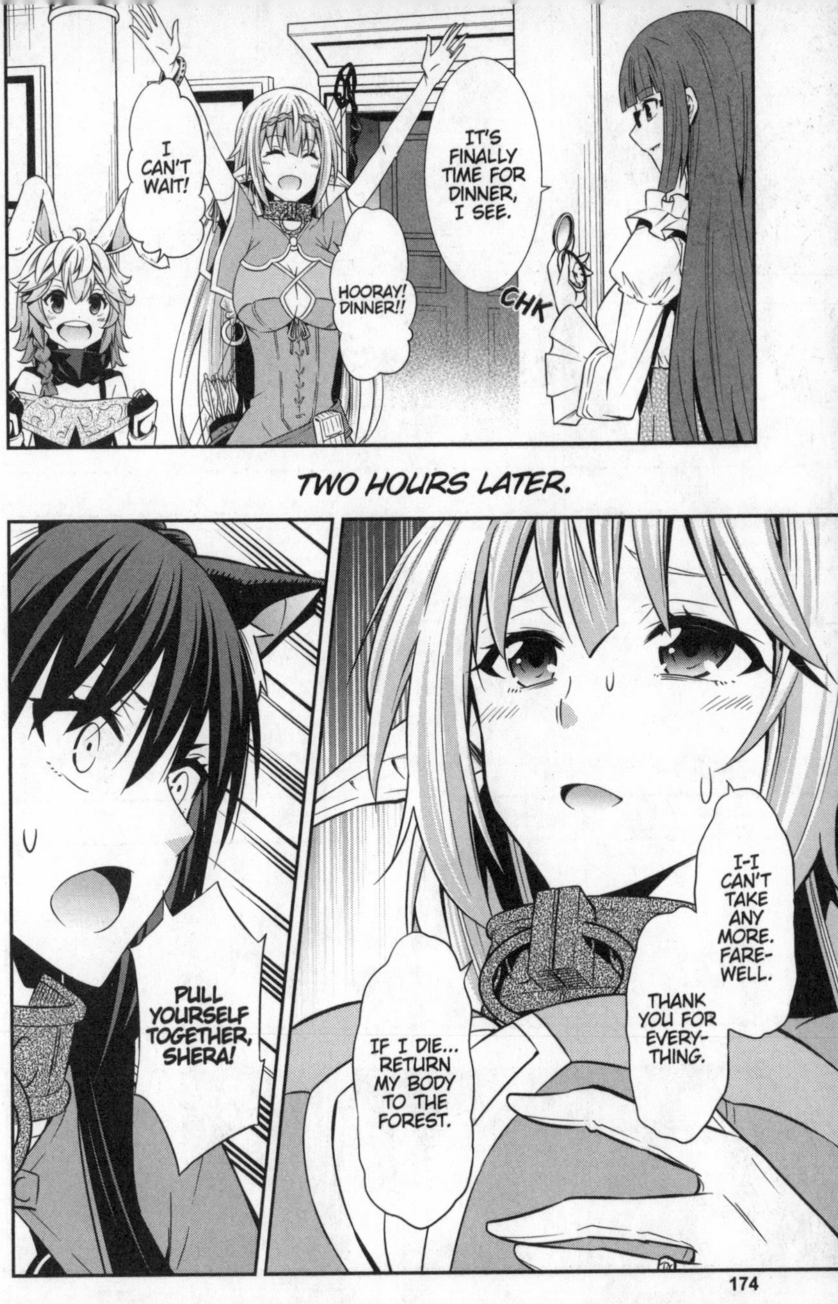
IT'S FINALLY TIME FOR DINNER, I SEE.
CHK
HOORAY! DINNER!!
I CAN'T WAIT!
TWO HOURS LATER.
I-I CAN'T TAKE ANY MORE. FARE-WELL.
THANK YOU FOR EVERY-THING.
IF I DIE... RETURN MY BODY TO THE FOREST.
PULL YOURSELF TOGETHER, SHERA!

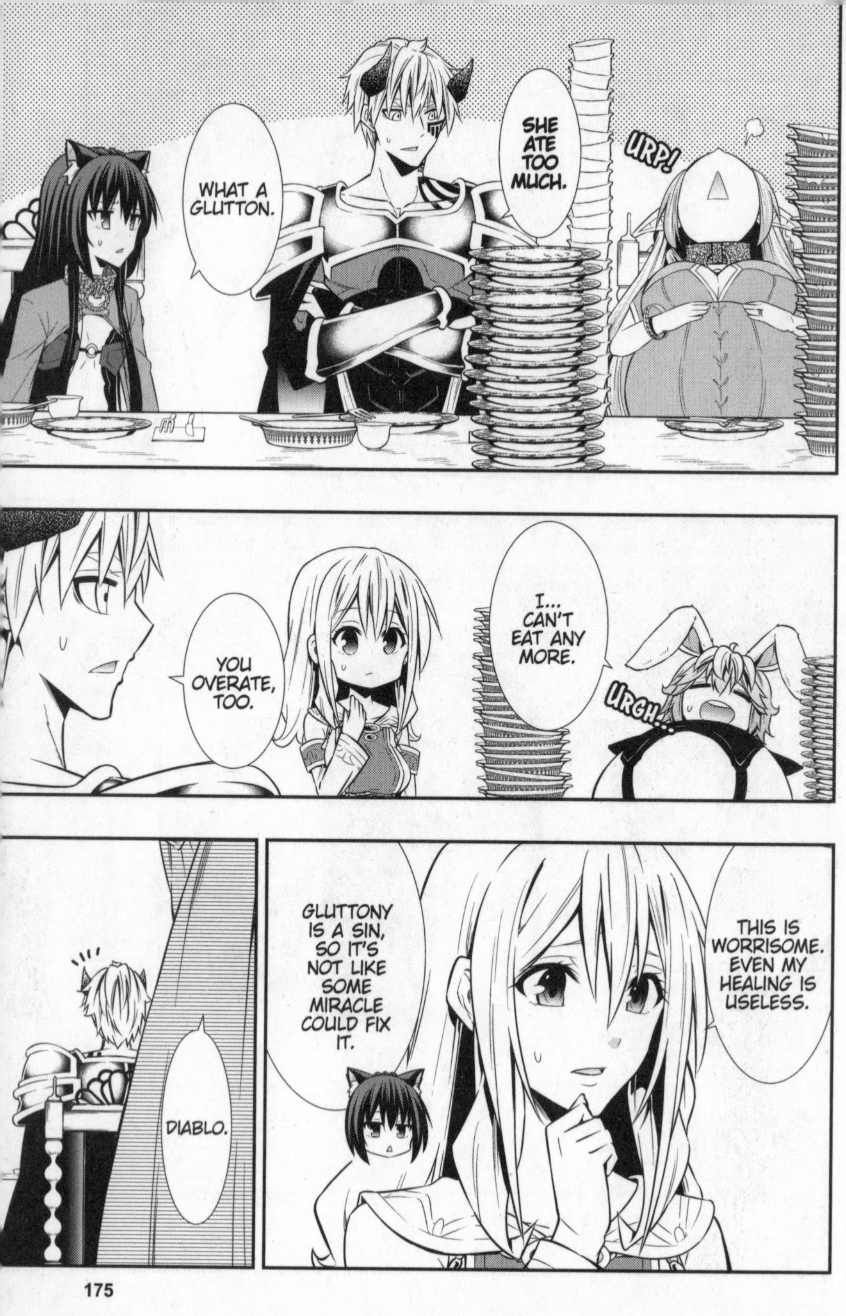
URP!
SHE ATE TOO MUCH.
WHAT A GLUTTON.
URGH...
I... CAN'T EAT ANY MORE.
YOU OVERATE, TOO.
THIS IS WORRISOME. EVEN MY HEALING IS USELESS.
GLUTTONY IS A SIN, SO IT'S NOT LIKE SOME MIRACLE COULD FIX IT.
DIABLO.

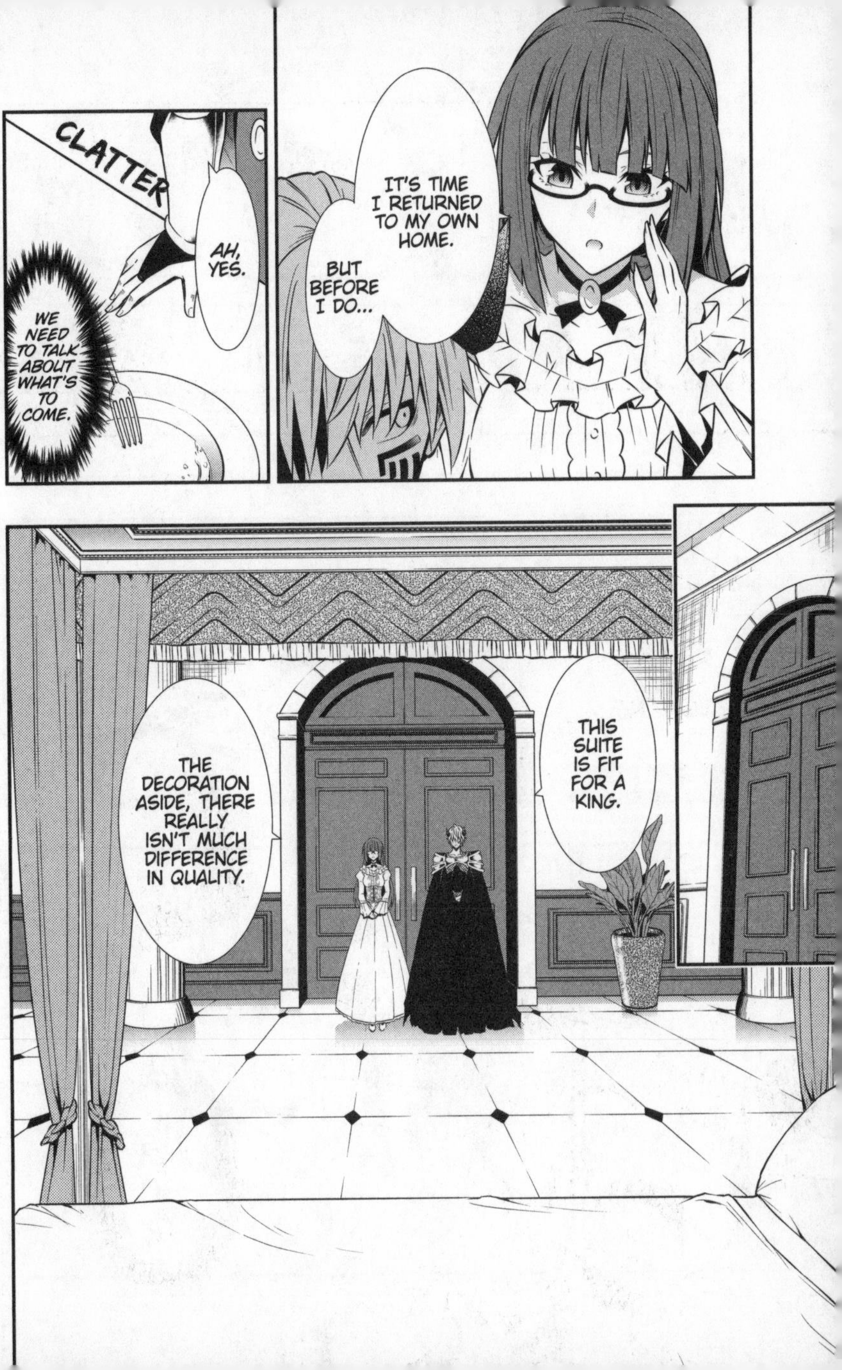
IT'S TIME I RETURNED TO MY OWN HOME.
BUT BEFORE I DO...
CLATTER
AH, YES.
WE NEED TO TALK ABOUT WHAT'S TO COME.
THIS SUITE IS FIT FOR A KING.
THE DECORATION ASIDE, THERE REALLY ISN'T MUCH DIFFERENCE IN QUALITY.

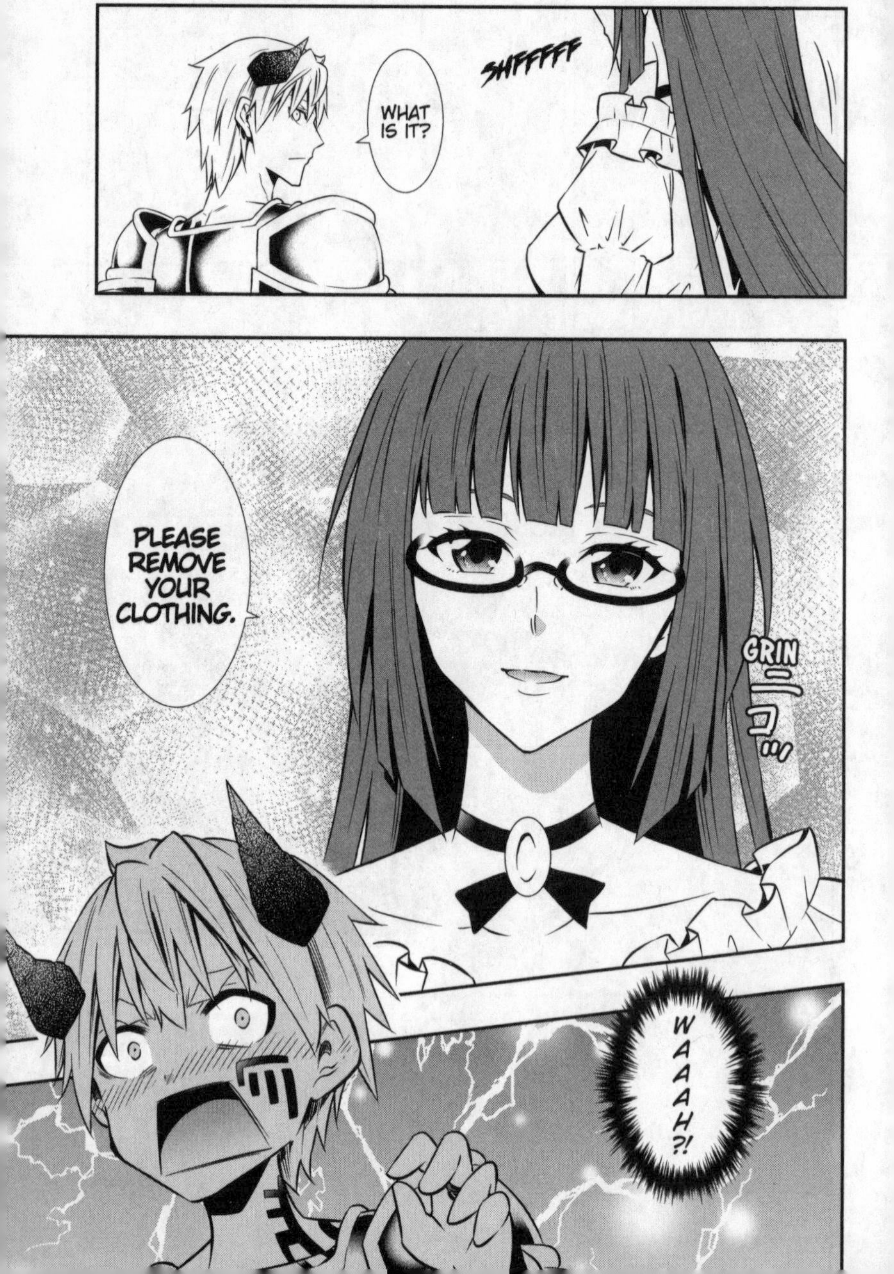
SHFFFFF
WHAT IS IT?
PLEASE REMOVE YOUR CLOTHING.
GRIN
ニコッ
WAAAAH?!

HOW NOT
TO SUMMON A
DEMON LORD

to be continued...

SPECIAL THANKS FOR VOLUME 13

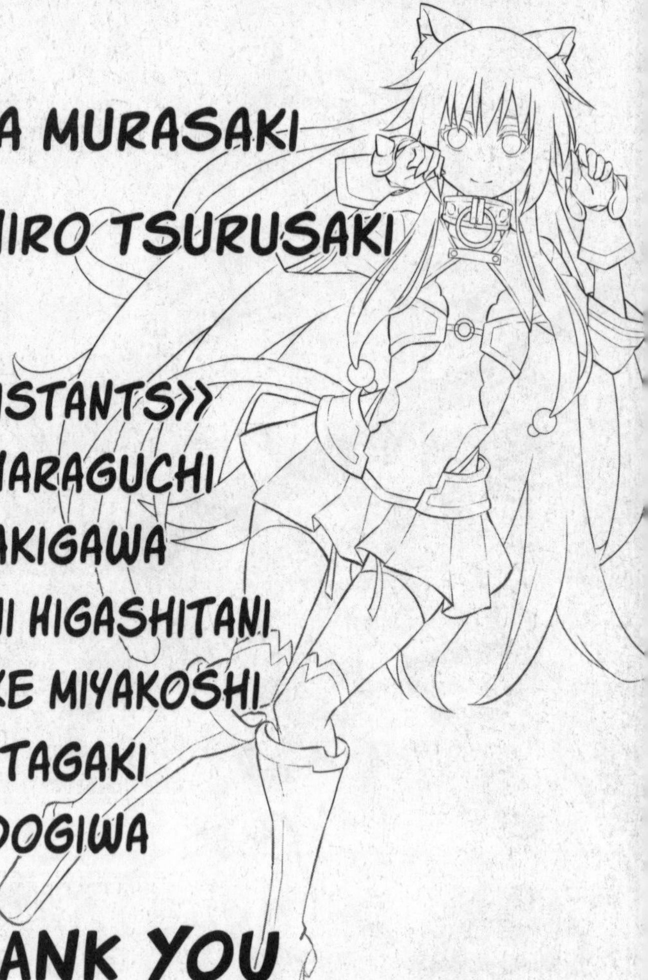

YUKIYA MURASAKI

TAKAHIRO TSURUSAKI

«ASSISTANTS»
DAIKI HARAGUCHI
YUU TAKIGAWA
MASUMI HIGASHITANI
DAISUKE MIYAKOSHI
MINA ITAGAKI
KOMADOGIWA

THANK YOU
FOR READING!

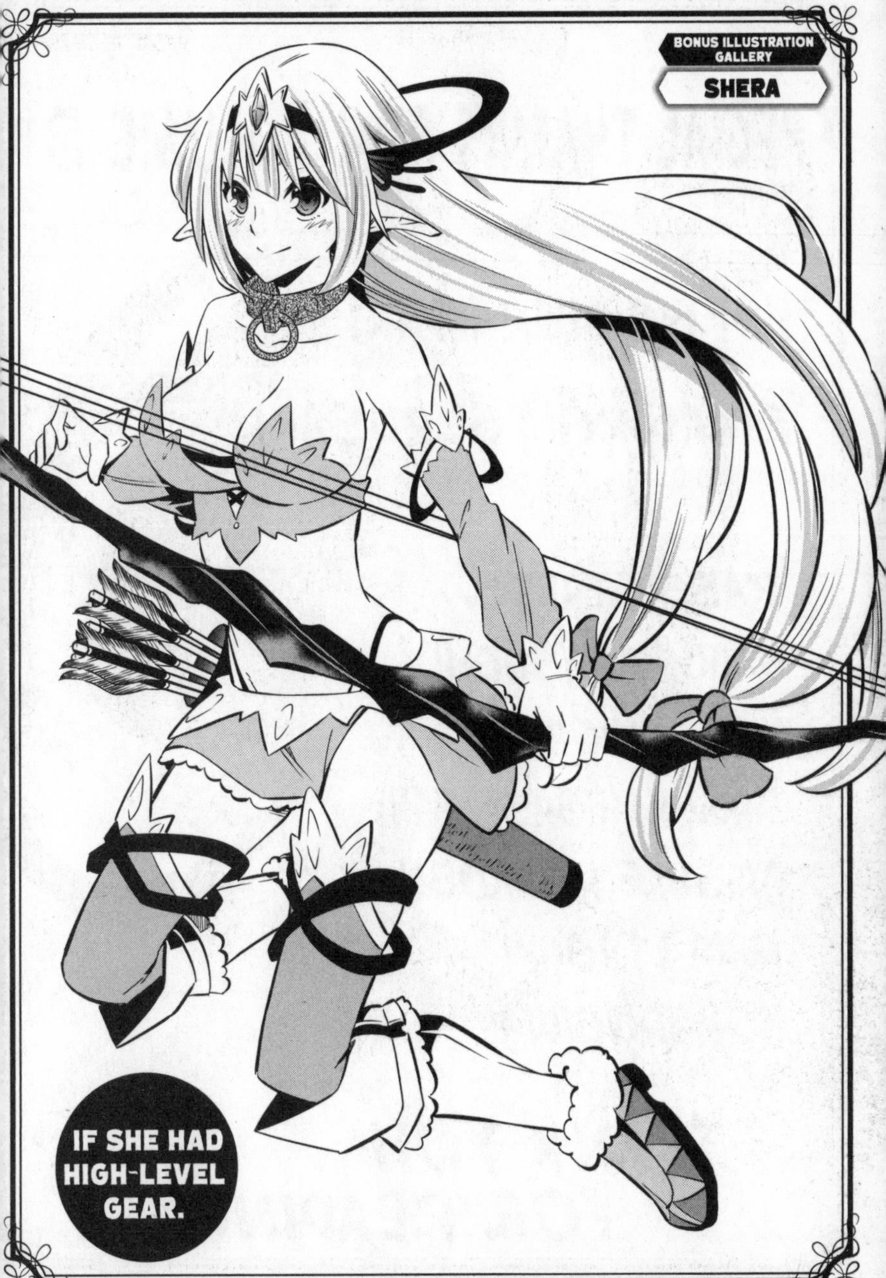
BONUS ILLUSTRATION GALLERY
SHERA
IF SHE HAD HIGH-LEVEL GEAR.

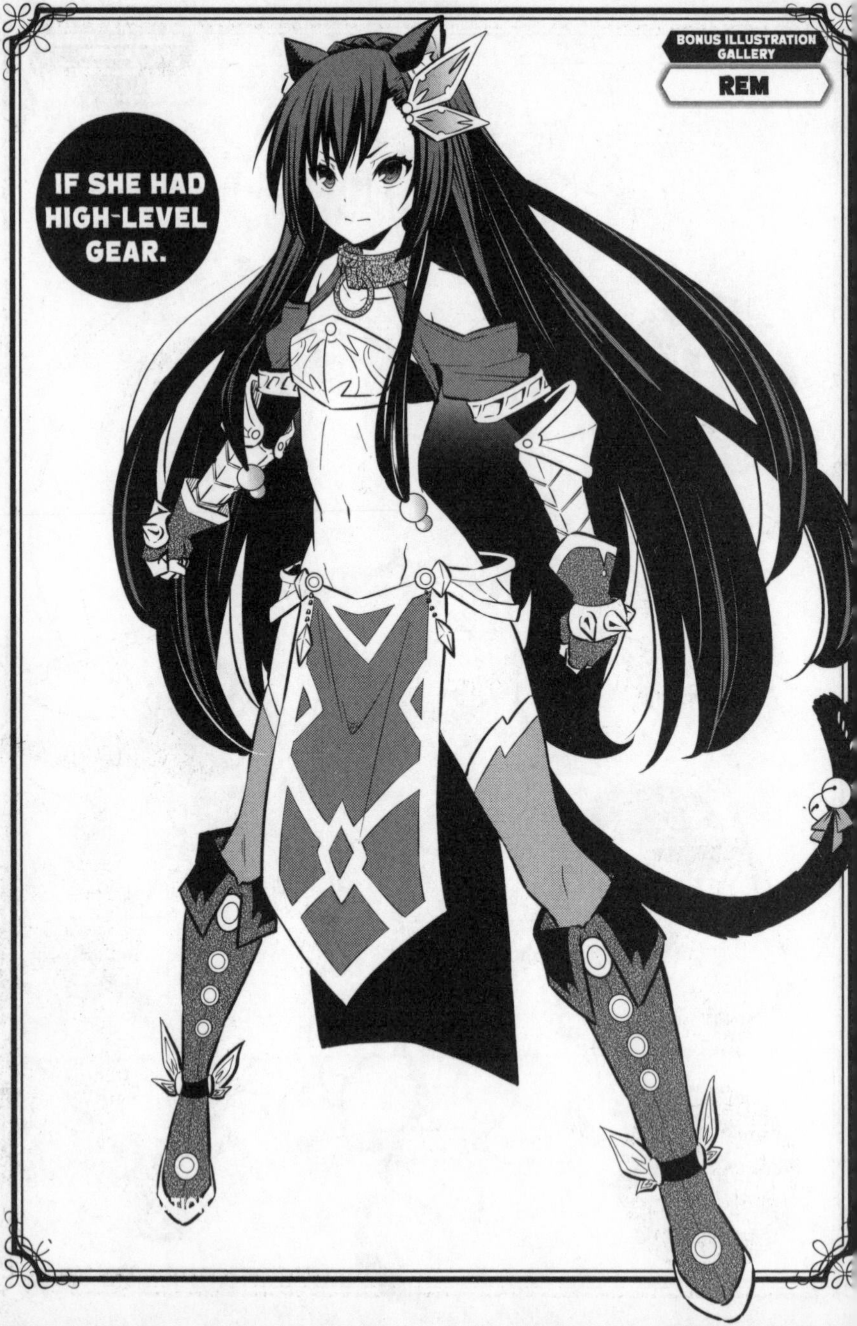
BONUS ILLUSTRATION GALLERY
REM
IF SHE HAD HIGH-LEVEL GEAR.

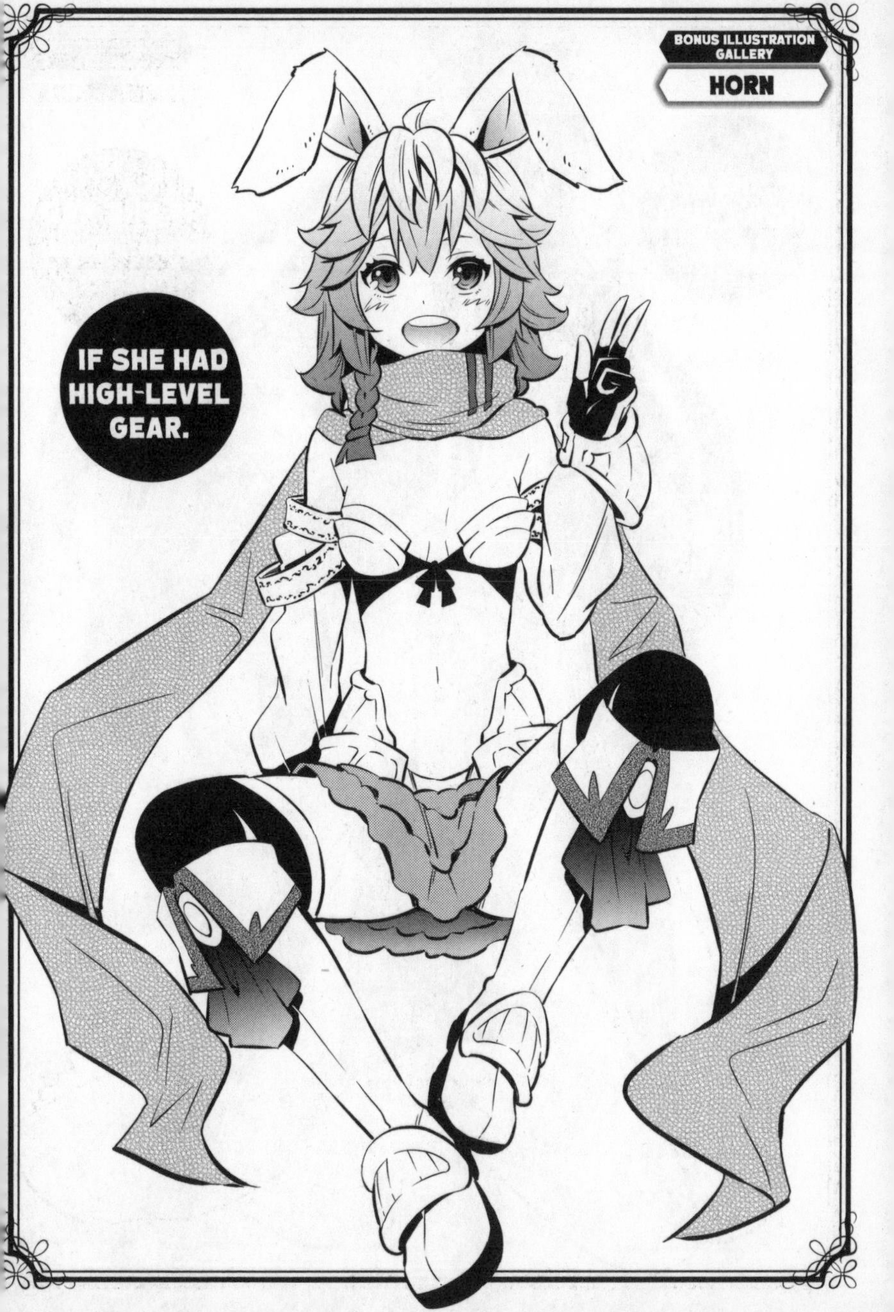
BONUS ILLUSTRATION GALLERY
HORN
IF SHE HAD HIGH-LEVEL GEAR.

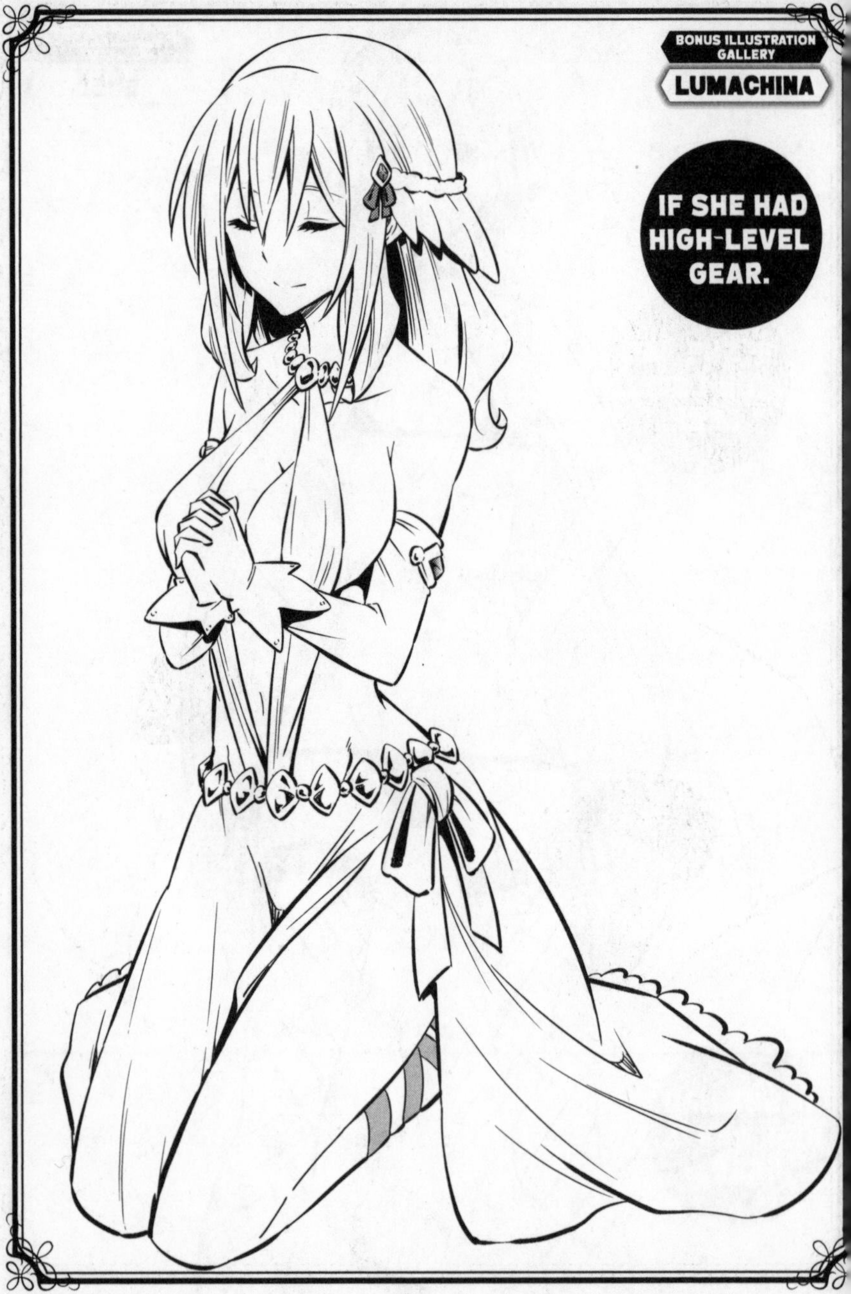
BONUS ILLUSTRATION GALLERY
LUMACHINA
IF SHE HAD HIGH-LEVEL GEAR.

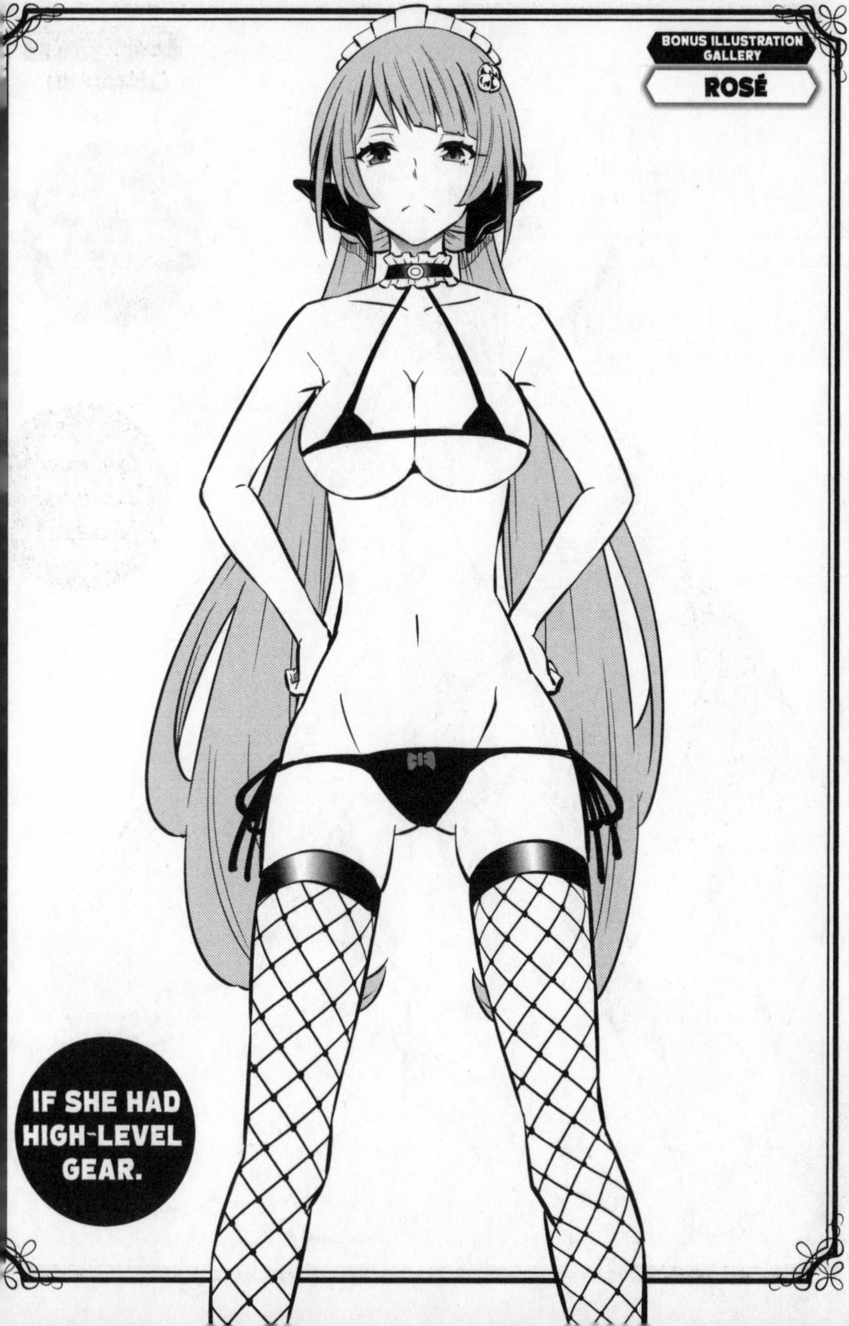
BONUS ILLUSTRATION GALLERY
ROSÉ
IF SHE HAD HIGH-LEVEL GEAR.

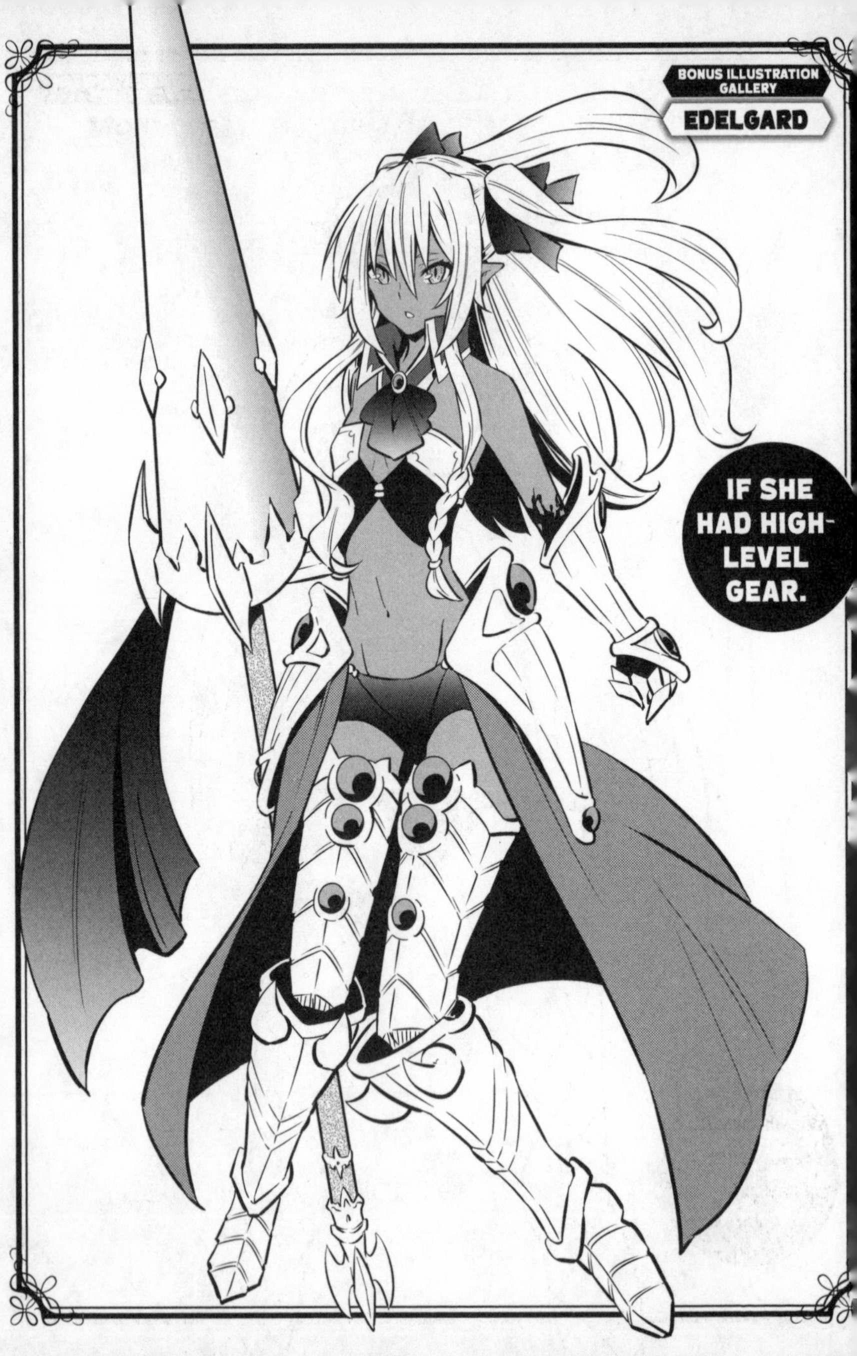
BONUS ILLUSTRATION GALLERY
EDELGARD
IF SHE HAD HIGH-LEVEL GEAR.

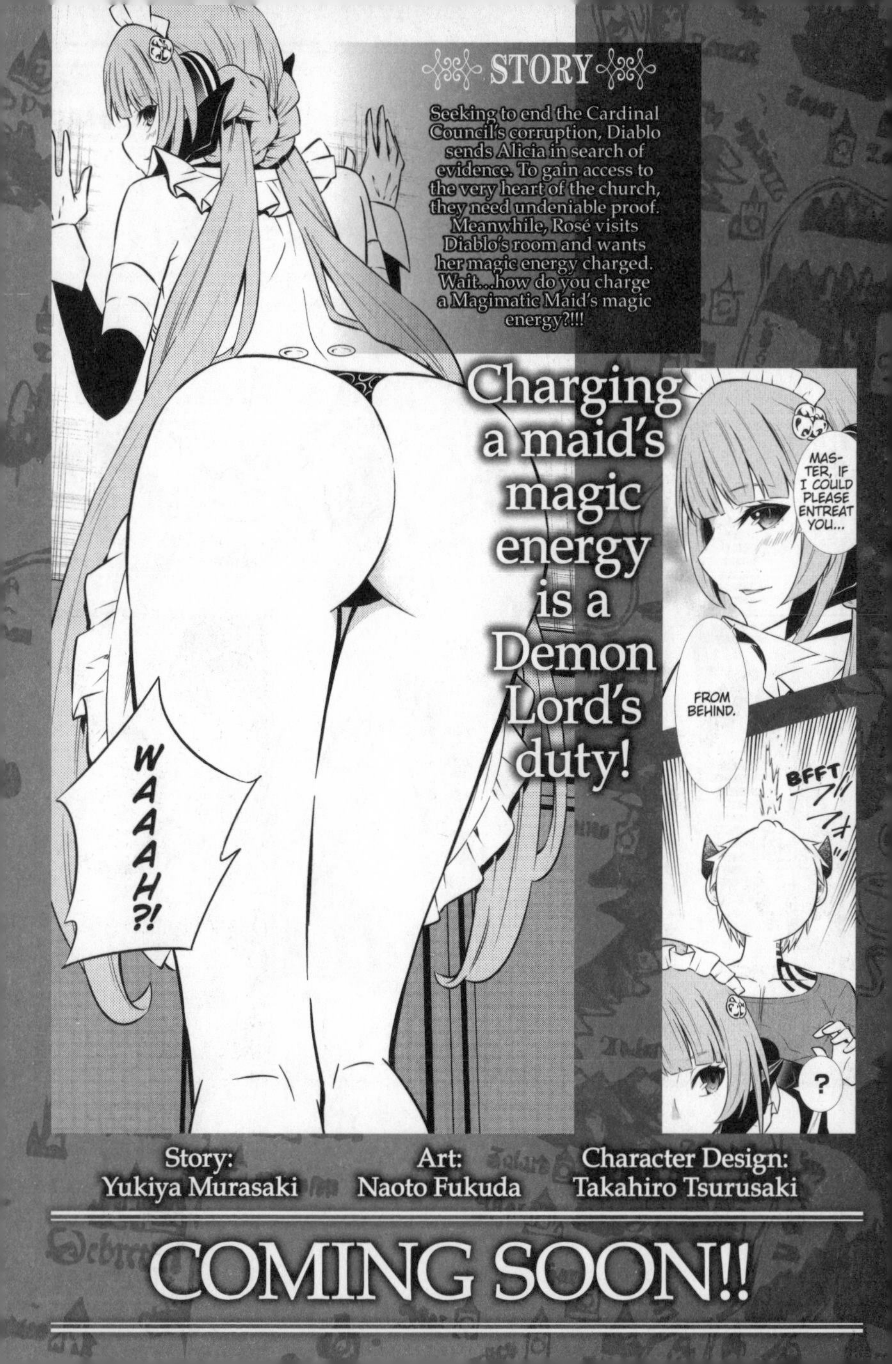
STORY
Seeking to end the Cardinal Council's corruption, Diablo sends Alicia in search of evidence. To gain access to the very heart of the church, they need undeniable proof. Meanwhile, Rosé visits Diablo's room and wants her magic energy charged. Wait...how do you charge a Magimatic Maid's magic energy?!!!
Charging a maid's magic energy is a Demon Lord's duty!
MASTER, IF I COULD PLEASE ENTREAT YOU...
FROM BEHIND.
BFFT
?
WAAAAH?!

Story:
Yukiya Murasaki

Art:
Naoto Fukuda

Character Design:
Takahiro Tsurusaki

COMING SOON!!

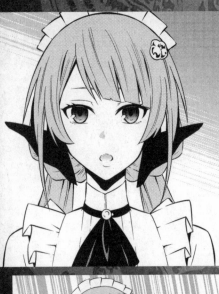

FOR SPEED CHARGING.
ROSÉ'S THE RXXMBA, AND I'M THE CHARGER!
THERE'S NOTHING INDECENT ABOUT IT!!
TH-BMP
TOUCHING HER FROM BEHIND IS OBSCENE.
NO! I'M SUPPLYING A COMRADE WITH MAGIC ENERGY!
TH-BMP
DON'T MAKE IT WEIRD!
TH-BMP
AUNGH?!
TWITCH

HOW NOT TO SUMMON A DEMON LORD

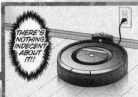

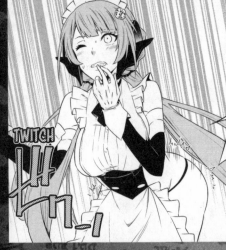

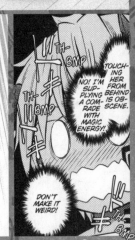

14

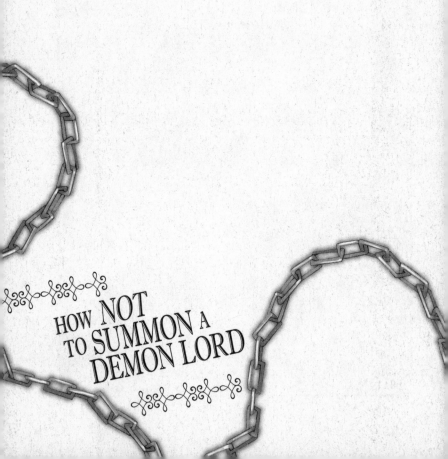

HOW NOT
TO SUMMON A
DEMON LORD

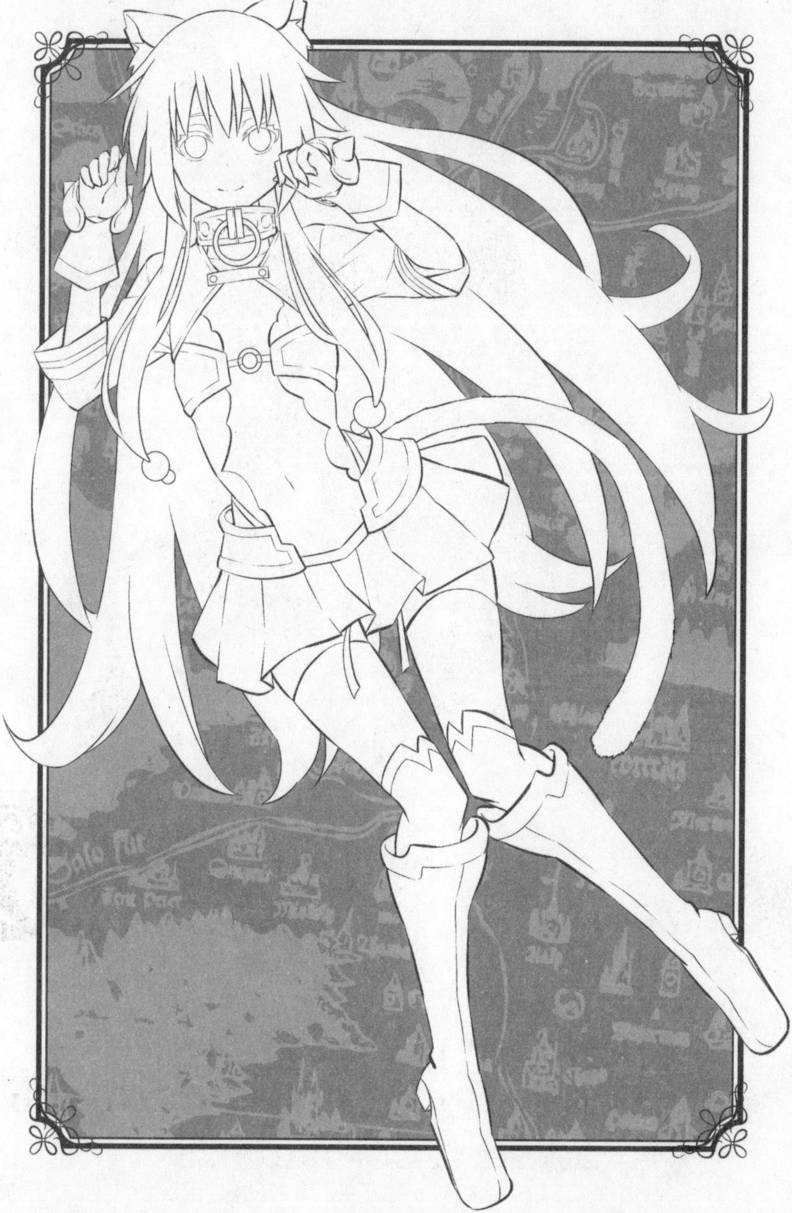

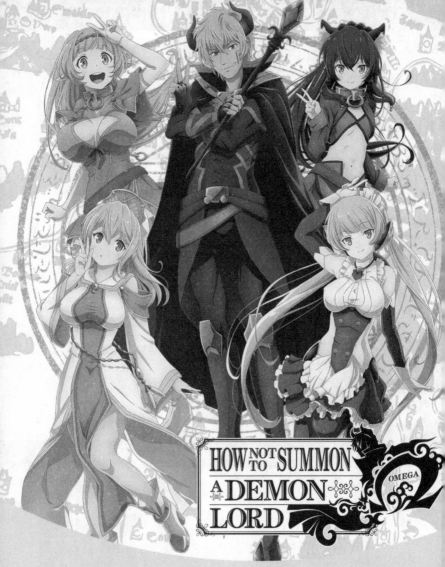

SEVEN SEAS ENTERTAINME[NT]

HOW *NOT* TO SUMMON ◦◦–A–◦◦ VOLUME 13
DEMON LORD
story by YUKIYA MURASAKI   art by NAOTO FUKUDA

W9-CFE-540
5/22

TRANSLATION
Kumar Sivasubramanian

ADAPTATION
Lora Gray

LETTERING AND RETOUCH
Christa Miesner

COVER DESIGN
Kris Aubin

EDITOR
Peter Adrian Behravesh
Kristiina Korpus

PRINT MANAGER
Rhiannon Rasmussen–Silverstein

PRODUCTION MANAGER
Lissa Pattillo

MANAGING EDITOR
Julie Davis

ASSOCIATE PUBLISHER
Adam Arnold

PUBLISHER
Jason DeAngelis

HOW NOT TO SUMMON A DEMON LORD VOLUME 13
© Yukiya Murasaki 2021, © Naoto Fukuda 2021, © Takahiro Tsurusaki 2021
All rights reserved.
First published in Japan in 2021 by Kodansha Ltd., Tokyo.
Publication rights for this English edition arranged through Kodansha Ltd.,
Tokyo.

Seven Seas press and purchase enquiries can be sent to Marketing Manager
Lianne Sentar at press@gomanga.com. Information regarding the distribution
and purchase of digital editions is available from Digital Manager CK Russell
at digital@gomanga.com.

Seven Seas and the Seven Seas logo are trademarks of
Seven Seas Entertainment. All rights reserved.

ISBN: 978-1-64827-385-8

Printed in Canada

First Printing: January 2022

10 9 8 7 6 5 4 3 2 1

FOLLOW US ONLINE: *www.sevenseasentertainment.com*

READING DIRECTIONS

This book reads from ***right to left***, Japanese style.
If this is your first time reading manga, you start
reading from the top right panel on each page and
take it from there. If you get lost, just follow the
numbered diagram here. It may seem backwards at
first, but you'll get the hang of it! Have fun!!

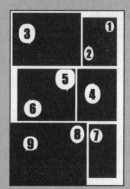